The Scythe of Saturn

THE SCYTHE OF SATURN

Shakespeare and Magical Thinking

LINDA WOODBRIDGE

UNIVERSITY OF ILLINOIS PRESS
Urbana and Chicago

This book is printed on acid-free paper.

Library of Congress Cataloging-in-Publication Data

Woodbridge, Linda, 1945–
    The scythe of Saturn : Shakespeare and magical thinking / Linda
Woodbridge.
        p.   cm
    Includes bibligraphical references and index.
    ISBN 0-252-02080-4 (cloth). — ISBN 0-252-06370-8 (paper)
    1. Shakespeare, William, 1564–1616—Knowledge—Occultism.
2. Magic in literature. I. Title.
PR3004.W66   1994
822.3'3—dc20   93-11755
                                                          CIP

Contents

Acknowledgments

The research for this book was generously funded by a grant from the Social Science and Humanities Research Council of Canada, which provided me with several graduate research assistants and money for travel, communications, and supplies. I am most grateful for this assistance.

I am also grateful to *Texas Studies in Literature and Language* and to *Renaissance Quarterly* for permission to reprint revised versions of essays originally appearing in those journals. Earlier versions of some of the material in this book were presented at the Creating Word Conference in Edmonton, Alberta; at the Pacific Northwest Renaissance Conference; at the Rocky Mountain Medieval and Renaissance Association; at the Elizabethan Fair at the University of Wyoming; and as part of the Edmund Kemper Broadus Lectures at the University of Alberta. I particularly thank those participants at those conferences and lectures whose thoughtful questions and comments sharpened my thinking.

Thanks are due to Naomi Liebler and Jeanne Roberts, readers for the Press, for their detailed and helpful critiques, to Ann Lowry and Becky Standard for their meticulous editing, and to Noeline H. Bridge for her preparation of the index.

Warmest thanks are owing to my family—Roland, Dana, and Rachel—who have been hearing about red, white, black, and the evil eye for too many years now and have remained patient and supportive through it all.

Introduction:
Recovering Enchantment

We work by wit, and not by witchcraft;
And wit depends on dilatory time.
                                        —*Othello*

Scholars specializing in the Renaissance easily regard Shakespeare as a contemporary. We read him in modern spelling. We have known him so long his language no longer sounds archaic—some of us drop the odd "fie" and "methinks" into our own conversation. We see modern-dress productions—Hotspur as Nicaraguan Contra, Dogberry as Texas sheriff. Marxists and new historicists keep trying to relocate Shakespeare in an early modern political and social world, but that very effort somehow makes him seem modern. Bringing to life the minutiae of sixteenth-century experience makes it seem contemporary, makes it familiar territory, and the new historicist habit of regarding everything as at base political is familiarizing too—a world in which every action, from travel to sexual intercourse, has political implications is *our* world.

With people who are not Renaissance specialists, it is quite otherwise. One has only to sit reading *Macbeth* on a bus to attract the attention of a fellow traveler who will report that he had to read Shakespeare in high school but never could make anything of the Old English. There is no point in trying to explain that *real* Old English, as in *Beowulf,* would give him even more trouble, that Shakespeare is technically *modern* English. Modern? he will puzzle. That stuff is *old.* It sounds like church. The historical accident that Shakespearean English is exactly contemporary with the King James Version that became fossilized as the language of church gives Shakespeare's English the resonance of Holy Writ. At least, that was so when churches still used the King James Version, with its sonorous "And Esau said to Jacob, Feed me, I pray thee with that same red pottage; for I am faint." For a generation nurtured on the Good News Bible, in which Esau demands "I'm starving; give me some of that red stuff," Shakespeare will sound even older than the Bible.

The man on the bus does us a service in reminding us that Shakespeare is old. Shakespeare is not our contemporary. In his day, witch trials were common. (Alan Macfarlane shows that witchcraft was not a matter of "sporadic and sudden 'epidemics,' outbreaks of 'superstition'" but of "everyday fears and constant accusations" [*Witchcraft* 90]; he presents evidence that cases brought to trial represented only the tip of the iceberg of suspected witchcraft.) Certain poor people, called sin-eaters, were paid to eat bread and beer passed over a corpse, to absorb (scapegoatlike) the dead person's sins and keep the ghost from walking (Aubrey 35–36). In 1604 "the House of Commons rejected a bill after the speech of its Puritan sponsor had been interrupted by the flight of a jackdaw through the Chamber—an indisputably bad omen" (Thomas, *Man* 78). As Anthony Fletcher and John Stevenson note, "the therapeutic work of an astrological physician like Richard Napier, who treated 2000 mentally disturbed patients between 1597 and 1634, was only possible in a mental world where for most people science, religion and magic were still fused" (12). The last words attributed to Shakespeare are a ritual curse on whoever disturbs his grave. The few remarkable thinkers, such as Reginald Scot, who tried to apply rational discourse to the project of debunking witchcraft beliefs were enormously outnumbered, and Scot met opposition from no less an authority than King James himself. In James's *Demonology* we see a mind far enough advanced in the new skepticism to argue that witches are deluded, thinking their own magic spells responsible for ill effects; but he seems less modern when he explains that the real agents are not witches but demons (see Clark 168). It used to be argued that as a Scotsman, James was more inclined toward magic than most English contemporaries, that he "descended as a persecutor from the north, enacted a savage new witchcraft statute, and was responsible for many hundreds of executions in England"; but historians now see James's witchcraft beliefs as being of a piece with widespread beliefs in England at the time (Clark 161). George Gifford, a cleric gifted with proto-anthropological insight, tried to oppose the scapegoating as witches of hundreds of people, mainly old women; yet as Macfarlane shows, "even Gifford had to admit the reality of witchcraft. In his two witchcraft works we are watching a mind trying to rise above the limitations and assumptions of its time, to argue its way out of a closed and circular system" ("Tudor Anthropologist" 145).

We often assume that Shakespeare's mind was capable of rising "above the limitations and assumptions of its time." But was it? Reginald Scot's debunking of magic was especially indebted to Cicero's *De Divinatione,* which "ridicule[s] prophecies which either do not come true or are contradictory, and [demands] to know how divine secrets could possibly be hidden in an animal's entrails" (Anglo, "Reginald Scot's *Discoverie*" 130), and in *Julius Caesar* Shakespeare presents Cicero as just such a skeptic. Yet portents in *Julius Caesar* do accurately portend, and prophecies prophesy aright—do we read debunking of magic here or not?

Sydney Anglo provides an excellent discussion of skeptical, antimagical strains in late medieval and Renaissance thought; he notes, for example, that skepticism is a component of Reformation thought, where "the comparison between Catholic rites and pagan magic, and the vanity of both, was [a] well-established tradition" (131; see also Von Rosador 7–8). The rich tradition of Renaissance Neoplatonic and hermetic magic, which offered an intellectual superstructure rationalizing magic, lifting it up above the level of mere folk superstition, is beyond the scope of my study: I am more interested in mere folk superstition. In *Power/Knowledge,* Michel Foucault recommends that more attention be paid to "naive knowledges, located low down on the hierarchy, beneath the required level of cognition or scientificity, . . . low-ranking knowledges, . . . popular knowledge, . . . a particular, local, regional knowledge, . . . discontinuous, disqualified, illegitimate knowledges" (82–83), and such knowledges are exactly my quarry in studying Renaissance popular magic and the traces it left on the mentalities of the age.

Historicizing Magic

Although trying to get a handle on the historical fortunes of magical thinking is frustratingly difficult, historicizing such questions as best we can is especially important, since studying magical thinking necessitates venturing into folklore and folklife, where Shakespeareans have not always trod carefully. An unfortunate ahistoricism in their approach has often discredited their use of folk materials: Shakespeare has too often been imagined drawing power from deep wells of occult meaning, in touch with the timeless cycles of the Folk, who went on dancing round their maypoles and frolicking under their Lords of Misrule, heedless of Tudor power, corn riots, enclosures, or civil war. Not even Barber's insistence on festive abuse or Bakhtin's attention to the lower bodily stratum has effaced entirely the sentimentality that has dogged nostalgia for folkways. Brisk correctives to Love of Quaintness appear periodically, like Keith Thomas's startling observation that much rural magical lore was derived from classical sources (*Man* 77). But Merrie England remains a pitfall. Quaintness nostalgia is in part the legacy of a deliberate glorification of rurality fostered by James I, with his promotion of rural pastimes, and taken up by poets such as Herrick (see Stallybrass, "'Wee Feaste'" 244).

To study magical thinking need not be to escape from history into a transhistorical folk consciousness; early modern folk consciousness is exactly what social historians and students of popular culture are currently exploring. "The rediscovery of the 'people,' often associated with the 'nativist' and 'folklorist' movements of the nineteenth century, has become a central concern of contemporary historians of popular movements in the pre-industrial period" (Fletcher and Stevenson 31).

The historicizing project of literary scholars (Greenblatt, Montrose, Marcus, Stallybrass) and historians (Thomas, Davis) has proved a valuable corrective, though the tendency of literary historicists to sidestep the maypole, to view the Folk synchronically as a contemporary proletariat rather than diachronically in its continuity with the magic and superstition of the medieval past involves losses as well as gains. Thomas's work is especially valuable because he attempts to position, historically, magical belief itself; we are better able to assess how far Shakespeare's audience might have believed unconsciously or semiconsciously in the magical efficacy of, say, scapegoating, after reading Thomas's account of how new antimagical and anti-ritual intellectual forces were colliding with and driving underground old habits of thought that still permitted reading gospels in fields for crop fertility, wearing rings with spirits imprisoned in them, transferring sickness from a child to a toad, sticking pins in wax models of victims, the royal touch for scrofula, magical divination to recover lost property, leaving of milk to propitiate household fairies, brewing of love potions, fortune-telling, ghost laying, witchcraft.

Protestantism did assail the medieval concept of religion, which had involved "a ritual method of living, not a set of dogmas" (Thomas, *Religion* 88), with an assault on ritual from maypoles to misrule. But despite Protestant efforts, "Reginald Scot wrote that every parish had its miracle-worker, and that some had seventeen or eighteen. Robert Burton . . . [asserted] that there was a cunning man in every village. At the turn of the sixteenth century well-informed contemporaries thus thought the wizards roughly comparable in numbers to the parochial clergy" (*Religion* 291–92). The clergy "were not above having recourse to magicians. Several medieval abbots and priors consulted sorcerers for the recovery of missing objects. . . . As late as 1640 a violent storm . . . was popularly thought to be the consequence of a visit made by the local Laudian clergyman to a conjurer to find out who had pulled down his altar rails" (*Religion* 325). Magical belief in the efficacy of scapegoating was a historical phenomenon, a medieval legacy; and the skepticism of dramatists who demystified scapegoating was historical too, born of the new rationalism. What I call magical thinking is a product of this historical collision: inherited medieval magical belief provided the structures, and dawning Renaissance rationalism drove them into the unconscious.

At least from the time of Aquinas and Scholasticism, with their attempt to reconcile faith and reason, rationalism as an ideology gained a toehold within official Christianity itself and over the ensuing centuries gradually attained ascendancy as a discourse guaranteed by the power of the state, "a power which the West since Medieval times has attributed to science and has reserved for those engaged in scientific discourse" (Foucault, *Power/Knowledge* 85). Magic, both because it was sometimes demonic and because it drew on powers outside the rational force field, became a subjugated discourse that, however, stubbornly held its ground for a very long time, an example of that "insurrection of knowledges that are opposed . . . to the effects of the centralising powers which are linked to the institution and functioning of an organised scientific discourse" (Foucault, *Power/Knowledge* 84).

Sometimes magical practice was legitimated by absorption into official church practice, such as religious processions through fields to promote crop fertility. Sometimes, in parishes remote from official centers of church and state power, magic must have been practiced innocently or in ignorance of its official proscription. In many cases, magical practices were surreptitious, a small revolt against or evasion of official sanctions. But I am most interested in the cases where, overt magic having been suppressed, its traces linger to structure the unconscious.

Magical Practices in the Plays

There is a fair amount of overt magical practice in Shakespeare's works. The commonest is prognosticatory—divination or prophecy by soothsayers, witches, and others. Such prophecies occur in *Cymbeline, 2 Henry VI, Richard III, King John, 1 and 2 Henry IV, Henry VIII, Troilus and Cressida, Julius Caesar, Macbeth,* and *Antony and Cleopatra.* Cleopatra's soothsayer is a palm reader, and Othello attempts to read Desdemona's palm. *Julius Caesar* has augury with animal entrails, birds as omens, a storm interpreted as portentous, and the practice of oneiromancy, or interpretation of dreams, to divine the future. Clarence's dream foretells the future in *Richard III,* which also offers onomancy, or divination through calculations based on names—the prophecy that Edward's heirs will be murdered by someone with a name beginning with *G.*

There is witchcraft, actual as in *Macbeth* or suspected as in *Errors*'s confused Syracusans who think Ephesus full of witchcraft or the scene where Ford suspects Mother Prat of being a witch in *Merry Wives.* There is magic to cause falling in love or to retain love—actual in the case of Puck's love juice or Othello's mother's handkerchief, suspected (and for all we know actual) in the charge by Brabantio in *Othello* and Egeus in *A Midsummer Night's Dream* that their daughters' love has been won through witchcraft.

There are magical cures: in *All's Well* the cure of the king has a magical aura, as Helena intones a kind of spell:

Ere twice the horses of the sun shall bring
Their fiery torcher his diurnal ring,
Ere twice in murk and occidental damp
Moist Hesperus hath quench'd his sleepy lamp,
Or four and twenty times the pilot's glass
Hath told the thievish minutes how they pass,
What is infirm from your sound parts shall fly,
Health shall live free and sickness freely die.
(II.ii.164–71)

In *Pericles,* Cerimon resurrects Thaïsa with the help of music, fire, napkins, and the mysterious contents of boxes; he refers to his "physic" as a "secret art," and it has a definite magical air: he speaks of "the blest infusions / That dwell in vegetives, in metals, stones" (III.ii.32–96). He has perhaps learned at the same school as Friar Laurence, who meditates as he gathers plants in a basket, "O, mickle is the powerful grace that lies / In herbs, plants, stones, and their true qualities" (*Rom* II.iii.15–16). Vegetives, herbs, and plants are one thing—one might grant such herbalism the status of protoscience rather than magic—but "stones," mentioned by both Cerimon and Friar Laurence, are quite another. Richard Kieckhefer describes books called "lapidaries" that explained the magical powers of gems: one kind, held in the mouth, induced prophecy; another cured gout and eye diseases; another defended against wild beasts (103). The lapidary, "a kind of user's manual for the wonder-working gems," had many practical uses: "A man who doubts the chastity of his wife, for example, can place a magnet against her head while she is lying in bed, and if she has been unfaithful she will fall on to the floor" (103–5). No doubt lapidaries were among the kinds of "authorities" by which a Cerimon learned his physic, and through such magic books practitioners such as Friar Laurence or *Cymbeline's* queen and Dr. Cornelius could learn to make poisons and sleeping potions. Again, perhaps the queen's poisons should be considered protoscience, since like a good modern experimental scientist she plans to test her "strange lingering poisons" on animals (I.v.1–35); but the queen's experiments retain a magical aura, if only from the fairy tale context—the play is clearly indebted to *Snow White's* tale type.

Among miscellaneous other magical practices in the plays are Bottom's transformation by fairies into an ass-headed monster; Joan of Arc's demonic dabblings in *1 Henry VI*; the Duchess of Gloucester's sorcery with hired conjurors, including the wise woman Margery Jourdain (called "a witch" in the *dramatis personae*) in *2 Henry VI*; the curses of Queen Margaret in *Richard III*, which turn from rhetoric into magic retrospectively, as we realize, one by one, that they are working; the human sacrifice in *Titus Andronicus* to appease the spirits of the dead; in *Julius Caesar* the magical practice of a barren woman's touching a runner in the races of the Lupercal; and *The Tempest*'s panoply of magical practices—the magically raised tempest, the charms that immobilize their victims, the use of a magic garment, staff, and books of spells, the control of fairies, the witch whose spells can control the moon.

To magical practice we can add belief in fairies, goblins, ghosts, and spirits—belief sometimes mocked, as in Hotspur's mocking Glendower's spirit mastery in *1 Henry IV* or Dr. Pinch bumbling through a comic exorcism in *Errors* or Falstaff's hiding his eyes from bogus fairies in *Merry Wives*. But such beliefs are sometimes justified by the appearance onstage of supernatural beings, as in *A Midsummer Night's Dream*, *The Tempest*, *1 Henry VI*, *Richard III*, *Julius Caesar*, *Hamlet*, and *Macbeth*.

Despite the common assumption that Shakespearean comedy deals in unreal and fantastic worlds, it is interesting that overt magical practice and supernatural beings occur in only about a quarter of Shakespeare's comedies, while they appear in 60 percent of his history plays and 60 percent of his tragedies.

In many cases, Shakespeare situates magic at a remove from his own culture, historical period, religion, or gender. *Julius Caesar*'s soothsayers, auguries, omens, portentous storms, and oneiromancy and *Titus*'s human sacrifice are set in ancient Rome. The Duchess of Gloucester's conjuring, Joan of Arc's fiends, Clarence's dream, King Edward's onomancy, and Macbeth's witches belong to the magic-besotted Middle Ages, an Other against which the Renaissance persistently (and rather smugly) defined itself. Sometimes in plays with medieval settings the Reformation ascription of superstitiousness to Catholics comes into play, as in King John's denunciation of a "meddling priest" with his "juggling witchcraft" (III.i.163–69). Joan of Arc's demonic magic and Queen Margaret's curses are the magical machinations of Frenchwomen; as French, as women, and as Catholics they are likely suspects. The French were always an enemy Other, and in Shakespeare, magical practice is often associated with women—Joan of Arc, the Duchess of Gloucester, Margery Jourdain, Macbeth's witches. This corresponds with the historical fact that magic was often associated with women (see Kieckhefer 29–33, 39, 59) and that the majority of accused witches were women. Krämer and Sprenger's *Malleus Maleficarum* (1486), the most influential Renaissance witchcraft treatise, has a section entitled "Why Superstition Is Chiefly Found in Women." Shakespeare even situates magical belief by reference to class: "The world's poor people are amazed / At apparitions, signs, and prodigies / Whereon with fearful eyes they long have gazed, / Infusing them with dreadful prophecies" (*Ven* 925–28).[1]

One might argue that by ascribing magical belief to people removed from himself—ancient Romans, Catholics, French, medieval men, women, the poor—Shakespeare means to demystify it. One is then left with the problem that Margaret's curses prove effective against their victims, and that Joan of Arc, the Duchess of Gloucester, and Margery Jourdain raise real spirits by their magic, which appear onstage and utter prophecies that come true, as do prophecies in some dozen Shakespeare plays, as noted above. By distancing himself from magical practice, was Shakespeare demystifying it, or was he engaging in the scapegoating process so common where early modern magical practice was concerned—blaming this evil on aliens or powerless segments of society?

Richard Hardin argues that Shakespeare's demonization of Joan of Arc was exactly such a blaming of aliens—a scapegoating that pandered to the anti-French prejudices of English audiences of his day, turning audiences into a mob with a propensity for collective violence, as described so often by René Girard: Hardin argues that "it is this mob that, projecting itself into the English heroes, is really closing in for the kill in Act 5. Shakespeare has collaborated with them in rewriting Joan's history. Her crime lies with their prejudices" ("Chronicles" 33). Hardin agrees with Girard that in *The Merchant* it is not Shakespeare but the Venetians who make Shylock a scapegoat; Shakespeare here reveals the ugliness of "a characteristically debased human effort to change one person into a monster so as to exonerate the group from its sins (i.e. the avarice and wrath of Venice)"; but Hardin does not think Shakespeare was exposing the scapegoating process in *Joan*'s case: "It seems doubtful that the author has so distanced himself in this play" (33–34). But what makes it doubtful? On what grounds do we make such distinctions? How do we know when Shakespeare himself is scapegoating a character and when he is inviting us to be horrified at his characters for doing so? The answer depends partly on where we situate Shakespeare with regard to magical thinking. How self-aware, how critical, how distanced was he? How "modern" was he?

Another difficulty in coming to terms with a magical mentality as it might be descried in Shakespeare and his audience involves the status of literary art vis à vis magical practice and belief. Demons, prophecies, and curses make good theater. Twentieth-century audiences would be disconcerted at the prospect that some four hundred years from now, scholars might conclude anything about the magical practices or beliefs of our culture by reviewing old tapes of "The Twilight Zone" or *The Exorcist*. Some people believe in Satan today, and others do not; either way, the *frisson* of horror we enjoy while watching *Rosemary's Baby* has virtually nothing to do with our everyday belief or disbelief in the supernatural. Though more people may have believed in magic in Shakespeare's day than in ours, how relevant is this when it comes to interpreting the effect of magical happenings in his plays? Literature after all stands off to one side of life, as new historicists sometimes forget. Despite the current orthodoxy that holds ideology to be nearly irresistible, Elizabethan audience members must often, I think, have suspended their everyday ideology and accepted a play's contract of belief: revenge tragedy asks Christian playgoers to suppress the text "vengeance is mine, I will repay, saith the Lord." In such a case, how helpful is it to historicize drama by digging out actual attitudes toward vengeance? Even though most Elizabethans believed in witches, can we assume that their response as audience members to *Macbeth*'s witches would correspond to their fears of the old woman next door in some direct, one-to-one relationship?

Kieckhefer shows that in the Middle Ages, where magical practice and belief saturated everyday life and magical episodes abounded in courtly romance, important differences of attitude occurred between real-life magic and literary magic: magic in the romances was much more playful and fanciful: "People at court clearly recognized that certain magical practices could be sinister and destructive; there is ample evidence that kings and courtiers feared sorcery at least as much as commoners did. In their imaginative literature, however, they were willing to accord it a different status and to consider without horror the symbolic uses of magical motifs" (95). In approaching the complexities of Renaissance attitudes toward Prospero's magic in *The Tempest,* Barbara Mowat reminds us not to forget a literary convention, the stage wizard: "the magic acts which we see Prospero perform—the placing of charms on Miranda and Ferdinand, the summoning of spirits to present shows, the use of magic to aid friends, and punish enemies, the creation and dissolution of a magic banquet—these acts are predictable stage-wizard magic" (292).

Magical Thinking

I have explored the important question of overt magical practice in the plays and its relation to actual magical practice and belief in Shakespeare's culture to give some sense of the pervasiveness of actual magic in Shakespeare and his culture but also to bracket this off: this is not, at least not mainly, my topic. The details of early modern magical practice are so fascinating that it is easy to be seduced into studying them in their own right: who could resist such compelling information as that "a man could be rendered impotent for the rest of his life by being so careless as to imbibe forty ants boiled in daffodil juice" (Kieckhefer 84)? However, resist such bypaths I must, for I am exploring not overt magical practice but the question of what difference it makes *to the literature* to know that Shakespeare and his audience belonged to a culture that believed in magic and in many forms of the supernatural. I think that the really interesting differences it made to the literature are not in certain superficial and flashy theatrical effects like Joan of Arc's spooky demons or Margaret's flesh-creeping curses but in the deep structure of what happens in the plays.

What do we make of Shakespeare's seeming obsession with threatened female chastity and of his preoccupation with siege warfare? I will argue that these reflect magical thinking—fear of bodily pollution, belief that the body can be protected by observing sexual taboos, belief that the body is an image of society. Why is political assassination sometimes redemptive in the overall scheme of a tragedy? I will argue that the ancient magic of scapegoating is mentally operative here. What is at work in Shakespeare's remarkable number of banishments? I will argue that the magical principle of expulsion of evil, found in early modern medical cures and exorcisms, also animates political banishments, and that it sheds some light, too, on the Battle of Agincourt. What lies behind Shakespeare's persistent characterization of good in terms of what is green and growing, evil in terms of what is withered and nonprocreative? I will argue that fertility magic is at work in this mentality, as it is in Shakespeare's sexualized landscape (males linked with trees, females with pools), and in the way that Shakespeare and his contemporaries use pastoral, grounding truth and even political probity in the world of the countryside. Why does Shakespeare stress the childlessness of Julius Caesar, Richard II, and Macbeth, political leaders with troubled regimes, all of them headed for assassination? I will argue that this emphasis reflects a magical linking of political power to sexual potency. Why are the colors red, white, and black so prominent in Renaissance love poetry? I will link this with ancient belief in the efficacy of these magical colors to promote fertility. Why are those in power so often complicit in organized misrule? I will trace this to the kind of magical thinking in which the older generation allows its consciousness to be tricked into believing that the younger generation's assumption of power is no more than a festive, carnival inversion—nonthreatening because temporary.

By magical thinking I do not mean conscious magical belief. *Magical belief* accepts the possibility of human supernatural agency, sometimes aided by divine or demonic forces, sometimes working by sheer force of will aided by magical words; *magical thinking* is the unconscious residue of such belief, which remains to structure experience even though true magical belief has atrophied in the individual psyche. In true magical belief, supernatural force occurs in various transactions between the material and the immaterial. Magic may involve the supernatural operation of the (immaterial) human will upon an immaterial entity such as illness or the polity, via a material intermediary (a human body, a glove, an animal) or the supernatural operation of the will upon a material entity (a neighbor's body) via an immaterial force (the gaze, magic spells, performative language). Human supernatural agency is also involved in self-protective magic—protecting oneself from pollution (a bodily harm magically defined) by observation of taboos, gustatory or sexual, or against other magical harm such as a neighbor's evil eye, via spells or amulets. In magical thinking, by my definition, though the conscious mind may have freed itself in large measure from true belief in magic or the efficacy of charms and rituals, all this has gone underground; it is unconscious. Magical thinking is like a concrete wall that remains standing after the forms into which it has been poured—true magical belief—have been knocked away. And even if the timber forms of true magical belief are still here and there left standing, what I am interested in is mainly the wall and not the forms, though I will need to discuss the forms to explain the shape of the wall. A concrete wall is a substantial matter, the skeleton giving shape to the building; and magical thinking, though unconscious, is at least as substantial and shape giving as the timbers of magical belief that formed it.

The Magical Unconscious

My understanding of the unconscious, like everyone's, is ultimately indebted to Freud, whose formulation "incompletely suppressed psychical material, which, although pushed away by consciousness, has nevertheless not been robbed of all capacity for expressing itself" is a good description of what I think was the position of magic in the thinking of many of Shakespeare's contemporaries (*Complete Works* 6:279). Freud thought that our *frisson* of horror at something "uncanny" betrayed magical thinking, the traces of magical belief left over from childhood and from more primitive stages of humankind:

> Let us take the uncanny associated with the omnipotence of thoughts, with the prompt fulfilment of wishes, with secret injurious powers and with the return of the dead. The condition under which the feeling of uncanniness arises here is unmistakable. We—or our primitive forefathers—once believed that these possibilities were realities, and were convinced that they actually happened. Nowadays we no longer believe in

them, we have *surmounted* these modes of thought; but we do not feel quite sure of our new beliefs, and the old ones still exist within us ready to seize upon any confirmation. As soon as something *actually happens* in our lives which seems to confirm the old, discarded beliefs we get a feeling of the uncanny; it is as though we were making a judgement something like this: "So, after all, it is *true* that one can kill a person by the mere wish!" or, "So the dead *do* live on and appear on the scene of their former activities!" and so on. Conversely, anyone who has completely and finally rid himself of animistic beliefs will be insensible to this type of the uncanny. . . . Our conclusion could then be stated thus: an uncanny experience occurs either when infantile complexes which have been repressed are once more revived by some impression, or when primitive beliefs which have been surmounted seem once more to be confirmed. . . . These two classes of uncanny experience are not always sharply distinguishable. When we consider that primitive beliefs are most intimately connected with infantile complexes, and are, in fact, based on them, we shall not be greatly astonished to find that the distinction is often a hazy one. (*Complete Works* 17:249)

Freud's formulation of magical thinking, in "The Uncanny," maps *repressed* childhood magical belief onto *surmounted* primitive or archaic magical belief, a kind of "ontogeny recapitulates phylogeny" of the world of magical thinking. The terms *ontogeny* and *phylogeny* were coined by Freud's younger contemporary Ernst Heinrich Haeckel, and the idea that each developing individual organism goes through all the phases of the evolving phylum (that human embryos at one point possess gills, etc.) is part of a nineteenth-century legacy of thought that also underpinned colonial paternalism— savages are analogous to children, and both need to be kept under the benevolent thumb of civilized adults. We are in the mental world of Sir James Frazer, with all its now embarrassing ethnocentrism, and we need to be careful in adapting Freud's notions not to fall prey in naive ways to the nineteenth-century prejudices encoded therein—we have more than enough twentieth-century prejudices to worry about without resurrecting older ones.

Also, I find the overemphasis on the sexual by psychoanalytic criticism as unhelpful as the overemphasis on the political by new historicists. In my adaptation of Freud's notion of an unconscious where magical belief has been repressed by a rational consciousness, I posit an unconscious not limited to phalluses, castration anxiety, and patricidal urges, but an unconscious more specifically early modern, where a medieval mentality has been repressed by an early modern mentality, a rural mentality repressed by an urban consciousness, and a Catholic mentality repressed by a Protestant consciousness. The Renaissance magical unconscious, however, should not be imagined as a sort of half-wit brother who periodically escapes from the attic of the unconscious to cause embarrassing scenes in the parlor of rational thought: the magical unconscious shapes consciousness because it is useful, because such older ways of thinking help make sense of a more modern world.

Hildred Geertz is surely right to protest against seeing magical belief or magical thinking in terms of individual psychology, and here again we must correct Freud's view of the individual consciousness by taking into account the social and historical embeddedness of consciousness. Geertz rejects the view that "although the origin of specific [magical] practices is historical in that we inherit each assemblage of customs and beliefs from our predecessors, their continued enactment and transmission to the next generation is to be explained in terms of the satisfaction of needs, either psychological or sociological" (79); she argues instead that beliefs are kept alive through the sheer force of culture itself, the plausibility lent to beliefs from the fact that we are brought up from childhood in them and surrounded by people who share them (84–85). But to this I would respond that psychological needs do not have to be individual: a group, a culture can have collective needs, collective anxieties, to which group magical thinking can be a response. Mary Douglas's theory that societies that feel threatened with invasion are likely to develop magical pollution beliefs, a theory I will use in chapter 1, is essentially such a theory of group needs, even group psychology.

The New in Terms of the Old, the Immaterial in Terms of the Physical

It should not surprise us that dawning modernity should structure experience by old magical blueprints, for as Ernst Gombrich has postulated with regard to the psychology of perception, the mind tends to apprehend the new in terms of the familiar. Gombrich provides an illustration from a sixteenth-century German artist who represented the Castel Sant' Angelo in Rome with wooden turrets like a German castle: "he selected from the drawer of his mental stereotypes the appropriate cliché for a castle" (70). Thomas Kuhn and others have shown that early modern science was often piggybacked on magical beliefs.[2] Harvey, who discovered the circulation of the blood, treated tumors by laying the hand of a corpse on them, and even later, Newton himself "made over a million words of notes on both alchemy and religious studies" (B. Vickers 15). Copernicus, father of modern astronomy, spoke the mythic language of Father Sky and Mother Earth: "The Earth conceives by the sun and becomes pregnant with annual offspring" (1.10.50). Gombrich's theory that familiar schemata help us understand what is new is often helpful in literature: in coming to terms with a modern political situation in the *Henry IV* plays, Shakespeare reached back into the Bible for the familiar schema of the prodigal son. One of literature's basic building blocks, metaphor, is at heart an attempt to elucidate the unfamiliar by reference to the familiar.[3] In understanding political assassination in terms of human sacrifice, international relations in terms of transfer-of-evil scapegoating, threats to national security in terms of bodily pollution, political stability and good government in terms of green trees and magical promotion of fertility, political rebellion in terms of old festive topsy-turviness, modern courtship in terms of fertility magic and eye magic, Shakespeare and his contemporaries were engaging in the time-honored human activity of making sense of the new in terms of the old, of assimilating the disconcerting world of modernity to the comforting world of traditional folkways. Humans are territorial animals, and unfamiliar territory, always threatening, is best entered by feeling cautiously ahead with one foot while keeping the other on native soil.

An extension of Gombrich's principle is that just as one conceptualizes the unfamiliar in terms of the familiar, one also conceptualizes what is cerebral and abstract in terms of the physical, the bodily. One cannot help noticing the persistent physicality involved in what I call magical thinking: the mental is repeatedly conceptualized in terms of the physical, the abstract in terms of the organic. Politics are envisioned in terms of blood sacrifice, the social activity of courtship in terms of bodily fertility, political stability in terms of a green countryside full of healthy sheep, foreign threats to British sovereignty in terms of protection of the body against penetration of its vulnerable orifices, mitigation of civil dissension in terms of expelling a disease from the body. Scapegoating depends on a conflation of the physical and the immaterial—as a load can be transferred from one person's shoulders to another's, so guilt can be transferred from one to another. Perhaps the most prominent strain in recent literary study has been attention to representations of the body, and I hope my study will contribute to that important work. As Mark Johnson notes, language repeatedly shows that "we understand the mental in terms of the physical, the mind in terms of bodily experience" (53), and that principle underlies much of the magical thinking I explore.

The Validity of Cross-cultural Reference

Since I am exploring a historical moment in a particular culture, this is probably the place to justify the fact that I have occasionally used materials from other cultures—ancient Greece, Persia, even Africa—to illuminate such practices as scapegoating. Sometimes one can point to a direct link between such cultures and Elizabethan England—Shakespeare's contemporaries knew about Greek sacrifice directly through some Greek and many Roman texts and about Hebrew sacrifice through the Bible; and less directly, the magical practices of the Mediterranean world influenced northern Europe for a millennium through Roman conquest, travel, trade. Cultural diffusion was a reality over centuries and millennia in Europe, India, the Middle East, and parts of Asia, as the genealogy of the Indo-European languages reminds us: where language could go, magical belief could go. Clarence Maloney points out the remarkable stability of evil-eye beliefs over a huge geographic area:

> There are so many aspects of the evil eye belief found contiguously from Scotland at one extreme of its main area of distribution to Sri Lanka at the other, that we must rely heavily on a diffusionist explanation. In Scotland, for example, where

this belief was described by Maclagan at the turn of this century, cattle and milk products and the churning process were especially susceptible to evil eye attack; the eye could make a cow's udder or a woman's breasts dry up, or cause milk to be devoid of butterfat. All this is true at the other geographical extreme, in India. A charm of a knotted red thread, or of hair, may be tied on children or on a pregnant cow both in Scotland and in South Asia. A fragment of the Bible may be sewn in the clothes as a preventative in Scotland, while in South Asia a fragment of the Koran or a Hindu incantation may be put in a receptacle and tied on children. In both regions the evil eye's malevolent effects may be cured by salt, and by spitting. Also in both regions its attack can be prevented by making deprecatory remarks about one's children or possessions, or by giving to charity. . . . In the two regions the belief serves similar functions in the folk etiology, is popularly regarded as preventing too much self-praise, and is explained as suppressing envy. (xiv)

But sometimes, as in most African materials I have drawn on, there is no demonstrable direct link with Elizabethan England. Should we therefore forgo all use of African analogy? Gone are the days when the "butterfly collecting" of a Frazer was acceptable: we no longer pile up examples of scapegoating or near scapegoating or possible scapegoating from all around the globe, attributing them to some universal entity such as the "primitive mind."[4] Having grown more respectful of the singularity of cultures, we no longer believe in pancultural phenomena uniting all humankind. The anthropologist Clifford Geertz has argued persuasively in his influential *The Interpretation of Cultures* against the existence of *any* universals that cut across all human cultures, except the ever-adaptable capacity to create culture, and many contemporary writers who draw on anthropology refuse to venture, for examples or analogies, outside the culture they are studying. But Geertz himself, in "Centers, Kings, and Charisma," draws an analogy between Elizabethan England and modern Java, and such analogies, as long as they do not blur distinctions or conjure cloudy human universals, can be very helpful. The anthropologist Victor Turner compares Ndembu liminality with the liminality of Shakespeare's fool and traces in many cultures the fertility-connected colors black, white, and red. *Never* to step outside our own culture is to court ethnological provincialism; to begin to understand any culture we need to see how it articulates with, resembles, or differs from other cultures. Therefore I have sometimes ventured into Mediterranean and African cultures and at times even further afield, trying always to be careful, and to link up such foreign evidence with Elizabethan evidence.

Magical Thinking and the New Historicism

New historicists have been interested in magical thinking, and in some ways this study forms a continuum with their work (though ultimately I have more quarrels with them than agreements). At the March 1991 meeting of the Shakespeare Association of America, Stephen Greenblatt presented a paper arguing for the presence in Shakespeare of a belief similar to tribal belief that no death is natural, that all deaths are attributable to enemy malice or sorcery. Arguing that nearly all male deaths in Shakespeare carry a suggestion of "answerability," he noted that Richard II's wish for Gaunt's death, Henry IV's wish for Richard II's, Henry V's killing Falstaff's heart have about them some aura of magical thinking ("Eating").[5] This perfectly fits my definition of magical thinking in comprising an unconscious residue of magical belief. Yet Greenblatt more typically argues that in adopting the forms of magical rites, the Renaissance "evacuated" them of magical meaning ("Exorcists"),[6] and this seems to me to lean too far toward the triumph of rationalism, making Shakespeare and his contemporaries more "modern" than they were. I suspect that we treat Shakespeare himself magically, as a kind of old/young figure, early modern but somehow modern. We complain of those who turn him into a cultural icon transcending time and yet we do it ourselves when we exempt him from the rigorous historicizing to which we subject his contemporaries: how many times have we read that Shakespeare demystified, exposed, treated with ironic detachment, parodied, inverted, played gracefully with the conventions and beliefs his benighted contemporaries adopted blindly? How far did Shakespeare evacuate or demystify magical belief? And how far, even though his characters at times mock and unmask magical belief, does magical thinking

remain subliminally operative? To what extent does magical thinking comprise the steel girders holding up the very edifice of his
plays? These questions will recur in these pages.

My most serious quarrel with the new historicists is with their
reducing history to politics. The study of magical thinking lays open
many areas of life other than the narrowly political, and too often
such areas have been closed out by politically dominated reading.

Fertility Ritual Revisited

Rather than assimilating all writings on the countryside to politics (by, for example, discussing pastoral only in the context of Elizabeth's politically manipulative rural progresses), we might with
equal justification assimilate the political to the overwhelming importance of crop fertility. Ritual misrule has most often been seen
in its political ramifications, as promoting or co-opting the rebellious urges of an oppressed populace. Yet saturnalian rites of misrule were from ancient times a species of fertility rite, promoting
crop growth and the survival of the human race. Rites promoting
human and crop fruition often peer through the "misrule" materials collected by Natalie Davis. Through charivaris, youth abbeys
punished husband- and wife-beaters, widows or widowers who re-
married, cuckolds, adulterers, newlyweds not yet expecting a child—
all offenders against sex and marriage. Davis thinks that charivaris
at second marriages, especially January–May marriages, expressed
society's displeasure at the removal of a youth from the pool of
marital eligibles and at a marriage unlikely to produce many children. Charivaris, saturnalian in age and status inversions—young
bachelors criticizing older married people—thus also seem linked
with fertility rites. One charivari custom, a parade through the
streets in which malefactors represented in effigy were buffeted
about the genitalia, recalls ancient Greek and Roman rites wherein
a slave was beaten about the genitals to ensure crop fertility (see
chapter 3). (Linking comic beatings in a wedding context with the
generative principle, Bakhtin cites the beating of a bride, including
her genitals, in Rabelais [205–6].) Even political charivaris turn out,
on close inspection, to address the fecundity of wives and land: at
Dijon in 1576 the king's grand master of streams and forests was

attacked in charivaris for beating his wife in May (a special month for women) and despoiling forests he was supposed to protect (Davis, "Reasons" 68). When Davis adduces examples of political revolt growing out of carnival, the fertility link holds: corn riots were often led by women or men dressed as women, often in black face (a hallmark of popular rites—see chapter 4); one revolt was led by a woman who said taxation was taking bread from her children ("Women on Top" 179, 156). One matter Davis does not discuss is that these revolts concerned distribution of harvested crops; one reason women were involved is that the female principle is often associated with harvesting rites.[7]

Carnival's feasting, reminiscent of fertility rites' insistence on plenty, is linked with another saturnalian feature—return of the dead. The archaic gesture of offering food to the dead persisted through the Middle Ages: "When honoring patrons and benefactors buried in the church, the clergy organized banquets and drank to their memory.... A Record of the Kvedlinburg Abbey openly states that the clergy's banquet feeds and pleases the dead.... The Spanish Dominicans drank to the memory of their deceased patrons, toasting them with the typical ambivalent words *viva el muerto*" (Bakhtin 79–80). We can read the return-of-the-dead motif politically, as I do concerning *Julius Caesar* (chapter 5) but we need not read it that way exclusively; its political side may not be its most interesting side.

The Scythe of Saturn

The tension, in Renaissance literature often amounting to murderousness, between human generations was easily mapped onto the political world: dominance by elders in the family provided Elizabethans with a primary model for political power. But the generational power struggle paradoxically enacts the goal of fertility rites, the regeneration of the race: the young must win the battle of the generations for the world to go on. This is what unites power-inversion rites like the Saturnalia and fertility rites like the Lupercal, and it provides a multivalent symbol that has given me my title. The scythe was the harvesting tool of a fertility god, Saturn, lord of seedtime and harvest; but it is also an iconographic sibling of the grim reaper's scythe, which descends in the history of emblematic art from the sickle with which Cronus castrated his father. Peeling off layers of story to find Greek myth under the Roman myth reminds us that Saturn and Cronus are one god: the god of harvest and the god of parent killing are the same. That fertility and the continuance of the race are not antithetical to but actually dependent on war between children and parents is more than the internal contradiction of a mingled myth: it is the terrible logic of life itself.

A nexus of fertility magic, murderous dismemberment, and generational strife recurs again and again in this study—in the idea of regenerative dismemberment in chapters 1 and 3 (where I discuss the link between dismemberment and harvest in *Titus Andronicus,* a play whose hero is a slayer of his own children and where one character is named Saturninus and another said to be governed in disposition by the planet Saturn); in the modeling of blood sacrifice, political and other scapegoating on a child's initial blaming of mother for life's shortfalls (chapter 2); in the topsy-turviness of generations—sometimes carnivalesque, sometimes violent and in earnest—in popular rites, in plays, and in life itself during the turbulent high Renaissance (chapter 5); in the genre of debate between an old man and a young in chapters 2 and 5—the debate was intimately linked with fertility magic; in the competition between an old suitor and a young in fertility-connected popular rites and in Shakespeare's sonnets (chapter 4). The Saturnalia, named after the god Saturn, was a fertility festival whose founding myths had to do both with a golden age of plenty and with murderous competition between generations. The lines *Iam redit et Virgo, redeunt Saturnia redeunt,* "the Virgin and the rule of Saturn are now returning," centrally important to the cult of Elizabeth, are from the most influential of pastorals, Virgil's fourth eclogue; the whole genre of pastoral was Saturnian in being at once a vision of a golden age and the scene of conflict between old shepherds and young. Given Elizabeth's appropriation of Virgil's "rule of Saturn" image, it is interesting that, as Kieckhefer reminds us, if great Jupiter was the planet governing France, Saturn was the planet governing England (125). The ambiguous scythe of Saturn, sign of dismemberment, murderous generational rivalry, and fruitful harvest, attracted me as a multivalent symbol expressing the disparate but interdependent kinds of magical thinking that interest me.

The Magic of the Potent Gaze

Another kind of magic that recurs in several chapters and that I am increasingly coming to regard as very important to Renaissance literature is the complex of beliefs involving the evil eye. The possessor of an evil eye can cause illness, deformity, or death to people, animals, or crops by simply staring at them; this evil eye is often attracted by praise. A person or thing put at risk by being praised is said to be "forspoken"; King James showed familiarity with such beliefs in his reference to "such kind of charms, as comely daft wives use for healing forspoken goods, for preserving them from evil eyes" (*Demonology* 11). Such beliefs are very widespread, being found throughout India, north Africa, the middle east, and Europe (John Roberts 234), and as ancient Sumerian texts show, evil-eye beliefs are over five thousand years old (Langdon 39). They appear in the Bible (see Prov. 23:6–8, Deut. 28:54–56, Matt. 20:15; see also Brav 46). Treatises on the evil eye available in the Renaissance include Enrique de Villena's *Tratado del Aojamiento,* 1422; Leonardus Vairus's *De Fascino,* 1589; Martinus Antonius Del Rio's *Disquisitionum Magicarum,* 1599–1600; and Joannes Lazarus Gutierrez's *Opusculum de Fascino,* 1653.[8] Since evil-eye beliefs were closely identified with witchcraft, many beliefs about the evil eye can also be found in Renaissance witchcraft treatises such as Johann Weyer's *De Praestigiis Daemonum.* In Shakespeare's day evil-eye beliefs were especially strong in Scotland, northern England, and other parts of rural England (see Maclagan, Davidson). Shakespeare refers to the evil eye when Pistol, disguised as a hobgoblin, tells Falstaff, "vile worm, thou wast o'erlook'd even in thy birth" (*Wiv* V.v.87) and when Portia tells Bassanio, "Beshrew your eyes, / They have e'erlook'd me and divided me" (*MV* III.ii.14–16). I will argue that evil-eye beliefs are important in *The Rape of Lucrece* and *Othello* and permeate Petrarchan love poetry.

The English term for casting the evil eye was *overlook;* Latin used the noun *fascinum* and and the verb *fascinare.* That we still use *fas-*

cinate, and other magical terms (*charm, bewitch*) for the act of inspiring love hints (as I will argue in chapter 4) at magical belief
submerged in our conceptions of sexual attraction; it is therefore
not surprising to find evil-eye beliefs lingering precisely in such sexually oriented texts as *Lucrece, Othello,* and love poetry. But the
implications of these beliefs are much wider.

Rulers' superstitious fear of the public gaze may be related to
fear of "overlooking." Though Elizabeth manipulated public ap-
pearances with genius, in many Shakespearean texts public figures
are profoundly ambivalent about being in the public view. Having
power over a large populace would seem to be one of the gratifica-
tions of "the sweet fruition of an earthly crown"; yet being much
gazed upon by that populace comes to be seen as harmful, an effect rather like the evil eye. Henry IV thinks that Hal has become
"common-hackneyed in the eyes of men," a fate shared with Richard II, who was "daily swallow'd by men's eyes"; when the people
tired of Richard, he was "seen, but with such eyes / As, sick and
blunted with community, / Afford no extraordinary gaze, / Such as
is bent on sun-like majesty / When it shines seldom in admiring
eyes" (*1H4* III.ii.40, 70–80). The "extraordinary gaze" has something magical in it. By the theory of eye-beams, vision occurred
when beams shot out from the eyes to illuminate what they fell
upon; in this passage, Henry IV imagines a gaze of the people falling on the king just as his sunlike majesty shines beams on them,
an ocular reciprocity like that between lovers (see chapter 4). The
king's sunlike gaze must remain stronger than the people's extraordinary gaze; a weakling like Richard is simply consumed by the
public gaze, cannibalized, "swallow'd by men's eyes"—the primitive fear of being eaten becomes entangled with fear of the gaze.

The public eye could serve directly for purposes of ritual humiliation, as in the public parading of prostitutes or scolds or as when
the Duchess of Gloucester is forced to walk barefoot on public
streets with papers on her back detailing her crimes: she says to
her husband, "Look how they gaze! / See how the giddy multitude
do point, / And nod their heads, and throw their eyes on thee! /
Ah, Gloucester, hide thee from their hateful looks" (*2H6* II.iv.20–
23). Gloucester's comment on her penance, "Sweet Nell, ill can thy
noble mind abrook / The abject people gazing on thy face, / With
envious looks, laughing at thy shame, / That erst did follow thy

proud chariot-wheels / When thou didst ride in triumph through the streets" (II.iii.10–14), is couched in Roman terms (riding in triumph, chariot wheels), recalling two purposes of Roman triumphal processions—to honor successful military heroes and to display the defeated in disgrace; both Antony and Cleopatra fear being displayed in such public humiliations (*Ant* IV.xiv.73–78, V.ii.55–57).

A tantalizing cultural and geographical link between the procession of disgracing and evil-eye beliefs is that both are found in dairy farming regions: in his cross-cultural survey of the contexts of evil-eye beliefs, John M. Roberts finds that the highest occupational correlation is with dairy farming (241), and David Underdown, writing of the skimmington ride (that procession of humiliation which shamed scolds, wife-beaters, husband-beaters, and quarreling couples) notes that "the geographical location, the name and the form of the ritual all seem to have some connection with dairy farming" ("Taming" 135). The same people, then, believed in the evil eye and used the public gaze as a punishment, and English rural people were among them. Even for a queen accustomed to using royal progresses through the countryside as what Louis Althusser calls "ideological state apparatuses" it would be difficult to avoid the ambiguous implications of being carried on display in a public procession, and the use of such public display as a punishment stems, I think, from magical beliefs about the danger of falling under the gaze of strangers.

The triumphal procession is not far removed from the procession of disgracing, as is suggested by Roman triumphs which, like the processions in which Richard II and Bolingbroke enter London (*R2* V.ii.23–28), are double processions of triumph and disgrace. In folk wisdom, praise itself can attract the evil eye; and even a triumphant figure parading before public eyes is in some ways a prisoner of their gaze, almost constituted by it. The gaze of the multitude is always obscurely threatening. As Eugene McCartney writes, "An overenthusiastic reception of an official was tantamount to praise of the kind that aroused the envy of the gods. . . . When Germanicus Caesar . . . was in Alexandria the cordial greetings of the populace greatly frightened him. He deprecated their acclamations of him as a god and threatened to appear before them less frequently unless they restrained themselves. According to Sir Walter Scott, Gustavus Adolphus was equally perturbed by the worship of a throng as he rode through the streets of Nuremberg. The novelist puts these words into the mouth of the great general: 'If you idolise me thus like a god, who shall assure you that the vengeance of Heaven will not soon prove me to be a mortal?'" (582). Can Coriolanus's horror at publicly seeking the praise of the multitude after his military triumphs also be seen in this light?

The evil eye was not only the malicious glance of an ill-tempered neighbor; it was often conceived as a larger principle of evil in the universe, as all the bad luck waiting to descend if one incautiously praised a friend or grew complacent in one's own happiness; the earliest texts depict the evil eye "as a roving independent entity" with "a deleterious effect upon both the rains from heaven and the milk from cows" (Langdon 39). As Eugene McCartney has shown, "the blasting effects of praise" come from three sources: "(1) the inadvertence or the ignorance of well-meaning people who let slip complimentary remarks; (2) the envy and malevolence of those who have the evil eye; and (3) the jealousy of the gods, who permit no mortal to be supremely beautiful or happy or prosperous without paying for his blessings by counterbalancing woes and adversities" (568). The third closely resembles hubris, that injudicious act of drawing attention to oneself that called down divine retribution in Greek tragedy. Othello seems too conspicuously to take pleasure in his happiness, and this fills him with superstitious dread: "If it were now to die, / 'Twere now to be most happy; for, I fear, / My soul hath her content so absolute / That not another comfort like to this / Succeeds in unknown fate" (II.i.191–95). His sudden dread draws on the old notion that happiness and misery alternate in cycles, and this is so because conspicuous happiness attracts misery—praise attracting the evil eye. Othello's public declaration of happiness is followed directly by a nervous disclaimer from Desdemona, "The heavens forbid / But that our loves and comforts should increase, / Even as our days do grow!" which resembles the apotropaic verbal formula often used to turn away the evil eye after an act of praise or a profession of well-being ("touch wood" is most familiar to us).[9] Desdemona's remark (and a further profession of "content" by Othello) are followed immediately by evidence that the couple's display of happiness has indeed attracted envy's evil eye: Iago says aside, "O, you are well tuned now! / But I'll set down the pegs that make this music." The moment may well be conceived psychologically—Othello is susceptible to suspicion precisely because he possesses the magical mind-set that makes spoken happiness dangerous. He gets trouble partly because (after parading his happiness) he is expecting trouble. But this does not devalue magic: psychological realism here depends on suppressed magical thinking.

If so central a concept as hubris, basic to our understanding of tragedy, is connected to superstitions about the evil eye and the danger of praising or of admitting to happiness, the literary implications of such superstitions deserve much more attention than they have received. And what about literary praise—is it dangerous? Whole genres such as eulogistic verse, conqueror plays, royal pageants flattering the queen, and formal praises of womankind have praise as their raison d'etre—does anything guard such genres against the blighting tendencies of praise? I have examined this issue in one such genre, love poetry of the Petrarchan tradition (chapter 4); I would be interested in seeing it explored in other genres.

Evil-eye beliefs provide a useful reminder that the magical mind-set is not necessarily "primitive," for as John M. Roberts has discovered through tabulating societies in which the belief occurs, "the cultures possessing the evil eye belief fall roughly in the upper half of our sample of 186 societies as far as cultural complexity is concerned"; evil-eye beliefs are associated with cultures possessing a high degree of technological specialization, complex social stratification, the practice of writing and the accumulation of written records, standardized coinage or paper currency, complex administrative levels above the local community, integrated land transport, and a fairly dense population (235ff.). In case we might jump to the conclusion that Othello is identified with the evil eye because he is an African, I would say it is more likely that the evil eye comes naturally to a play set in one of the great centers of evil-eye belief, Italy. One would hesitate to call Renaissance Italy a primitive culture. Magical thinking can be highly sophisticated; to demonstrate its prevalence in Shakespeare and his culture is not to look for primitivism.

The persistent presence of evil-eye beliefs, the obsession with eyes in Renaissance love poetry, and the strongly visual appeal of such poetry lend support to Marshall McLuhan's theory that with the coming of print, an ear-oriented culture replaced an eye-oriented culture. McLuhan argues that during the sixteenth century, the shift to print culture from oral tradition (and from a manuscript culture limited to a clerical elite) brought with it a widespread conceptual reorientation from the aural to the visual. "Nonliterate cultures," he argues, "experience such an overwhelming tyranny of the ear over the eye that any balanced interplay among the senses is unknown at the auditory extreme, just as balanced interplay of the senses became extremely difficult after print stepped up the visual component in Western experience to extreme intensity" (28). Like many theorists of orality and literacy, McLuhan overstates the conceptual restructuring that accompanies literacy. Regarding oral cultures as visually deficient ignores the tremendous visual acuity of the hunter-gatherer who tracks animals by tiny signs or spots minute berries in dense foliage. To generalize to the human brain from changes in verbal communication systems (from oral to literate) is probably too large a leap; but this does not render unimportant the changes in verbal communication systems. And there is definitely something to the notion of the ascendancy of the eye in the early modern period; picking up on "Heidegger's characterization of the early modern age as an effort to conceive of the world *as* a picture," Barbara Freedman uses the Lacanian theory of the gaze to investigate the Elizabethan "spectator consciousness" (9). In chapter 4 I will explore a highly visual genre, the sonnet sequences of Renaissance love poetry, and show how their visual orientation manifests itself in a semiotics of red, white, and black color coding, in pervasive imagery of eyes and sight, in a suppression of sound, the tongue, the oral. It is not surprising to find in such poetry, where the eye is all powerful, symptoms of the evil eye, and I will argue that such symptoms are pervasive. The red, white, and black color symbolism evidences the presence of fertility magic, and the poems are full of eye magic as well.

The Wand of Literature

The possibility that literature itself might as late as the Renaissance have constituted a magical intervention into social relations—and I will be raising this most explicitly in chapter 4 when I suggest that the Petrarchist's praise of his mistress can be construed as malicious magic—provokes questions about language as magically efficacious. Anglo-Saxon literature rejoiced in charms and spells and often appropriated the paraphernalia of Christianity for magical purposes. *Solomon and Saturn I* uses the Pater Noster as a charm; the letters of "Pater Noster" are individually powerful against the devil: "By smashing his face and causing his teeth to scatter throughout hell, S, letter of glory, . . . sends the fiend into hiding"; T stabs the devil's tongue (O'Keeffe 48, 57). That writing itself was magically powerful "was acknowledged in various ways in the literature of Anglo-Saxon England" (O'Keeffe 51). The professional writers (or singers) of the age, the Anglo-Saxon scops, were "Lord of the Word in a world in which words had not yet lost their magic power" (J. E. C. Williams 93). How far had the magic ebbed out of words by Shakespeare's day? Renaissance professional writers did not claim sacred status; yet throughout the early modern period people used charms, spells, talismans with magic writing on them. It may be at our peril that we neglect the possibility that literary works themselves could at times possess magical efficacy or at least that the aura of such efficacy gave them, in their own day, a special charge that we are no longer aware of. "Is it any wonder," as Louis Montrose asks, "that in the ambiguous and pervasively occult mental world shared by most Elizabethans, theatrical performances should have affinities with religious services and magical rites?" ("Purpose" 61).

The kinds of magical thinking I discuss here do not begin to exhaust the subject. Heather Dubrow has discussed traces of "apotropaic magic, the type of ritual aimed at averting danger" in Stuart epithalamia (*Happier Eden* 81). Shakespeare's many references to reading character in the face may reveal a mind-set more magical than we would at first assume: Ihon Indagine's treatise on physiognomy, translated into English in 1558, regards physiognomy as a species of divination, along with palm reading and astrology, and when Duncan regrets not being able to "read the mind's construction in the face" or when Othello reads Desdemona's palm, we should recall that these were common magical practices in Shakespeare's time.[10] In my essay "Patchwork: Piecing the Early Modern Mind in England's First Century of Print Culture," I argue that the Renaissance habit of piecing together a number of borrowed plots owes something to belief (also visible in patchwork quilting) that magical power accrues from joining together objects owned and used by illustrious forebears and that writing and printing technologies, multiply interconnected with the technologies of cloth, encouraged the transfer to literature of ancient magical beliefs attending cloth making. Many other facets of early modern magical thinking could be explored, and even those I do take up here remain to be explored in many other writers: for reasons of manageability, I have restricted my focus mainly to Shakespeare, treating some other Renaissance writers, especially in chapter 4, but not to the extent I would have liked.

Why Shakespeare? the reader might ask. Those truly interested in magical thinking might more profitably study works less canonical than these central texts of Renaissance high literature: they might study folk tales or other popular genres or oral tradition. In fact, that is what I will be doing next—I have begun work on a group of early sixteenth-century anonymous texts I believe to be oral-derived and am already experiencing the frustration of trying to penetrate into an oral world that vanished four hundred years ago. Keith Thomas writes almost despairingly of the prospects for learning much about "illiterate Englishmen who lived three or four centuries ago" or being able to "recreate their mental world." This involves "searching for invisible mental structures, . . . underlying inchoate and ill-recorded systems of thought, which are only articulated in a fragmentary way, . . . structures of which the average member of the society concerned is, almost by definition, unable to give a coherent account, any more than he can describe the analytical structure of the language which he speaks" ("Anthropology" 104, 106). Yet a culture containing both orality and literacy offers one way to approach the mental world of the oral, of the Folk: through traces it left on the literate culture. An ideal place to look for such traces would be in writers who grew up, if not in a village, at least in a country town with close access to rural culture; writers educated enough to write well but not educated to so advanced a level that their minds were completely interpellated by intellectual ways of structuring reality—ideally, writers not university educated. Writers hospitable enough to popular culture that they felt comfortable using folk tales as sources; writers who wrote large bodies of works, enough for patterns of thinking to emerge clearly. If there is any English Renaissance writer who fits this description better than Shakespeare, or is more ideally suited to preserving the traces of the mental world of the Folk, I cannot imagine who that writer would be. My main quarry is what magical thinking can tell us about Shakespeare; but those interested in what Shakespeare can tell us about magical thinking, about the submerged mental world of his culture, will also find material in these pages.

Defining Magic

Though magical thinking rather than magical belief comprises my main focus, the one does depend on the other, and it would be irresponsible not to make some attempt to define magic or to give some account of the theory and controversies surrounding the study of magic in this period. The topic is immense, and I can do no more here than to sketch in its outlines lightly.

It is not easy to define magic in this period or to distinguish it firmly from religion on one side, protoscience on the other. Some Renaissance thinkers placed magic in a religious framework and tried to situate it in a theological superstructure where evil magic was invariably linked with demonic pacts; others took a "scientific" tack, assuming that magic operated mechanically, following something like the laws of nature. From the late Middle Ages on, Kieckhefer says, writers

> endeavored to work out the boundaries between natural and demonic magic. What is remarkable is how much power they were willing to concede to the occult powers in nature, without positing demonic intervention. Certain thirteenth-century and later writers recognized that the evil eye (or "fascination") might work in natural ways. Some, relying on Arabic sources, explained this phenomenon by arguing that the human soul can in many ways affect other persons: the soul is superior to the body, and has power over its own body and other people's as well. (182)

Here magic, given a "scientific" explanation, shades off into natural occurrence. Authors on folk medicine "do not reflect explicitly on the relationship between medicine and magic, nor do they indicate which of their cures have 'occult' as opposed to ordinary power. . . . If they claimed that cat faeces could cure baldness or a quartan fever, they would support this claim not so much with theoretical explanation as with appeal to their own experience" (Kieckhefer 66). The same went for charms; as Kieckhefer says,

> when speculative minds in the later medieval centuries began reflecting on natural magic, one of the questions that they considered was whether words by themselves, just like certain herbs and other objects of nature, held special powers. Many people believed that verbal formulas could have such inherent power, and these charms would be prime examples. Thus, for *some* medieval people charms would count as magic. Other people would have been hard pressed to distinguish between them and purely religious prayers. And perhaps the majority of users would simply not have reflected on the question: if the charms worked, that was more important than how they worked. (74–75)

The boundary between religion and magic has always been fluid, and the degree to which early modern religion partook of the magical is a contested question. Many regard belief in ritual's magical efficacy as the hallmark of primitive thought, and the anthropologist Luc de Heusch adduces, as a historic moment when the magical was yielding to the symbolic, the medieval-Renaissance transubstantiation debate: was communion "merely commemorative, symbolic, or . . . an efficacious act, just like sacrifice" (195)? But the anthropologist Mary Douglas contrasts the merely commemorative communion practices of early Christians with later Catholicism's superstitious regard for ritual: "magical practice, in [the] sense of automatically effective ritual, is not a sign of primitiveness . . . ; nor is a high ethical content the prerogative of evolved religions" (19). Denying that "primitive" people believe in their rites' automatic efficacy, she notes that early Christians prayed for miracles, but could not lay them "under automatic control":

> sprinkling of holy water could not guarantee a cure. The power of miraculous intervention was believed to exist, but there was no certain way of harnessing it. . . . Each primitive universe hopes to harness some such marvellous power to the needs of men. . . . [In the Christian miraculous period] miracle did not only occur through enacted rites, nor were rites always per-

formed in the expectation of miracle. It is realistic to suppose an equally loose relation holds between rite and magic effect in primitive religion. (*Purity* 59–60)

The "primitive" mind, Douglas argues, believes in magic as we believe in money, knowing at some level of consciousness that belief itself creates efficacy. The historian Keith Thomas argues, however, for a more naively instrumental attitude in medieval Christianity: "the Church's teaching was usually unambiguous on this point: prayers might bring practical results, but they could not be guaranteed to do so. In practice, however, the distinction was repeatedly blurred in the popular mind. The Church itself recommended the use of prayers when healing the sick or gathering medicinal herbs. Confessors required penitents to repeat a stated number of Paternosters. . . . The medieval Church thus did a great deal to weaken the fundamental distinction between a prayer and a charm" (*Religion* 28, 46–47). Thomas finds widespread evidence of a magical component persisting in early modern Christianity, despite the anti-ritual program of Protestantism. This suggests that a mind-set persisted, operating unconsciously or semiconsciously, inherited from many centuries of magical belief and practice, and not eradicable merely by Protestant preachers' inveighing against superstition or Puritans' abolishing morris dancing and Christmas.

During the late sixteenth century and the seventeenth century, Thomas argues, "in England magic declined in a double sense: the clergy abandoned all claims to be able to achieve supernatural effects; and the practice of the various magical arts diminished in prestige and extent" ("Anthropology" 99). But some argue that Thomas placed "the decline of magic" too early; noting that "Thomas's argument that by 1700 it is possible to draw a distinction between religion and magic is persuasive with regard to the gentry elite but not with regard to the people at large," Anthony Fletcher and John Stevenson declare that "in the English village there was probably no appreciable decline of magic before 1800" (8). Divination, such a widespread magical practice in Shakespeare's time, was still going strong in the many prophecies in popular literature in the eighteenth century, to the point where it was possible to say that "the commoner's world, despite the corrective efforts of Protestant divines and the diffusion of scientific knowledge, revolved within a universe of magic" (Valenze 85). Sometimes we can trace into later centuries a direct continuity with sixteenth-century prophecy beliefs, as in the continuing popularity of Mother Shipton, a Tudor folk prophet whose prognostications first appeared in print in 1641 and then went through nearly thirty editions into the nineteenth century (Valenze 77). Regional folklore studies such as Deane and Shaw's *The Folklore of Cornwall* or Palmer's *The Folklore of Warwickshire* show that superstitious beliefs persisting in the twentieth century display a remarkable continuity with beliefs we know existed in the sixteenth.

Reviewing Thomas's *Religion and the Decline of Magic,* Hildred Geertz (ignoring Thomas's declaration of the continuity of magic and religion in medieval times and perhaps exaggerating his contention that the two became severed by 1700) maintained that Thomas did not go far enough in recognizing the permeability of the line between religion and magic. Thomas's response was that he "did not suggest that magic was always distinct from 'religion,' . . . [but] that a reclassification took place during the [early modern] period, . . . whereby those elements in religion which ultimately came to be regarded as magical were gradually identified as such, first by the Lollards, then by the Reformers, [and] that a fundamental change took place in the idea of religion itself, as the emphasis came to be placed on formal belief rather than on a mode of living" ("Anthropology" 96). Controversies still surround the nature, extent, and date of the shift in "magical" attitudes within religion, but that magical belief was still a potent presence in society in Shakespeare's day is demonstrable.

The fluidity of Renaissance ideas on magic appears in the slipperiness of terminology; as Thomas notes, "the term 'witchcraft' was used loosely in Tudor and Stuart England, and was . . . applied to virtually every kind of magical activity or ritual operation that worked through occult methods" ("Relevance" 48). That being so, Hildred Geertz has objected to the very use of the term *magic,* not only as an oversimplification, but on grounds of its complicity in an ideological struggle; I will discuss this presently. Thomas, however, defends the term:

> "Magic" was relatively slow to emerge as a single label for a number of different activities. In the Middle Ages it was more

common to speak separately of "enchantment," "necromancy," "conjuration" or "sorcery" than to refer simply to "magic." The word existed both in Latin and in English, but commentators and clerics tended to list the magic arts separately;
only in the sixteenth century did it become common to group
them together under a single head. Nevertheless, I felt no in-
hibition about using the expression "magic" as a convenient
label for bracketing together a variety of specific practices
which contemporaries usually associated together, which had
been classified as "magical arts" since classical times. ("Anthropology" 94–95)

The disagreement on terminology between Thomas and Geertz
stems partly from a difference in outlook between a historian and
an anthropologist. As Thomas notes, historians often retain terms
that have become contentious or even taboo among anthropologists,

for example, "ritual," "belief," "witchcraft," "kinship," and
"religion." All of these have been rejected, as least by some
[anthropologists], because they are culture-bound categories
which are alien to the thinking of many societies and which,
if used on a universal scale, turn out to lack any constant or
intrinsic content. ("Primitive," of course went much earlier
because of its condescending evolutionary overtones; it has
been replaced by such debatable substitutes as "tribal," "traditional," "undifferentiated," "preliterate," or "having a low
level of material culture.") And with this rejected ballast has
gone "magic." ("Anthropology" 93)

But terms such as *magic*, Thomas argues, "though unsuitable for
export, . . . may be good enough for home." His intention has been
"to write English history, not to engage in cross-cultural analysis"
("Anthropology" 94). Without losing sight of the problematic nature of *magic*, I will justify my use of it by an argument similar to
Thomas's: Shakespeare uses the word *magic*—along with *enchantment, conjuration, sorcery, belief, witchcraft, religion*, and even
primitive; and he certainly doesn't have any truck with *undifferentiated, preliterate*, or *having a low level of material culture*. What
is good enough for Shakespeare is good enough for me.

The problem of defining *magic* is not merely semantic, of course.

Douglas argues that ever since the nineteenth century, "anthropologists have been saddled with an intractable problem: . . . magic is defined for them in residual, evolutionary terms" (*Purity* 18); in something resembling the Whig view of history, rationality is seen to be rousing itself from the slumbers of centuries, shaking off the fogs of magic and superstition, and marching forward into modernity. Douglas prefers to see something more like historical oscillation between "magical" beliefs such as those surrounding pollution and more "modern" attitudes emphasizing ethics, interior experience of God, a scientific approach to nature, and so forth. Not only did early commemorative communion rites precede more "magical" and superstitious attitudes toward communion, but Greek thought in the Homeric period "seems to have been relatively free of ritual pollution, . . . while clusters of pollution concepts emerge later and are expressed by the classical dramatists" (*Purity* 27). Where the word *decline* in Thomas's *Religion and the Decline of Magic* indicates a permanent turning point, Douglas might see it as the beginning of a cycle. I think that Shakespeare demonstrably wrote at a time of important change for magical thinking, whether it was the beginning of a new cycle or the beginning of the end. I emphasize, though, how early in the process of change his work comes, how incompletely transformed was magical thinking in his time. From time to time in this study I will argue that magical thinking is incompletely transformed even in our time.

Geertz puts her objections to the "decline of magic" hypothesis in more political terms than does Douglas:

What the Reformation and Enlightenment added up to in the end—to simplify outrageously—was the climb in intellectual status of a conception of the nature of religion which stressed the central necessity of a coherent doctrine and the emptiness of ritual. At the same time, in other circles, there was an increase in the market value of a view of the pursuit of knowledge which was empiricist and experimental. The result was an across-the-board downgrading of alternative views of religion and knowledge. The concept of "magic" as Thomas uses it when he himself is speaking is a direct descendant of these controversies, as a term for some of these downgraded alternatives. It is not the "decline" of the practice of magic that cries out for explanation, but the emergence and rise of the label "magic." (76)

By lumping a number of practices together as magic and positioning them sometimes against religion as a more coherent system, sometimes against technology as an instrumentally effective system, Thomas (Geertz thinks) is "tak[ing] part in the very cultural process that he is studying" (77). She argues that "the construct 'magic' as used in much of today's thinking about exotic belief systems draws its aura of factualness from its place in our own culture and its legitimacy from the social prestige of the cultivated groups who employed the construct as an ideological weapon in the past. The same is true for the notion that 'primitive ways of thought' contrast with 'modern'" (88).

Thomas has responded that although "today both scientists and theologians agree in using the term 'magic' negatively and pejoratively, to group together and disparage such practices as they currently regard as irrational or useless," this was not necessarily the case in early modern England: it is "quite wrong to suggest, as does Geertz, that the only contemporaries who used the term 'magic' were those who rejected it. If that had been so we should never have encountered women claiming to be 'good' witches or intellectuals boasting of their magical powers" ("Anthropology" 91, 97–98).

The problem of coherence bedevils the study of early modern magic. Geertz seems to contradict herself: she objects to Thomas's lumping together various early modern occult practices under the one label "magic" but at the same time she insists that such practices belonged to a "closed system" every bit as unified and coherent as a fully articulated theology: if it is so closed, unified, and coherent, why not call it "magic"? The conflict is not Geertz's alone: the resistance to a unifying label like "magic" is common (cf. D. F. Pocock's "if categorical distinctions of the Western mind are found upon examination to impose distinctions upon [and so falsify] the intellectual universes of other cultures then they must be discarded. . . . I believe 'magic' to be one such category" [2]); but no less common is an insistence that early modern magical beliefs formed a unified, coherent whole: as Fletcher and Stevenson note, Stuart Clark and others insist that early modern people "lived in a mental world that mostly made perfectly good sense to them and engaged in rituals which were . . . [not] merely the fragmentary cultural debris of earlier ways of thinking" (8). Thomas argues staunchly against this view:

> To the wizard, as to his clients, the source of his power was often unclear. Recourse to him did not necessarily reflect subscription to some alternative view of reality, any more than a visit to an orthodox physician indicated a clear grasp of the principles of Galen. Men went in a spirit of "try anything which works." . . . I am not convinced that a more sensitive observer would find behind [early modern magical rites] a view of reality comparable in coherence to that offered by the theologians. . . . It remains to be established whether these charms and rituals always constituted a coherent system or whether, as is implied in the old-fashioned definition of "superstition," they were just unintegrated remnants of older patterns of thought. At present it would seem common sense to assume that in a changing society mental coherence is no more to be expected than social coherence. ("Anthropology" 103, 106)

The defense of folk magic as "coherent," that is, as forming a unified and internally logical system, arises from the laudable wish to avoid ethnocentric condemnation of folk culture or condescension to the mind-sets of plebeians, peasants, the disadvantaged classes. But why should coherence and unity be so revered? Is this not itself the prejudice of a modern educated elite? (And more specifically, of an elite still not fully emancipated from the sway of structuralism?) Such reverence for unity runs on parallel rails to the demand for thematic unity in a literary work, a notion that held sway at about the same time this debate began raging among Geertz, Thomas, and others (the midseventies). In literary study, the ideal of unity and coherence has ebbed under attacks from Richard Levin (*New Readings*) and flagged in the general post-structuralist climate that valorizes decentering over unity. The notion of coherence, however, persists in the study of magic, though it is, I think, a misguided defense of the Folk. I think Thomas is right that "what we are faced with in this period is not one single code, but an amalgam of the cultural débris of many different ways of thinking, Christian and pagan, Teutonic and classical; and it would be absurd to claim that all these elements had been shuffled together to form a new and coherent system" (*Religion* 627–28). But I do not see this as an embarrassment to the folk consciousness. One might argue that inventive, system-free bricolage is the glory and strength of proletarian thinking; or one might argue that pilfering and patching is exactly the way high culture behaves in the Renaissance. In my essay "Patchwork: Piecing the Early Modern Mind" I argue that breaking down earlier culture into tiny units for reassembly was a hallmark of Renaissance culture, from the invention of printing to the indexing of books to the keeping of commonplace books to the assembly of multiple-plot plays. And one could reach beyond the Renaissance: the theory of intertextuality holds that piecing together random scraps of culture with no coherent overall system is what we do every time we read. Amalgamating shards of cultural debris from different traditions is often precisely the way culture works.

The uneducated did not articulate large belief systems in print or even in writing, and where their beliefs and rituals differed from those of educated people, a conflict existed that can (with caution) be mapped onto other developing class conflicts of the period—the early modern effort to stamp out magic was in part a class conflict. What worries Hildred Geertz in Keith Thomas's "decline of magic" formulation is that the ultimate winners in this conflict—the educated—have been able to impose their view of history, through labeling the belief system of the uneducated of their day as no system at all, as a meaningless collection of ad hoc superstitions, and it is from this, she thinks, "that our contemporary cultural concept of magical beliefs as a hodgepodge of unempirical illusions must have emerged" (88). But rather than rehabilitating respect for early modern commoners by claiming that their magical beliefs were part of a coherent system, I would argue that there is nothing inherently embarrassing about a hodgepodge of unempirical illusions—at worst it is no worse than the systematically unified structure of unempirical illusions that is Christian theology, and at best it has the potential, like chaos in recent scientific thinking, to be infinitely creative.

To import coherence and unity as yardsticks in dealing with folk culture is itself a serious imposition of alien ideology. Though I have grouped together various cultural practices and assumptions under the general heading of magical thinking, I do not view them as constituting a coherent, unified system. They are often interrelated, and I will show how some overlap with others, feed into each other, loop back over the same territory. But that is not to say that they form a closed system, and I do not see why we should seek coherence where it does not exist out of a wish to be ethnologically correct and fair to the Folk any more than we should ignore, from the same motive, the fact that magical thinking is often vicious, self-serving, and cruel.

Magic and Social Class

Class differences between the educated and the uneducated, though slippery and shifting,[11] are an important consideration in the study of magical thinking. It is among the educated that we find both magic and religion occasionally subjected to skeptical scrutiny, as in Reginald Scot's skepticism about witchcraft or the suspicion of a Marlowe or a Raleigh that religion was invented for political purposes, to "keep men in awe"; and it is also among the educated that we find ambitious attempts to systematize and rationally account for magic, as in the hermetic theorizing of the Neoplatonists.

This may be partly an artifact of literacy (and print culture) versus orality; lower classes may appear lacking in skepticism only because they did not articulate their beliefs in print or writing, and so posterity lacks direct access to them. Without denying the reality of the class conflicts or the ideological struggles that are involved in the Renaissance discourse of magic, I want to deconstruct the binary opposition between old magic and new rationality, between educated views and uneducated practices by showing that similar concepts such as the transferability of evil underlie both folk magic and canonical literature. My book is a study of literate culture, but I am trying to tease out of canonical texts of literary high culture some habits of mind common to literacy and orality, to educated and uneducated in the early modern period. The very ideological conflict involved in the attempt to stamp out magic betrays an unwanted continuity: to say "your beliefs are magic, mine are theology" is a kind of scapegoat thinking, an attempt to project upon an enemy Other the qualities one wishes to disown in oneself. It is because such similar thinking underlies theology and magic that the educated must demonize magic in the uneducated: the boundaries that preserve Protestant Christianity in a special category, distinct from Catholicism, paganism, or superstition, can effectively be policed by exaggerating the differences between Protestantism and folk magic, by sanctifying the former and damning the latter. As I will explain in chapter 2, this is exactly what is involved in what I call scapegoat thinking, and I think that the assault on magic—both by Renaissance clerics and by modern writers who valorize the "modern" emergence from magic as a rational sun shining through the foul and ugly mists of superstition that did seem to strangle it—is itself deeply involved in magical thinking.

Prognostication and Almanac

My approach to this subject, though I hope not quite a "hodgepodge of unempirical illusions," will cheerfully "amalgamat[e] shards of cultural debris from different traditions," and in drawing now on Freud, now on anthropology, now on history, now on critical theory, will seek by a resourceful bricolage to weave together "the fragmentary cultural debris of earlier ways of thinking." This subject is too large and complex to make profitable a "psychoanalytic approach" or a "Marxist approach," and anyway I share Foucault's wariness of global applications of such "totalitarian theories":

> It is not that these global theories have not provided nor continue to provide in a fairly consistent fashion useful tools for local research: Marxism and psychoanalysis are proofs of this. But I believe these tools have only been provided on the condition that the theoretical unity of these discourses was in some sense put in abeyance, or at least curtailed, divided, overthrown, caricatured, theatricalised, or what you will. In each case, the attempt to think in terms of a totality has in fact proved a hindrance to research. (*Power/Knowledge* 80–81)

Arguing for "the *local* character of criticism," Foucault calls for "an autonomous, non-centralised kind of theoretical production" (81). It is this that I have tried to achieve, since the decentralized, discontinuous, fragmentary, shifting discourse of Renaissance magical thinking seems to demand it.

My book is structured so that the first two chapters deal mainly with what is sometimes called apotropaic magic but which I will call simply protection magic: the erecting, by magical means, of an invisible protective barrier around a body, a house, a village, a nation to ward off external evils; in cases where external evils have already penetrated, they must be expelled through exorcisms and banishments or decoyed away in foreign wars. Chapters 3 through 5 deal mainly with life-promoting magic, with some excursions back into protection magic. Especially for the sake of the chapter "Black and White and Red All Over," with its many references to obscure authors of opaque orthography, I have modernized all spelling and capitalization except (bowing to convention) Spenser's and Chaucer's (and even there I have modernized *u, v, i,* and *j*). I hope this will make for ease of reading and reduce the gulf between writers made quaint by their habitual appearance in old spelling and Shakespeare, whose usual appearance in modern spelling helps us forget that he, like his fellows, was the child of a magical age.

It is something I hope we will stop forgetting. Symptomatic of the age in which Shakespeare lived, a time when rationality vied with magic, wit with witchcraft, in a European mind that was shifting gears, Shakespeare's last great hero was a mighty magician, whose final act was to renounce his magical power. Shakespeare's work, like his age, is a fabric whose rationality, realism, skepticism, and worldliness often strike us as modern; but there's magic in the web of it.

Notes

1. I am taking "poor" to mean "impoverished"; if it means "unfortunate," the statement being made about magical belief is much more sweeping.

2. Brian Vickers gives a useful account of the scholarship on this subject, and the debates surrounding it, in his introduction to *Occult and Scientific Mentalities in the Renaissance.*

3. As the linguistic philosopher Mark Johnson argues, metaphor is "a pervasive mode of understanding by which we project patterns from one domain of experience in order to structure another domain of a different kind. So conceived, metaphor is not merely a linguistic mode of expression; rather, it is one of the chief cognitive structures by which we are able to have coherent, ordered experiences that we can reason about and make sense of. Through metaphor, we make use of patterns that obtain in our

physical experience to organize our more abstract understanding" (xv). This concept, which provides for language something quite similar to Gombrich's theory of spatial perception, will be important in chapter 1.

4. This older-style anthropology, as Thomas analyzes it, consisted of "wrenching particular aspects of a system out of their cultural context and arbitrarily grouping them together with superficially similar aspects of other systems; [it] ended up by studying non-existent entities, brought into being by the ill-considered application of a single label to social phenomena which in fact differed radically from society to society" ("Anthropology" 93).

5. Alan Macfarlane argues that "England, even in the sixteenth century, had developed from the Azande-type situation where it is believed that 'Death has always a cause, and no man dies without a reason' [that is, intervention by divine will or human malice] to a more complex set of beliefs where 'natural' illness and death were accepted. In other words, not every death needed an explanation in personal terms: some people, for instance the very old or infants, might die or be ill from causes unrelated to divine or human will" ("Tudor Anthropologist" 146). But note that this applied only to a minority of cases—the very old and infants: Elizabethan beliefs were not very far removed from tribal beliefs that no death is natural.

6. Perhaps his classic example is that "Catholic clerical garments—the copes and albs and amices and stoles that were the glories of medieval textile crafts—were sold during the Reformation to the players. . . . A sacred sign, designed to be displayed before a crowd of men and women, is emptied, made negotiable, traded from one institution to another." ("Sign"/ "designed" seems an unintentional pun here, though a quite wonderful one.) "The official church dismantles and cedes to the players the powerful mechanisms of an unwanted and dangerous charisma" ("Exorcists" 171, 177).

7. In his book on early modern food riots in England, Buchanan Sharp shows that "women played important roles, including that of leader, in the riots in Kent at Wye (1595), at the port towns on the Medway (1605), and at several locations in 1631, as well as in food riots at Southampton (1608), at Maldon, Essex (March, 1629), and in Berkshire (1631)" (35–36).

8. Major resource works on this topic include Frederick Elworthy's *The Evil Eye*, 1895, and Siegfried Seligmann's *Der Böse Blick und Verwandtes*, 1910, though Elworthy's is subject to the same kind of cautions as is Sir James Frazer's work, with which it is contemporary and on which it sometimes draws. A useful collection of essays by anthropologists is *The Evil Eye*, edited by Clarence Maloney, and Alan Dundes has put together a di-

verse collection by specialists from psychoanalysts to ophthalmologists, *The Evil Eye: A Folklore Casebook.*

9. One classical formula was *praefiscine dixerim* ("I would speak without bewitchment" [McCartney 577]); Jews say "'*Keinahora*' (no evil eye)" when a child or treasured possession is praised (L. Jones 155); in other cultures the formula is often a variant of "God bless you" or "God save the mark."

10. I am indebted here to graduate student Cam Balzer, who has done some interesting work on physiognomy and Shakespearean drama.

11. Thomas is rightly uneasy about Geertz's "simple distinction between literate and illiterate," insisting that "the boundaries between them are far from clear-cut" ("Anthropology" 107). Students of orality and literacy long ago abandoned Albert Lord's insistence on an absolute divide between the worlds of oral and literary composition.

1

Protection and Pollution: Palisading the Elizabethan Body Politic

That island of England breeds very valiant creatures.
—*Henry V*

To island dwellers like the Elizabethan English, Shakespeare's description of Lucrece's death must have held a peculiar horror:

> And bubbling from her breast, it [the blood] doth divide
> In two slow rivers, that the crimson blood
> Circles her body in on every side,
> Who, like a late-sack'd island, vastly stood
> Bare and unpeopled in this fearful flood.
> Some of her blood still pure and red remain'd,
> And some look'd black, and that false Tarquin stain'd.
>
> (1737–43)

The goriness of those blood rivers, the creepiness of their "slow" movement, even the chilling vision of blood turned black through pollution might have paled, in those immediately post-Armada days, beside the specter of a sacked island. That the woman is the island provides a clue to the impact of the Lucrece story on Elizabethans. *The Rape of Lucrece, Titus Andronicus,* and *Cymbeline* offer vivid testimony to the truth of anthropological theories that treat the human body as an image of society. This is the first kind of magical thinking I will identify; it is what Freud called "incompletely suppressed psychical material, which, although pushed away by consciousness, has nevertheless not been robbed of all capacity for expressing itself" (*Complete Works* 6:279), and is one of what Keith Thomas calls "invisible mental structures, . . . underlying inchoate and ill-recorded systems of thought, which are only articulated in a fragmentary way" ("Anthropology" 106). The notion of the body as an image of society is one of those concrete walls giving shape to the building of thought after the timber forms of true magical belief have been knocked away.

Viewing through an anthropological lens these three texts, and also that *bête noire* of colonial-discourse theorists, *The Tempest*, also helps explain why England identified with Rome, why Shakespeare so favored the themes of siege warfare and threatened women, and why cartographers put so much water on Renaissance maps of England. By way of some tangled bypaths, including beliefs about the evil eye, about impregnation through the ear, and about the dangers of bathing, I hope to show that encoded in some common tropes and metaphors of this age is deeply ingrained magical thinking in which the body and the body politic are beleaguered and protected, metaphorically and magically.

First let me sketch the anthropological theory and link it with some background material on England's love affair with Rome. Implicit in Arnold Van Gennep's sweeping synthesis of territorial passage rites with personal rites of passage like initiations or weddings is that many cultures make analogies between the spatial and the temporal. Noting Shakespeare's interchangeability of temporal and spatial vocabulary, Edward Berry notes that nearly half of Shakespeare's uses of "space" refer to time (139). Life's events can be plotted as on a map; a human life is like the land.

The anthropologist Mary Douglas, addressing the problem of why many societies guard the body's orifices so zealously that an unsanctioned penetration—a breach of chastity, eating forbidden food—is a pollution,[1] argues that the body is "a symbol of society" and finds "the powers and dangers credited to social structure reproduced in small on the human body" (*Purity* 115). Philosophers and art historians have long recognized the body as a cosmic structuring principle: Panofsky concludes that despite "mathematical or philosophical foundations, perspective and proportional systems are still iconologies of space and of the human body" (see Argan 298). The linguistic philosopher Mark Johnson argues that our sense of bodily balance provides a schema giving rise to "our understanding of balanced personalities, balanced views, balanced systems, balanced equations, the balance of power, the balance of justice, and so on" (74–87), that the body's sense of verticality in space bestows on language "the *verticality* schema," which involves

> a very simple, but pervasive, metaphorical understanding: *more is up*. . . . We understand *quantity* in terms of the *verticality* schema. . . . *Prices keep going up; The number of books published each year keeps rising; His gross earnings fell; Turn down the heat.* . . . If you add more liquid to a container, the level goes up. If you add more objects to a pile, the level goes up. *More* and *up* are therefore correlated in our experience in a way that provides a *physical* basis for our *abstract* understanding of quantity. (xv)

Johnson's use of "schemata" resembles Gombrich's—in both cases the familiar (here, bodily experience) provides conceptual frameworks for understanding the less familiar (abstractions like quantity). And Johnson's linguistic findings dovetail with Douglas's anthropological theory when he shows how language suggests that various senses of boundedness are based on body sense: "Our encounter with containment and boundedness is one of the most pervasive features of our bodily experience. We are intimately aware of our bodies as three-dimensional containers into which we put certain things (food, water, air) and out of which other things emerge (food and water wastes, air, blood, etc.)" (21).

Douglas sees bodily margins as Van Gennep and Victor Turner see the no-man's-land between territories and the liminal phase between life stages—as powerful, dangerous marginal states. Fear of bodily pollution expresses fear for the fabric of society: "It seems that our deepest fears and desires take expression with a kind of witty aptness. To understand body pollution we should try to argue back from the known dangers of society. . . . Symbolism of the body's boundaries is used in [a] kind of unfunny wit to express danger to community boundaries" (*Purity* 121–22). Among Douglas's examples are the Coorgs of India, ensconced in a mountain fastness, whose culture was deeply oriented toward fear of pollution.

The early American land-as-woman metaphor (see Annette Kolodny's provocatively entitled *The Lay of the Land*) was a species of the Renaissance body/state analogy. In what Peter Stallybrass calls "the geography of the body" ("Patriarchal Territories" 138), Donne calls his mistress "my America, my new found land," and Shakespeare calls Lucrece's breasts "ivory globes circled with blue, / A pair of maiden worlds unconquered"; Lucrece's smoothness is "like a goodly champaign plain" (407–8, 1247). Leonard Barkan surveys the metaphor of cosmos and commonwealth as the body (Plato saw the cosmos as a living creature, astrologers described Aries as the head, Libra the buttocks, Pisces the feet, of a great body). The body/state analogy "was already a commonplace in Plato's time not only among political philosophers using anatomical descriptions but also among physicians describing anatomy in social or political terms" (69), but it was Renaissance England that saw "the heyday of the anthropomorphic image of the commonwealth" (75).

Magical notions of body and society, of pollution and dangerous margins, emerge often in Shakespeare, but with particular force in *Lucrece, Titus,* and *Cymbeline,* where women's bodies are metaphors for societies threatened. All three texts involve Rome, which offered early modern England a potent symbol of invasion that spoke poignantly to England's sense of itself.

As the Romans Do

A binary image of Rome, almost Lévi-Straussian in its precise mirror inversion, haunted the European imagination for a thousand years: Rome the implacable invader, thrusting its masculine armies deep into the virgin territory of the Goths, its soldiers raping the queen of Britain's daughters; and Rome the invaded, the sacked city, ravaged by Goths. But history offered a potent tool for deconstructing this binary opposition: the opposed images represented successive phases of Roman history, and poised between them, as a historical "time out" like calendric intercalary days, was a third Rome, Augustus Caesar's, a Rome that had finished its invasions, acquired its colonies, and was enjoying its empire in peace, a Rome yet unsacked. This compound image, its binary oppositions mediated by a liminal zone of history, fascinated Renaissance England partly because England spun from it images of itself. As John Velz notes, the ancient world was the setting for one third of the Shakespeare canon—"two of the comedies, both of the narrative poems, four of the five romances, and six of the eleven tragedies" (1). The many readers who have seen Elizabethan politics in Shakespeare's Roman politics (see Velz) confirm the link between England and ancient Rome. Besides the "ubiquitous presence of Rome in Elizabethan culture" (Miola 11), a classicism shared with all Europe, England often identified more specifically with Rome, as when Roman civil wars were compared with the Wars of the Roses (Barroll 328–29).

Titus and *Lucrece* display Rome in both aspects, as invader and invaded. Each opens with the typically Roman activity of soldiers invading someone's territory—Titus returns home from "weary wars against the barbarous Goths" (I.i.28); Lucrece's husband is among Romans besieging Ardea. Yet the sense of an invaded Rome predominates. In *Lucrece,* Tarquin, having seized power in a bloody coup, is reigning tyrannously; *Titus* opens on armed men battering the "city walls"; "Open the gates and let me in," cries Saturninus (I.i.26, 65), who soon becomes emperor and rules tyrannously; his marriage to the Queen of the Goths and adoption of her unlovely sons creates a reconstituted family that brings the barbarian to the gates. *Lucrece* culminates in an army marching on Rome bearing Lucrece's body and ousting the tyrants; late in *Titus,* an army of Goths surrounds Rome; the tyrant is killed. Though the Rome of these texts is a complex mixture, part thrusting, martial masculinity, part woman in danger of ravishment—now invader, now invaded—the image of besieged Rome predominates. If Douglas's theory is correct and if Shakespeare has imaginatively captured the episteme of a siege-mentality culture, we should expect, for such a society, images of the human body threatened with unsanctioned penetration and pollution. This is exactly what we find. In *Titus,* where Rome's margins are threatened, a woman is raped and dismembered; Lavinia's invaded orifices and mangled margins are aptly symbolized by the horrifying "marginal stuff" (Douglas, *Purity* 121), blood issuing from her mouth. In *Lucrece,* tyrant and rapist are father and son; that coup and rape are parallel usurpations, the poem makes clear: Tarquin approaches Lucrece "like a foul usurper" who means "from this fair throne to heave the owner out"

(412–13); debating whether to rape her, "now he vows a league [i.e., peace treaty] and now invasion" (287); he "march[es] on to make his stand / On her bare breast, the heart of all her land" (438–39). Military siege is the governing image of *Lucrece,* which opens upon "the besieged Ardea" and which imagines the rape as a siege. Tarquin fears Lucrece's husband will dream of "this siege that hath engirt his marriage" (220). When "the Roman lord marcheth to Lucrece' bed" (301), Shakespeare imagines a medieval or Renaissance city siege, with its scaling of turrets and battering rams: "her bare breast . . . / Whose ranks of blue veins, as his hand did scale, / Left their round turrets destitute and pale"; "His hand, that yet remains upon her breast—Rude ram, to batter such an ivory wall!— may feel her heart—poor citizen!—distress'd" (440–41, 463–65). "I come," he announces, "to scale / Thy never-conquered fort" (481–82). An analogue of the rape is a painted siege of Troy, again a Renaissance city siege: "The laboring pioner / Begrim'd with sweat" (1380–81). And in a Chinese box of siege/rape analogies, this siege was occasioned by a rape: the Greek army has assembled "for Helen's rape the city to destroy" (1369; see N. Vickers, 106ff.; Dubrow, *Captive* 93–95).

In *Lucrece* as elsewhere, Shakespeare envisions Rome as "the enclave of civilization ringed round with a protective wall, outside of which the dark forces of barbarism lurk" (Velz 11); Heather Dubrow suggests that Lucrece "comes to represent the center of civilization that is threatened by barbarians"; in a sense "violence is not really outside the wall," since Tarquin is a Roman (*Captive* 94–95); but so firmly is the siege trope attached to Rome that Shakespeare's imagination configures even Roman enemies as invaders. As in *Titus* we first see the Roman Saturninus arriving from foreign wars and beating on Rome's doors, so Tarquin, arriving at Lucrece's house from an outlying camp, has the air of an external invader: "Throughout the poem Shakespeare depicts Tarquin as the invading barbarian who comes to raze Lucrece's city. . . . Although he is a 'Roman lord,'" he is "alien and hostile" (Miola 27).

Further evidence of the underlying mental structure of the body as society: William Heckscher notes, "The woman who had been dishonored was easily equated with a city or fortress that had been conquered by the enemy. . . . From classical antiquity onward, cities and fortresses had . . . been considered to be of the feminine sex.

The Virtues of Prudentius's fifth-century *Psychomachia* were . . .
maidens inhabiting and defending their *Tugendburgen*. . . . The classical *triumphator* entering a city was often greeted by a group of
women, or a single woman, representing the city. . . . The daughter
of Sion appears frequently in sixth-century representations of the
Entry into Jerusalem" (26–27). As Dubrow notes, "Given the common association of gates with the vagina, the notion of rape is latent in the image of the attacked city" (*Captive* 94). And cities wear
female attire: "outskirts" is a Renaissance coinage.

A Woman's Place Is in the Home

The invasion of defended territory may be domestic as well as
national or civic—as countries may be invaded and cities besieged
and sacked, a house may be burglarized. Among more specialized
cases is illegal entry into a game preserve: "He is no woodman that
doth bend his bow / To strike a poor unseasonable doe" (*Luc* 580–
81); "Hast not thou full often struck a doe, / And borne her clean-
ly by the keeper's nose?" (*Tit* II.i.93–94); raped Lavinia is a poach-
er's deer (II.i.117, ii.26; III.i.91–92). Metaphors for Lucrece's
body—house, fortress, mansion, temple, tree bark, "emphasize the
protective and enclosing function of the body," which "surrounds
the soul and wards off danger" (Maus 70). All territorial invasions
invite literary analogues of bodily violation, and rape in Shakespeare
calls forth comparisons with all kinds of territorial invasion.

Lucrece riots in images of sex as burglary.[2] In the rape scene, the
analogy is explicit, as Tarquin burgles his way to Lucrece's bedcham-
ber, forcing the locks of doors. Lock forcing, analogue of the rape,
calls forth a metaphor of rape: "Each [lock] by him enforc'd re-
tires his ward" (302–3). Even more suggestive than this rape of the
lock is the way Tarquin opens the last door: "His guilty hand
pluck'd up the latch, / And with his knee the door he opens wide"
(358–59)—why, unless to emphasize the parallel between such
breaking and entering and the rape itself, should Tarquin open the
door with his knee?

Stallybrass discusses the way the body may be conflated with the
house that enguards: "Surveillance of women concentrated upon . . .
the mouth, chastity, the threshold of the house. . . . Silence, the

closed mouth, is made a sign of chastity. And silence and chastity are . . . homologous to woman's enclosure within the house. . . . This 'Woman,' like Bakhtin's classical body, is rigidly 'finished': her signs are the enclosed body, the closed mouth, the locked house" ("Patriarchal Territories" 126–27).

As Douglas reminds us, "Van Gennep . . . saw society as a house with rooms and corridors in which passage from one to another is dangerous. Danger lies in transitional states" (*Purity* 96). Turner's term *liminal* for such states comes from Latin *limen,* threshold. The bride carried across the threshold embodies the spatial/temporal analogy—spatially, she enters new territory; temporally, she enters a new phase of life. (A common superstition reflects the danger inherent in threshold states: "Men that stumble at the threshold / Are well foretold that danger lurks within" [*3H6* IV.vii.11–12; cf. *LLL* III.i.115].) Burgling his way toward Lucrece, Tarquin meets resistance in locked doors and threshold guardians reminiscent of myth's monstrous figures;[3] metallic threshold guardians seem animate:

> The locks between her chamber and his will,
> Each one by him enforc'd retires his ward;
> But, as they open, they all rate [i.e., berate] his ill,
> Which drives the creeping thief to some regard.
> The threshold grates the door to have him heard;
> Night-wand'ring weasels shriek to see him there;
> They fright him, yet he still pursues his fear.
>
> (302–8)

The paradox of the seemingly passive threshold grating actively against the seemingly active opening door foreshadows the paradoxical power of seemingly passive Lucrece to effect the ultimate downfall of her rapist.

Lucrece dies by creating, with a knife, a new bodily orifice leading to her heart. No orifice leads to Tarquin's heart; the orifices of his ear open on no passageways reaching that far. Though Lucrece pleads, "his ear her prayers admits, but his heart granteth / No penetrable entrance to her plaining" (558–59). But then, women have more orifices than men to start with, which may be why the female body offers the more frequent image of society endangered. If Tarquin begins, however, as an image of impenetrable body and soul, he ends invaded and sacked. He finally realizes that he has invaded himself, raped his own soul, a soul he imagines as a woman polluted:

His soul's fair temple is defaced,
To whose weak ruins muster troops of cares,
To ask the spotted princess how she fares.
She says her subjects with foul insurrection
Have batter'd down her consecrated wall. . . .
Ev'n in this thought through the dark night he stealeth,
A captive victor that hath lost in gain.

(719–30)

As Tarquin's invasions, first (as the usurper's heir) of the Roman political state and then of Lucrece's body, make him paradoxically a prisoner, a "captive victor," so the violent penetrations of Lucrece, first by rape and then by knife, paradoxically free her, restoring her to the safety of defended territory. The image with which I began captures this paradox in all its complexity. Lucrece's body becomes a sacked island—the ravished female body as an image of society not merely endangered but wrecked: "The crimson blood / Circles her body in on every side, / Who, like a late-sack'd island, vastly stood / Bare and unpeopled in this fearful flood." But symbols of encirclement mark the reintegrative *agregation* phase of Van Gennep's rites of passage, and the river-ringed island suggests the liminal zone buffering defended territory. Lucrece has saved her reputation, even her soul, and the island is at least in part an image of safety and protection. Lucrece's death frees Rome from tyranny, as Lavinia's rape ultimately frees Rome from tyranny in *Titus*.

Trunks, Girdles, and Ears

The endings of the two early works, personally bleak if politically redemptive, contrast with *Cymbeline*'s comic resolution. In the early, invasion-obsessed texts, redemption comes through killing or expelling the invader. *Cymbeline* still stresses England's danger from invasion, but suggests another way out, not expulsion but peacemaking; as I shall show, it is a distinctly Jacobean solution.[4] Invasion is averted partly because *Cymbeline* is a comedy but partly because a new Jacobean ideology, as we shall see, was downplaying the threat of invasion. England throughout most of *Cymbeline* is still a nation under siege: the Britain that always identified with Rome here takes on Rome's identity as the besieged, while Rome wears its invader face. Rome's dual nature is thus divided between two societies, England adopting the aspect with which Elizabethans had most readily identified.

Lucrece's image of a "late-sack'd island" would strike a sympathetic chord in *Cymbeline,* where memory of Julius Caesar's invasion of the island Britain is still fresh. This invasion, however, was almost unsuccessful, for Britain was defended actively by its very surrounding liminal zone, the sea:

> Your isle . . . stands
> As Neptune's park, ribb'd and paled in
> With rocks unscalable and roaring waters,
> With sands that will not bear your enemies' boats,
> But suck them up to th' topmast. A kind of conquest
> Caesar made here, but made not here his brag
> Of "Came and saw and overcame." With shame—
> The first that ever touch'd him—he was carried
> From off our coast, twice beaten; and his shipping,
> Poor ignorant baubles, on our terrible seas,
> Like egg-shells mov'd upon their surges, crack'd
> As easily 'gainst our rocks.
>   (III.i.18–29)

Britain courts Roman invasion again, as Cymbeline refuses to pay the tribute. The queen's son defies the Roman emissary, declaring that if Rome invades Britain, "you shall find us in our saltwater girdle" (III.i.79–80). Though the image is unheroic for a moment of high patriotism, and its speaker is the lumpen villain Cloten, it is perfect for the play: seawater protects an endangered society, and military invasion is compared with getting inside a person's clothing—endangered society as a body protected by clothing against rape. My colleague James Marino suggests that Cloten's image hints at the magical virginity-protecting girdles of medieval romances like *Bevis of Hampton* and *Emare.* Clothing, like the body, can be an "image of society." As Georges Vigarello shows, in Renaissance plague time pores "needed permanent protection from attack," which "rendered the shape and nature of clothing in time of plague all-important: smooth fabrics, dense weave and close fit. . . . Men and women alike longed to have smooth and hermetically sealed clothes enclosing their weak bodies" (10); compare this with the storming-the-Bastille image of French Revolutionary times: "Our clothes are like fetters," B. C. Faust wrote in 1792; "they are the invention of the barbarian and Gothic centuries. You must break these fetters if you wish to become free and happy" (B. C. Faust in Vigarello 140).

When the Romans invade, they press into Britain at an inlet, Milford Haven, and try to penetrate through a lane whose narrowness is repeatedly emphasized. A stand being made at the cervix of this lane, British society, direly endangered, is saved. Here, the attempted invasion of a country is paralleled by the attempted invasion of a woman's body. One male character tries to seduce the heroine, another to have her murdered, a third to rape her. A fourth attempted invasion, through her mouth, is averted when the poison turns out to be a sleeping potion. She is also nearly poisoned through the ear, slanderously told that her husband has been untrue; a similar poison is poured into her husband's ear. Such ear poisoning was a penetration like rape: to a long succession of medieval thinkers, the ear had seemed vaginal; the Virgin Mary supposedly conceived through the ear (cf. Cleopatra's "Ram thou thy fruitful tidings in mine ears, / That long time have been barren" [II.v.24–25]). Cloten's plan to penetrate Imogen's ear with music is fraught with double entendre: "I am advis'd to give her music o' mornings; they say it will penetrate. *Enter Musicians.* Come on; tune. If you can penetrate her with your fingering, so; we'll try with tongue too" (II.iii.11–15).

The series of close calls that make Imogen's story so like the Perils of Pauline reiterate Britain's near misses: the royal line is nearly wiped out by the kidnapping of the princes and near murder of Imogen; tyranny is averted by the queen's timely suicide; the Roman army is fended off in the act of breaching Britain's maidenhead at that narrow lane. Imogen's perils are Britain's.[5]

Threshold crossings objectify this repeated pattern of danger averted. Seducer Iachimo is carried across the threshold of the chamber where Imogen sleeps. Would-be rapist Cloten is carried across the threshold of the cave where Imogen sleeps. (Underlining the connection between these two scenes, in both chambers the sleeping Imogen is called a "lily" [Skura, "Interpreting" 213–14].) But just as the threat of Roman invasion is headed off through the deaths of many soldiers at the neck of a lane, so the threat to Imogen from the sexual miscreants who keep being carried into her chamber is contained by images of death: the resemblance of Iachimo's trunk to a coffin suggests the ultimate death of his evil aspirations; and Cloten arrives in Imogen's chamber quite deceased, having recently been beheaded. Iachimo's conveyance is insistently called a "trunk": Cloten's beheaded trunk, a visual pun, recalls the earlier incident; of his body a character cries, "Soft, ho, what trunk is here / Without his top?" (IV.ii.354–55). Perhaps this is a species of that "unfunny wit" to which Douglas alludes. The constant danger threatening this young woman who spends too much time sleeping next to trunks is symbolized by the menacing penetration of domestic thresholds—a burglary (Iachimo's) that is an analogue of attempted seduction or rape, itself an analogue of military invasion. In Douglas's terms, danger to society is expressed by danger to the body; in Van Gennep's, different kinds of "passage" have a similar structure and vocabulary of symbols; in Turner's, the indeterminacy of a liminal state expresses vulnerability.

"God Breathed and They Were Scattered"

The unconscious mental structure I have so far been teasing out might well be described simply as a metaphoric system with roots in bodily experience, to use Mark Johnson's terms; what is there about them that is specifically magical thinking? The magic lies in the way that such bodily penetration causes pollution, a soiling that is magically conceived. Shakespeare sees Lucrece's rape as a pollution: "'To kill myself, . . . what were it, / But with my body my poor soul's pollution?'"; her body is a "polluted prison" (1156–57, 1725–26). In tribal societies, pollution may be removed by simple purification rites, but for Shakespeare rape is so severe a pollution that its only purifier is death: "My blood shall wash the slander of mine ill," resolves Lucrece (1207), as Titus kills his rape-polluted daughter. Lucrece uses "stain" eighteen times, alongside "blot," "spot," "blur," "blemish," "attaint," "scar," and "pollution": Coppélia Kahn argues that "though Lucrece uses moral terms such as sin and guilt, she actually condemns herself according to primitive, nonmoral standards of pollution and uncleanness" ("Rape" 49). (On guilt versus shame and sin versus pollution, Ian Donaldson, Harriett

Hawkins, and Heather Dubrow have written perceptively.) It is startling to find in a Christian writer the pagan force of "some of her blood still pure and red remain'd, / And some look'd black, and that false Tarquin stain'd" (1742–43). Augustine, a thousand years earlier, seems more Christian, even more modern, in arguing that soiled flesh was irrelevant if Lucrece's mind was pure: Shakespeare's arresting image of blackened blood as a sign of pollution seems more at home amongst the Yoruba or the Ndembu.[6] Did something in his society make it hospitable to primitive pollution beliefs—even more so than the rest of European Christendom?

By Douglas's theory, a society bound up in pollution beliefs and obsessed with protecting orifices should be a society endangered, besieged, vulnerable at its margins. What could more accurately describe Elizabethan England, a second-rate military power in perennial danger from great powers like Spain, a Protestant country obsessed with the threat of papal takeover and nourishing a paranoid certainty that foreign Jesuit infiltrators were penetrating every available national orifice? Sequestered like the Coorgs in their mountain fastness, Elizabethan England had a sense of itself as an island, perpetually threatened with invasion but defended by its liminal zone, the sea.

Victor Morgan sees the sixteenth-century boom in English map making as owing partly to "the international situation throughout the greater part of the century, with the recurring threat of invasion"; many royally sponsored maps were of coasts and their fortifications (136). The map on which Elizabeth stands in the Ditchley portrait emphasizes the south coast. Saxton orders his county maps to give early focus to the south coast. His map of England highlights its island nature: England occupies about half the plate; the rest is given over to seas with prominently lettered names—Oceanus Britannicus, Mare Hibernium, Oceanus Germanicus—and filled with some thirty-five ships, plus sea monsters, fish, crabs, and mermaids (Evans and Lawrence).

Today we can still say that England was last successfully invaded in 1066, but Elizabethans were not complacent—they saw the sea as rising up to defend them against repeated near invasions, a real and constant threat. (Today's periodic outcries against the channel tunnel suggest that England's fear of penetration has not even yet wholly abated. The specific fear that rabies will make its way into England via the tunnel is a species of the quasi-magical fear of disease sent in by a neighbor-enemy, to be discussed in chapter 2.) The historical moment when this sense was strongest, the 1588 defeat of the Armada, coincided closely with the beginning of Shakespeare's career. Although the Spanish fleet enjoyed particularly good weather during its progress through the English channel, encountering storms only during the retreat along the Irish coast, the great sea storm scattering the Spanish fleet quickly entered the mythology of this attempt on England's virtue: England protected by its saltwater girdle.

> "God breathed and they were scattered," runs the legend on one of Queen Elizabeth's Armada medals. A Dutch medal records a similar sentiment, and the learned poets who celebrated in Latin verse the triumphant preservation of the Virgin Queen and the Protestant faith were so busy extolling the divine partisanship which drowned some thousands of Spaniards by a specially provided tempest that they scarcely had time to mention the English fleet. Of course, better ships and better guns had won the battle before the Spaniards had any trouble with the weather. . . . The great storm which destroyed the Spanish Armada joined the other legends. (Mattingly 390)[7]

A medal struck the year after the Armada defeat shows Elizabeth on one side, an island emerging from storm on the other (Strong 138); several portraits foregrounding Elizabeth feature a drowning Armada in the background. Of one of them, Louis Montrose writes,

> The demure iconography of Elizabeth's virgin-knot suggests a causal relationship between her sanctified chastity and the providential destruction of the Spanish Catholic invaders. . . . The royal body provides an instructive Elizabethan illustration of Mary Douglas's cross-cultural thesis that the body's "boundaries can represent any boundaries which are threatened or precarious." . . . The inviolability of the island realm, the secure boundary of the English nation, is thus made to seem mystically dependent on the inviolability of the English sovereign, upon the intact condition of the queen's body natural. ("Elizabethan Subject" 315; cf. Marcus, *Puzzling* 62)

Shakespeare often writes about England besieged, threatened at its watery borders, sometimes saved by "our terrible seas." Elizabethans knew Caesar's invasions from the *Gallic Wars* and from many embellishing legends and pseudohistories (see Nearing); considering the many available elements of legend—from magical swords to Geoffrey of Monmouth's "admirable old Britons . . . ready to die for country" (Nearing 904)—Shakespeare's focus on the role of the sea is all the more significant. When in *King John* the French try to invade England, their ships are wrecked on the Goodwin Sands, a liminal zone Shakespeare returned to—one of Antonio's ships is wrecked there in *The Merchant of Venice*. John of Gaunt's classic description of England (*R2* II.i.40–68) offers many familiar elements—the emphasis on England as an island, the island envisioned as a natural fortress, England imagined as naturally on the defensive (even the sea here an invader), besieged nation as walled house or moated castle, the land-as-woman trope, the idea that an England once conquering others has now conquered itself by tolerating tyranny—as Rome in *Titus* and *Lucrece* is both conqueror of foreign lands and conquered itself by tyrants, as *Lucrece*'s rapist has raped his own soul. When England turns against itself, in Shakespeare's many civil wars, the *Lucrece/Titus* phenomenon appears: subjects who turn against their ruler are configured as foreign invaders. To maintain the less disturbing fiction that the enemy is without, rebels are laundered by foreign travel and appear as invaders from abroad: Bolingbroke invades from France, Hotspur (hailing from the perilous north) invades from Wales. Later I will explore the way Henry V transforms civil unrest into foreign threat; the sleight of hand that transforms the Cambridge conspiracy into a French plot employs this move brilliantly.

We might link Shakespeare's passion for siege warfare, evident in so many texts from the English history plays to *Troilus and Cressida,* with his remarkable interest in sexually besieged women—the many women raped or threatened with rape, the seduction attempts, the four plays in whose main plots a woman is falsely accused of sexual misconduct (*Othello, Much Ado, Cymbeline, The Winter's Tale*). The biblical story of Susanna, sexually besieged by men who accuse her of sexual misconduct, thus combining sexual siege with siege of sexual reputation, attracted Elizabethans; perhaps reflecting the age's interest in this kind of female culture hero, Shakespeare's daughter was named Susanna. Siege of body and of reputation are linked when Tarquin forces Lucrece to submit by threatening to accuse her of adultery with a servant if she does not. Shakespeare's preoccupation with slander may be connected to its being a poisoning through the ear, another vulnerable orifice, subject to his culture's fear of danger to the opened body. A long tradition links ear penetration with vaginal penetration. Origen thought Mary "had conceived Jesus the Word at the words of the angel"; in medieval lyrics, Mary conceives through the ear, a way to preserve her as *virgo intacta* (Warner 37). Poisoning or wounding through the ear is common in Shakespeare, sometimes literal (as in Hamlet Senior), sometimes figurative, as in Iago's "I'll pour this pestilence into his ear" (*Oth* II.iii.362). Shakespeare's concern with sexual slander recalls this link between ear and vagina.

Protection Magic, from Defensive Ear to Aggressive Eye

This nexus of ideas, turning on the identification of body with society, is no chastely intellectual analogy but bears unmistakable traces of protective magic. To illustrate more concretely how such magic operates, I will devote a few pages to one of the most widespread of magical practices, amulets and charms against the evil eye, which comprise a bodily protection against a magical weapon: the supernaturally powerful gaze of an enemy. A repeated motif in the texts I have been examining is the helpless victim stared upon by an enemy's malevolent eye: Imogen asleep, falling under the evil gaze of her enemy Iachimo, an episode from which all her later tribulations grow; Lucrece asleep, "overlooked" by an enemy whose aggressive eye is emphasized. Let us look closely at the passage in *Lucrece*.

On entering Lucrece's chamber, Tarquin is identified with the "night-owl" (360), a bird often connected with the evil eye because of its prominent eyes (Siebers 64). Tarquin "gazeth on her yet unstained bed" and walks around it, "rolling his greedy eyeballs in his head"; his eyes mislead his heart (365–69). When he gazes directly upon Lucrece, something about her acts like an amulet against his evil eye: "his eyes begun / To wink, being blinded with a greater light: / Whether it is that she reflects so bright, / That dazzleth them, or else some shame supposed; / But blind they are, and keep themselves enclosed" (374–78). The notion of reflection here is crucial: the light that dazzles Tarquin is a reflection of his own gaze. We could see this as simply emblematic of his inner moral state ("some shame") or as a residue of protective magic: many charms against the evil eye involve wearing mirrors about the body to deflect harm from oneself and also to redouble the malevolent gaze back upon the enemy. "Dazzleth," suggesting at this date both blinding by strong light and mental confusion (OED), recalls the baffling effect of amulets against the evil eye; as Tobin Siebers notes:

> Confronted with the uncanny force of amulets, [Plutarch] theorizes that the 'strange look of them attracts the gaze, so that it exerts less pressure on its victims.' . . . Amulets engage the forces of attraction; they defeat fascination with fascination. Relics, amulets, and talismans embody those forces that they supposedly counteract, and are effective because they direct evil against itself. Certainly, the ambivalent logic of amulets is baffling; . . . their purpose . . . is to create confusion. The word 'amulet' . . . derives from the Latin *amolior* or "to baffle." (7)

We have not seen Lucrece going to bed; she is not shown arming herself against dangers while asleep; but protective charms of the "now I lay me down to sleep" variety were practiced in Shakespeare's time; Imogen murmurs one before falling asleep in the scene where Iachimo is to "overlook" her: "To your protection I commend me, gods. / From fairies and the tempters of the night / Guard me, beseech ye" (*Cym* II.ii.8–10). Whatever magical protection guards Lucrece against her tempter of the night, its effect is temporary, for Tarquin's dazzled eyes "must ope," and they ope "to kill; / And holy-thoughted Lucrece to their sight / Must sell her joy, her life, her world's delight" (383–85). Shakespeare continues to emphasize Tarquin's malevolent gaze: "She lies, / To be admired of lewd unhallow'd eyes"; through his eyes, as if we were voyeurs, we see a blazon of Lucrece, her "hair, like golden threads," her "breasts, like ivory globes," "her coral lips"—the whole Petrarchan inventory, seen through the evil eye (393–420). (I will return to the evil eye in Petrarchan convention in chapter 4.) The aggressive gaze becomes temporarily a substitute for rape: "his rage of lust by gazing qualified" (424), and then the eye becomes a pirate chief, inciting to rape and pillage:

> His eye, which late this mutiny restrains,
> Unto a greater uproar tempts his veins:
> And they, like straggling slaves for pillage fighting,
> Obdurate vassals fell exploits effecting,
> In bloody death and ravishment delighting,
> Nor children's tears nor mothers' groans respecting,
> Swell in their pride, the onset still expecting:
>   Anon his beating heart alarum striking,
>   Gives the hot charge and bids them do their liking.
>
> His drumming heart cheers up his burning eye,
> His eye commends the leading to his hand.
>   (426–36)

Feeling his hand on her breast, Lucrece awakes, "breaks ope her lock'd-up eyes, / Who, peeping forth this tumult to behold, / Are by his flaming torch dimm'd and controll'd"—her own gaze is baffled by the strength of Tarquin's evil eye, and well might she imagine him in magical terms, as "some ghastly sprite" (446–51). Her first instinct is, self-protectively, to close her eyes (458); as I will show in chapter 4, the evil eye is especially damaging to a gaze that returns it. And an important facet of the magical thinking connected with eyes is the unconscious conviction that what one cannot see does not exist: Lady Macbeth exhibits such thinking when she cries, "Come, thick night, / And pall thee in the dunnest smoke of hell, / That my keen knife see not the wound it makes" (I.v.50–52), as does Macbeth: "I am afraid to think what I have done; / Look on 't again I dare not" (II.ii.49–50).

That Shakespeare was thinking specifically of the evil eye in *Lucrece* is suggested by his endowing Tarquin with the gaze of the best known of animal evil-eye possessors, the basilisk, or cockatrice: as Lucrece pleads, he fixes her "with cockatrice' dead-killing eye" (540).

In the terms of magical thinking, Lucrece was vulnerable from the start, because her husband foolishly praised her:

> her husband's shallow tongue,—
> The niggard prodigal that praised her so,—
> In that high task hath done her beauty wrong,
> Which far exceeds his barren skill to show:
> Therefore that praise which Collatine doth woe
> Enchanted Tarquin answers with surmise,
> In silent wonder of still-gazing eyes.
>   (78–84)

Should we take "enchanted" literally, to mean bound with a magical spell? Is Tarquin's malevolent gaze engendered by Collatine's praise? Praise was thought to attract the evil eye:

> The pronouncing of compliments and curses has always been intimately related to the cause and cure of the evil eye. The custom of addressing children by opprobrious names is one manifestation of the fear of praise. . . . In southern India, mothers paint black spots on their children's faces, chins, cheeks, and eyelids to deter compliments. . . . A compliment is a show of desire. . . . If a misfortune befalls someone who has been praised, he may attribute it to the compliment. His illness is thus explained, while the hostility that must naturally appear in such situations can be dispelled by requiring the admirer to undo the offense through an act of ritual dispraising. (Siebers 41–43; see also Elworthy 12, 32; McCartney)

Such an interpretation would seem to make Tarquin himself the victim of magic—possession of the evil eye befalls him as an enchantment. The evil eye has been seen from ancient times to operate either as an act of the will or unconsciously: in some, "the faculty of the evil eye was natural, whose baneful look was unconscious; [their] eye threw out *radios perniciosos,* which by a sort of mesmeric power acted upon the nervous system of the victim" (Elworthy 33; see also Brav 48–49, Siebers 48).[8] While not wanting to absolve Tarquin of responsibility for the rape, I would also invoke Siebers's theory that evil-eye accusations are constructed by a community against an individual: it is possible that Tarquin is being constituted as a scapegoat (see chapter 2). René Girard argues that "Shakespeare partially deconstructs the republican scapegoating of Tarquin, since he distributes the violence equally between the rapist and the husband" (*Theater* 27). Shakespeare makes clear that Lucrece's husband, through his foolish praise, bears significant responsibility for her rape. We could interpret this politically—the rape of Lucrece is politically unifying, providing an excuse for expelling a malefactor; solidarity is achieved by uniting against a common enemy. Or we could interpret it in gender terms: the poem's blaming the husband is a way of holding the patriarchal system, with its view of women as property, responsible for the abuse of women. Whatever our interpretation, meaning is mediated through magical thinking, whether of the evil eye or of scapegoating. It may be only a metaphor, or it may be residual belief, driven into the unconscious, in the possibility of harm at a distance, through praise or the gaze—belief in the need to hedge the body round with protective magic.

In other Shakespearean texts too, we may detect submerged evil-eye belief. Given that "in England, squinting eyes and deformed people, especially hunchback, supposedly possess the evil eye" (Siebers 89), it is significant that hunchbacked Richard's mother says of him, "O my accursed womb, the bed of death! / A cockatrice hast thou hatch'd to the world, / Whose unavoided eye is murderous" (*R3* IV.i.54–56). The Gobbo, or hunchback, was a favorite amulet against the evil eye (Elworthy 331). Launcelot Gobbo, in a play set in Italy (a center of evil-eye belief), utters the apotropaic formula "God bless the mark!" a common protection against the evil eye, when speaking of Shylock: "the Jew my master, who, God bless the mark, is a kind of devil" (*MV* II.ii.23–24), perhaps reflecting a facet of evil-eye belief: as Moss and Cappannari note, "the Jewish people as a whole were viewed as the Devil incarnate and the source of the evil eye. The Jews of England were forbidden to attend the coronation of Richard the Lion-Hearted (1189) for fear that an evil eye might harm the crown. So feared was the purported power of the Jew that the German word for evil eye remains *Judenblick* (Jew's glance)" (8). The only other Shakespearean character to use the expression "God bless the mark" is another Italian connected, I think, with the evil eye—Iago (*Oth* I.i.34). A closely allied protective formula, "God save the mark," is used by a third Italian character, Juliet's nurse, as she recalls recoiling in horror from a dead body (*Rom* III.ii.53).

The ill-wisher motivated by envy is closely linked with the cast-er of the evil eye: as Siebers notes, "The evil eye and envy join in the Latin *invidia* from *invidere*, to look at too closely and thus to envy" (144). Freud wrote in "The Uncanny," "One of the most uncanny and wide-spread forms of superstition is the dread of the evil eye. . . . Whoever possesses something that is at once valuable and fragile is afraid of other people's envy, in so far as he projects on to them the envy he would have felt in their place" (*Complete Works* 17:240). Iachimo is such an envious ill-wisher, and so is Iago. Siebers's definition of envy—"The envious person wishes to destroy what brings others pleasure" (146)—is echoed in many Renaissance texts (cf. the words of Envy in Marlowe's *Dr. Faustus*—"I cannot read and therefore wish all books were burned" [II.ii.2]) and makes up at least one piece of the crazed mosaic of Iago's psyche. Envy's close connection with the evil eye appears in iconography, where envy is often many-eyed: for example, Envie in Book 1 of Spenser's *The Faerie Queene* wears a garment "ypainted full of eyes" (1.4.31.2); Spenser's Envie is also linked with animals often associated with the evil eye, the large-eyed toad and hypnotic-eyed snake (1.4.30.3, 1.4.31.4). The belief that the evil eye can best be foiled by turning its force back on itself appears in many proverbs about envy: "'Envy is a beast that will gnaw its own leg. . . .' 'Envy cuts its own throat.' 'Envy will eat nothing but its own heart'" (Siebers 147); a version attaches to Spenser's Envie, who "chawed his owne maw / At neighbours wealth, that made him ever sad; / For death it was, when any good he saw" (1.4.30.5–7).

Envious Iago's evil eye gleams as he malevolently gazes upon helpless Othello, who is writhing on the floor in "an epilepsy" (IV.i.51). Epilepsy often signals "the presence of the fascinator; in Ethiopia, hysterical symptoms once required that the relatives of the victim seek out the fascinator among them in order to effect a cure" (Siebers 60). As Iago gazes upon the entranced Othello, he intones a kind of charm, "Work on, / My medicine, work!" (IV.i.45–46), a reference to his metaphorically poisoning Othello through the ear, but also perhaps to the effect of his evil eye. Iago administers his poison in two doses, in the two halves of Act III, scene iii; in the first, Othello is disturbed by Iago's insinuations but still under rational control; in the second, he is raving, screaming for "blood, blood, blood!" Iago attributes the change to the progressive effect of his poison ("the Moor already changes with my poison" [III.iii.325]), but it is significant that between the two episodes—in the exact center of the play—Desdemona loses what looks like a magical protection against the evil eye: the handkerchief. This amulet, of which we are told "there's magic in the web of it," magic instilled by an Egyptian charmer, has the magical effect of controlling a husband's eye: Othello's mother was told by the charmer that "if she lost it, / . . . my father's eye / Should hold her loathed." The talisman passes to Desdemona to serve her in the same magical way. As the most powerful sign against the evil eye is the representation of an eye (Siebers 7), so Desdemona is charged to make the handkerchief "a darling like your precious eye" (III.iv.55–69). She loses it, and immediately afterwards Othello believes Iago's insinuations and begins calling for her blood; her husband's eye "holds her loathed." The handkerchief is lost because Othello distractedly pushes it away when Desdemona offers it as a cure for his headache; readers have always read his "I have a pain upon my forehead here" (III.iii.283) as a reference to cuckold's horns, but it may not be irrelevant that the most frequent immediate effect of the evil eye on adults is "a piercing headache" (L. Jones 159; cf. Hand 187). One evil-eye belief is that possession of the evil eye is contagious; as the victim of a vampire becomes a vampire, so a victim of the evil eye can afflict or kill others: just as the evil-eyed Iago looms over the epileptic Othello, so at the end, an Othello whose eye holds his wife loathed looms over the sleeping Desdemona.[9] The scene resembles Tarquin's gazing on the sleeping Lucrece, and as Tarquin's eyes rolled, so Othello's gaze is fearfully abnormal: "I fear you," Desdemona cries; "For you are fatal then / When your eyes roll so." As if Iago's self-gnawing envy were contagious, Othello chews himself: "Why gnaw you so your nether lip?" (V.ii.37–43). In the evil-eye assault upon Desdemona, we see again the besieged woman whose endangerment was such a hallmark of this period.

Have we been right to regard Othello's description of the handkerchief's magical properties as no more than a rhetorical ploy to impress on Desdemona the heinousness of losing this love gift? To what extent is there magic in the web of it? Seeing that the magically protective handkerchief was Othello's first gift to Desdemona, was Brabantio entirely wrong to suspect some witchcraft in the course of this courtship? The loss of an amulet protecting against the evil eye leaves the owner vulnerable, and she is killed, in a play which bears other marks of evil-eye belief, such as the convergence of envy and epilepsy or the two references to Othello's turning to stone (IV.i.192–93, V.ii.63), which is the effect of Medusa, in a myth closely connected with evil-eye belief. Of course the turning to stone is a metaphor for hardening of the heart, but is it only a metaphor? The very metaphors of this age often seem steeped in magic and superstition; and the word *superstition* comes from the Latin *superstitio,* "standing in paralysis and stupefaction over an object or person" (Siebers xv), like one turned to stone by the evil eye. Even in a play such as *Julius Caesar,* which in a number of passages interrogates superstition, we have that token of the evil eye, epilepsy, and as Caesar comes away from his epileptic seizure he catches the disquieting sight of Cassius bending his malevolent gaze upon him. This is what I call magical thinking—magical belief lingering below the surface of consciousness.

In an age when people were tried and burned for "overlooking" their neighbors and other maleficent practices, we cannot blandly assume that Shakespeare was always rationally aloof from the superstitions that animated his neighbors. In his obsession with endangered chastity, with vulnerability to invasion whether through city wall or vagina or ear or eye, we glimpse the subterranean contours of magical belief that was still aboveground in the consciousness of the many Renaissance people who carried protective amulets. What I am addressing in this chapter is a mental phenomenon that is part metaphor, part intellectual construct, part protection magic.

Of Map-Makers, Virgins, and Pores

Evil-eye beliefs illustrate how protection magic works, and as I will explain in chapter 4, in some contexts the eyes themselves are regarded as orifices dangerously vulnerable to penetration. I want to explore further the national implications of such protectionism. Douglas's thesis that societies threatened at their borders obsessively protect bodily orifices suggests a profound link between two prominent concerns—with siege warfare and England embattled and with threatened female bodies. The link was not Shakespeare's alone: this piece of magical thinking—the need to guard against invasion through antipollution measures—was built into his culture.

Renaissance maps often identified England with the female body. The frontispiece female figure Britannia in Drayton's *Poly-Olbion* is clothed in a map. Elizabeth in the Ditchley portrait stands on a map of England; jewels carbuncling her dress resemble in color and distribution the map's towns and forests, and the south coast below her feet disconcertingly resembles toes. In a portrait in Hardwick Hall (Strong and Oman 32) Elizabeth's petticoat is adorned with fish and sea horses like the sea creatures surrounding England in Saxton's country map. Elizabeth appears as defender against papist invasion in a Dutch engraving superimposing her body on a map of Europe (Strong 116).

Though this society officially lionized the masculine invader Henry V, its unease about Henry is suggested by Shakespeare's ambivalent treatments of him. And in a passage in *Henry V* Henry hesitates to become an invader because of England's traditional vulnerability to invasion, especially via Scotland, when her kings are away: "We must not only arm t' invade the French, / But lay down our proportions to defend / Against the Scot, who will make road upon us / With all advantages." The Archbishop of Canterbury minimizes the danger: England is a house walled against thieves ("They of those marches, . . . / Shall be a wall sufficient to defend / Our inland from the pilfering borderers"), but Henry sees threat of invasion as a condition of English history:

> We do not mean the coursing snatchers only,
> But fear the main intendment of the Scot,
> Who hath been still a giddy neighbor to us.
> For you shall read that my great-grandfather
> Never went with his forces into France
> But that the Scot on his unfurnish'd kingdom
> Came pouring, like the tide into a breach,
> With ample and brim fullness of his force,
> Galling the gleaned land with hot assays,
> Girding with grievous siege castles and towns;
> That England, being empty of defense,
> Hath shook and trembled.
>
> (I.ii.137–54)

Here the great masculine invader himself sees England as a vulnerable nation always subject to sieges.

Even at its most invasive, as in its aggressive Irish policy, Elizabethan England expressed fear of invasion through an insecure border: "All over Catholic Europe, as well as in Ireland, Elizabeth was regarded as illegitimate, and unlikely to remain for long on the throne she had wrongfully ascended. Catholics were convinced that, when the time was ripe, Philip II of Spain, or some other powerful Catholic sovereign, would unseat her on the pope's behalf. With her position so weak, she saw a disobedient Ireland as a constant menace to her security. . . . Elizabeth could not allow Ireland to become a base for hostile fleets and armies" (Somerset Fry 116). Irish lords kept up "a continual correspondence with the queen's enemies in France, Spain and Scotland"; Ulster assisted refugees from the Spanish Armada, and a Spanish army landed in Ireland in 1601 (Somerset Fry 117, 127, 134). Sir Philip Sidney warned in 1577 that the Irish "will turn to any invading force" (Myers 37), and the enclave of English in the Irish pale had the palisaded mentality of a surrounded minority subject to constant border raids.

The tissue of cultural signifiers I have been describing was not unique to the Elizabethan age. The island trope looks back beyond the Norman invasion to Julius Caesar's. Metaphors comparing siege warfare with the siege of a lady's heart permeate medieval literature in many countries, and besieged cities are compared with sexually embattled women in cultures besides England and times other than the Renaissance. The siege mentality seems to have affected Europe to the point where even pores became vulnerable orifices, and people quit washing; bathing, popular in the Middle Ages, was almost completely discontinued in the sixteenth and seventeenth centuries. Vigarello attributes the new mentality largely to fear of the plague: the skin

> was seen as porous, and countless openings seemed to threaten. . . . The plague had only to slip through. . . . The body had less resistance to poisons after bathing, because it was more open to them. It was as if the body was permeable; infectious air threatened to flood in from all sides. "Steam-baths and bath-houses should be forbidden, because when one emerges, the flesh and the whole disposition of the body are softened and the pores open, and . . . pestiferous vapour can rapidly enter the body and cause sudden death" [Houel, 1573]. . . . The

architectural metaphor played a central role, with the body seen as a house invaded and occupied by the plague. (Vigarello 9)

But there is a peculiar intensity to the almost paranoid self-palisading of the English Renaissance psyche—something akin to what Canadian literati used to call a garrison mentality. And England, for a Protestant country, was oddly obsessed with virginity. Countless literary examples spring to mind, from Spenser's Knights of Maidenhead to the virgins slaughtered during *Tamburlaine*'s city siege, and lingering as late as virginity's magical power in *Comus*. Who spurred on the army to meet Armada invaders? The Virgin Queen, ideal image of Invaders of England versus Embattled Woman. The Land as Woman, society as a body threatened at its orifices—such deeply ingrained ideas help explain why Elizabethans valued virginity, why England needed a virgin queen.

All Europe was influenced by what Douglas calls "the exaggerated importance attached to virginity in the early centuries of Christianity": "The idea that virginity had a special positive value was bound to fall on good soil in a small persecuted minority group"; such social conditions encouraged symbolism of the body as "an imperfect container which will only be perfect if it can be made impermeable" (*Purity* 157–58). Marina Warner documents the persecution (one hundred thousand early Christians martyred) and virginity's growing centrality in medieval dogma, which stressed "technical, physical virginity, . . . the closed womb, . . . the 'fountain sealed,' an unbroken body, and not . . . a spiritual state of purity" (63). Though Augustine's view of rape was more spiritual than Shakespeare's, this architect of the doctrine of original sin laid the foundations for the cult of sealed-up virginity. His belief that original sin is transmitted by male genitals during intercourse made sin a venereal disease; it linked sexual penetration with admission of evil to the human interior. Saint Methodius wrote: "Anyone who intends to avoid sin . . . must keep all his members and senses pure and sealed—just as pilots caulk a ship's timbers—to prevent sin from getting an opening and pouring in" (Warner 54, 73). Medieval belief that the hymen sealed off the uterus abetted the idea of a virgin as a sealed vessel. Medieval women's passion for fasting sealed the body from food and from the passage of other substances through orifices: fasting saints like Joan the Meatless ceased to menstruate and were believed not to defecate, urinate, sweat, or emit tears; of one it was said, "neither saliva nor sputum emanated from her mouth nor any mucus or other fluid from her nostrils"; another "discharged no filth or dandruff from her hair" (Bynum, 91, 100, 122, 211). Here was truly one of Douglas's societies to "develop taboos and pollution beliefs around anything—from feces to menstrual blood—issuing from a bodily orifice" (*Purity* 115). But in most Protestant countries, virginity as an ideal was yielding, in the Renaissance, to marriage. England joined in this movement, as many cultural documents show (marriage sermons, romantic comedies); but in England virginity persisted as a potent ideal in the virgin queen cult and in works of many Protestant writers. And where married love emerged as the ideal, writers became obsessed, like Shakespeare, with sexually besieged wives. It is tempting to conclude that Douglas's theory is right and explains a lot—the Elizabethan mentality resembled the early Christian mentality because similar political and social conditions of the two groups fostered similar anxieties. Here is a kind of magical thinking that lies below the surface of consciousness—the sense that rape (even sex itself) is a pollution, that an anxious and threatened society can magically protect itself by defending (in political symbolism, in literature) the orifices of the body.

Augustus, Brutus, and the Back Door

But the sky began to change in 1603. Forthrightly enunciating a new ideology in his first speech to Parliament in 1603, James promised to avoid wars and declared the island Britain more secure from invasion than ever before. He also announced a policy of not persecuting Catholics, whose threat to the nation he saw as diminished: rather than demonizing them as would-be rapists, potential invaders of the national body, he minimized them as the last remnants of an amoebic dysentery lingering in the national alimentary canal, a "Sect, lurking within the bowels of this Nation" (*Political Works* 274). His one reference to his predecessor did not mention her virginity (270–76).

This speech put an ingenious spin on the island trope: union of

England and Scotland would create a true nation-island immune to invasion. Abolishing its main landlocked border would give Britain sea on all its boundaries:

> These two countries being separated neither by sea, nor great river, mountains, . . . but only by little small brooks, or demolished little walls; . . . And now in the end and fullness of time united, the right and title of both in my person, . . . whereby it is now become like a little world within itself, being intrenched and fortified round about with a natural, and yet admirable strong pond or ditch, whereby all the former fears of this nation are now quite cut off: the other part of the Island being ever before now not only the place of landing to all strangers, that was to make invasion here, but likewise moved by the enemies of this State by untimely incursions, to make enforced diversion from their conquests, for defending themselves at home, and keeping sure their back-door, as then it was called, which was the greatest hindrance and let that ever my predecessors of this nation got in disturbing them from their many famous and glorious conquests abroad. (*Political Works* 272)

James thinks England's status as besieged island has long hampered its expansion into empire; the island of his beleaguered predecessors he sees as a house, the Scottish border its unsecured back door. (*Henry V*, recall, had dwelt on the perennial danger of invasion through Scotland.) The passage even hints at invasion as bodily penetration, given the Renaissance slang meaning of back door. (The trope persists in our century: in the 1989 European elections, the British Conservative party campaigned on an isolationist platform; radio commercials threatened that closer alliance with Europe would bring left-wing policies to Britain "through the back door," thus recalling the Elizabethan palisading mentality that guarded all the doors of England's island "house.") But his rule, James says, has changed all that; and well he might wish to minimize the threat from the north, having himself recently penetrated the inner chambers of the English monarchy through the same Scottish back door. But what was the change? The new Jacobean ideology was not a simple shift from fear of invasion to a joyful prospect of invading others: James's pacifism, stressed in this speech, undermines talk of "famous and glorious conquests." As the address deconstructs, by introducing pacifism, its own opposition Besieged Nation/Conquering Nation, so James's ideology deconstructed Rome's opposed images as invader/invadee, by focusing on the historical liminal zone of Augustus.

Elizabethan England conceptualized itself mainly as a "feminine" society, vulnerable to invasion. In Jacobean England, official ideology played down the threat of invasion, comparing England with Rome the possessor of empire, enjoying the golden age of Augustus. James's first speech to Parliament heightened his peacemaking efforts by painting the Wars of the Roses, then more than a century past, as but recently ended; this helped create the desired Augustan atmosphere. Remember that there were always three concepts of Rome and of England: first, the "masculine" invader concept, whose frequent signifiers were Julius Caesar and Henry V; second, the "feminine" invadee concept, whose signifiers were Lucrece and Boudicca's ravished daughters; and third, the perhaps hermaphroditic "peaceful empire" concept,[10] symbolized by Augustus Caesar and King James. James's ideology belonged to the third concept. That he identified with Augustus rather than Julius Caesar is crucial: in focusing on the Augustan moment in Roman history, James emphasized peaceful possession, rather than acquisition, of empire. As the old binary oppositions invite the language of sexual difference I have here employed *sous rature,* James's deconstruction of this oppositional system invites the language of, as it were, sexual indifference: James's own bisexuality is as revealing a cultural signifier as Elizabeth's virginity.[11] James's ideology favored not the "feminine" image of endangered England, but not the "masculine" invader image either: it posited the peaceful colonial power.

The ideology's colonial side preceded and shaped reality, for at this moment in history the image of empire was premature: at the time of James's first speech to Parliament, Britain's empire consisted of a colony in Newfoundland, claimed in 1583 but as yet without settlers. Early reports from infant colonies are among the sources of *Cymbeline*'s close contemporary *The Tempest,* 1611, a play whose complexity and ambivalence have often been ignored in recent criticism, where it has gradually become a touchstone of the western colonial discourse, a central image of European invasion of the nonwhite world.[12] Prospero, be it remembered, finally abandons his colony, allowing it to revert to its precolonial state; if this mentality sadly did not shape reality, it remains unlikely that pacifist James would have conflated colonization and invasion; he found in colonization a peaceful alternative to invasion. His word *plantation* conjures more the fertility rites of an agrarian society than the invasion mentality's rites of war.[13]

This rural dimension of Jamesian ideology points toward a world of pastoral, with all its disparate possibilities. Pastoral can serve the interests of the powerful: Raymond Williams's *The Country and the City* shows how the ideology permeating Jacobean country house poems like Jonson's "To Penshurst" legitimated extreme social inequality and sanctioned exploitation of rural labor by the smooth expedient of erasing it from view. James himself sponsored the revival of rural sports and rites as a method of co-opting discontent with his reign; and the age of "rustication" on a large scale, with mass exports of convicts to the colonies, was not so very far in the future. Yet pastoral can also offer a standpoint for dissent, for criticizing power; it was the decentered perspective of a society founded partly on the model of pastoral retreat from a corrupt civilization that eventually empowered the American Revolution. At the Jamesian moment in history, the rural, pastoral component of the prevailing ideology contained the seeds of conflicting movements.

Jacobean England expanding into empire fancied itself heir to the Roman Empire. The title of Speed's 1611 atlas, *The Theater of the Empire of Great Britaine,* alluded to Ortelius's *Theatrum Orbis Terrarum:* as J. B. Harley argues, "*Orbis*" there means both "world" and "Roman Empire," and "the authority of the Roman Empire . . . attach[ed] by implication to the English Empire" (39). Emrys Jones shows that James carefully fostered the identification, especially in his "favourite self-appointed role of Peacemaker. *Beati pacifici* was his motto, and he loved to be called, and poets duly obliged him, the second Augustus" (90); James was portrayed in Roman dress as early as 1590 (Goldberg, *James* 46). As David Bergeron shows ("*Cymbeline*"), the popular mind linked the Jacobean era with Augustan Rome.

Jamesian ideology incorporated that traditional link between England and the ancient world, the Brutus-Trojan myth; significantly, Brutus was a colony founder. But this myth encoded a vulnerability more typical of the Lucrece than the Augustus paradigm: Brutus founded Britain because his own city, Troy, had been destroyed, and not only had Brutus come from a vulnerable society, he had created one, by dividing Britain—Learlike—into three kingdoms. Mythic common ancestor of Rome and Britain, Troy shared Rome's dual image of besieged city and mother of empire: Aeneas founded Rome after fleeing sacked Troy; his grandson Brutus dubbed the Ur-London New Troy. Jacobean ideology identified James with Brutus as well as Augustus, but as he downplayed England's "feminine," vulnerable image, James borrowed Brutus's nation-founding image without its vulnerability. Appropriating the title "new Brutus," James created himself as an anti-Brutus: uniting England and Scotland reversed Brutus's dangerous division. Image makers promoted the theme: Munday's *Triumphs of Re-united Britania*, 1605, notes that "*England, Wales, & Scotland,* by the first *Brute* severed and divided, is in our second *Brute* reunited" (7). But so entrenched are a culture's semiotic codes, even in times of change, that image makers could not entirely forget Brutus's vulnerable side: Heywood's *Troia Britanica: or, Great Britain's Troy* (1609), rejoicing that in James "three kingdoms, first by Brute divided, / United are, and by one scepter guided" (437), also develops a parallel between the sack of Troy and the rapes or near rapes of Helen.

Throughout a poem and five plays about Rome, Shakespeare "makes continual reference to Troy, the city that gave birth to Rome" (Miola 17).[14] Since he most often represents Troy as a besieged, sacked city, this identification underlines the basic vulnerability of Shakespeare's Rome. The ecphrasis so prominent in *Lucrece* evokes Troy's destruction. Katharine Maus justly notes that "for Shakespeare the sack of Troy is a culturally primal event" (81). Shakespeare's return, in works early and late, to the Rome/Troy complex of ideas suggests deep resonance between the Rome/Troy culture he imagined and the English culture he experienced. Across his career he more typically represents that culture in its vulnerable aspect, at risk of invasion, than in James's imperial aspect; but his treatment does shift during his Jacobean phase.

Elizabethan Shakespeare typically imagines a "feminine" embattled society, like Douglas's Coorgs—the Lucrece paradigm; but in Jacobean works like *Cymbeline* he shifts toward the Augustus (not the Julius Caesar) paradigm. This reflected, I think, his culture's changing sense of itself. The change did not occur overnight; it was a subtle shift, a tilting rather than a revolution—jaundiced views of virginity emerge in works before 1603, jaundiced views of Augustus Caesar in works after 1603 (witness *Antony and Cleopatra*'s Caesar). The change was not universally applauded: James's pacifism and bisexuality disturbed many; transvestism in the streets disturbed even James. The change did not flow down from the top, the sole creation of Jamesian ideology: like most social change, it welled up from many sources. The ideology was no more innocent than most ideologies: the bad faith behind pacifist pronouncements was only too clear in Ireland's continuing agonies. But the vision of peace without self-palisading and plantation without invasion held great potential; it offered much to women, to the New World, to relations between sexes and between nations, to England's sense of itself. Like a Wordsworthian spot of time, the Jacobean intercalary period offers one of history's shining worlds of possibility.

Of Salamanders and Hermaphrodism: Life in the Interstices

Mary Douglas's *Purity and Danger*, in a neat piece of puzzle solving, decodes the Hebrew abominations of Deuteronomy and Leviticus. To thousands of years' efforts to solve the puzzle of what a pig shares with a salamander that both should be abominated, Douglas adds her solution: abominated animals are those that fail to fit one clear category. "Any class of creatures which is not equipped for the right kind of locomotion in its element is contrary to holiness. . . . Anything in the water which has not fins and scales is unclean" (55). Pigs, which have cloven hooves but do not chew the cud, fail to conform to the category of cattle, "the model of the proper kind of food for a pastoralist" (54). As Turner encapsulates this theory of Douglas's, the unclear is unclean.

Fear and avoidance of creatures that stray out of class boundaries is symptomatic of that boundary obsession that generates pollution beliefs—in a society that feels endangered, clear boundaries divide Jew from Gentile, as an invisible wall guards bodily boundaries, protecting orifices. "The discrimination of statuses obsessed the guardians of the Elizabethan social order" (Montrose, "Purpose" 56), as sumptuary laws dictated dress for social classes. (Tellingly, sumptuary laws were repealed at the beginning of James's reign). Extraordinary efforts during this period to maintain the line between humans and beasts recall Douglas's theory of boundary-blurring creatures: "It was bestial to work at night, for the same reason that burglary was a worse crime than daylight robbery; the night . . . was 'the time wherein man is to rest, and wherein beasts run about seeking their prey.' It was even bestial to go swimming, for . . . it was essentially a non-human method of progression. As a Cambridge divine observed in 1600: men walked; birds flew; only fish swam. . . . Monstrous births caused such horror [because] they threatened the firm dividing-line between men and animals" (Thomas, *Man* 39). Such *human* self-palisading is contemporary with other instances of category fortification we have seen. It was during the early modern period that "most farmers finally moved the animals out of their houses into separate accommodation," and bestiality became a capital offense in England in 1534. Bestiality was a "sin of confusion; it was immoral to mix the categories"; the many tales of monstrous human-animal births "show that, in popular estimation at least, man was not so distinct a species that he could not breed with beasts. It was because the separateness of the human race was thought so precarious, . . . that the boundary had been so tightly guarded" (Thomas, *Man* 39–40, 135). Also feared was whatever blurred the

> categories of "wild" and "tame." . . . The encroachment of wild creatures into the human domain was always alarming. . . . In 1593 it was feared that the plague in London would get worse because a heron perched on the top of St. Peter's, Cornhill, and stayed there all afternoon. In 1604 the House of Commons rejected a bill after the speech of its Puritan sponsor had been interrupted by the flight of a jackdaw through the Chamber—an indisputably bad omen. The attitude resembled that of those African peoples amongst whom misfortune is expected whenever the world of the bush encroaches upon that of human settlement. (Thomas, *Man* 78)

The Israelites abominated some foods; Elizabethans abominated some women. Organizing women into clear categories—maid, widow, wife, whore—it abominated the unmarried nonvirgin partly because she confounded the distinction between maid and wife (see my *Women* 84). In Douglas's terms, such women would have been considered polluted not because sex was inherently staining but because in a society that demands clear boundaries, to confound the line between categories is to become an abomination as sure as the finless salamander or the flying ant.[15] The raped wife, too, is decategorized. Because her extramarital sex is unsanctioned but unwilled, she is neither chaste wife nor adulterer. Her classlessness— or boundary-crossing double class—like rape's "stain," leaves her polluted, potentially contaminating to others. She inhabits a liminal zone between two classes.[16] All margins are dangerous.

Book 1 of Spenser's *Faerie Queene,* on Holiness, the only nonsecular book in that educative epic, constructs sin (the antithesis of Holiness) largely as pollution. The words *filth, filthy, dirty,* and their variants and cognates loom larger here than anywhere else in *The Faerie Queene.* In the depth of his sinfulness, the Redcross Knight lies in a dirty dungeon reeking with a "filthie banefull smell" (1.8.39.9) and his regeneration involves cleansing and ritual purification: he goes to the House of Holiness "the filthy blots of sinne to wash away" (1.10.27.7). Error's body is a receptacle of sin, imaged as filth, pollution: her body is "full of filthie sin" (1.1.24.7). The personification Lechery is called "filthy" and Gluttony rides on a "filthie swine" (1.4.24.4, 1.4.21.2). The icon of holiness is a virgin, Una, and sin is represented by filthy orifice violations—the promiscuous couplings of Duessa—and also many mouth violations: the monster Error and personified Gluttony eat grossly and unnaturally (Error eats gobbets of raw flesh and the pages of pamphlets) and both vomit (Error "spew[s] out of her filthy maw" a stinking flood of raw flesh, papers, and live frogs and toads [1.1.20.1]).

As her name suggests, Una possesses a unitary nature, but the forces of sin, as Duessa's name suggests, possess double, hybrid natures: Archimago is a shapeshifter who can change into a bird, fish, or fox (1.2.10), Error is half woman, half snake, Gluttony and Lechery are animal-like (1.4.21, 1.4.24), and in the remarkable passage in which the beautiful young Duessa is stripped naked, her filth is connected with her being several kinds of hybrid:

> Her misshaped parts did them appall,
>   A loathly, wrinckled hag, ill favoured, old,

Whose secret filth good manners biddeth not be told.

Her craftie head was altogether bald,
    And as in hate of honorable eld,
    Was overgrowne with scurfe and filthy scald;
    Her teeth out of her rotten gummes were feld,
    And her sowre breath abhominably smeld;
    Her dried dugs, like bladders lacking wind,
    Hong downe, and filthy matter from them weld;
    Her wrizled skin as rough, as maple rind,
So scabby was, that would have loathd all womankind.

Her neather parts, the shame of all her kind,
    My chaster Muse for shame doth blush to write;
    But at her rompe she growing had behind
    A foxes taile, with dong all fowly dight;
    And eke her feete most monstrous were in sight;
    For one of them was like an Eagles claw,
    With griping talaunts armd to greedy fight,
    The other like a Beares uneven paw:
More ugly shape yet never living creature saw.
                    (1.8.46.7–1.8.48)

After resisting the literal-minded thought that in those days scarlet robes could do wonders for a girl of few natural endowments, the reader cannot help being struck not only by the filth—the disgusting "marginal stuff" (dung, filthy matter issuing from the breasts)—but also by the hybridization. The unclear is unclean. The word *loathly* alerts us to a reversal of the "loathly lady" folk tales, where a repulsive old hag turns young and beautiful—here is an inversion of the regenerative old/young figure of ritual (see chapter 5). Since even old women less often go bald than men, the baldness hints at a gender hybridization, and Duessa also crosses the boundary into the animal world, sporting parts of fox, eagle, and bear, and (at least metaphorically) even crosses into the plant kingdom—her skin is rough as maple rind.

In this centrally important Elizabethan text, then, holiness is linked with virginity and unitary nature, sin is constructed as pollution, and the polluted and sinful have double, hybrid natures. And they inhabit margins: Error lives in a cave—liminal zone between the underworld and the world of everyday reality; Archimago dwells in "a little lowly Hermitage . . . / Downe in a dale, hard by a forests side, / Far from resort of people (1.1.34.1–3); the Redcross Knight first pays court to Duessa in a "desert waste" under two trees considered "unlucky ground" by local shepherds (1.1.2.28–42).

Marginalia at the Center

All margins are dangerous. But, Douglas says, to be in the margins is to be "in contact with danger, to [be] at a source of power" (*Purity* 97). Vladimir Propp reminds us how many folk heroes disobey interdictions, transgress boundaries, which is dangerous but necessary for a hero to grow up and triumph. The dangers that boys in tribal cultures undergo in initiation, Douglas says, "express something important about marginality. . . . To go out of the formal structure and to enter the margins is to be exposed to power that is enough to kill them or make their manhood. . . . The danger that is risked by boundary transgression is power" (*Purity* 96, 161).

In *Titus* and *Lucrece*, rape and mutilation lead to the downfall of a tyrannical government and to Rome's political salvation. Like smashing an atom, smashing these women releases tremendous power. When bodily violence propels them into dangerous margins, when ceasing to be chaste wives they transgress confining boundaries, they release an uncanny power upon the world. In chapter 2, I will discuss the paradox that shedding blood can cleanse pollution, and in chapter 3, I will pursue in more depth, in *Titus Andronicus*, the magical thinking that credited rape and dismemberment with fertilizing and renewing power.

Releasing power through blood sacrifice is tragedy's ancient heritage from magic. Modern female readers may prefer comedy's way of releasing power. All through *Cymbeline*, Imogen tiptoes along a chasm of rape and death, but escapes violation and murder, and England escapes invasion. Imogen transgresses boundaries in happier ways—eloping, running off to Wales, confounding sexual distinctions by dressing as a boy, transgressing theatrical conventions in being Shakespeare's only transvestite heroine who is not a virgin.[17] This last, a break with her comedic sisters, signals a difference not generic but historical. That this symbol of Endangered

Britain is a sexually experienced woman is a sign of change. Are the orifices not to be so desperately guarded as before? Can Britain escape invasion without a royal virgin as a rallying symbol? Britain escapes here because the Britons trounce the Romans at the narrow lane, but also because Britain pays the tribute and makes peace. Has the invasion mentality ebbed? This is the last invasion attempt in Shakespeare.

In *The Tempest,* Shakespeare's last globe-trotting Italians, like the classical Romans before them, make themselves at home on whatever islands they come upon. The virginity magic of Prospero's "virgin knot" threat proves temporary: Prospero does not favor perpetual virginity, but wants his daughter to marry. The menace has bleached out of the invaded-island theme: the storm wrecking the intruders' ship, as storms defended Britain (at least in imagination) from Caesar's ships and the Armada, is here controlled by the island's sovereign, and the threat of rape, by Caliban, is contained. The virgin will marry; the besieged island is abandoned. Prospero returns to the mainland to rule without the aid of boundary-protecting magic.

We know, as Shakespeare did not, what lay ahead for the island Britain. The besieged virgin of Renaissance imaginings would become the thrusting masculine conqueror, threatening the New World with ravishment. As Rome moved from invader stage through Augustan liminal zone to invaded stage, so Britain would move from invaded stage through Jacobean liminal zone to invader stage. Colonization would reveal its brutal face, indistinguishable from invasion: the "plantation" James saw as a peaceful alternative to invasion soon displayed invasion's panoply of signifiers—rape, pillage, genocide. The British Empire, like the Roman, would thrust deep into the world's virgin territories; many read *The Tempest* as a document heralding that advance. But while Jacobeans helped invent English colonialism, the play does not fully inhabit that discourse; like Jacobean ideology, it dwells in a liminal zone. No longer an ideology of feminine endangerment, not yet one of masculine rapacity, James's ideology deconstructed a worldview that offered only these equally unpleasant alternatives. *The Tempest* belongs to a precolonial discourse: to locate it fully within the discourse of colonialism, as do Paul Brown or Francis Barker and Peter Hulme, is to miss the power accruing from its position in the interstices of literary history. The late comedies conjure a world poised between society as threatened virgin and as thrusting rapist, a world redeemable without rape and mutilation of women, where territorial integrity can fit comfortably—a loose-fitting saltwater girdle—without being tested through invading other nations.

Cymbeline closes with peace, concluded without the need for magical purification rites: "Let / A Roman and a British ensign wave / Friendly together. . . . / Never was a war did cease, / Ere bloody hands were wash'd, with such a peace" (V.v.481–87).[18] Shakespeare had always identified England with Rome, and his last Roman play unites them; this union weds the "third Rome," which desists from invading, with the "third England," saved from invasion—Augustan Rome meets Jacobean England. Toward the end of his career Shakespeare, living in a charmed moment in a changing culture, envisioned a society neither invaded nor invader, neither raped nor rapist, neither polluted nor polluter, which has truly become what John of Gaunt earlier wanted it to be: "this happy breed of men, this little world, / This precious stone set in the silver sea, / . . . This blessed plot, this earth, this realm, *this* England."

At this moment, the need for talismanic protection was suspended. It was as if Shakespeare the writer were personally on a trajectory of what Keith Thomas has called "the decline of magic." It is no wonder that his last hero, himself a magician, ends by breaking his staff and drowning his book. However, the change was not merely personal but cultural, a subtle shift in the design of those invisible—and residually magical—mental girders that structured the mind of the age.

Notes

This chapter is a significantly revised version of "Palisading the Body Politic," which appeared in *True Rites and Maimed Rites: Ritual and Anti-Ritual in Shakespeare and His Age,* ed. Linda Woodbridge and Edward Berry (Urbana: University of Illinois Press, 1992), 270–98, and in *Texas Studies in Literature and Language* 33 (1991): 327–54.

1. Douglas defines pollution as "ritual uncleanness" brought on by violation of some taboo (*Purity,* chap. 1).

2. See lines 16, 33–34, 838, 1056, 1067–68; see also Dubrow, *Captive* 92–93. *Cymbeline,* too, imagines sex as burglary (see I.vi.15, II.ii.41–42).

3. Fineman notes that doors, wind, and glove objectify the rape (40).

4. Marcus's reading of the play as a "sustained political allegory" of Jacobean political concerns (*Puzzling*) is a more topical approach than mine.

5. The Roman emissary arrives in Britain to demand tribute just before the Roman seducer arrives in Britain to attempt Imogen's virtue. Imogen represents British womanhood against the claims of a Roman, Frenchman, Dutchman, and Spaniard that their own countrywomen are superior (I.iv). Told that her husband has been consorting with Roman prostitutes, Imogen replies wanly, "My lord, I fear, / Has forgot Britain" (I.vi.112–13), meaning "he has forgotten me," a natural identification of herself with Britain. Believing her dead, Posthumus repents of having commissioned her murder and joined the Romans invading Britain: "'Tis enough / That, Britain, I have kill'd thy mistress [Imogen as the king's daughter]; peace, / I'll give no wound to thee" (V.i.19–21).

6. As Douglas argues elsewhere, however, it is a mistake to regard as advanced or civilized an "internalized" view of transgression as moral guilt and as primitive or uncivilized an "external" view of transgression as taboo violation. Instead she locates the taboolike attitudes in claustrophobic societies obsessed with boundary protection (*Natural Symbols* 102).

7. In the spate of books published in 1988 for the Armada's four hundredth anniversary, this verdict stood. The most revisionary, Fernández-Armesto's (which was not reviewed very favorably), tries to resurrect the weather as a determining factor, but mainly cites poor weather on the voyage from Spain; even he admits that twice during the battle itself the weather *helped* the Spanish (202–3, 205, 238; see also Hart-Davis 198).

8. Deut. 28:54–56 shows the evil eye operating without the will of the possessor: God threatens, as a curse for disobedience to the divine will, an evil eye that men and women will helplessly turn on their own families.

9. In one frenzied passage, Othello also hints that he has been charmed by Desdemona's eyes: he rushes off to murder her with the cry "Strumpet, I come. / Forth of my heart those charms, thine eyes, are blotted" (V.i.34–35).

10. I have elsewhere discussed the hermaphrodite symbol's centrality in Jacobean culture, including female cross-dressing in London (see *Women*, part 2). Some Elizabethan women also cross-dressed—scattered references appear from about 1570—but the fashion blossomed in Jacobean times. Elizabeth's cross-dressing at Tilbury might tell against hermaphrodism as a typically Jacobean symbol; but Susan Frye notes a complete lack of contemporary evidence that Elizabeth *did* cross-dress at Tilbury: this image of Elizabeth was, tellingly, a Jacobean creation. Determined to find hermaphrodism in Elizabeth, Marcus exaggerates from small hints—Eliza-

beth's holding a truncheon at Tilbury, Marcus inflates into the "donning of male battle gear" (*Puzzling* 63).

11. Building on Mary Douglas's theories, Kirsten Hastrup suggests "that the ambivalent feelings of most people towards transvestism, and to a lesser extent towards homosexuality, are founded on the fact that the people designated by these terms defy the normal categorisation of male and female. . . . If transvestism and homosexuality are concepts of danger, in the sense that they are notions relating to ambiguous areas of classification, then virginity and heterosexuality may be said to be notions of purity, in that they operate with distinct categories of men and women" (52).

12. Skura's "Discourse" usefully assembles (n.1) and cogently criticizes the many "colonial discourse" treatments of the play. She argues that English colonialism of later centuries has anachronistically colored readings of the play: in fact the play marked, in 1611, the very beginning of a colonial discourse that was significantly altered as early as Purchas's remarks in 1625. She questions whether "colonialism was already encoded in the anomalous situation in 1611," when "there were in England no literary portrayals of New World inhabitants and certainly no fictional examples of colonialist discourse. . . . Insofar as *The Tempest* does in some way allude to an encounter with a New World native, . . . it is the very first work of literature to do so. . . . If the play is 'colonialist,' it must be seen as 'prophetic' rather than descriptive" (52–58). For another perceptive recent critique of the "colonial discourse" interpretation of the play see Willis, "Shakespeare's *Tempest*."

13. Jim Black drew my attention to this Jamesian usage.

14. Miola details many links among our three Roman works: the wager on the wife's chastity (*Luc, Cym*), Tarquin's and Iachimo's similar approach to sleeping victims, the configuration wicked queen/lustful son (*Tit, Cym*). Other readers too have noticed close affinities among these works: "The Lucrece story and the Titus Andronicus story look like alternative versions of the same archetype" (G. K. Hunter 184). The Rome/Troy works grew out of a discrete body of material, encoded to conflate harm to the state with bodily harm. That great Jacobean endangered heroine in endangered Britain, *Cymbeline*'s Imogen, bears the name of the wife of Brutus of Troy (see Goldberg, *James* 240).

15. Other boundary blurrers: the leper is "a walking oxymoron; violating the sacrosanct boundary between life and death, he had long been a figure of anomaly and hence of pollution"; leprosariums were on the outskirts of the city (Mullaney 33); the actor "was a willful confuser of categories"—as Gosson charged, "in stage plays for a boy to put on the attire, the gesture, the passions of a woman, for a mean person to take

upon him the title of a prince, . . . [is] to show themselves otherwise than they are" (Montrose, "Purpose" 55).

16. As Dubrow shows, *Lucrece* "repeatedly describes ambiguous intermediate states, such as the sensation of being both dead and alive or the dilemma of being at once chaste and unchaste, and these examples of 'strange harmony' are mirrored by syneciosis," in phrases like "lifeless life" (*Captive* 82). Dubrow is interested in identity loss in the rape victim; but such interstitial states can also be attributed to society's rigid categories.

17. Given Posthumus's banishment, it is possible that his marriage to Imogen was never consummated; but his description of their life together suggests restraint but not abstinence: "Me of my lawful pleasure she restrain'd / And pray'd me oft forbearance" (II.v.9–10). "Oft" is not "always."

18. Emrys Jones thinks that "the peace-tableau with which *Cymbeline* ends . . . pays tribute to James's strenuous peace-making policy" (89), and Wickham offers, "The drift away from revenge tragedy and towards regenerative tragi-comedy in the first decade of James's reign . . . has its true origins in the political consciousness of the British peoples saved from foreign invasion and civil war by the peaceful accession of James I in 1603" (36).

2

Magical Politics: Shakespeare and the Scapegoat

"The tragic paradox is the paradox of violence, the problem of the positive value of suffering, sin and death," Jean-Pierre Guépin muses, contemplating Greek tragedy. "How can the sad ending, . . . [the] whole atmosphere of crime and lamentation, be reconciled with a spring performance in honour of the giver of plenty, Dionysus?" (xiii, xi). The answer may be that the hero's death does bring "plenty," because it works magically to ward off evil from society. Is Renaissance tragedy redemptive, the hero's death curative for the community? Is Shakespeare's tragic hero a classic scapegoat?

Surveying ritual readings of Shakespeare in 1962, Robert Hapgood found "the association—not equation—of the death of the tragic hero with the sacrifice of the scapegoat king . . . the soundest and most suggestive contribution which the ritualists have made" (120). In the best-known scapegoat reading of Shakespeare, John Holloway in 1961 had seen tragedy's "vertebrate structure" as "human sacrifice" (98): Coriolanus is driven away like a classical scapegoat, his death a *sparagmos* ("tear him in pieces"); the hero goes "from being the cynosure of his society to being estranged from it; . . . what happens to him suggests the expulsion of a scapegoat, or the sacrifice of a victim" (135). Scapegoats have been found in other genres too. History-play kings "are loaded at their end with . . . collective responsibility for the many kinds of evil which have been freed (by whatever agency) during their reign" (Henn 84). "By dying [Henry IV] will cleanse England: 'And now my death /

Changes the mood' (*2H4* IV.v.198–99); simply and without fuss he accepts the role of scapegoat" (Leggatt 84). Shylock and Antonio, *Merry Wives*'s Falstaff, and Pericles have been called scapegoats (Girard, "Entrap"; Spens; Jeanne Roberts; Barber, *Shakespeare's Festive Comedy*; Thorne). Barber thinks fools are scapegoats "consolidat[ing] the hold of the serious themes by exorcising opposition" (*Shakespeare's Festive Comedy* 232). I have argued that the stage misogynist, "not unlike the classical pharmakos or scapegoat [carries] doubts, fears, and antagonisms [toward women] out of the play with him" (*Women* 290). Guépin distinguishes tragic from comic scapegoats: in tragedy our sympathy is with the scapegoat, but in comedy we acquiesce in his expulsion (116); in Guépin's terms, René Girard's compromise—that only the refined sympathize with the scapegoat Shylock—*The Merchant of Venice* would be a tragedy for the refined, a comedy for the vulgar ("Entrap" 109).

Though the word *scapegoat* was not in secular use before the nineteenth century, scapegoat rites were practiced in early modern England and were prominent enough in biblical and classical texts to offer paradigms for secular experience in literature. The Renaissance knew the world of sacrifice, through the Old Testament and the classics, which reinforce each other: as Walter Burkert notes, "Semitic . . . sacrificial rites offer the closest parallels to Greek ritual" ("Greek Tragedy" 103). Heinrich Bullinger's "Of the Sacraments of the Jews," 1550, shows Renaissance familiarity with ancient Hebrew, Greek, and Roman sacrificial practices. Richard Marienstras notes that travelers' accounts like Hakluyt's (however embellished) acquainted Elizabethans with heathen sacrifice in their own time. Elizabethans may well have seen tragedic slayings in terms of human sacrifice.

Though not all scapegoating involves blood sacrifice, some familiarity with ancient blood rites appears in Shakespeare's surprisingly frequent use of blood sacrifice, mostly in imagery, occasionally as incident. To give period color to a Greek or Roman play, he uses sacrifice as shorthand (*Tro* V.iii.17–18; *Ant* I.ii.165; *Cor* I.vi.9). Human sacrifice occurs in *Titus Andronicus*: "Alarbus' limbs are lopp'd, / And entrails feed the sacrificing fire, / Whose smoke, like incense, doth perfume the sky" (I.i.145–48), a religious rite appeasing the souls of slain warriors (cf. *Cym* V.v.73). Shylock's threatened revenge takes on something of an aura of human sacrifice, partly because Antonio's last-minute reprieve recalls the Abraham and Isaac story the guild plays dramatized: the boy reprieved from sacrifice by a substitute atonement.

In the three late romances set among classical gods and oracles, moments of solemn joy—reunion of spouses or of parents with lost children—spark allusion to blood sacrifice. Diana directs Pericles to "do upon mine altar sacrifice" (V.i.244), a ritual that leads to Pericles' reunion with his wife. To celebrate finding his lost children, Cymbeline will "smoke the temple with our sacrifices," crying "Laud we the gods, / From our blest altars" (V.v.400, 478–80). Of the oracle consulted about estranged spouses, Dion cries, "O, the sacrifice! / How ceremonious, solemn, and unearthly!" (*WT* III.i. 6–7; on pagan ritual in *WT,* see Laroque, "Pagan"). A similar moment in tragedy is Lear's reunion with Cordelia: "Upon such sacrifices, . . . / The gods themselves throw incense" (V.iii.20–21). And even in nonpagan contexts, imagery of human sacrifice abounds (see *Mac* IV.iii.16–17; *Rom* V.iii.304; *TN* V.i.126; *Tro* IV.iii.9–10; *Jn* II.i.419).

Scapegoating is one among many reasons for sacrifice: sacrifice may also be practiced for fertility, divination, as a thank offering, as a gesture of dedication to a god, or appeasement of the dead. We find few formal scapegoat rites in Shakespeare; scapegoating typically operates subliminally, as a mode of magical thinking.

Some Efficacious Scapegoatings in Shakespeare

Some plot motifs suggest scapegoating. The ritual victim's *sparagmos* appears in Macbeth's beheading and the mob killing of Coriolanus. Aufidius's standing on Coriolanus's body recalls an ancient Albanian rite: "the body is carried away . . . , and then they all trample upon it, . . . as a mode of purification" (Strabo 2:234). The noisy ritual procession to drive away demons or collect them for transfer to a scapegoat (Vickery 26) appears when deposed Richard and new King Henry enter London in procession. With much shouting the city's (and nation's?) evils are transferred to Richard: "Rude misgovern'd hands . . . / Threw dust and rubbish on King Richard's head" (*R2* V.i.5–6). The dust and rubbish suggest pollution, and the public transfer of this filth to the expelled monarch reveals an underlying kind of magical thinking in which Richard's political faults, such as allowing flatterers too much say in government or leasing out land in a manner unbefitting royalty (*R2* II.i.59–60), are redefined magically, as pollution.

A minor motif in many plays, scapegoating is central and to some degree efficacious, I think, in *Titus Andronicus, Romeo and Juliet, 1 and 2 Henry IV, Coriolanus, Richard III*, and *Macbeth*. In the first five, evil—in every case civil dissension—is transferred to a victim. In the last two, kings are slain. In *Richard II* and *Julius Caesar*, scapegoating also seems central, but is not efficacious.

Titus Andronicus, Romeo and Juliet, 1 and 2 Henry IV, and *Coriolanus* share one skeletal structure: a troubled society is saved, wholly or partly, by sacrificing or expelling a scapegoat who is not a monarch. In all these, the trouble is internecine more than external: *Titus*'s strife over who shall be emperor, *Romeo and Juliet*'s feud, civil war in *Henry IV*, class war in *Coriolanus*. One cannot speak, of course, of permanent efficacy, of a society saved once and for all; and often in these plays we have the impression that the troubles temporarily cured by the sacrifice of a scapegoat are deeply structural in the society the play depicts and will recur. This is, in part, what makes scapegoating so troubling a phenomenon—the sense of its futility in the long run, the melancholy recognition that in the fallen world of civic and national strife, every generation will need its scapegoats.

As Gail Paster notes, "the entire Andronici family serves as the ritual scapegoat," though Titus is at the center (75). As I will discuss in chapter 3, human sacrifice in *Titus* is efficacious: Rome is saved. Here is one of many cases where the threads of scapegoat magic prove nearly impossible to unpick from the threads of fertility magic.

Romeo and Juliet are the innocent sacrifice familiar to Greek tragedy: the "sacrifice of young people to save family or city or nation in a situation of social crisis . . . is a common theme in Euripides" (H. Foley 65). Their deaths, though not a religious rite as in Greek tragedy, have a kind of religiomagical effect: the feud ends, Verona is saved. Innocence here is crucial: to dismiss the lovers' feelings as puppy love is to miss a vital emotional effect: because it is puppy love we respond to Romeo and Juliet as virtual children, innocent victims.

The rejection of Falstaff (foreshadowed in *1 Henry IV*, enacted in *2 Henry IV*) gives the *Henry IV* plays a pattern not unlike "the periodic ejection of the repulsive old man who, among the Rukuba, takes over the monstrous aspect of sacred power after having been identified with the chief" (de Heusch 156). Falstaff has indeed been identified with the chief: clearly Hal's father surrogate, he plays the king's role in the tavern scene; he also represents Hal's disreputable side that must be externalized and banished before he can be king. At the end, Falstaff's own considerable weight is augmented by transferred evils—the prince's wildness, civil dissension recently raging, perhaps Lancastrian illegitimacy itself, are expelled with that poor old king surrogate, and *Part Two* ends with a monarch legitimized, a kingdom at peace.

Coriolanus is driven away *and* slain: banished from Rome, killed in a communal act of violence. Evil is transferred: Coriolanus exacerbated but did not solely cause Rome's class tensions, yet when he leaves, tensions cease, in "a happier and more comely time / Than when these fellows ran about the streets, / Crying confusion" (IV.vi.28–30). He has borne civil dissension out of the city.

In these five plays, scapegoating effects at least formal harmony. To René Girard, a tragedy like Euripides' *Bacchae* recreates a primal event of curative violence when a crowd "hurled itself on one individual," who polarized all "the fears, anxieties, and hostilities of the crowd. His violent death provided the necessary outlet for the mass anguish, and restored peace. [In] the ritual sparagmos . . . the community tries to mimic the gestures that effected its salvation" (*Violence* 131–32). Girard thinks that tragedy, imitation violence, mediates between ritualized and real violence. Whatever its relation to sacred rites or societal violence, scapegoating in these five plays does what Girard suggests: restores peace at least temporarily.

Only two king slayings redeem society. In both, we see a society deeply mired in a state resembling pollution. In Richard III's nightmare England, no one is safe from murder, arbitrary criminal charges, summary execution; in Macbeth's Scotland children are butchered and distrust runs so deep it is unsafe to speak without elaborate testing preambles like Malcolm's to Macduff. God supports the kings' opponents—saintly Richmond in *Richard III*, the English in *Macbeth*, whose king glows with supernatural mana. The deaths of Richard III and Macbeth bring redemption: "Civil wounds are stopp'd, peace lives again" (*R3* V.v.40); once Macbeth is slain, "We may again / Give to our tables meat, sleep to our nights, / Free from our feasts and banquets bloody knives" (III.vi.33–35). I want to put these examples on the table before turning to some theory on scapegoating; I will return to these plays in more detail.

Scapegoating: Some Theorists

The scapegoat theory provides a psychological mechanism for the redemptive quality of suffering or death, and tragedy does have some link with ancient ritual sacrifice.[1] But most scapegoat readings of Renaissance texts are disquietingly sketchy. How consciously did writers use the notion of human sacrifice? What exactly is a scapegoat and how did scapegoating function in a community? The word is bandied about without definition, as if everyone knows what a scapegoat is; or we are tossed an all-inclusive footnote to the works of Sir James Frazer. Even the redoubtable Derrida, in "Plato's Pharmacy," relies almost exclusively on Frazer and on Jane Harrison, those elderly authorities, for information on scapegoats. Perhaps because it lacks solid theory, scapegoat interpretation (despite periodic forays) has never really taken hold in Shakespeare studies. (For a discussion of problems in the work of scapegoat theorists from Frazer to Girard, see the introduction to Woodbridge and Berry's *True Rites and Maimed Rites*.) Drawing on the work of Pierre Guépin, Luc de Heusch, and Helene Foley, theorists who (though unfamiliar among Shakespeareans) seem to me more useful than most scapegoat theorists usually cited now, I will try here to put the theory on a sounder basis, so that other interpreters can approach Shakespearean scapegoating with more precision.

We can begin with scapegoat thinking—some in the form of overt magical practice, some submerged as magical thinking—in early modern England. Occasionally, blood sacrifice was practiced: one reads of toads sacrificed in curing rites, and the ritual bludgeoning to death of a tied-up cock on Shrove Tuesday suggests an expiatory sacrifice, since "shrove" is related to shriving, or being absolved of sins, and Shrove Tuesday was the threshold of that expiatory season Lent. It has been argued, by Violet Alford and others, that the folk-drama sword dance, with its mimed beheading, represent-

ed a former blood sacrifice. Bloodless rites wherein evil was transferred were, however, more common than blood sacrifice. In one
overtly magical scapegoat rite practiced in Shakespeare's time, a
poor person was hired to attend a funeral and take on the deceased's
sins, keeping the dead person's ghost from walking; sin was transferred via bread and beer, passed over the corpse and then consumed
by the sin-eater. The seventeenth-century historian John Aubrey,
who details instances of the rite, likens it to "the Scapegoat in the
old law," quoting Lev. 16; "this custom (though rarely used in our
days), yet by some people was observed even in the strictest time
of the Presbyterian government" (35–36). Scapegoating at a more
submerged psychological level was also common: "At the local level
the clergy did not hesitate to identify the scapegoat responsible for
the community's sufferings. When 190 persons died of the plague
at Cranbrook, Kent, in 1597–98, the vicar of St. Dunstan's church
entered his diagnosis in the parish register: it was a divine judgement for the town's sins, and in particular for 'that vice of drunk-
enness which did abound here.' [He identified two culprits by
name.] . . . At Hitchin the minister blamed the plague of 1665 on
the local prostitute" (Thomas, *Religion* 100). Such blaming was
natural to scapegoat thinking, to which transference of evil is basic. In rural England, illness was often transferred to plants, animals, or objects until quite recent times: students of folklore have
noted transfers of illness into rushes that are floated downstream
(Thistleton-Dyer 163), into snails or tree trunks (R. Palmer 65),
dogs, potatoes, or rings (A. R. Wright 70, 72). Warts were transferred to sticks; whoever picked them up got warts (A. R. Wright
70). The many transference cures Palmer records in *The Folklore
of Warwickshire* are late survivals of folk beliefs Shakespeare grew
up with. Some early modern witchcraft charges arose from such
cures: "The 'good' witch who . . . cured [a client] by transferring
his disease to another person, might well be regarded as a 'bad' one
by the injured party" (Thomas, *Religion* 520).

John D. Niles writes of the long tradition of transference rites
in medieval fertility rituals and in the cures in medieval English folk
medicine. In one fertility ritual,

> the celebrant is instructed to take unknown seed from beggars
> and to return them twice as much. . . . The celebrant is engaged

in an act of magic by transference. He is making a symbolic trade of his own 'bad' seed for the 'good' seed of the almsmen. The logic of the trade is that of symbolic transference of bad luck from one party to another. Magic by transference is a commonplace of folk belief from early times and is well illustrated by other Anglo-Saxon charms, Storms 10, for example, a charm to prevent the recurrence of miscarriage. Here the woman who has not been able to give birth to a live child is instructed to take some earth from her child's grave and hide it well in a wrapping of wool. She then sells the wool to a chapman. Because the chapman has bought the wool, symbolically he has 'bought' the bad luck as well. In this charm . . . , the importance of the trade lies not in what is gained but in what is given away. To some moderns, the logic of magic by transference may seem ungenerous; and yet magic in general is not noted for its generosity. The point is to effect a cure. (52–53)

Elizabethans were also familiar with biblical scapegoating. Tyndale coined the word *scapegoat* in his 1530 translation of Leviticus, to render the Hebrew *Azazel*. God's sacrificial instructions in Leviticus, familiar to Renaissance writers, are worth quoting in full:

He shall take . . . two kids of the goats for a sin offering . . . and present them before the Lord. . . . And Aaron shall cast lots upon the two goats; one lot for the Lord, and the other lot for the scapegoat [*Azazel*]. And Aaron shall bring the goat upon which the Lord's lot fell, and offer him for a sin offering. But the goat, on which the lot fell to be the scapegoat, shall be presented alive before the Lord, to make an atonement with him, and to let him go for a scapegoat into the wilderness. . . . And Aaron shall lay both his hands upon the head of the live goat, and confess over him all the iniquities of the children of Israel, and all their transgressions in all their sins, putting them upon the head of the goat, and shall send him away . . . into the wilderness: And the goat shall bear upon him all their iniquities unto a land not inhabited: and he shall let go the goat in the wilderness. (KJV 16:5, 7–10, 20–22)

The translation of *Azazel* as "sent-away goat" is old—the Vulgate has *caper emissarius,* the Douay "emissary goat," Coverdale (1535) "free goat" (Yerkes 246).[2] But "one lot for the Lord, and the other lot for Azazel" suggests Azazel as a rival deity, perhaps a desert demon. (A few take "Azazel" as "wilderness"; the word occurs nowhere else.) The goat ritual occurred on Yom Kippur, Day of Atonement; both goats were to atone for and remove evil. The two correspond closely to the two types of Shakespearean scapegoat, the slain and the driven-away. The slain goat might be a simple gift to God, to atone for sin; but it seems more a substitute for the people, on whom to deflect God's wrath over sin, in a vicarious atonement. The sin-laden goat, like the transference cures that do not involve bloodletting, carries evil beyond community borders. Tribally, disease and evil are often traced to foes; perhaps the Hebrew scapegoat carried evil back to Azazel, its origin, as in a Ugandan rite in which a disease was carried back to the foe when a bodily defective person was abandoned in enemy country (Roscoe 342). An early modern analogue, the witch bottle, carried back to a witch the malady that the witch had given to a neighbor; it often contained nails with which to fix the malady to the witch (Merrifield 163–78). The two-goat rite's duality (like the leper purification [Lev. 14:7], in which one bird was released, one killed), corresponds to the two ways we use "scapegoat": (1) the figure blamed for community ills and driven away and (2) human sacrifice. They are closely related, as the Hebrew rite suggests; but the expulsion operates mainly by transference, the slaying by substitution.

The Transference Principle: The Expelled Victim

Frazer aptly, though with his usual condescension, calls the idea of transference a "confusion between the material and the immaterial, between the real possibility of transferring a physical load to other shoulders and the supposed possibility of transferring our bodily and mental ailments to another" (*Scapegoat* v). Examples of private physical healings are Pliny's account of Romans transferring fever by fixing a patient's nail-parings on a neighbor's door (61) and a Devonshire rite, reported in the nineteenth century, wherein a sufferer gives his or her ague to a neighbor "by burying under his threshold . . . the parings of a dead man's nails" [Thistle-ton-Dyer 150]. In a public, political rite of transference, Romans cured civil dissension by nailing discord to a wall (Livy 73). In Roman Britain, curses were nailed up to fix them to a victim, a practice with a long later history; the Latin for such curses was *defixio*, the fixing of evil on a victim (Merrifield 138ff.). In Shakespeare's day nails were common in witchcraft, to transfer and fix evil. (Both fingernails and carpentry nails are widely involved in such magic; that the same word was used for both from earliest times in most Germanic languages [OED] suggests a long cultural identification between the two.)

In ancient Greece, a slave was beaten and turned outdoors with the words "out with hunger, in with wealth and health" (Plutarch 495–97); in Athens plague was placed on poor people who were cast out or sacrificed (Aristophanes, *Frogs* 111). Rome's scapegoat Mamurius Veturius was sent to the land of enemies of Rome (Usener 122–23); as in the Ugandan and perhaps the Hebrew cases, he seems to carry evils back to their origin, the neighbor-enemy. Medieval human scapegoats included a barefoot sinner in Thüringen, a goat-clad child or puppet in Switzerland (Aeneas Sylvius 423–24; Usener 109ff.). Some scapegoats were driven away, some killed, usually outside the village or at a boundary: the rite strove to get illness well away from the community. Holloway sums up: "The essence of a scapegoat rite is that the evil in a particular society is transferred to a certain individual, and then eradicated from the society through his destruction or expulsion" (141), and this is broadly true, though important differences exist from culture to culture, and even within a single culture the phenomenon is very complex: transferred evils may be bodily (fever, plague), agricultural (drought, floods), political (civil dissension), or moral (sins of the people). When we try to tease out from this kind of magical thinking Thomas's "invisible mental structures, . . . underlying inchoate and ill-recorded systems of thought," three principles seem involved: evil is detachable, transferable, and indestructible.

First, detachability. Reflecting material/immaterial confusion, magical thinking often sees evil as material. Renaissance "alchemic operations . . . [were based on] the fundamental idea of the transferability and material detachability of attributes and states—the same idea [as in] a more naïve and primitive stage in such notions as that of the 'scapegoat'" (Cassirer 67).[3] But even the immaterial is detachable. Greek sacrifice of virgins before war externalizes interior states—a killing of innocence and the feminine in the warrior (H. Foley 89). In the magical thinking that blames all trouble on evil spirits or enemy sorcery we may detect evils already detached from the self.[4] In "The Scapegoat Psychology," Neumann suggests that tribal thinking often experiences evil as alien (*Depth* 54–55); in a less universalist mode, the anthropologist Mary Douglas reports that the Dinka (who sound like tribal post-structuralists disbelieving in the autonomous subject) do not "distinguish the self as an independent source of action and of reaction":

> The self acted upon by emotions they portray by external powers, spiritual beings who cause misfortune of various kinds. So . . . to do justice to the complex reality of the self's interaction within itself the Dinka universe is peopled with dangerous personal extensions to the self. This is . . . how Jung described the primitive world view . . . : "An unlimited amount of what we now consider an integral part of our own psychic being disports itself merrily for the primitive in projections reaching far and wide." (*Purity* 84)

Folk tale enemies and helpers seem projections of the hero's qualities; such a preliterary mode partakes of thinking that underlies scapegoating—belief that attributes are detachable from oneself. Such thinking also underpins allegory, where the hero's detached virtues and vices (or, as in *Everyman,* bodily attributes—Strength, Beauty) are externalized in other characters; Catherine Belsey reads such fragmentation of medieval dramatic figures as evidence of what she calls the discontinuous subject—and indeed discontinuity of personality is a precondition for the kind of magical thinking in which one part of the personality can be externalized and alienated from the rest. Allegorical plays like *The Interlude of Youth* mediate between a world of magical belief and the world of *Henry IV.* Hal's ability to detach riotousness from himself and fix it on Falstaff displays the residuum of a tribal mentality, mediated by precursors like Riot, the allegorical tempter in *The Interlude of Youth,* recipient and embodiment of Youth's detachable evil. Hotspur, Hal's changeling (*1H4* I.i.85–89), externalizes Hal's interior state, performing actively what Hal does by passive resistance:

he rebels against Hal's father. Once Hal's rebelliousness is transferred to scapegoat Hotspur, who is killed, Hal and his father are reconciled. In *Henry V,* riot and rebellion are separated from Hal for good; as riotous Falstaff dies and a set of rebels are executed, Hal sloughs off his cocoon of youthful guilt.

In *Cymbeline,* Cloten is Posthumus's double. They are foster brothers; Cloten descants on their similarity (IV.i); he dies in Posthumus's clothes, his body taken for Posthumus's (see Brewer 140). Like Cloten, Posthumus desires Imogen sexually and also wants to abuse her. His sexual desire is only slightly less frustrated than Cloten's—he is banished, and she often denied him sex anyway—and if Cloten wants to rape and kick Imogen, Posthumus plans to kill her. The political behavior of both is ambiguous: Cloten helps his mother to dominate the king (see III.i); Posthumus joins the invasion of Britain. Posthumus's ugly marital and political attitudes are externalized in Cloten: soon after Cloten's death, Posthumus repents of wanting to murder Imogen and fights on the British side.

Second, evil is transferable. Detached from me, it may be transferred to my neighbor, sometimes via a material intermediary like the sin-eater's bread and beer. Girard says the recipient must be enough like the donor to facilitate the transfer, enough unlike the donor to assuage guilt—noncommunity members (slaves, captive soldiers) are preferred scapegoats (*Violence*). Sam Keen argues that war propaganda demonizing enemies as monstrous (giant or dwarf, animal-like, machine-like) makes them enough unlike us to be scapegoated. But the need to do this acknowledges the extent to which enemies are like us: we demonize foes "because we are *not* instinctually sadists; . . . we have to make them horribly unlike us" before we can kill them (178). Noting that Athenians kept degraded people to serve as scapegoats, Derrida examines the insider/outsider paradox: the scapegoat "represents the otherness of the evil that comes to affect or infect the inside by unpredictably breaking into it. Yet the representative of the outside is nonetheless *constituted,* . . . chosen, kept, fed, etc., in the very heart of the inside" ("Plato's Pharmacy" 133).

Transfer of evil to enemies is deeply implicated in war. A territorial species, we fear the strangers beyond our borders (we believe they caused our illness) and hate them (after we have projected our evils upon them, they grow the more loathsome in our eyes). Keen's

Jungian approach to the causes of war fits perfectly with my scapegoating principle of the transferability of evil: "Paranoia involves a complex of mental, emotional, and social mechanisms by which a person or a people claim righteousness and purity, and attribute hostility and evil to the enemy. The process begins with a splitting of the 'good' self. . . . By this sleight of hand, the unacceptable parts of the self—its greed, cruelty, sadism, hostility, what Jung called 'the shadow'—are made to disappear and are recognized only as qualities of the enemy" (19). Keen sees fear of enemy malice as a product of blaming our evil on foes: "paranoia, far from being an occasional individual pathology is the normal human condition" (17); "blaming, 'projection' as psychologists call it, is learned early and remains a primitive defense mechanism, a way by which we magically split the self and claim the good for ourselves and disown all that our parents consider bad" (94)—like children who blame their own misconduct on naughty imaginary friends. Thomas traces the same projection in attitudes toward animals: "'As drunk as a dog,' the proverb said. But who has ever seen a drunken dog? Men attributed to animals the natural impulses they most feared in themselves—ferocity, gluttony, sexuality—even though it was men, not beasts, who made war on their own species, ate more than was good for them and were sexually active all the year round" (*Man* 41).

Patristic misogyny ascribed to women the rampant sexuality celibate male authors repressed in themselves; Marianne Novy (285) discusses how women are scapegoated because "we punish others for our own faults"; *Lear*'s beadle whips a prostitute for indulging the lust he feels himself (IV.vi.160–65). Prospero, several readers believe, displays "the psychology of colonials who projected their disowned traits onto New World natives" (Skura, "Discourse" 44). In the most common scenario for witchcraft charges, the accuser, "guilty of a breach of charity or neighbourliness, by turning away an old woman who had come to the door to beg or borrow some food," projected his own guilt on her; assuming she bore him malice since he had wronged her, he accused her when some affliction struck (Thomas, *Religion* 660ff). As Alan Macfarlane notes, the reason for the alleged attack by a witch "was almost always an unneighbourly action on the part of her . . . victim" ("Tudor Anthropologist" 147).

Characters in *Richard II,* true to scapegoat thinking, pass guilt along like a hot potato: Bolingbroke and Mowbray accuse each other of Woodstock's murder, and Richard is happy to see guilt rest with one of these; Gaunt blames Richard himself. Later, Bolingbroke blames Richard's death on Exton, who (laden with guilt) is driven away like an emissary goat: "With Cain go wander thorough shades of night" (V.vi.43); the evil is then transmitted to the whole community as civil wars descend like murder-caused plagues in Greek myth. Many well-known readings of Shakespeare detect characters in the act of projecting their own guilt onto others: Leontes' belief in Hermione's lust for Polixenes projects his own lust for Polixenes; Iago's tale of Cassio's lust for Desdemona and deceptive loyalty to Othello projects these qualities in himself.

We can see a similar character-splitting in a non-Shakespearean text, Marlowe's *Dr. Faustus*. Implicit in the tale type dealing with sale of one's soul to the devil is that the devil is not really necessary: the protagonist's sensuality, pride, and other sins are enough to cause damnation without a demonic pact. Already in the folk-tale tradition, the devils appear as projections of evil located within the protagonist's character, and the scapegoating mentality whereby one projects one's disowned qualities onto another is highly visible in *Dr. Faustus*. In his last hour, Faustus casts about for someone—anyone or any force but himself—to blame for his hellish predicament: "You stars that reigned at my nativity, / Whose influence hath allotted death and hell"; "Cursed be the parents that engendered me!" (V.ii.152–53, 175). His momentary "No, Faustus, curse thyself" gives way (before the line is out) to "curse Lucifer / That hath deprived thee of the joys of heaven" (V.ii.176–77). But the transfer of evil that comes most naturally is to Mephistophilis: "O thou bewitching fiend, 'twas thy temptation / Hath robbed me of eternal happiness" (V.ii.95–96). The very existence of Mephistophilis, Lucifer, and other material powers of evil seems spun out of Faustus's magical wish fulfillment, the scapegoat mentality that constructs evil as alien to the self. It is Mephistophilis who insists that hell is within, and he is in a good position to do so, since he is Faustus's internal evil rendered external by magical thinking. Faustus's character lacks boundedness, integrity in the sense of wholeness and unity: as princely delicates and a procession of catered dinners flow in through his mouth, so his evil flows out into a second personality, like a child's naughty imaginary friend. Schizophrenic tendencies find expression in Faustus's self-distancing habit of referring to himself in the third person and addressing himself by name. Pompa Banerjee, who sees Mephistophilis as a projection of Faustus's evil, argues that the identity of the two appears in the fact that Faustus's dying soliloquy opens with the words "Ah, Faustus" and closes with the words "Ah, Mephistophilis."

In *Macbeth* we see a magical thinking in which guilt is transferred to an inanimate object, a knife, just as in the Greek Bouphonia rite a community's guilt was transferred to a sacrificer's knife that was thrown into the sea. In a complex piece of magical thinking, Lady Macbeth draws upon eye magic to protect herself from her own guilt by closing her eyes to the murder (magically, what cannot be seen does not exist), and at the same moment she rhetorically transfers both her strategic blindness and her guilt to the murder weapon: "Come, thick night, / And pall thee in the dunnest smoke of hell, / That my keen knife see not the wound it makes" (I.v.50–52). Macbeth, too, transfers guilt to a knife: first he hallucinates a dagger and then he draws his own dagger; syntax leaves unclear whether it is the imaginary or the real dagger he addresses as if it were human: "Thou marshall'st me the way that I was going, / And such an instrument I was to use" (II.i.43–44). What is clear is that he is making himself out to be marshalled, directed toward murder by an anthropomorphosed weapon to whom he talks—a transfer of guilt onto an inanimate object that is given the aura of volition by being addressed as "thou."

Third, evil is indestructible. One cannot discharge evil into the atmosphere: it must go somewhere, into an object or being, as evil spirits entered the Gadarene swine. Evil detached from me not only may but must be transferred to my neighbor. Exorcists often become possessed, since demons leaving a body seek the nearest refuge (Oesterreich 92–93). As in the principle of conservation of energy in physics—energy can change form but cannot be destroyed—so evil can shift its residence but cannot wholly dissipate. Richard II captures such compensatory logic, describing his transfer of power to Bolingbroke in an image of two buckets in a well, one rising as the other sinks (IV.i.185–90). Bolingbroke transfers to Richard the evil of his own powerless exile. The logic of indestructibility demands transfer: the health of one demands the sickness of another. The paradox of sacrifice—improving one's health by another's bloodletting, ensuring life by killing—reflects this principle: evil must be transferred because it cannot be destroyed. Indestructible evil in Shakespeare's histories spreads across the land, a pollution descending on those yet unborn, like biblical curses falling on the second and third generations.

The technique of "splits" noted above—Henry IV/Falstaff, Hal/ Hotspur, or Posthumus/Cloten—suggests belief that evil is transferable and indestructible: characters cannot reform by discharging ill behavior into the air, but evil must enter another character who is killed or exiled. Such thinking underlies Hal's claim "My father is gone wild into his grave, / For in his tomb lie my affections" (*2H4* V.ii.123–24). Henry, who so often employs surrogates, ends with Hal's guilt shifted onto his own corpse. Hal is a chip off the old block in many ways, not least his facility in scapegoating others; but Henry never appreciated Hal's compliment of imitation, and had he known of this last maneuver, he would have gone wild to his grave indeed.

The Medical Model for Transference

Transferring evil depends on a sense of alterity, a rift between self and other, inside and outside (of a body or a city). It is no accident that similar rites attend physical illness (nail parings tacked to a door) and illness in the body politic (dissension nailed to a wall): the body, we recall, often serves as an image of society. The linguistic philosopher Mark Johnson believes that "our sense of *out* orientation is most intimately tied to our experience of *our own* bodily orientation" (33). Susan Sontag, arguing that "if it is plausible to compare the polis to an organism, then it is plausible to compare civil disorder to an illness," cites such comparisons in Plato, Machiavelli, and Hobbes (*Illness as Metaphor* 76).

Expelling evil from a community seems modeled on expelling illness from a body. (The model is perfect when the community evil is plague.) The Greek term for an illness-causing object extracted from the body, *katharma,* was also used as a variant of *pharmakos,* scapegoat (Girard, *Violence* 86). Contagiousness, with which the Renaissance was familiar, fits the idea that evils come from a neighbor-enemy. As in tribal belief where illness comes from enemy sorcery, medieval Jews were blamed for causing plague by poisoning wells or rivers (see Elton; Girard, *Scapegoat*, chap. 1); "Catholics, whose sorcery was thought to have been responsible for the Oxford gaol fever of 1557, were reported in 1641 to have sent a plague-sore in an envelope" (Thomas, *Religion* 667). Syphilis, carried about Europe by travelers, often soldiers, could also be blamed on aliens. As Sontag writes, "It was the 'French pox' to the English, *morbus Germanicus* to the Parisians, the Naples sickness to the Florentines, the Chinese disease to the Japanese. . . . There is a link between imagining disease and imagining foreignness. . . . The foreign place of origin of important illnesses . . . may be no more remote than a neighboring country. Illness is experienced as a species of invasion, and indeed is often carried by soldiers" ("AIDS" 89). (The African genesis theory of AIDS Sontag sees as a variation on this tune.) Elizabethans had a garrison mentality (see chapter 1), partly for fear of invasion (the Armada), and partly because plague and syphilis were raging. As we saw in chapter 1, magical thinking can serve to maintain the less disturbing fiction that the enemy is without; as subjects who turn against their king are configured as foreign invaders, so disease comes only from abroad. And the European plagues from measles to smallpox that wiped out natives in North America were seen as body invasions paralleling European military invasions: natives called them "invisible bullets" (Greenblatt, "Invisible Bullets" 26; Ackerknecht 38).

The time was ripe for scapegoating plays; plague-year *Macbeth*, with its efficacious king slaying, repeatedly imagines evil as illness (see Fitz, "Mental Torment"). Shakespeare often exploits the fact that "ill" meant both "sick" and "evil." His curses involve sending illness into an enemy's body; Shakespearean characters use the cursing formula "a plague upon . . ." a total of forty-eight times. Civil dissension, appropriately, is imagined as an internal parasite: faced with the quarreling factions headed by Gloucester and Winchester in *1 Henry VI*, King Henry warns, "civil dissension is a viperous worm / That gnaws the bowels of the commonwealth" (III.i.72–73).

Renaissance medicine often worked by expelling evil from the body, through bleeding or violent purges like hellebore; exorcism too expelled evil from the body. As Mircea Eliade shows (*Shamanism*), body invasion by demons or foreign objects is one of two basic archaic concepts of illness (the other is soul theft). Expulsion of the foreign is basic to shamanic curing, and exorcists sometimes induce vomiting (Oesterreich 178); bleeding is almost universal in primitive medicine (Ackerknecht 99). Both body invasion and soul theft involve the kind of garrison mentality we saw in chapter 1—health depends on staying safely ensconced in the body and keeping intruders out. The body-invader concept, unlike more typically Asian soul loss, was widespread among primitive peoples of Europe and the Americas, as Forrest Clements's distribution maps indicate. Clements argues that world distribution patterns show the body-invader concept to be ancient, possibly Paleolithic; he cites the universality of the cure (sucking, exhibition of a supposedly extracted object) as evidence that the concept diffused from one or two locales (212–13; cf. Eliade, Ackerknecht, Maddox). Even if England had lacked a homegrown concept, the body-invader concept would have been familiar through many biblical exorcisms that interpret illness as possession by spirits.[5] The invasion concept appears in recent times: in nineteenth-century Cornwall, "pellers" (expellers) extracted illnesses caused by ill-wishers (Deane and Shaw 117); Oesterreich's massively documented *Possession and Exorcism* traces accounts of demonic possession from biblical times to his time of publication, 1921. Susan Sontag thinks the invasion concept even now underlies attitudes toward cancer, "metaphorically, the barbarian within, . . . often experienced as a form of demonic possession—tumors are 'malignant'" (*Illness* 61, 69). Drama has drawn on such thinking since Aristotle: catharsis is modeled on the medical purge. Given the longevity and wide geographic distribution of such magical thinking, it is not far-fetched to suspect that Shakespearean externalizations and expulsions of evil were experienced with something of the force of magic.

The notion of a medical purge as the cure for political evil surfaces at crucial moments in Shakespeare. Brutus, who calls assassins "sacrificers, . . . not butchers," avows "we shall be called purgers, not murderers" (*JC* II.i.166, 180). Killing Macbeth will be "our country's purge" (V.ii.28; cf. V.iii.52). In the *Henry IV* plays, steeped in scapegoating, Hal vows to "purge" himself of offenses and the Archbishop thinks the cure of a diseased nation is to "purge the [Lancastrian] obstructions which begin to stop our very veins" (*1H4* III.ii.20; *2H4* IV.i.54–66).

Part of early modern political magic was the belief that rulers could heal. As Marc Bloch shows, in every medieval European country "kings were considered sacred, and in some countries . . . they were held to possess miraculous powers of healing" (3); such ideas continued in full force in the Renaissance. Belief in the ruler's touch curing scrofula "retained a profound vitality" into the seventeenth century (Bloch 4–5).[6] Elizabeth and James touched for scrofula, even though, as Deborah Willis points out, this "resembled the magical healing techniques [of wizards] that orthodox authorities . . . were busy trying to eradicate"; though early in his reign James "pronounced that 'neither he nor any other King can in truth have power to heal the disease called the Evil, the age of miracles being past,'" advisors soon prevailed on James to practice this magical rite (see Willis, "Monarch" 148–49).

Banishment as a Magical Expulsion of Evil: The Potency of Language

The physical body being analogue to the body politic, I suggest that in Shakespeare, banishment is a quasi-magical act by which a ruler purges the country of enemies, sending them away (often to a neighbor-enemy as in the Ugandan scapegoating) as diseases were extracted from the body by medicine and exorcism. Rulers in Shakespeare expend much energy in banishing those they consider enemies of the state.[7] Banishing Suffolk, Henry VI uses the language of contagious disease: "He shall not breathe [i.e., breathe out, spread] infection in this air / But three days longer, on the pain of death" (*2H6* III.i.287–88); drawing on the idea of the medical purge, Duke Frederick calls banishment of traitors a "purgation" (*AYL* 51). Like a Dr. Faustus drawing a magic circle on the ground, rulers decreeing banishment often draw a protective circle around themselves by specifying the distance from them a banished offender must stay: Duke Frederick specifies twenty miles for Rosalind (*AYL* I.iii.41–43), Henry V ten miles for Falstaff and friends (*2H4* V.v.65). This quarantine is a kind of protective magic akin to what we saw in chapter 1, the body or the state surrounded by an invisible, magical barrier—the besieged island trope—and it was regularized by law: in Shakespeare's time "the verge," a circle of twelve miles, surrounded the monarch wherever she went and affected the legal system in the circumscribed area. It was because the queen happened to be within twelve miles of Deptford that Marlowe's murder came under the jurisdiction of the queen's coroner (Bakeless 187). In this legal device can be glimpsed the remnants of a magically protective circle surrounding the monarch, and it is significant that banished persons are required to stay beyond such a circle. Pronouncements of banishment loom large among speech acts of Shakespearean rulers; in magical thinking, a ruler preserves the commonweal's health by purging it, through banishments, of infectious evils in the person of national enemies—scapegoating par excellence.

Pronouncing banishment is a performative in J. L. Austin's sense: what turns an imperative like "leave the country" into a performative like "we banish you our territories" (*R2* I.iii.139) is the speaker's royal authority, secured by the ruler's monopoly of violence, by subjects' willing obedience, and by supernatural power. Such power may be grounded theologically in divine-right beliefs or magically in belief that a ruler's mere words can affect the material world, a trace of that archaic phase of language in which, Northrop Frye says, "quasi-physical power [was] released by the utterance of words" (*Great Code* 6).

The early Lear habitually speaks in terms of command: "*Attend* the lords of France and Burgundy; . . . *Give* me the map there. *Know* that we have divided / In three our kingdom; . . . *Tell* me, my daughters. . . . Our eldest-born, *speak* first" (I.i.34–54; emphasis mine). Instant obedience renders his imperative verbs virtual performatives. That Lear views his political power as magical power is clear from his later language, when commanding yields to cursing, a performative more overtly magical. Like banishments, curses took effect within a circle, called a "compass," drawn verbally around the curser (see *R3* I.iii.43; *Titus* V.i.126), and like banishment, curses aimed to clear this area of noxious enemies. In magical thinking it is but a short step from banishing Kent to cursing Goneril with sterility; I think both are meant to carry for Lear significantly more magical force than we usually ascribe them. He puts Goneril away from himself—"We'll no more meet"—with a sense of extracting an illness: "thou art . . . a disease that's in my flesh, / . . . a boil, / A plague-sore, or embossed carbuncle / In my corrupted blood" (II.iv.219–24).

And Lear tries to control the weather by performative utterances, commanding winds to blow and thunder to cease. To us these seem mere rhetorical flights, yet in Shakespeare's day witches were thought capable of controlling the wind, and medieval liturgical books had offered charms to drive away thunder (Thomas, *Religion* 32). If a charm learned from a book could control thunder, how much more easily might the words of a king do so, given his supernatural healing powers and magically performative habit of "doing things with words"? When Lear considers bidding "the thunder-bearer shoot," commands the "all-shaking thunder" to "strike flat the thick rotundity o' th' world," and is later dumbfounded to find that "the thunder would not peace at my bidding" (II.iv.226, III.ii.6–7, IV.vi.101–2), something more is involved than the progress of an egomaniacal old man toward a more realistic self-assessment. This is a failure of magic. A radical disenchantment of monarchy, in whose magic many of Shakespeare's contemporaries believed, might have been subversive in the reign of King James who himself touched for the king's evil; but can we be sure Shakespeare is disenchanting?

The unstable status of magical belief and of notions of potent language bedevils interpretation of other Renaissance texts too, for example Marlowe's *Dr. Faustus,* which explores the magical efficacy of words and signs. Ravished with the "heavenly" powers of "lines, circles, signs, letters, and characters," Faustus draws a circle on the ground and chants a fifty-five-word Latin conjuration to the impressive accompaniment of thunder (I.i.51–52, iii.16–23). When Mephistophilis appears and then disappears on command, Faustus preens himself: "I see there's virtue in my heavenly words: / . . . How pliant is this Mephistophilis, / Full of obedience and humility!" (I.i.29–32); "virtue" in this sense was a technical term referring to operative magic. But Faustus is soon disabused of the notion that his words are performative, that they caused the thunder or the appearance of Mephistophilis: when he demands of that urbane demon, "Did not my conjuring speeches raise thee?" Mephistophilis replies:

> That was the cause, but yet *per accidens,*
> For when we hear one rack the name of God,
> Abjure the Scriptures and his Saviour Christ,
> We fly in hope to get his glorious soul; . . .
> Therefore the shortest cut for conjuring

Is stoutly to abjure the Trinity
And pray devoutly to the prince of hell.
(I.iii.47–57)

In an irony rich with interpretive potential, the university-educated Renaissance magus speaks out of a medieval magical mind-set, assuming the mechanical efficacy of magical words, while the representative of the new interiority, proffering a theological rather than a magical interpretation of Faustus's speech act, is the viceroy of Satan. However, sometimes Mephistophilis affirms the magical potency of words, as when the clown Robin, by uttering a few words of Latin, manages to call up Mephistophilis all the way from Constantinople. The devil complains, "How am I vexèd with these villains' charms! / From Constantinople have they brought me now, / Only for pleasure of these damnèd slaves" (III.iii.32–34). And Faustus, too, at the end of the play forgets that it was not his conjuring speeches and magical know-how that raised Mephistophilis: his penultimate line is "I'll burn my books!"

Discrepancies exist between Mephistophilis' "that was the cause, but yet *per accidens*" and his rising at the charms of clowns and between Faustus's learning that his conjuring speeches had no performative force and his later belief that all his troubles resulted from his learning to conjure out of a book. Such discrepancies may be explained by the notoriously corrupt state of the text,[8] by Faustus's self-deluding personality, by conflicting generic codes ("stage wizard" genre versus morality play), or in various other terms. But we should not neglect the possibility of slippage owing to the unstable cultural status of magical belief and magical thinking in the Renaissance. Tension between a magical mentality and a more rational mentality was characteristic of this period, and we should not align Marlowe with the rational camp simply because he was a university graduate—after all, Faustus is a university graduate too, and he is more prone to magical thinking than the devil himself.

Transfer of Evil Demystified?

In my Introduction, I complained that critics are too ready to assert that Shakespeare demystified, exposed, treated with ironic detachment, parodied, inverted, played gracefully with conventions and beliefs his superstitious contemporaries adopted blindly. Might not Lear have simply lost his mana when he gave away his crown? Greenblatt speaks of Renaissance rituals from which the magic has been "evacuated" ("Exorcists"); but how do we know how much magic has been evacuated in the case of Lear's banishments, cursings, and weather magic? His magical thinking may be meant simply to characterize an early medieval monarch, but it is equally likely that Shakespeare himself believed, at least semiconsciously, in the magic. A mixture of belief, half-belief, unconscious, or semiconscious belief in magic must have existed in any given heterogeneous audience at any performance, and some of *Lear*'s effects depend on such beliefs. I think that in historicizing the play we should allow for considerably more magical belief than we usually do; in the process of historicizing, political readings often edge out all other considerations, and it is easy to forget that in this age politics itself was distinctly magical.

Some have seen Shakespeare as demystifying the scapegoating process; but we cannot be sure he was not himself habituated to magical thinking. He lived, after all, in an age when witches were feared and sin could be transferred to a scapegoat from a dead body via bread and beer. I fear we have come to regard Shakespeare as our contemporary to the point of forgetting that magical thinking was much more viable in his age than in ours. (And there is a generous portion of magical thinking even in our own political scapegoatings, our own attitudes to war or disease.) C. L. Barber poses the problem clearly with regard to one major scapegoating: regarding the scapegoating of Falstaff as Shakespeare's rather than Hal's, he thinks the play fails in not demystifying Hal's ritual magic; the cynical, might-makes-right attitude is "too pervasive in the whole society of the play" to be banished "merely by getting rid of Falstaff." Elsewhere Shakespeare makes clear that "rituals have no *magical* efficacy. The reason for his failure at the close of *Part Two* is that at this point he himself uses ritual, not ironically transformed into drama, but magically"; this is "a retreat into magic by the *dramatist,* as distinct from his characters" (*Shakespeare's Festive Comedy* 217–19). But this is not an isolated intrusion of magical thinking: the Henriad is shot through with such thinking, and I am not convinced that it consistently is demystified.

Falstaff is not the only scapegoat to whom Hal/Henry V tries to transfer guilt. Excusing himself to his father, Hal prays "God forgive them that so much have swayed / Your majesty's good thoughts away from me" (*1H4* III.ii.130–31), a neat shift of blame. Though as *Henry V* opens he has already laid claim to French lands, he instructs churchmen to justify the claim, noting that if they do so, the war will be their fault: "Take heed how you impawn our person, / How you awake our sleeping sword of war" (I.ii.21–22). Though the tennis ball mock is in retaliation for Henry's aggression, he uses it to blame the war on the French: "many a thousand widows / Shall this his mock mock out of their dear husbands, / Mock mothers from their sons, mock castles down" (I.ii.285–87). The prospect of his soldiers running amok with rape and pillage of civilians in the siege of Harfleur, he blames on Harfleur: "you yourselves are cause" (III.iii.19)—imagine, building a city directly in the path of Henry's army. The blame for soldiers' dying unshriven in battle he shifts onto their own shoulders (IV.i.146–47). Such transfer of evil need not characterize Henry personally; it is part of the Lancastrian project of detaching the evil of usurpation from their dynasty.

The sending away of evil begins with Henry IV's plan to prevent further revolts against his ill-won throne by "lead[ing] out many to the Holy Land, / Lest rest and lying still might make them look / Too near unto my state" (*2H4* IV.v.211–13). Alexander Leggatt writes, "If this is to be taken at face value, it is damning. There is no sense of guilt here, and certainly no religious dedication; merely a cynical, self-protective strategy. But is it the whole truth? . . . The first announcement of the crusade [in *R2*] seemed a desperate but sincerely meant response to the shock of Richard's death" (83). I will go further and note that on first mention the proposed journey sounds not like a crusade, but (given its purificatory aim) like a pilgrimage: "I'll make a voyage to the Holy Land, / To wash this blood off from my guilty hand" (*R2* V.vi.49–50). However, the magical thinking behind crusades and pilgrimages is similar—evil is dumped far from the home community. At any rate, rebellion overtook the plan to get the rebels away from England; but the dying Henry IV advises Hal to try again: "Busy giddy minds / With foreign quarrels, that action, hence borne out, / May waste the memory of the former days" (*2H4* IV.v.213–15). The crucial "hence borne out" is vintage scapegoat thinking: trouble borne away from here, sent to the neighbor-enemy. As the next play opens, Henry V is apparently acting on this advice: invading France seems a kind of magical thinking, a carrying of evil (Lancastrian illegitimacy and rebellions against it) away from England—another magical way of securing the island kingdom.

Detaching evil from England is the whole point of Henry's constructing the Cambridge conspiracy as a *foreign* threat: the rebels have "for a few light crowns, lightly conspired / And sworn unto the practices of France / To kill us" (II.ii.89–91). Only one line in the play subverts this mystification: Cambridge's "for me, the gold of France did not seduce" (II.ii.155). If we read only *Henry V* we may well succumb to the mystification: we must know *Henry IV* to see that the Cambridge rebellion is a continuation of *civil* rebellions against usurping Henry IV. Hotspur in *1 Henry IV* was revolting on behalf of Mortimer's claim to the throne, and the Cambridge revolt is more of the same—an internal English rivalry, not a French plot. We must know Mortimer's account of the plot in *1 Henry VI* to see that Cambridge in *Henry V* was revolting on behalf of a stronger claim to the crown than Henry's, and that Cambridge, who is executed for treason early in *Henry V*, was posthumously to become patriarch of the Yorkist dynasty (grandfather of two Yorkist kings)—the Lancastrians' great opponents.

Did Shakespeare mean us to recall the other plays, or was *Henry V* to stand on its own? If we do recall them, Henry's sleight of hand is clear: the really significant action of the play, for consolidating the Lancastrian dynasty, is foiling the Cambridge rebels. Indeed, after the crushing of this attempted revolt it was to take the Yorkist dynasty a whole generation to get back on its feet and begin to challenge the Lancastrians once again. The death of the Duke of York in the Battle of Agincourt, also a setback for the Yorkist dynasty, is emphasized in *Henry V* as a valiant act of patriotism; on its significance for Lancastrian-Yorkist power relations, the play is strategically silent. So obscure does Shakespeare keep the Lancaster-York rivalry in this play that we must consciously labor to recall that Lancaster and York were the opposing sides in the Wars of the Roses, whose early skirmishes are played out in the *Henry IV* plays and *Henry V* and which blossom into full war in the *Henry VI* plays and *Richard III*. Henry V's constructing the Battle of Agincourt as the play's significant action is a brilliant piece of evil transfer—the threat to England is construed as external, as French, transferring everyone's attention from narrowly averted civil rebellion to a war abroad: evil "hence borne out." (As I noted in chapter 1, Henry also constructs the main threat to England while he is abroad not as civil revolt but as Scottish invasion—another neat piece of attention shifting [I.ii.136–54].)

But the play's structure abets the mystification: Agincourt is given a climactic position, the Cambridge plot disposed of early. And if Shakespeare meant to demystify Henry's sending of evil from England, why did he plant so few clues in this play to the Cambridge plot's true nature? The Chorus accepts Henry's view that the rebels were motivated only by French gold:

> O England! . . .
> France hath in thee found out
> A nest of hollow bosoms, which he fills
> With treacherous crowns; and three corrupted men,
> One, Richard Earl of Cambridge, . . .
> Have, for the gilt of France,—O, guilt indeed!—
> Confirm'd conspiracy with fearful France.
>
> (II.Cho.22–27)

Civil trouble is neatly carried away from England and deposited on the doorstep of France. Whose mystification *is* this, Henry's or Shakespeare's?[9]

Similar problems arise again and again in Shakespeare, whenever assassinations, executions, and other political scapegoatings form part of a play's action. Such problems, for example, dog our reading of Brutus and his political assassination cast as a religious sacrifice: is he a cynical manipulator of sacrificial beliefs? Or a believer in sacrifice as redemptive for Rome? Brutus lived in an age when some people fervently believed in the efficacy of sacrifice, of scapegoat magic, and practiced it; but his was also an age when rationalists were questioning sacrificial modes and scapegoat thinking. Shakespeare lived in such a transitional period too. How do we position a Brutus or a Shakespeare in transfer-of-evil scapegoat thinking? Is Barber right that Shakespeare typically makes clear that "rituals have no *magical* efficacy"? I fear we must often reach an aporia on this question, and historicizing the issue cannot settle it, since early modern culture was a text divided against itself, magical belief and rationalism too intermingled to be separated.

The Neighbor-Enemy: Shakespeare's French Orientalism

I have shown how *Henry V* displaces English civil dissension onto France. France is centrally important to the English history plays. Edward Said shows how over many centuries the "Orient" has functioned as Europe's "cultural contestant"; as Derrida notes that in binary systems a "superior" group maintains its identity by setting itself off from an "inferior" group—e.g., masculinity maintained by eschewing the "effeminate"—so Said notes that "European culture gained in strength and identity by setting itself off against the Orient" (3–4). One is reminded of Keen's Jungian theory of evils projected onto enemies and of Sontag's comments on diseases attributed to neighbor-enemies. I suggest that in Shakespeare's history plays, France is to England what in Said's terms the Orient is to Europe.

Elements of the oriental stereotype discussed by Said are present in Shakespeare's characters: lascivious sensuality, lying and untrustworthiness, lack of energy and initiative, cowardice, intrigue, cunning, cruelty to people and to animals, and despotism. French sensualists range from Charles in *1 Henry VI,* wantoning with Joan of Arc (who confesses to several "lustful paramours" [III.ii.53]), to the Dauphin in *Henry V,* sexually decadent enough not to resent his fellow officers' insinuations that he is sleeping with his horse. (Indeed, he has written the animal a sonnet.) For lying and untrustworthiness, literal orientalism surfaces in the Renaissance idiom "to turn Turk," meaning to change sides or break an oath (see *Ado* III.iv.52; *Ham* III.ii.274), and French orientalism speaks the same language: Joan of Arc notes dryly of turncoat Burgundy, "Done like a Frenchman: turn, and turn again!"(*1H6* III.iii.85); in *King John,* the French king changes sides in a war twice in one day, for political advantage; Alençon advises Reignier to make a truce with England and "break it when your pleasure serves" (*1H6* V.iv.164). To the English, the French seem "a fickle wavering nation" (*1H6*

IV.i.138) because after being conquered they fight on: this French Resistance becomes "Charles, Alençon, and that traitorous rout" (*1H6* IV.i.173)—traitorous because unfaithful to English conquerors. Elizabethan writers painted the Irish, too, as fickle, irresponsible, and treacherous for rebelling against their English conquerors; the note would be struck again with regard to conquered New World populations.

French soldiers lack energy and initiative, not bothering to relieve besieged Harfleur, lounging about the night before Agincourt in pampered enervation, preening themselves on expensive armor and fancy horses while the manly English fast and pray. The French are cowardly, "leap[ing] o'er the walls in their shirts" fleeing the English. One English hero can keep the entire French nation at bay: "All France with their chief assembled strength / Durst not presume to look [Talbot] once in the face." The Dauphin calls his own troops "dogs, coward, dastards," bravely declaring that he wouldn't have fled if they hadn't. (A true French oriental, the Dauphin speaks of Mahomet and wants to build a pyramid [*1H6* II.i.38 s.d.; I.i.139–40, I.ii.23–24, 140, vi.21–22].)

Intrigue and cunning are French stock-in-trade; Joan infiltrates a town dressed as a peasant; the master gunner's ingenious method of picking off Salisbury is decried by Talbot as "treacherous"; the Countess of Auvergne tries to kidnap Talbot after a false display of hospitality, a guile she sees as oriental, comparing herself with "Scythian Tomyris," murderer of Cyrus (*1H6* II.ii.16, iii.6). French cruelty is ubiquitous, from Joan's exulting over Talbot's "stinking and fly-blown" corpse (*1H6* IV.vii.76) to the perfidious killing of the boys with the luggage in *Henry V.* Even cruelty to animals appears: while the kind-hearted English let their horses graze with their bits in their mouths, even though this makes them look a little uncouth, the cruel French "mount [their horses], and make incision in their hides" (*H5* IV.ii.49–50, 59).

As for oriental despotism, Shakespeare links French rule with despotism stereotypically ascribed to Turks. In his first speech as king, Henry V recalls the Turkish Amurath, who on becoming sultan had his brothers strangled: "Brothers, you mix your sadness with some fear. / This is the English, not the Turkish court; / Not Amurath an Amurath succeeds, / But Harry Harry" (*2H4* V.ii.46–49). The French ambassador, however, accustomed to despotism at home, asks if he can speak freely; Henry replies, schooling the French infidel in Christian conduct, "We are no tyrant, but a Christian king" (I.ii.239–41).

The French are barely to be deemed Christian. They are Catholics, after all, and Shakespeare neglects the fact that the English were Catholics too at the time in which the plays are set. French Catholicism is represented as a tissue of superstitions, almost as foreign to English Protestants as was Islam. Saint-ridden France foolishly worships Joan of Arc: "we'll set thy statue in some holy place, / And have thee reverenc'd like a blessed saint" (*1H6* III.ii.14–15). Shakespeare continues the proto-Protestant interpretation of King John he inherited from Bale and from *The Troublesome Reign of King John:* John answers the papal legate's arrogant demands with a stout

> no Italian priest
> Shall tithe or toll in our dominions;
> But as we, under heaven, are supreme head,
> So under Him that great supremacy,
> Where we do reign, we will alone uphold
> Without th'assistance of a mortal hand;

the pope's is a "usurp'd authority" (*Jn* III.i.153–59). John dismisses Catholicism as "juggling witchcraft" (III.i.169), and when the legate threatens to exercise the pope's magical powers by cursing John and by cursing King Phillip if he remains allied to John, John stands firm while French Phillip knuckles under to juggling witchcraft. The play's two dangerous foreign enemies unite—at the papal legate's instigation France claims the English crown and sets off to invade England. Early modern orientalists caricatured Mohamet as an impostor of Christ; Reformation England caricatured other nations' Catholicism as devilcraft. Catholic France in the histories is as good as in league with the devil: Joan is aided by demons, and Henry V says the Cambridge rebels were seduced not only by the French but by a "cunning fiend" (*H5* II.ii.111–12). Of Henry V's death in France, Exeter wonders if "the subtle-witted French / Conjurers and sorcerers, . . . afraid of him, / By magic verses have contriv'd his end" (*1H6* I.i.25–27). The need to rely on supernatural help, "art and baleful sorcery" like Joan's, is a result of French indolence and cowardice: "This happy night the Frenchmen are secure, / Having all day carous'd and banqueted. / . . . Coward of France, how much he wrongs his fame, / Despairing of his own arm's fortitude, / To join with witches and the help of hell!" (*1H6* II.i.11–18).

France throughout the histories is England's "cultural contestant," inferior of course, cowardly and cruel, but great enough to be a worthy opponent. The opening of *Henry V* creates a binary opposition: an emblem of the two nations with their high cliffs (Dover, Calais) facing off across the channel: "Within the girdle of these walls / Are now confin'd two mighty monarchies, / Whose high upreared and abutting fronts / The perilous narrow ocean parts asunder" (I.Pro.19–22). In its status as a fortified island, discussed in chapter 1, England is confronted directly by one enemy whom only a narrow channel keeps at bay: France. Reminiscences in the plays create the impression that making war in France has been the ordinary occupation of English rulers from time immemorial: "You shall read that my great-grandfather / Never went with his forces into France / But that the Scot on his unfurnish'd kingdom / Came pouring"; "Your grandfather of famous memory, . . . and your great-uncle Edward the Plack Prince of Wales, as I have read in the chronicles, fought a most prave pattle here in France" (*H5* I.ii.146–49, IV.vii.91–94). England often has colonies in France; after conquering Rouen, Talbot sounds like a nineteenth-century imperial officer establishing efficient British administration in some oriental colony unable to look after itself: "Now will we take some order in the town, / Placing therein some expert officers" (*1H6* III.ii.126–27).

France is England's dark double: many of its evil qualities have clearly been projected on it from what England fears in itself. The French are lascivious, yes; but on the English side, Suffolk commits adultery with the queen of England (of course, she *is* French), and the Bishop of Winchester is called "lascivious, wanton" (*1H6* III.i.19). The French *are* lying double-crossers, but then two English kings (Henry VI, Edward IV) wriggle out of state marriages; Prince John in *2 Henry IV* executes opponents who surrender under assurance of amnesty. The French king does change sides twice in *King John,* but so do the English earls Salisbury and Pembroke. If the French lack energy and initiative, Henry VI wringing his hands on a molehill and Richard II sitting on the ground to tell sad stories are not outstanding models of action. If the French are cowards, the English have their Falstaffs, Pistols, and Nyms. If the French are known for intrigue and cunning, it is English plotters who lay a trap for the Duchess of Gloucester. If the cruel French kill the boys with the luggage, Henry V orders French prisoners killed. If Joan is in league with devils, the Duchess of Gloucester conjures spirits. French monarchy recalls oriental despotism no more than does the reign of Richard III. The difference in all these cases is that vices are never called typically English; the same vices in the French are singled out as typically French, just as vices in men are ascribed to individual viciousness, vices in women called typical of the sex. Again, is this foreignizing of vice a scapegoating perpetrated by the characters? I suspect it is perpetrated by Shakespeare; the magical thinking is his.

French wars are central to *1 Henry VI, Henry V,* and *King John;* the other histories feature only English civil strife. French wars always have a symbiotic relationship with English civil strife. *1 Henry VI*'s French wars are lost because of English civil strife: Talbot, mainstay of the forces fighting the French, dies because the English regents in France fall out with each other and fail to send relief troops. Henry VI unsuccessfully tries Henry IV's strategy of busying giddy minds with foreign quarrels: he tries to get warring English factions to "go cheerfully together and digest / Your angry choler on your enemies"—French enemies (*1H6* IV.i.167–68). Henry V's whole French campaign is motivated by a need to unify the nation and distract attention from civil wars. In *King John* English factionalism is so severe that some English nobles fight on the French side and France nearly invades England. Conveniently for the usual English attempt to blame civil strife on a foreign foe, here the French actually back a rival claimant to the English throne. Falconbridge's closing speech emphasizes that England is vulnerable in foreign conflict only when divided by civil strife at home: "England never did, nor never shall, / Lie at the proud foot of a conqueror / But when it first did help to wound itself" (V.vii.112–14).[10]

Just as so many of the English in the plays try to heal civil dissension by uniting England against the French, so in *King John* Salisbury entertains the idea of uniting England and France, both Christian after all, against pagans: upon "a pagan shore, / . . . these two Christian armies might combine / The blood of malice in a vein of league, / And not . . . spend it so unneighborly" (V.ii.36–39). The constant intra-European fighting helps explain why the Orient was useful as Europe's cultural contestant.[11]

If the traditional double tetralogy (leaving aside the anomalous *King John*) is read in the order in which the kings reigned, two plays of French wars stand as a centerpiece, with three plays of civil strife on either side; read in the order of composition, the two plays of French wars bracket the sequence, with six plays of civil strife between. Read in the latter order, in the first play, *1 Henry VI*, France is lost because of civil strife in England; in the last, *Henry V*, France is won and civil strife in England staved off by the euphoria of victory in France and by the sleight of hand absorbing the Cambridge rebellion into the French threat. The primary evil in the English histories is civil strife, a domestic evil; the orientalizing tactic of constructing France as a perfidious, magic-dabbling neighbor-enemy is the result of a perception by three successive kings, Henries IV, V, and VI, that the way to cure civil strife is to reconfigure evil as a foreign threat, to unite factions at home against an enemy abroad. If sometimes Shakespeare brilliantly exposes such reconfiguration as a political mystification, at other times he seems himself to succumb to it.

It is tempting to apply these same terms to the Elizabethan situation: in Shakespeare's day the English were projecting onto the Spanish and onto continental Catholicism whatever civil unrest existed at home, just as Shakespeare's English history plays reconfigure civil strife as foreign threat. And plenty of civil unrest existed at home: not only the relatively shallow political instability that allowed for an abortive Essex rebellion but the deeper unrest shaping up between social classes, which would eventuate in civil war. If we return now to Mary Douglas's interest in societies that feel threatened from without, armed with some of the theory of scapegoating I have been exploring, we can hypothesize that in many cases the very sense of threat from without is a state mystification or a psychological defense mechanism (or both), rewriting trouble at home as threat from abroad. A common reaction to threat from outside is to band together; and if the true problem is internal disunity, then positing a threat from outside, if it causes internal banding together, has achieved the desired result.

Even paranoids can have real enemies, and sometimes the threat from outside is real; but it is probably sensible to adopt a policy of looking for internal dissension every time one sees an external scape-goating. In this light, it is highly significant that, as I have shown above, virtually every history play or tragedy in which the scape-goating of an individual seems to prove efficacious—*Titus Androni-cus, Romeo and Juliet, 1 and 2 Henry IV, Coriolanus, Richard III, Macbeth*—involves a society troubled at least to some degree by *internal* strife. All of them involve expelling or killing an insider, not a foreigner, which often seems to be a way of saying "this in-sider was really an outsider," a way of disowning internal troubles and declaring them alien.

To sum up on the transference principle, the same thinking un-derlies scapegoating and Renaissance medicine: transfer of evil, cur-ing by expelling evil or illness, sending it back to the enemy whose sorcery caused it. Such thinking united political expedience and magic in unstable proportions. I will turn now from the transfer-ence principle to the substitution principle, moving from the sent-away goat to the slain goat.

The Substitution Principle: The Slain Victim

When a victim is not exiled or banished but slain, we have some-thing resembling blood sacrifice. What is blood sacrifice all about? Among various models for sacrifice (restitution for offense, dem-onstration of piety by forfeiting the precious), the most useful for human sacrifice is substitution: a victim may substitute for all com-munity members committing death-meriting offenses. Such think-ing expresses itself in language as synecdoche, wherein the part stands for the whole. The sacrifice most relevant to Renaissance lit-erature is that of Jesus: scapegoating, laying human sin on Jesus, is central to Christian theology. In a 1550 sermon on Hebrew sacri-fice, Bullinger took as types of Christ the Leviticus scapegoats, pas-chal lamb, holocaust (burnt offering), grain offering, and poured-out-wine sacrifice (179–94). Jesus blurs the line between the two meanings of "scapegoat"—sent-away and killed goat, transferred evil and substitution. Evil is clearly transferred, and like other sent-away scapegoats, he was removed from the community: Golgotha was at a distance from Jerusalem, and all four gospels emphasize, in near identical wording, that he was "led away" to crucifixion

(Matt. 27:31; Mark 15:16; Luke 23:26; John 19:16). The removal prompts Paul to compare Jesus' death with Hebrew sacrifice: "Those beasts, whose blood is brought into the sanctuary by the high priest for sin, are burned without [i.e., outside] the camp. Wherefore Jesus also, that he might sanctify the people with his own blood, suffered without the gate" (Heb. 13:11–12). The removal beyond community borders recurs in the ascension; a German scapegoat rite on Ascension Day commemorated "the departure from earth of Him who . . . took away the sins of the world" (Vickery 14). Christ was both taken away and slain: the death of Christ the deity is a version of the slain god, and the death of Christ the King a version of tribal king slaying.

King killing is analogous to god slaying. On divine versus human victims, the faded gods theory holds that heroes and kings degenerated from gods of myth; the euhemerist theory regards gods as originating in outstanding humans, elevated by myth; and as for king slaying versus slaying of a commoner—often poor, deformed, or criminal—elevationists again confront degradationists. Some think king slaying evolved from sacrifice of commoners—if human life is precious, the king's is the most precious. An ideal scapegoat, a king can "represent the whole population, and the value of the sacrifice is often measured by the worth of the victim" (Guépin 90). Others see king slaying as a rite from which sacrifice of commoners degenerated. On human versus animal sacrifice, de Heusch sees humans as the supreme sacrifice: "When the stakes of a sacrifice are of a collective and cosmological nature [e.g., catastrophic drought] . . . the preferential victim is none other than man himself" (205); others think all animal sacrifice has degenerated from human sacrifice.

The substitution principle underlies sacrifice, and one kind of victim often substitutes for another: a king may be replaced by a criminal or an ox; instead of a human being, the Zulu slay a sheep, the Minyanka a dog (de Heusch 63, 179). The switch may be comically sly: as de Heusch shows, African cattle herders, valuing oxen highly, tell the gods an ox has been sacrificed when it is only a chicken. A king's death can substitute for that of his people; a surrogate can die in his place. In scapegoat thinking, aspiration toward such awesome grandeur as king sacrifice can coexist with the sly, thrifty impulse to spare the king and make do with a chicken, if the gods blink.

Skeptics have cast serious doubt on ritual king killing;[12] and even in examples offered by believers it is honored more in the breach than the observance—more substitutes than kings are slain. But if ritual slaying is rare, political assassination is common; when assassination acquires a ritual aura, we suspect deliberate mystification, but we might also invoke Gombrich's theory that the mind assimilates new experiences to familiar schemata: one who (like Brutus) thinks assassination will benefit the community may unconsciously be assimilating murder to the world of sacrifice, where killing is beneficial. Shakespeare himself may unconsciously do this; political scapegoatings were a common enough phenomenon in his time.

L. B. Smith discusses some early modern scapegoatings: Empson and Dudley "were sacrificed at the commencement of Henry VIII's reign because they seemed to personify the financial extortion of the government of the first Tudor.... They had been too zealous in a government from which the new king was attempting to disassociate himself"; Cromwell suffered "because the king needed a scapegoat in 1540 for his discarded religious and foreign policies" (475–77). Steven Mullaney describes Cesare Borgia's scapegoating of his lieutenant de Orco, whose bisected body was displayed, in 1502, in a province he had cruelly subdued. Knowing Borgia had ordered the oppressions, the people still accepted the body as "a convenient object for their hatred and fear, a much-desired catharsis that would 'purge their spirits'—a scapegoat who, like any scapegoat, is effective because he is at least a partial fiction, a symbolic object constituted as such by an entire community" (88–92). Mullaney's comparison of the de Orco scapegoating with that of Angelo in *Measure for Measure* is apt, since that play offers a textbook example of the operation of substitution in Shakespeare: Angelo substitutes for Vincentio as Duke, Mariana for Isabella as lust object; Barnardine is to substitute for Claudio as victim, but instead Ragozine substitutes for Barnardine. Angelo resembles Frazer's temporary kings who spare the monarch literal or figurative execution for waning vitality; Vincentio's inability to enforce laws suggests such waning, and Angelo's lust suggests the sexual license typical of such temporary rulers. Claudio is scapegoated by the state, sentenced to death to atone for city lust and prostitution. Especially seeing that human sacrifice and capital punishment are related (see below), Claudio seems a sacrifice for the city's sins. A condemned criminal is chosen as his substitute; Ragozine's natural death, obviating sacrifice, recalls God's providing a ram that Abraham need not sacrifice Isaac. By scapegoating's substitution logic, if the play had a sixth act the Viennese might have worked their way down to a chicken.

In *Twelfth Night,* Malvolio serves the same function for Olivia, who must control reveling guests, that Angelo serves for Vincentio, who must control licentious subjects; like Vincentio—but more effectively because sooner—Olivia uses a surrogate, Malvolio, who becomes a comedic scapegoat, enforcing household laws while drawing onto himself the inmates' rebellion against authority.

Deflection onto a surrogate works well in allegory; as Angus Fletcher shows, Spenser's Talus is "the agent of violence, acting for Artegall in such a way that Artegall himself never has to dirty his hands in the violence of law enforcement. That such crude violence is not directly part of Artegall's own function is evidence . . . of Spenser's poetic control over an embarrassingly unmagnanimous characteristic. The poet can control Talus far better than he could control fits of rage and savage vengefulness in his titular hero" (37–38).

Henry IV handily shunts evil onto others: he banishes Exton, who acted on his behalf in killing Richard; in battle he attires in his coats nobles who are killed in his place, like Abyssinian, Ethiopian, and Persian king impersonators who protected the king by drawing evil spirits' fire (see Bourboule). Taking a cue from father, Henry V shifts from his own shoulders that burden of inherited guilt, the Lancastrian regime's illegitimacy, by sending old companions to prison after blaming Falstaff for his own misconduct and by executing rebels and a thief. Removing the guilty with public display, Henry casts the monarchy as a bastion of probity, a scapegoating in which the hand is notably quicker than the eye. In *Henry VIII,* surrogates Wolsey and Gardiner are sacrificed in fear of kingly tyranny. In *The Tempest,* Alonso is a criminal king, abettor of usurpation; but since he will be Miranda's father-in-law, a surrogate, Sebastian, absorbs his guilt: unlike Sebastian, Alonso repents. Mamillius replaces Leontes as "sacrificial victim whose death renews the society" (Latimer 134; cf. Tinkler).

Shakespeare's equivalents of tribal king substitutes are often criminals—Henry IV has murderer Exton and highwayman Falstaff;

Henry V has Falstaff and thief Bardolph; Vincentio has prisoners Barnardine, Ragozine, and Claudio. As criminal doubles of the high-ranking, surrogates can expose, in caricature, the guilt of their doubles. As a substitute father figure for Hal, Falstaff serves as a double for Henry IV; his theft of crowns on their way to the royal exchequer reminds us that his kingly double has stolen the crown. Bardolph loots French churches; Henry V, for whom Bardolph serves as criminal surrogate, ravages the French countryside. Barnardine, one of a series of substitutes, neglects to repent on execution day; he doubles for Vincentio, who has neglected the governing of his realm.

Life and Prosperity through Blood and Violence

Sacrifice, though among the most widespread of rites, is a distinctly odd practice. It paradoxically tries to subdue violence "through the application of violence" (Girard, *Violence* 20). Sacrifice is "an endeavour to remedy evil with evil, or to wash away murder with murder. Purification with blood, the most common form of cleansing to Jews, and Greeks, has rightly been called a pollution by Heraclitus, 'as if somebody who had fallen into mud would clean himself with mud'" (Guépin 166–67). Some sacrifices are considered criminal, and "if the sacrifice is regarded as a crime, how can its effects be beneficial?" (Guépin xii). Why is this seemingly irrational behavior so prevalent?

Several theories strive to explain. Sacrifice may make ceremony of a fact of life: animals eat "organic matter, must destroy, kill, either plants or other animals, in order to live; one lives by the death of others" (Guépin 209); sacrifice asserts "that death is the price of life" (de Heusch 188). Or sacrifice may free life-giving energy: the life force of animals, "liberated by sacrifice, [is] put into general circulation for man's benefit" (de Heusch 149); Holloway suggests that in Shakespearean tragedy "the vital energy of the victim is redistributed among those he leaves behind" (141). Life force may be imbibed by ritual cannibalism, as in Dionysiac rites, or by theophagy, god-eating, as in the Christian communion.

Adducing the common belief that happiness and misery alternate in cycles, Guépin suggests that a sacrificer "inflicts on himself tolerable pain in order to ensure a reversal from evil to good, or to prevent the opposite" (177). Sacrifice inoculates against evil, like a mild cowpox immunizing against severe small pox. Belief in the alternation of happiness and misery animates the iconographic tradition of the wheel of Fortune, and Wylie Sypher notes a particular Renaissance transformation of it, appropriate to a dawning capitalist and trading society: "The rotational action of Fortune is also a force in that bleak play, *Timon of Athens,* where the cyclic course of time is traced in the reverses that bring down the wealthy—glittering gold here transposing the medieval aristocratic view of Fortune into a new Renaissance context, the 'quick blows of Fortune' struck in the free and open market, as they are in *The Merchant of Venice*" (12). Fortune's wheel contributed to the development of tragedy, and it is possible that this particular superstition accompanied the wheel into tragedy: that whatever "strange attractor" impels Fortune's wheel to turn will be momentarily satisfied with a sacrificial offering.

The impulse to fight fire with fire—to cleanse bloody crime with blood sacrifice—underlies not only sacrifice but other kinds of protection magic such as amulets; as Tobin Siebers points out, "Amuletic logic, *similia similibur curantur* (like cures like)," accounts for the widespread use of eye images as amulets against the evil eye (8; see also Westermarck 1:459).

So much for general theories of sacrifice; why should a *king* be killed, physically, in effigy, or by surrogate? Two main theories are on offer. First, king slaying, while appearing to destroy society's most powerful member, actually enhances royal power. "Far from ending royalty, the sacrifice of a king assures the perpetual regeneration of its power" (de Heusch 124). Though the king dies, royalty is renewed. As kings were regarded as magical guarantors of health, many tribal societies regard the king as also "the guarantor of prosperity and the fertility of crops" (de Heusch 101). In medieval Europe, too, "kings were in their divine capacity considered to possess a certain power over nature": Halfdan the Black of Norway was "'of all kings the one who had brought most success to the harvests'"; Danes believed that "by touching children and crops, a worthy prince could ensure a man fine offspring and fine harvests" (Bloch 32). As Jonathan Goldberg notes, "the root of *authority* is *augere,* to make grow" (*James* 52). Kings were marked by magical signs right into the Renaissance: James I bore on his body "from earliest infancy marks which heralded his high destiny: a lion and a crown" (Bloch 4–5, 145). Frazer thought the motive for king killing was "fear lest with the enfeeblement of his body in sickness or old age his sacred spirit should suffer a corresponding decay, which might imperil the general course of nature" (*Dying God* v; for an alternate view, see Fontenrose 12). Of such claims to power over nature, Douglas comments drily, "Political power is usually held precariously and primitive rulers are no exception. So we find their legitimate pretensions backed by beliefs in extraordinary powers emanating from their persons" (*Purity* 3).[13] But regenerative killing of the enfeebled has analogues even in animal sacrifice: Dionysians sacrificed a goat losing his procreative power: "A five year old [goat] is no longer fit for use. . . . Every four years the old he-goat must be renewed" (Burkert, "Greek Tragedy" 100). In Shakespeare, political power's link with the leader's sexual potency appears in "sterile" leaders who are killed (Julius Caesar, Richard II, Macbeth) and in those whose withdrawal from power is linked with sexual abstinence: Duke Senior (*AYL*), Vincentio, Prospero, Titus, Richard II, Lear—(widowed, celibate, or separated from their wives); Meredith Skura insightfully discusses this pattern ("Discourse" 61-62). To allay fear of the king's waning power as fertility bestower, Henry VIII scapegoats the first of six wives for his own infertility. (The blame shifting here is even clearer if one knows about X and Y chromosomes.)

According to the first theory, then, king slaying, while appearing to destroy society's most powerful member, actually enhances royal power. The second theory, diametrically opposed to the first, is frequently proffered by the same theorists, with little attempt at reconciliation: king slaying, appearing to destroy society's most powerful member, aims to do just that. "The ritual killing of the king . . . is the ultimate expression of the prohibitions that hedge in his excessive power" (de Heusch 99). De Heusch, in short, holds simultaneously that the king is killed for enfeebled and for excessive power. More on this paradox presently. The Nigerian Kuba and Rukuba, de Heusch notes, force kings to commit incest and cannibalism; investiture rites make "the holder of power a 'being at fault,' . . . a marginal being, outside the group for which he is now responsible . . . he is the guarantor of prosperity and the fertility of crops, yet it is as if he could not act upon natural forces unless he presented himself as a desocialized, even monstrous figure. . . . In order to protect themselves from the excesses of this uncanny force, . . . [the] sacred king is surrounded by a network of prohibitions" (100–101).[14] Victor Turner would regard such a king as both sacred and dangerous, like all liminal figures. The ultimate protection against his danger is to kill him.

Mythic god killing may express a desire to limit or rebel against godly power; the myth of Dionysus's killing may express human resistance to the gods' sacrality. Breaking a divine interdiction intended to keep humans in their place eventuates in god slaying in Christian myth; in Dogon myth, the Fox, like Adam and Eve, steals "divine signs" to equal god, an act leading to god sacrifice, which atones for "the disorder that a rebellious creature, hungry for power and knowledge, brought into the universe" (de Heusch 20, 198). Such ostensible myths of human guilt are subversive: that a god dies for humanity's attempt to steal power acknowledges the human power to kill a god indirectly.

Myths of a human refusing to honor a god Guépin dubs "resistance myths" (e.g., Pentheus/Dionysus). Divine figures may also defy each other on behalf of humankind: Prometheus stole from heaven, as did the Dogon Ogo, whose theft accomplished "the founding act of civilization (the invention of agriculture) through transgression" (de Heusch 156). Resistance to divine tyranny proves fruitful for humankind. Ogo is the "ultimate agent of inquiry and of development" (de Heusch 158); Eve's or Pandora's transgressions may be taken as a *felix culpa,* as acts of creative resistance. Such fruitful transgression, which fed into literature through oral figures like folk-tale heroes (great interdiction breakers) is a subversive strain in many cultures' myths.

King and god slaying, then, may be blows against tyranny. Kings make ideal tribal scapegoats for the same reason governments make ideal scapegoats for us: they were designed for the job. Being scapegoats is among their main functions. We create leaders to govern us and to be abused by us. We need someone to blame for life's griefs; accepting blame ourselves is both unpleasant and false: most troubles are beyond our personal control. Not wanting to believe life's troubles beyond *anyone's* control, we create governments. Giving them enough power that we can blame them for failures of prosperity and order relieves our frustrations and reassures us that order and prosperity are achievable, if only we had competent leaders. It banishes the terrifying specter of an uncontrollable world, just as witch trials gave the illusion of control: "Witches are potentially controllable; the caprices of environment are not" (Kluckhohn 197). A national economy's vagaries may be as resistant to human control as malevolent demons in tribal thought; but because we do not want to think so, we create governments to scapegoat for a languishing economy.

We are prepared for this move, having scapegoated our earliest government: mother. Since mother in most cultures is a child's nurturer in helpless youth, the child believes her powerful as we believe governments powerful and blames her for failure to control life's exigencies. Dorothy Dinnerstein argues that "woman, who introduced us to the human situation and who at the beginning seemed to us responsible for every drawback of that situation, carries for all of us a pre-rational onus of ultimately culpable responsibility forever after"; women are "scapegoats . . . for human resentment of the human condition" (234). Small surprise that some of Shakespeare's most troubled societies are menaced by women—Joan of Arc, the countess of Auverne, Margaret of Anjou, Lady Macbeth, the witches. The ritualized antifeminism that crops up in certain periods of literary history, such as the early seventeenth century, points to a scapegoating of women in response to cultural anxieties arising from rapid social change. Jacobean city comedy, so often intensely cynical about women, offers other scapegoats too—usurers, lawyers, lying travelers, smokers; but the targeting of the other groups is more directly explainable in terms of current economic, legal, and historical conditions, some of this as specific as the introduction and spread of tobacco. But women as a group are such a generalized target as to suggest a deep psychological tendency to blame the world's evils on one's first authority figure, mother. That such magical thinking persists into our own time is suggested by the vicious turning against women we have witnessed in our own very recent troubled times; as Susan Faludi analyzes it, "When the enemy has no face, society will invent one. All that free-floating anxiety over declining wages, insecure employment, and overpriced housing needs a place to light, and in the '80s, much of it fixed itself on women" (68). Commenting on Faludi, Gayle Greene invokes the classic scapegoat model: "From this *comédie humaine* there emerges a picture of an economy in trouble, a system failing fast and thrashing about in search of an enemy; a resorting to that most primitive mechanism for dealing with fear, scapegoating" (169). Dinnerstein's theory of the child's sense of mother's power, the tendency to blame her for what goes wrong, helps make sense of why women are so often scapegoated in this way.

Returning from mother blaming to the resistance against tyrants: real tyranny does exist, of course; but the need to blame failure on someone powerful suggests that society also constructs its rulers as hateful tyrants because it needs someone to blame. The anthropologist Max Gluckman reports a song performed at a Zulu ritual: subjects chant "King, alas for your fate, / King, they reject thee, / King, they hate thee" (122). Leaders *exist* to be hated; it isn't personal, but structural. "The ceremony states that in virtue of their social position princes and people hate the king, but nevertheless they support him." Similarly with the Swazi: it is with "songs of hate and rejection [that] the Swazi *support* their king" (Gluckman 128). Such songs suggest that hate absorption is a leader's function. The deliberate turning of a king into a "sacred monster," discussed by de Heusch, follows the same pattern as the demonizing and alienating of an enemy Other: the declaration of evil as alien enables the scapegoating process.

A ruler must be believed powerful, whether powerful or not. But once we have bestowed power, we fear it will be used against us, rulers waxing as menacing as malevolent demons. "All power, when it calls itself sacred, . . . becomes terrifying" (de Heusch 216). We give leaders power because we fear chaos; we restrict that power because we fear tyranny. And though real tyranny is common enough, our fear of tyranny also results from projection of our own disowned qualities onto the king, in exactly the way we project them onto an enemy—we make rulers monstrous and alienated just as propaganda makes enemies into malevolent giants. We fear the leader's power partly because, in the insecurity of our fear of chaos, we have magnified that power, and partly because evils will always exist, and to blame is to explain, to blame is to achieve the illusion of control. Calling the leader a tyrant justifies our blame.

We the people constitute our leaders as tyrants in the same way that mobs, according to Girard in *The Scapegoat,* constitute some person as a scapegoat; in the same way that the collective imagination of a superstitious crowd, according to Siebers, constitutes a stranger as possessor of the evil eye. One of my quarrels with the new historicism is that in granting hegemonic authority a near-omnipotent power and a self-serving motivation that approaches malevolence, this school of cultural theory is complicit in the constituting of political leaders as wielders of the evil eye, as hateful tyrants. Scapegoating political leaders helps to rationalize killing the king.

Take for example Stephen Greenblatt's bitter denunciation of the suffering royal insomniacs Henry IV and V:

> Perhaps in a society in which the overwhelming majority of men and women had next to nothing, the few who were rich and powerful did lie awake at night. . . . The sufferings of the great are one of the familiar themes in the literature of the governing classes in the sixteenth century. . . . We are invited to take measure of his suffering, to understand . . . the costs of power. And we are invited to understand these costs in order to ratify the power, to accept the grotesque and cruelly unequal distribution of possessions: everything to the few, nothing to the many. The rulers earn . . . their exalted position through suffering. . . . At such moments 2 *Henry IV* seems to be testing and confirming an extremely dark and disturbing hypothesis about the nature of monarchical power in England: that its moral authority rests upon a hypocrisy so deep that the hypocrites themselves believe it. ("Invisible Bullets" 40–41)

If hypocrites believe what they are saying, are they still hypocrites? Though rulers do mystify their power, rulers are ideology's objects as well as its perpetrators. Even in exposing Henry's mystification of power, Greenblatt contributes to that mystification: he magnifies Henry's power by intimating that Henry alone stands outside and above ideology. And Greenblatt's abuse of Henry reveals the old scapegoat, king-sacrificing belief that only our leaders prevent solution of society's problems.

If fear of political chaos is partly a useful construction by the ruling class, fear of political tyranny is partly a useful construction by those who are ruled. These fearsome poles may be partly imaginary; but imagining them serves the purposes of various parties in society, and any government must somehow steer a course between them. Various mechanisms adjust between chaos and tyranny: king slaying, fixed terms of office, elections, assassinations, usurpations, civil wars, mandatory retirement; saturnalian rites curb tyranny by reminding the king what it is like to be a subject.[15] Political scapegoat thinking is two-edged, forming "antinomies" like those Hazard Adams posits: somebody strong should be in control/we must fear the strong who seek control; the king must die because he is too weak/the king must die because he is too strong. Thus the old ethnographic question of whether kings are very often (or ever) ritually killed may be irrelevant: scapegoat thinking underlies political assassination *and* sacrifices on altars.

Killing a surrogate—or in our terms, demanding the resignation of cabinet ministers—is useful insofar as a king has some governing function: killing a king invokes a threat of chaos. The subject may be as relieved as the king when the monarch is not killed, or when after saturnalia the world turns right side up: our rage for order makes chaos as fearsome as tyranny. Angelo, who is enforcing the laws, absorbs public ire, and wrath is deflected from Vincentio, who should have been a firmer leader; the realm, after veering toward chaos, now veers toward tyranny. By the end of *Measure for Measure* Vincentio is better placed to steer between chaos and tyranny, the happy result of scapegoating a surrogate.

In Buchanan Sharp's study of early modern harvest failures and food riots we can see a persistent pattern wherein social protest—over grain hoarding, supply to London or overseas markets at the expense of starving provinces, inadequate relief programs—is aimed not at the highest authorities but at surrogates. "In the earlier period the rioters' attacks were almost all directed at carriers of corn and scarcity was occasionally blamed on the dealings of millers and other middlemen" (35); rioters of 1629 wanted to

> bring their distress to the attention of the King. In this talk could be heard echoes of a long tradition in English popular risings stretching back through Ket's Rebellion of 1549 to the Peasants Revolt of 1381: the King, if he were made aware of them, could solve the problems of the poor; to reach his ear a rising of some sort was required. In that way the poor could

bypass the evil or corrupt officials who stood between the people and their King and kept from him accurate knowledge of his subjects' distress. (48)

Justices of the peace "consistently and conscientiously enforced those aspects of the Book of Orders intended to insure that stocks of grain in private hands were surveyed and brought to market, the market supervised, and the needs of the poor attended to first" (55), and it is predictable that as surrogates, as representatives of authority, the justices themselves would come to be scapegoated. In 1596–97, As Sharp writes, the justices themselves

> were included among the grain hoarders blamed for the continuing high prices and scarcity. . . . Some justices may have deserved such castigation, but there is no evidence that dereliction of duty was widespread; indeed, on only one other occasion—during the desperate months following the 1630 harvest failure—were such charges made. It is much more probable that these accusations and exhortations demonstrate the seriousness of the situation and the government's desperation in the face of an unprecedented string of bad harvests. The justices, like cornbroggers, millers, maltsters, and brewers, became a convenient scapegoat. (56)

Harvest failure is not only physically traumatic but represents a failure of all the magic that went into religious processions through the fields, sprinklings of holy water to promote crop growth, rain-promoting magic, protection of fields against witches, and the rest of the Renaissance fertility magic I will discuss in the next chapter, and considerable psychic distress must have resulted from this chaotic specter of the loss of human control over nature. Under the circumstances, a direct attack on royal authority was unlikely—the need to believe that somebody strong is in control runs deep in such times of crisis. But so does the need to blame a *human* agency for the food shortage, for if humans caused it, humans can cure it, which is much less frightening than the alternative of human helplessness before nature. A human must be blamed, but it must be a surrogate, not the highest authority.

The two reasons for killing the king—that he is too weak and that he is too powerful—can be reconciled. We must replace a leader who, unable to end a drought or regulate the economy, is too weak to obviate our fear of chaos; and we must replace a leader who tyrannizes. Tyranny is a central concern of Shakespeare's, and not only in histories: even *As You Like It* has the double oppression "tyrant Duke"/"tyrant brother" as its opening situation (I.ii.300). *Tyrant* and its derivatives appear in thirty-one of Shakespeare's thirty-seven plays. We might well ask whether this concern signals a civil-libertarian mentality or betrays Shakespeare's own complicity in the construction of rulers as scapegoats, the charge of tyranny bordering on the sort of vague and mythic guilt that is the *signum diaboli* of the constructed public enemy. The energies of the English history plays dance like metal filings in a magnetic field between poles of chaos and tyranny, the people repelled by the tyranny of a Richard or a Henry, then repelled by the chaos of civil war. King slaying has one foot in fertility rites, one in politics; a king's magical powers may fail at the very moment his political powers wax excessive. This situation sounds rare, but occurs in two Shakespearean leaders, Richard II and Julius Caesar.

Caesar is killed for being too weak and too powerful: too weak in that his fertility-guaranteeing power has failed, too powerful in that he grows tyrannous. Like the sick king in the opening of medieval romances that Jessie Weston long ago connected with fertility rites, Caesar is ill, of falling sickness, as *Julius Caesar* opens; the failure of his mana is hinted in his wife's infertility. And tyranny threatens: Caesar flirts with a proffered crown; just before he dies, he is behaving like an absolute monarch. The duality of king killing rationales in scapegoat rites helps explain why Cassius's speech to Brutus stresses both Caesar's weakness ("His coward lips did from their color fly"; he cried like "a sick girl") and excessive power ("This man / Is now become a god" [I.ii.115–26]). Cassius may mean only that it is ironic for Caesar to claim such political power in the face of such physical weakness; but scapegoat thinking suggests that both strength and weakness are frightening in a leader—strength imperils the people's liberty, weakness their health and prosperity. Richard II's weakness ("We were not born to sue, but to command; / Which . . . we cannot do") makes for a troubled land, its malaise expressed as a failure of fertility: "Noisome weeds . . . without profit suck / The soil's fertility from wholesome flowers" (I.i.196–97, III.iv.38–39); and Richard is childless. But excessive power appears in his tyrannical, arbitrary acts—canceling a trial by combat, banishing nobles and reducing the sentence upon a second thought, seizing a duke's inheritance. As in tribal scapegoating, the sacrifice of Richard is prompted by both weakness and strength.

Macbeth's killers worry only about tyranny, not weakness, and whether he has children is famously uncertain; otherwise he too would fit the pattern: he is associated with sterility ("the sere, the yellow leaf") and is a tyrant. The conjunction of weakness/sterility and strength/tyranny in rulers like Caesar, Richard II, and Macbeth might be viewed psychologically, the drive to power a consequence of failed fertility experienced as sexual inadequacy—tyranny as compensation for infertility.

Innocence and Guilt

The problem of guilt has greatly muddied the question of slain kings as scapegoat figures. A. P. Rossiter, like many, demands an innocent victim: Richard II's guilt (his implication in Woodstock's murder) "greatly reduces the possibility of regarding [him] as a . . . sacrificial-king" (36–37). But does it?

Among imaginable kinds of victim—spotless innocent, tainted criminal, random victim—the third has most appealed to our post-Darwinian age. The victim is chosen by lot in Shirley Jackson's much-anthologized "The Lottery"; the early Girard sees this as the basic scapegoat: "The English word *scapegoat* designates . . . the spontaneous violence that strengthens a threatened community at the expense of a random victim" ("Lévi-Strauss" 35–36; in Girard's *The Scapegoat* this random victim theory disappears: he insists that all scapegoats are innocent). But this does not take us far with Shakespearean tragedy, where most candidates for scapegoat are kings or military leaders—hardly random victims. Shakespeare's tragic victims are carefully chosen, the situations tailor-made, the one set of circumstances with which they are least equipped to cope: Othello is vulnerable to Iago's insinuations as Hamlet would not be. This is not randomness. (Even Leviticus's randomness—one of two goats is chosen by lot—is highly restricted: the two were earlier chosen from many others.) Heinrich Bullinger discounted the randomness even of lotteries: "The lots are guided by the Lord's will" (196). For our purposes, I believe, the random victim can be disregarded.

The Hebrews favored unblemished animal victims—perhaps analogous to innocent humans. The youth of Leviticus's goats—kids, not adults—may imply innocence, perhaps a presexual state in that proverbially oversexed animal. In Christian theology, the king/god Jesus was preeminently innocent. (Girard's view that all scapegoats are innocent stems partly from the fact that his prime example of a scapegoat is Jesus.) In Greek tragedy, virgins are sometimes sacrificed. But many cultures' scapegoats have been diseased, defective, sinful, or criminal. De Heusch's African examples favor the guilty or imperfect (179). (Frazer's vast data, though haunted by dubious and suspect examples, tend in this same direction—toward the blemished rather than the perfect.) Such patterns expose as simply muddled a statement like Girard's "either Oedipus is a scapegoat and not guilty of parricide and incest, or he is guilty and is not . . . [a] scapegoat" (*Scapegoat* 123).

Shakespeare, though more likely to be aware of Hebrew/Christian theory, in fact favors the guilty victim. Young, innocent victims (Romeo, Juliet) are far outnumbered by those guilty in varying degrees, from Richard III to Macbeth. The guilt of Shakespeare's tragic heroes, or at least their initiative in the chain of events leading to their deaths, is a departure from Aristotle, who insists "pity is aroused by unmerited misfortune." Where Shakespeare got his ideas of guilty scapegoats is unknown, but we cannot dismiss the guilty victim as not a scapegoat. Familiarity with the tainted scapegoat appears in Antonio's "I am a tainted wether of the flock, / Meetest for death" (*MV* IV.i.114–15).

Girard's theory that all scapegoats are innocent and are called guilty to assuage persecutors' consciences does not help much, unless we regard Shakespeare as their persecutor. One *might* try this with a Richard III (Shakespeare lied about historical Richard, or accepted Hall's and More's lies); but this goes far outside the play's world and involves a Gosson-like confusion between fiction and lying. (Is Shakespeare lying when he tells us Orlando saved Oliver from a lion? Girard, who regards as "forgery" literature that reports what never happened, would answer "yes.") One could try to acquit tragic heroes of guilt, but "this way madness lies." Figures like Macbeth, a guilty scapegoat, are embarrassments to Girard's reductive theory. Girard is on firmer ground in arguing that in choosing victims, societies often persecute on nonmoral grounds: "sickness, madness, genetic deformities, accidental injuries, and even disabilities" (18); but Renaissance platonism took physical deformity as an index of moral depravity: in Richard the withered-armed hunchback and Falstaff the abnormally fat, physical defect mirrors moral defect.

In sum, a Shakespearean tragic victim need not be blameless to serve as a ritual sacrifice. Some (Romeo, Juliet) are almost wholly innocent, some (Richard III, Macbeth) almost wholly guilty; in all three plays an efficacious sacrifice redeems society. Some victims mingle innocence and guilt: Richard II, tyrannous and implicated in murder, may be a criminal king, but he is a legitimate, anointed king: unlawful deposition and cruel murder finally lend him the air of an innocent victim; negligent, tyrannical Lear achieves new innocence when victimized by his daughters and cognizant of his own guilt. These more ambivalent plays lack a sense of society redeemed.[16] Redemptive scapegoat plays boldly demarcate good and evil, innocence and guilt, without much moral chiaroscuro: innocent Romeo and Juliet and guilty Richard III and Macbeth make effective sacrificial victims as morally ambiguous Richard II and Lear do not. Even so, our sympathy with suffering Macbeth, and the aura surrounding the great criminal, threaten to undermine *Macbeth*'s redemptive effect by morally overcomplicating our response to the hero. Shakespeare corrects for this by keeping Macbeth offstage during Act IV and by viewing some atrocities through victims' eyes: promoting a black-and-white response to the "tyrant" and "butcher," Macbeth's victims are shown as exaggeratedly innocent sacrifices, Macbeth a guilty sacrificer who must be slain.

As guilty victims go, Macbeth may be a rather less satisfying scapegoat than Richard III, in that while Richard's evil is only one part of the sickness and pollution of his society, ravaged by a century of civil war, Macbeth seems largely responsible for the sickness of his society—since he murders a legitimate and good king, it might be argued that Macbeth himself creates the need for himself as a sacrificial victim, which would seem to undermine the whole point of scapegoating. However, Scotland is sick before Macbeth begins his career of crime: the play opens on a civil rebellion, and that Macbeth inherits the title of the Thane of Cawdor, one of the rebels, underlines the fact that his treachery against the king does not initiate but merely continues a national scenario of unthanelike uprisings. Again, we have civil dissension, the kind of situation that most often evokes a scapegoat cure.

Not only in Macbeth's case, but in every case where a sacrifice seems to redeem society, we should examine the relevance of the guilt: is the victim's guilt directly responsible for the trouble from which society is seeking to redeem itself, or is the guilt irrelevant or only partly relevant to this trouble? If the victim's guilt is directly and solely responsible for the trouble, then expelling or killing the victim is not really a scapegoating at all, but a rational remedy for a problem with no supernatural dimensions. But if such causality is not demonstrable, if the victim's guilt is not the cause (or not the sole cause) of the trouble, then the guilt may be simply an excuse allowing the killers to assuage their consciences; this is true scapegoating because it involves magical thinking—the killing is efficacious not because it removes the cause of trouble but because it is a blood sacrifice operating magically to remove pollution. If victims are wholly innocent, the thinking is purely magical; if they are guilty in some degree, we must ask whether their guilt is adequate to account for the trouble removed by their deaths. And here we can see easily that in *Richard III, Coriolanus, Macbeth, Henry IV,* and other plays, the victim's death or expulsion cures evils much more extensive than can be accounted for by the victim's own guilt. Shakespeare sometimes attempts to account for such magical-seeming cures by rational means—Romeo and Juliet's deaths, for example, though called "sacrifices" (V.iii.304), are seen to be curative for Verona because the patriarchs Montague and Capulet, remorseful over their children's deaths, agree to end the feud. But the very extensiveness, in the Shakespeare canon, of victims' deaths that prove curative in a much larger sphere than that which the victim could realistically influence suggests that magical thinking was subliminally operative. It is a kind of magical synecdoche, in which the part stands for the whole, and excising a guilty part can cure a guilty whole.

Guépin explores advantages and disadvantages of innocent and guilty victims. The gods may value an innocent victim for its purity and because the sacrifice involves giving up something precious;

but killing an innocent makes the sacrificer guilty. "Sacrifice is always dangerous, because in principle every killing sets the law of talion into motion: the killer must be killed." (The chain of revenge following *Titus Andronicus*'s initial sacrifices shows this law operating.) Choosing a guilty victim avoids charges of reasonless killing, but death as "a form of capital punishment" does not work quite like a sacrifice (more on this presently). Myth often compromises, combining innocent victim with guilty: an innocent victim is "avenged by the punishment of the slayer, who serves as the criminal victim when he is killed" (Guépin xii, 68).

The question of guilt arises with sacrificers as well as victims. Tribally and in early civilizations, guilt attends both animal and vegetable sacrifice.[17] Evil's transferability, essential to expelled-victim rites, can also be brought into play to dispel guilt attending sacrifice. Guépin discusses shifting of blame for sacrifice: to the victim, the gods, the community, aliens, or powerless minorities. Guilt may be deflected onto the victim if he or she is deemed guilty of a crime or "consents" to die. The Greeks caused the sacrificial beast to nod its head in consent (H. Foley 29); the African Lele believe a sacred animal gives itself up voluntarily to capture and sacrifice (de Heusch 37). In early seventeenth-century country-house poems "birds and beasts find their fulfilment in yielding themselves up to be eaten by man" (Thomas, *Man* 29), a kind of consent to being sacrificed. At Tudor executions for treason, "innocent and guilty at the moment of death almost invariably acknowledged their real or imaginary offenses [and] . . . proclaimed their worthiness to die"—L. B. Smith discusses the state's methods of extorting such statements (476ff.). Responsibility is shifted to the gods when, say, an oracle ordains sacrifice; Euripides and Sophocles often implicate the gods in this way. The community may absorb blame in a communal victim stoning. In the Greek Bouphonia's explanatory myth, the ox murderer who fled to a foreign city had to return before a plague would cease. The community then stoned another ox—murder expiated by replaying the murder, guilt atomized among many murderers; the total guilt was somehow less than the sum of its parts.

Sacrifice may be blamed on aliens—*The Bacchae*'s violent Maenads are barbarians. As a powerless group, women are often blamed, thus becoming guilty sacrificers as in other contexts they are guilty victims. Insofar as witchcraft sometimes involved guilty blood rites (or the accusation thereof), it is significant that the great majority of accused Elizabethan witches were women.[18] Other guilt-deflecting strategies are innocence by reason of insanity (in the Bacchic frenzy, "the awful crime was committed . . . in madness" [Guépin 59]); the claim that the victim is not really dead ("resurrection [as of Dionysus or Jesus] is one of the most drastic ways of disclaiming responsibility" [Guépin 100]); masks to obscure sacrificers' identity from avengers; and the resort to tradition—sacrifice reflects hallowed ancestral myths and rituals. Strategies may coexist: guilt over the Bouphonia ox murder was fixed to an alien (as suggested by his fleeing to a foreign city), to the victim (the ox had criminally eaten offerings), to the gods (an oracle revealed the plague's cause and ordained sacrifice), to individuals (the priest, various participants); guilt was distributed among community members (communal stoning) and concentrated in a sacrificial knife that was thrown into the sea. Finally, resurrection: the ox's skin, stuffed with straw, was hitched to a plow. The sacrifice of Jesus was consented to by the victim, ordained by God, abetted by the community ("Crucify him!"), and mitigated by resurrection; and medieval Europe blamed it on a powerless minority, the Jews.

Among many such guilt-deflection strategies in Shakespeare, *The Merchant*'s near human sacrifice is blamed on a member of an alien people, Shylock, as are many of *Titus*'s atrocities—on Aaron the Moor, the Goth Tamora and her sons—again, the foreignizing of evil. As the Bacchae's sacrifices were excused on grounds of insanity, so Hamlet excuses his murder of Polonius: "Hamlet does it not. . . . / Who does it, then? His madness" (V.ii.234–35). Guilt is deflected from Macbeth's killers by classic moves: blame is placed on the victim (he was tyrannical); on supernatural powers (the witches, Hecate); on women (Lady Macbeth, the witches). Like ancient Greeks, Macbeth's sacrificers arrive masked (behind boughs). Seduction by a false prophecy, as in *Macbeth,* is "a recurrent topos in accounts of treason," displacing "the source of seduction from the rebels to an oracular utterance" in an "infinite regress of others who are to blame" (Mullaney 119). Here again is scapegoat thinking: the substitution principle, serial displacement of blame. The verbal subterfuge of euphemism, too, had deflected guilt from ancient sacrificers—Plutarch says the first animal sacrificers, "terrified by what they did," called it simply "'making' or 'doing'" (Guépin 101)—and the Macbeths as killers of Duncan are reluctant to use plain words like "murder," preferring euphemisms: "I have done the deed"; "'tis time to do 't," a pronoun like "it" (and squeamishly abbreviated to "'t" at that) substituting for the noun "murder," a linguistic equivalent of the substitutions central to scapegoat practices.

In the double tetralogy, whose central evil is civil dissension—always an evil amenable to scapegoat cures—guilt over the king sacrifice of Richard II, which spreads evil in the land, is deflected by the usual strategies over the course of eight plays. An alien race is blamed (the French), as are powerless minorities (women); the victim is blamed (Richard was tyrannical), as are supernatural powers (demons aiding Joan of Arc and the Duchess of Gloucester; numerous prophecies play the oracular role). Guilt spreads during *Henry VI* until it involves nearly every community member; then in *Richard III* it is concentrated in one figure, as evil in the Bouphonia contracted from the whole community to a knife that could be thrown into the sea: "As in *Henry VI* Englishmen killed each other, so as the myth has developed Richard is killing everybody. The corruption has gathered into one place, and one stroke will finish it" (Leggatt 52).

The King and the Criminal

The criminal surrogate in king sacrifice, as among the ancient Athenians and Leucadians or in the Persian Sacaea, offends one's sense of the king and the criminal as opposites. Foucault reminds us that "crime attacks the sovereign . . . since the force of the law is the force of the prince" (*Discipline* 47); justice institutionalizes the sovereign's revenge. Military presence is common in executions, since "in every offence there was a *crimen majestatis* and in the least criminal a potential regicide. And the regicide was . . . the total, absolute criminal" (53–54). But the criminal is also an inverted, Lévi-Straussian transformation of a king, a through-the-looking-glass king: at a pole opposite the king "the body of the condemned man . . . gives rise to his own ceremonial and he calls forth a whole theoretical discourse, . . . to code the 'lack of power' with which those subjected to punishment are marked. . . . The condemned man represents the symmetrical, inverted figure of the king" (29).

The king's and criminal's complementary identities arise from the impulse to criminalize the king (recall de Heusch's kings forced to commit cannibalism or incest) that enhances the king's power by alienating him from ordinary mores, making him "a sacred monster" (de Heusch 101); it also diminishes guilt when the people sacrifice or abuse him. And they also arise because a criminal "is surrounded by something of an aura of sanctity. . . . [A condemned man] is hated for his crime, but at the same time something awesome surrounds him that magnifies his personality to almost superhuman proportions" (Guépin 84). In 1845, three pieces of rope with which a criminal had been hanged were sold in Cornwall to heal wounds (Deane and Shaw 120)—like the curative magic of objects the king or queen has touched. Superstitions attending executed people and objects of execution might well animate Christianity itself: Richard Kieckhefer finds magical elements in the ascription of power to "an executed man, Christ, and to the cross on which he was executed," noting that "people in the Roman world often ascribed special power to those who had died violent or untimely deaths; the spirits of these victims were especially sought in necromancy"; both Apuleius and Lucian refer to "the notion that nails from a cross possess magical potency" (36).

Jean-Pierre Vernant finds king and criminal united in *Oedipus Rex,* where sterility and plague are caused by the king's patricide and incest, of which he is unconscious, like the unwittingly criminal Nigerian kings: the divine king, "the purifier and saviour of his people becomes one with the defiled criminal who must be expelled like a *pharmakós* or scapegoat so that the town can regain its purity and be saved. . . . If Sophocles chooses the pair *túrannos-pharmakós* [king-scapegoat] . . . it is because the two figures appear symmetrical and in some respects interchangeable in their opposition. Both are presented as *individuals* responsible for the *collective* salvation of the group" (97, 103).

Erich Neumann thinks that execution of criminals has the same public psychological effect as scapegoating of aliens: we feel that evil, external and alien, has been eliminated; also, a king makes an ideal scapegoat because outstanding ones are perceived as alien (*Depth* 52–54). In mutual alienation from society, opposites meet:

sacred and condemned, king and criminal. In the Athenian custom of periodic ostracism, an ostracized man's only crimes were "the very superior qualities which had raised him above the common herd. . . . [Aristotle] declares that man is by nature a political animal; so whoever is found to be by nature *ápolis* is either . . . a degraded being, less than a man or else . . . above humanity, more powerful than man" (Vernant 106–7). In the Persian Sacaea, a condemned criminal becomes the king's double, with access to the royal harem. A criminal surrogate draws the subjects' fire, absorbing their fear of the king's tyranny. King and criminal are like Jungian "splits": the criminal, expendable and hateable, becomes a target for the subjects' fear. The criminal is the king's dangerous side, objectified: evil being transferable, tyranny is transferred to the criminal, and with the criminal's execution, fear of the sovereign's tyranny subsides. "The king unburdens his responsibilities upon an individual who is [an] inverted image of all that is negative in his own character. This is indeed what the *pharmakos* is; the king's double, but reversed like the carnival kings" (Vernant 104). Carnival indeed: criminalizing the king is a saturnalian move, a Bakhtinian uncrowning.

Jesus was sacrificed by judicial execution: this king died a criminal's death. Execution often resembles sacrifice: like a victim, "the condemned person is cleansed in a bath; he gets special, clean clothes; his illnesses are cured; he is well fed with a last meal; he must be filled with repentance, so that he dies of his own free will. During the execution silence is observed" (Guépin 84). Criminals were once forced to proclaim their guilt at crossroads and before churches on their way to execution (Foucault, *Discipline* 43)—as the Greeks caused the beast to nod its assent to sacrifice. Gallows processions resemble sacrificial processions. *Sparagmos*—ritual tearing apart of the victim—occurred in judicial executions, where the victim was drawn and quartered. The widespread distaste for executioners smacks of the ancient blaming of the sacrificer for the sacrifice.

I hope I have shown that the tendency to discount any redemptive scapegoat function in a figure who is guilty of some crime is quite wrongheaded. King and criminal are complementary; and Shakespeare recognized in *Richard II, Richard III,* and *Macbeth* that the ideal public scapegoat is the criminal king.

Greek Tragedy and the Principle of the Secular Scapegoat

Because human sacrifice is much more visible in Greek than in Elizabethan tragedy—Euripides alone probably affords more examples of human sacrifice than all of Elizabethan drama—Greek tragedy offers clearer insight into the implications of giving scapegoat interpretation to secular slayings. Discussing human sacrifice in fourteen plays, Helene Foley notes, "In the very plays in which Euripides' characters reject the fickle and immoral Olympians, religious rituals (prayer, suppliancy, ritual offerings, and festival) and especially sacrifice continue to play a central and often surprisingly positive role" (21). Such deaths have a sacrificial aura: "The voluntary sacrifices of virgins in tragedy mimic proper sacrificial procedures. The victim is pure and goes willingly to death in propitious silence" (40). Greek tragedy often adopts technical terms from religious sacrifice: Medea's child slaughter is called a sacrifice (Guépin 1–2); "vase-paintings constantly show Medea killing her children at an altar" (Burkert, "Greek Tragedy" 118). In drama and its source myth, secular events unfold like ritual, as when the pattern of the sacrificer deemed a criminal and killed in his turn appears in Clytemnestra's killing Agamemnon for his sacrifice of Iphigenia. Burkert posits the origin of Greek dramatic masks in those that sacrificers wore to evade retribution (114–15).

Agamemnon's killing Iphigenia to ensure propitious winds is a religious sacrifice, as Romeo and Juliet's deaths are not. But the Greeks linked religious sacrifice with tragedic deaths, applying the same language to both; and when Capulet calls Romeo and Juliet "poor sacrifices of our enmity" (V.iii.304), was not Shakespeare too linking religious sacrifice with the heroes' deaths? In Euripides, ritual remains, though religion has been stripped away: "As the intellectual revolution transformed Greek theology, popular and deeply rooted ritual practices apparently remained relatively unchanged. And Euripides is not alone in insisting on the preservation of ritual performance while debunking theological superstructure. Plato, too, although his views of the Greek gods are both elusive and clearly not traditional, . . . expresses no doubt about the need for ritual and for specific ritual practices" (H. Foley 22). Separating religion from ritual paved the way for drama's secular scapegoat. Greek theory sometimes views ritual as primarily of social benefit (see H. Foley 31); it was thus available to tragedy, even wholly secular tragedy.

What remained after the severance, for Greeks and Elizabethans, must often have been a kind of hypothetical magic. If sacrifice and scapegoating stemmed from early magical practices and later theological principle, but were extended into secular life even without magical belief because they were socially useful, society has tacitly agreed to hypothesize magical effect in order to reap social benefits. In this kind of schizophrenic doublethink, one brackets off from one's own rational scrutiny one's belief in magic or one's willingness to pretend one believes in magic. Or we could conceive of it as hypocrisy, a pretense to magical belief enabling some social benefit. It is hard to come to terms with such states of mind in ourselves, let alone to reconstruct them for Greeks or Elizabethans. Would Shakespeare's audience have accepted Macbeth as a scapegoat because they knew the logic of sacrifice, either theologically (Christ's sacrificial atonement) or magically (animal sacrifice as practiced in contemporary witchcraft or curing rites)? Or would nascent rationalism have obliterated or at least complicated such a response?

Problematic Scapegoating

The scapegoating concept, often illuminating, should not be applied unreflectingly. *Pace* Holloway, the paradigm will not stretch to cover all tragedies. Many end with no saved society. Some create no society in need of saving—*Othello*'s society, for example, does not cry out for redemption. Brabantio does emit an air of "some of my best friends are blacks but I wouldn't want my daughter to marry one," but Venetian society in general is not especially racist, even compared with our own, and of what other crimes is it guilty? Is it so sick that human sacrifice must cure it? *Antony and Cleopatra,* following Plutarch, treats Egypt and Rome cynically, but conditions in Alexandria or Rome are hardly so desperate that expiatory sacrifice of the heroes must cure them.

Even in tragedies with a troubled society, the hero's death is not always redemptive. Without royal permission, no one can enter or leave *Hamlet*'s police state, a land of heavy drinkers, advisors like

Polonius who shift loyalties quickly, venal courtiers who "have free-ly gone / With this affair along" (I.ii.15–16), a fickle populace. *Hamlet* may enact the purging of a corrupt society (Jorgensen 49). Hamlet thinks in terms of reform (I.v.189–90), though this society is beyond ordinary reform: it is polluted, in the archaic magical sense, by a royal fratricide and requires a human sacrifice. But sac-rificial efficacy founders on Fortinbras, too much a Hotspur mind-lessly pursuing glory, too much a pawn in his own nation's power politics, to confirm Denmark as redeemed or give us a sense that the land's pollution has been purified.

That the feuding families will die out, their only children sacri-ficed, blunts *Romeo and Juliet*'s redemption, as in Euripides "the cause for which the victim dies is frequently dubious and the con-sequences of the ritual death are often ambiguous" (H. Foley 66). As Philip Brockbank says, in *Romeo and Juliet* "a poignantly lyri-cal death, of some significance to the community, is also a disgrace-ful outrage brought about by human malignancies and inadequa-cies" (14). If *Lear*'s society needs cleansing from pollution, how purificatory is the ending? Most of society is wiped out, not re-deemed, and the depressive Edgar-Albany coalition inspires little more hope than Fortinbras; "the atrocity is more conspicuous than the sacrifice" (Brockbank 15).

The Ides of March coincide tantalizingly with the March 14 Ro-man scapegoat cum fertility rite of Mamurius Veturius, wherein a man was beaten and driven out of the city to ensure crop fertility. Death at this season casts Caesar as a scapegoat, and his society does need redeeming—a fickle populace shifts allegiance from one leader to the next and dictatorship seems inevitable. The adjura-tion "fall upon your knees, / Pray to the gods to intermit the plague / That needs must light on this ingratitude" (I.i.53–55) hints at mythic scapegoat scenarios: a city stricken with plague for a trans-gression. But if Caesar's death is meant to cure Rome, as Cassius and Brutus hope, the failure is absolute. When Brutus explains that he killed Caesar because no one should play Caesar, the crowd cries, "Let him be Caesar." Similarly in *Richard II*, king sacrifice brings no healing but generations of civil war.

Shakespeare often subverts ritual expectations, as when ritual-ized murder accusations fail to deflect Richard II's guilt onto a crim-inal surrogate and mass violence breaks out—Girard's "sacrificial crisis." Richard's seemingly honest attempt to enlist divine aid to expose a murderer raises expectations that political tensions will be discharged by scapegoating one of these nobles. But the ensuing private scene corrects this public scene: Gaunt, blaming the murder on Richard himself, lifts the lid from boiling cauldrons of hidden motive. Why has Gaunt let his son accuse Mowbray without telling him of Richard's complicity? Or *does* Bolingbroke know, and does he accuse Mowbray in order to reassure Richard he does not intend to accuse him? If so, why? In this world of political chess moves and private machinations, if scapegoat rites have not disappeared, they have been re-viewed through cynical political lenses.

One character may scapegoat another out of self-interest: witness Hal's scapegoating of Falstaff, the tribunes' of Coriolanus. Caesar's murder, cast by Brutus as sacrifice ("Let's carve him as a dish fit for the gods"), may be what Foley, in a Greek context, calls "corrupt sacrifice": "murders thinly disguised as sacrifice and symptomatic of a social environment in which violence is proliferating uncontrollably"—figures such as Clytemnestra "deceive themselves as to the justice . . . of their acts by calling their crimes performed with tainted motives 'sacrifices'" (40–41), a description possibly applicable to Brutus. (Stirling argues that Shakespeare prepares for Brutus's dubious ritualizing by undercutting ritual early in the play [44–45].)

Scapegoating is often a villain's maneuver. The ouster of king surrogates—a time-honored political scapegoating, as when the fall of Wolsey and Gardiner deflects wrath from Henry VIII—is clearly a villain's tactic when Richard III tries to scapegoat Hastings and Buckingham (their fall fails to deflect public hatred from his tyranny). Claudius heads off insurrection by aiming Laertes' wrath at Hamlet. Since scapegoating is so often a villain's trick, we view it with a jaundiced eye in a character like Hal: it becomes hard for a dramatist to use scapegoating redemptively. Girard thinks tragedy by its nature destroys scapegoat rites by demystifying them (*Violence* 136). The frequency with which scapegoating is a villain's move raises interesting moral questions about the instances in which Shakespeare himself seems to be performing the scapegoating.

At least some of the time, the Renaissance was disturbed by guilt shifting. (However ready the age was to scapegoat women, Christians who attended to the Bible had to admit that God was unim-

pressed with Adam's attempt to scapegoat Eve after the unpleas-
antness with the apple.) The scapegoating process is disquieting, as
Jeanne Roberts notes: "Banding together against an outsider does
indeed unite a community, and driving him out does create a temporary sense of unanimity. But it is perhaps the least rational of all
means of achieving concord and the most short-lived. . . . Both these
scapegoating plays [*Wiv* and *MV*], in spite of the surface serenity
of their endings, leave their audiences with a lingering uneasiness"
(*"Merry Wives"* 109).

How much of this uneasiness would Shakespeare's audience have
felt? So much was changing. Scapegoating depends on guilt's detachability; but the Christian (especially Puritan) concept of sin was
increasingly interior. Making sin a matter of the private heart robbed
formal rituals of their force. Protestantism was suspicious of rites;
waning ritual in the church must have affected ritual's artistic efficacy in drama. Protestantism heightened the antimagical movement
that began before the Reformation: for example, "For More, as for
John Foxe a few decades later, the Christian repudiation of the Jewish blood sacrifice was proof that God abhorred unnecessary blood-
shed" (Thomas, *Man* 161). Because sin has scarred Lady Macbeth's
heart, her instinctive purification rite, hand washing, has no effect.
The anti-ritual, antimagical movements of early modern life were
surely a major reason that scapegoatings, which occur often in this
literature, are mostly without formal ritual; scapegoat thinking is
a mental artifact, a fossil of earlier modes of thought, stripped of
legitimacy and even of logic but stubbornly ingrained.

Had Renaissance culture reached a stage like that of Greek culture that questioned the morality of sacrificial rites but kept using
them in plays? Greek sacrifice was legal, but there was "something
intrinsically repellent about a divine/human relationship in which
communication so often occurs in terms of violence" (H. Foley 45).
Foley thinks Greek tragedians "exploited the violence that lay at
the heart of the sacrificial ritual" to question gods and religion (45).
Sacrificial ritual often breaks down. *Oedipus Rex* does not "reach
a Girardian resolution, since Oedipus himself, not the community,
violently discovers and attempts to make himself a scapegoat";
whether he will exile himself remains unclear (57). At *The Bacchae's*
close, "Thebes will not enjoy peace and order . . . but will continue to face additional dangerous external Dionysiac invasions" (57).

Pentheus's death, called a sacrifice, is "an aberration," "a perversion of the controlled civic norm. In a wild rather than civic context the unwilling victim is torn apart by the hands of maddened women rather than despatched with due ceremony and a sacrificial knife by men. . . . The benefits of the ritual clearly fail to accrue to the sacrificers, and Pentheus does not serve as a *pharmakos* to save his city" (H. Foley 211). In *The Bacchae*, "The eating of the son by the mother is the reversal of giving birth and feeding. . . . The eating of the god, the rite of death and renewal, becomes in the end a cruel killing of son by mother. The ritual turns into a ritual murder" (Kott, *Eating of the Gods* 200, 207).

In his own society, like the Greeks' still imbued with magical thinking though intellectuals combated it, where do we position Shakespeare? Knowing how easily even twentieth-century minds can slip into magical thinking, there is little reason other than bardolatry to assume that Shakespeare never slipped into it.

We cannot ascribe only to a "decline of magic" the failure of scapegoating to purify society in tragedy. Scapegoating also fails, in Greek and Renaissance drama, because pity for the hero overwhelms our sense of magic, eroding any relief at the harmony that death restores. In *Oedipus Rex,* that the plague ends when the murderer is found is forgotten amidst "lamentations over the fate of Oedipus" (Guépin 116). An audience overwhelmed by Romeo and Juliet's deaths doesn't care that Verona is now free of civic strife.

As we will see, "fertility" readings often fail in tragedy: seeing a hero's conflict with an antagonist as summer's combat with winter does not salvage a sense that though the hero dies, the race will go on. Tragedy is too insistent on sterility and we are too involved with the hero. Vestiges of fertility magic only increase tragedy's bleakness. And scapegoating, which promised to help account for tragedy's strange satisfactions, encounters the same barrier: magical benefits to the community are overwhelmed by the hero's tragic fate.

Scapegoat theory is not the answer to every critic's prayer. De Heusch warns against pressing it too far even for sacrifice: "The expediting system of the scapegoat is peripheral to the sacrificial pattern. It does not constitute the centre of gravity for all sacrifice as René Girard thinks" (211). Nor is it the skeletal structure of all Shakespearean tragedy, as Holloway thinks. But within its limits scapegoat theory can be very suggestive.

Bullinger saw scapegoat rites as dramas of Christ's sacrifice; better than, say, a mystery-cycle crucifixion play only because God was the dramatist—not because scapegoat rites differed inherently from plays: "This manner of representing our redemption [the Yom Kippur scapegoat rite] . . . did please God, by sacraments, rather than by pictures . . . or by stage-plays; which are at this day greatly set by, although scarce godly" (194). This Reformation cleric's dislike of the stage does not efface his linking of drama and ritual: an audience attuned to scapegoating through its religion, its reading, its popular rites, might well approach with a scapegoat mentality a king-killing play.

Redemption may, finally, occupy the plane of art. Though the scapegoat effect is often vitiated, a tragedy's community left unredeemed, maybe defining its community as Venice or Verona is too narrow: maybe it should include audience and readers. Scapegoat theory helps explain one effect of tragedy, a sense of reprieve: we must all die like the hero, but not yet. The dying human being is like "the surrogate victim vis-à-vis the community. . . . The death of the individual has something of the quality of a tribute levied for the continued existence of the collectivity" (Girard, *Violence* 255). We, the collectivity, may feel that the hero's death prolongs our life because (as Guépin says) enduring misery now ensures prosperity tomorrow. The hero's death is our vicarious misery: the hero is a surrogate victim, not for the play's society, but for us.

The Bacchae suggests that the "spectator of rather than the actor in Dionysiac theatre may benefit from tragic experience. . . . The sacrifices made by art and ritual substitute for actual violence" (245), and in relocating the tragic catharsis in the spectator, we of course arrive back at Aristotle. In a world of surrogates and displacement, this displacement onto spectators is the ultimate surrogate, the ultimate displacement. Where rite substitutes for real violence, where a king replaces a god and has his own criminal substitute, who may be replaced by an ox, where one person's guilt shifts to the shoulders of another, the final displacement is to shift all this onto drama. To remove violence from life, we displaced it onto ritual magic; now we displace it onto art. Lear suffers and dies not to redeem Albany or Edgar, Goneril or Regan: he suffers and dies for us. He suffers in our place; not so that we may delay facing up to our own deaths, but so (if we have brought with us a heart that watches and receives) we might learn what he has learned without having to suffer as he has suffered.

But all this presupposes that we accept the efficacy of surrogate victims in the first place. Why should victims be required to cure the troubles afflicting humankind? Why should we not simply refuse assent to magical thinking, declining the archaic premise that the sacrifice of an ox will appease the gods, that killing a chicken will somehow make things go better for everyone? But if we refuse the logic of magical thinking, does that not destroy the redemptive effect we experience in some tragedies? In my conclusion, I will argue that we in the twentieth century still structure experience by some of the old magical schemata that structured early modern experience, and it may be that our continuing experience of tragic redemptiveness rests on such magical foundations. If some tragic effects do rest on magical thinking, then to the extent that we manage to shake off such thinking we will cease to be able to appreciate tragedy in traditional ways. If we see through scapegoating as a despicable or pitiable piece of magical thinking, we are left, in tragedy, with a bleak nihilism in place of whatever redemptive sense the genre once provided. If we do not repudiate magical thinking, we will never be fully rational; but if we do repudiate it, we destroy the tragic effect. As I will argue toward the end of this book, however, our modern minds are still steeped enough in magic that (for now anyway) the kind of tragedy that depends on scapegoating still has a future.

Notes

1. Walter Burkert, an authority on ancient Greek ritual, judges correct the ancient etymology of "tragedy": "song at the sacrifice of a goat" ("Greek Tragedy" 88). (The alternate theory linking tragedy with goatish satyr plays has the authority of Aristotle, but Gerald Else argues forcefully against it [15].)

2. Animal scapegoatings have had a long history in various cultures: in late nineteenth-century India, for example, cholera was charmed into a buffalo driven from the village (Crooke 142); a white cow was a scapegoat in Egypt (Dena 57ff.); a toad carried away flu in Togoland (Seidel 24).

3. Benign powers were also transferable. Jesus became aware of the woman healed by touching his garment when he felt power flowing from

him—a concept of power transfer no more under conscious control than a flow of electricity. In medieval France, a woman whose son was ill "made her way through the crowd from behind the king, and without his noting it, managed to pull off a part of the fringe of the royal cloak. She soaked it in water, and then gave this water to her son to drink. The fever immediately abated, and the disease was cured" (Bloch 15–16). The curative power transfer here is strictly material.

4. The scapegoat mentality came naturally to a society deeply habituated to assigning blame for all occurrences, even those we would regard as solely attributable to nature—disease, crop failure. Alan Macfarlane shows how for many in this period "witches were to blame for a large proportion of the pain and misfortune in the environment" ("Tudor Anthropologist" 146).

5. See Mark 1:23–27, 5:2–10, 9:17–27; Matt. 7:28–33, 17:14–21; Luke 1:35–45, 8:26–39, 13:10–13; Acts 14:13–16 (Oesterreich 7–8).

6. Overt magical practice at the royal level can be traced to the earliest days of the conversion to Christianity in medieval Europe: as Richard Kieckhefer explains, "While pagan priests were forbidden to continue their rites, it was harder to eradicate elements of pagan belief from the kings, who continued to be seen as descended from the gods and as sources of magical power and protection for their realms. There was little the Christian priest could do about these vestiges from the earlier culture" (45).

7. Banishees include Mowbray and Bolingbroke in *R2*; Duke Senior, Rosalind, and Oliver in *AYL*; Valentine in *TGV*; Falstaff and company in *2H4*; the Duchess of Gloucester and Suffolk in *2H6*; Henry VI in *3H6*; Margaret in *R3*; Alcibiades in *Tim*; Posthumus (and earlier Belarius) in *Cym*; Kent in *Lr*; Sycorax before the opening of *Tmp*; Titus Andronicus's sons; Coriolanus; and Romeo. Significantly for the charge of political overreaching leveled at Julius Caesar, he is assassinated in the act of declining to repeal a banishment.

8. All those mentioned, however, exist in both 1604 and 1616 editions.

9. Jeff Opland has argued that the tradition of eulogy partakes of magical thinking related to ancestor worship; one sings the praises of a dead ruler or hero of the tribe in hope of enkindling heroic fervor in the tribe, a kind of resurrection of the ruler or hero (26ff.). Such a eulogistic purpose in singing the praises of a national hero such as Henry V appears more baldly in *The Famous Victories of Henry V,* but I doubt if it is wholly absent from *Henry V.*

10. The motif appears even in plays with no French wars: *2H6* invokes "the French bogeyman—who will, Clifford threatens, invade England if it suffers civil war (IV.viii.41–50). . . . [He] appeals to the patriotism that means not love of one's country but fear and hatred of the foreigner, . . . for

Bolingbroke's reason: busy giddy minds with foreign quarrels. Once the rebellion has been quashed, no more is heard of the reconquest of France" (Leggatt 17).

11. The desirability of European unification to fight the oriental neighbor-enemy was evident during the sixteenth century: while Europeans fought among themselves, Turks were invading Hungary. Vives's *De concordia et discordia* argued that Christian princes "should not engage in internecine warfare but should instead unite against the Turks" (Patterson 88).

12. See especially Fontenrose. Many accounts of king sacrifice exist, however; e.g., the medieval Scandinavian *Ynglingasaga* where "King Domaldi was offered 'for good seasons', his blood offered to the gods; King Olaf Tretelgia of Sweden was burned in his palace as an offering to the god Woden" (Caie 14). Nigerian tribes seem to have killed kings in the twentieth century; the Jukun killed theirs every seven years (de Heusch 100).

13. Bloch speculates that medieval rulers "conceived the idea of trying their hand as wonder-workers [especially in the royal touch], in order to strengthen their rather fragile prestige. Persuaded as they were themselves of the sanctity conferred on them by their function and their royal lineage, they probably thought it a simple thing to claim this kind of power" (243).

14. As Bloch shows, part of a king's sacred monstrousness was his indeterminate, decategorized status, neither layman nor priest. "The king, being the Lord's Anointed, cannot be called a layman," one medieval writer puzzled (110). This recalls Mary Douglas's theories about the power and danger lurking in such states, discussed in chapter 1.

15. Again, "primitive" thought can inform modern behavior: Alan Ryan discusses Douglas's theory about American litigiousness ("people use the legal system to express the primitive conviction that they have been attacked and that somebody is therefore to blame") and Ernest Gellner's theory of our ambivalence toward social science: "we want social control, and we fear that those who possess the necessary know-how will exercise that control by manipulating the ignorant and the powerless" (971). During Japan's bribery scandals several years ago, not Prime Minister Takeshita but his aide committed suicide; such "sacrifices" of aides rather than rulers, typical of Japanese political and business atonements, mediate between tyranny and chaos.

16. Hewitt's cautious application of scapegoat theory may be as far as it is safe to go with *Lear*: "To suggest that, because they took part each year in the driving out of some kind of scapegoat, [a Renaissance audience] would approve of Lear's expulsion is patently ridiculous. But it is

reasonable to deduce that they transferred from the ceremony to the play a feeling of the inevitability of the old king's expulsion" (19). But this "feeling" must have been frustrated when the king killing brought no redemption—and when the play violated its folk-tale roots by allowing its Cinderella figure to be hanged.

17. See H. Foley 46–47; Burkert's *Homo Necans* and "Greek Tragedy" 109; Thomas, *Man* 288–89; Robertson Smith 303; Bronowski 8; Guépin 181, 200.

18. Much scapegoat thinking is involved in witchcraft: projection of evil onto one who has been harmed (accusing one to whom one has denied alms), evil's materiality and transferability (rites with nail parings or hair clippings), the curative, sacrificial power of witch killing. But witches seldom served as community scapegoats: "It was very unusual for large-scale disasters, like famine, plague or fire, to be blamed on a witch" (Thomas, *Religion* 667).

3

Green Shakespeare

I'll show thee every fertile inch of the isle.
—*The Tempest*

A nation, a people, even the cosmos, as we saw in chapter 1, was regularly envisioned in Shakespeare's day as a great body. To political theorists, the state had a head (and the Senate might be a belly); to astrologers, the universe had feet and buttocks. In chapter 2 we saw that dissension in the state was conceived analogously to disease in the body, and the cure was the same: expulsion of invaders and banishment of dissidents were at one with bodily purges and exorcisms. Descartes was yet unknown, and the mechanistic universe was a thing of the future: to Shakespeare's contemporaries, the known world was alive, sentient, organic. And along with a conception of the state as a physical body went a deep responsiveness to green, organic nature.

Shakespeare wrote in an age of deforestation—the ships of his great trading nation had masts cut from the tallest old trees, and the iron industry used oak to produce charcoal for smelting; wood was also used in the soap, glass, and copper-refining industries (Merchant 62–63). Sheep enclosures encroached on traditional common land, depopulating rural villages. Large fen drainage projects were underway (see Holmes). Urbanization was rapid, and displaced villagers dwelt bemusedly in a London choked with smog, the worse since smoky sea coals were burned owing to a shortage of wood. Capitalism was gaining a firm foothold in the countryside itself; in fact, it was with the putting-out system for textiles, to make use of cheap rural labor unregulated by town guilds, that protocapitalism began (see Coleman, Kriedte). In this chapter dealing with Shakespeare and the countryside, my first admission must be that in Shakespeare's day green nature was shrinking.

But fertility and sterility are even more prominent in the language of Shakespeare than in the Greeks—which is one reason Shakespeareans went on courting "ritual" long after classicist suitors had left it standing at the altar.[1] The classicist Gerald Else was incredulous at finding, as late as 1965, critics of English literature still promulgating as fact Gilbert Murray's theory of the origin of tragedy in fertility rituals, dealt a severe blow by Pickard-Cambridge in 1927, and many Shakespeareans were among those seduced by ritual: Northrop Frye's "fertility" theories of Shakespearean comedy, based on Francis Macdonald Cornford, remain influential to this day. Gone are the days when Gilbert Murray could view a Shakespeare play as a thinly veiled fertility rite or celebrate Hamlet as a spring god: classicists have heavily documented the scholarly crimes and logical lapses of Cornford, Murray, and Jane Harrison, who were indeed overenthusiastic, mistaken about many details, naive about the relation between rite and literature, reductive in tracing all dramas (even all myths) to one archaic ritual (whose very existence they failed to prove), led astray by Frazer's dubious anthropology. But in rejecting their flaws and excesses, and admitting that it is difficult to find fertility rites practiced in Shakespeare,[2] we can still see that Shakespeare's plays are deeply committed to fertility as an idea and an organizing principle; artifacts of an age that viewed nature through mental spectacles more magical than ours, they link human fruition with earth's fecundity. Some vestiges of fertility magic rode into the plays in medieval sources; but some magic seems subliminally active in Shakespeare's own writing, like hidden computer codes—again, traces of magical belief have gone underground into the unconscious to become what I call magical thinking.

Though I am moving now from the concerns of the first two chapters, magic protecting the body and the body politic, into the life-promoting magic of fertility rites, the division is mainly one of convenience, and there is considerable overlap between these types of magic. Life must be protected if fecundity is to be promoted; a good example of the overlapping functions of magic is the hawthorn, which was gathered and hung up on May Day as part of fertility-promoting rites (maypoles, gown-greening); as both John

Aubrey (15) and Reginald Scot (152) note, the hawthorn was placed on the doors of houses as a defense against witches. Another place where life protection and growth promotion meet is in plowing rites. Rites performed on Plough Monday to ensure crop growth were still called "Plough Witching" in Cambridgeshire in the early 1900s (Niles 47); that such fertility rites from earliest times involved protective magic against witches is evident in a very complete text that has luckily survived from Anglo-Saxon times of the *Aecerbot,* or field-remedy rite. As John Niles explains of this "major communal rite," "its very first lines claim emphatically that the rite is effective against witchcraft. 'Here is the remedy by which you can improve your fields, if they will not grow properly, or if any harm has been done to them by sorcery or witchcraft. . . . May the eternal Lord grant him [the landowner] . . . that his produce may be safe against every foe, and secure against every harm from witchcraft sown throughout the land'" (46).

That witches were linked in the popular imagination both with sterility (harming crops and human sterility) and with filth—they indulged in filthy practices such as kissing the devil's anus and brewed disgusting concoctions full of unclean meats such as bats, toads, and even human organs—suggests that in some ways sterility can be identified with pollution. (Mary Douglas, in *Purity and Danger,* makes strong connections between witchcraft beliefs and pollution beliefs.) In classical myths such as the Oedipus story, a polluting crime causes famine in the land and sterility in women. Avoidance or removal of pollution is often a necessary condition of fertility. Throughout this study of fertility, then, life-promotion rites should be understood to include certain elements of protection against magical harm.

The Dropped Acorn and the Haunted Pool

Shakespeare's plays rejoice in fertile lands, like "fruitful Lombardy, / The pleasant garden of great Italy" (*Shr* I.i.3–4).[3] Keith Thomas identifies the Renaissance love of landscape with "the ancient classical ideal which associated beauty with fertility. In the sixteenth and seventeenth centuries it was always the fruitful and cultivated scenery which travellers admired" (*Man* 255). Shakespeare links human with vegetable ripeness: "Not yet old enough for a man, nor young enough for a boy; as a squash is before 'tis a peascod, or a codling when 'tis almost an apple" (*TN* I.v.153–55).[4] The many agricultural images perhaps reflect his youth in a countryside still practicing seasonal agrarian rites. In *The Tempest*, where nature is harsh—in twelve years Prospero has established no more than what anthropologists call a hunting and gathering economy—a utopian vision of nature yielding fruits without hard work (II.i.145–66) is derided as a muddled vision; the more potent utopia Prospero conjures is agricultural, with "wheat, rye, barley, vetches, oats, and pease," "nibbling sheep," "barns and garners never empty," "vines with clust'ring bunches," "harvest," a reapers' dance, and a fertility goddess, Ceres (IV.i; see Fitz, "Vocabulary"). The picture is idealized, but unlike Jonson or Carew, Shakespeare does not erase from it the rural workers whose sweat keeps garners full: he remembers the "sunburnt sicklemen of August weary."[5]

Sometimes human/plant sympathy seems older than agriculture, as if in dim memory of forest-dwellers' rites. Is there a touch of Druid ancestry in Shakespeare's many likenings of humans to trees? The powerless are "shrubs, no cedars"; a youth is a "sapling" (*Tit* III.ii.50, IV.iii.45). Sap is a human life force—"There's sap in 't yet," Antony declares (*Ant* III.xiii.193). In the Welsh forest primeval, *Cymbeline*'s imagery riots in human/tree metaphors.[6]

Thomas thinks that Elizabethan use of protective plants on ritual occasions,

> box, rosemary and bays at weddings and funerals; holly, ivy and mistletoe at Christmas; willow branches on Palm Sunday . . . might almost be called religious. The English no longer worshipped sacred groves, for early Christian missionaries had always been hostile to . . . "holy" trees; and in the eleventh century the Church had made it an offence to build a sanctuary around a tree. Yet green branches were carried in procession on May Day or at Midsummer. . . . In popular folklore many trees had a protective significance which made it unlucky to cut them down. (*Man* 75)

Orchard keepers and woodcutters used anthropomorphic terms: "a fruitful cross was called 'a wife'; one without seed was a 'maiden' or 'widow.' . . . A tree too old to yield useful timber a 'dotard'" (215–19).

The oak, sacred to Jove and Thor and revered by Druids, Shakespeare calls Jove's tree (*3H6* V.ii.14; *AYL* III.ii.233; *Tmp* V.i.45); he alludes playfully to its sacredness in Herne the hunter's procession around his oak at midnight in *Merry Wives,* though seriousness may underlie the fun: "Traditionally in mythology [the oak] is associated with strength, with shelter, with awesome size, and frequently with gods. Underneath this oak, as under the oak where Oliver finds regeneration in *As You Like It,* . . . [we] find a scene appropriate both to divine judgement and to mercy and forgiveness" (Jeanne Roberts, "Falstaff" 10).

Most parishes had famous trees: Thomas tells of the Shire, Greendale, and Kidlington oaks, and "the indulgent oak in Staffordshire . . . which, it was claimed, bestowed immunity from prosecution upon the parents of any bastard child begotten under its boughs." Many trees were associated with national heroes: the oak "where Edward I had convened his Parliament in 1289; Herne's oak in Windsor Great Park; Chaucer's oak in . . . Newbury, supposedly planted by the poet himself; the oak . . . off which glanced the arrow which shot William Rufus; and the Boscobel oak, which sheltered Charles II" (*Man* 216–17). Most English national heroes were associated with the oak; why Chaucer got an oak and Shakespeare had to settle for a mulberry tree is a mystery.

Forest scenes typify comedy, as Frye shows: *Shrew* opens in a forest, and action often moves, midplay, to a forest from court or town (*A Midsummer Night's Dream, Two Gentlemen of Verona, As You Like It, The Merry Wives of Windsor, Cymbeline*); nonforest comedies (*Much Ado about Nothing, Twelfth Night*) feature orchards within town. Tragic scenes in forests may presage renewal: bough-laden troops herald Scotland's renewal in *Macbeth;* in *Titus*'s forest begins a symbolic action restoring Rome.

From Orlando sitting under his tree "like a dropp'd acorn" (*AYL* III.ii.231–32) to Ferdinand threatened with being fed on acorn husks and forced to carry logs, male romantic heroes are linked to trees—interesting in view of George Long's theory that the sacred tree beside a holy well or spring in many cultures is a phallic symbol, the well a symbol of female reproductive power. Long notes a fertility rite called well-dressing, a sacred service beside a village well decorated with flowers and bearing religious inscriptions. These are variants of worldwide holy-spring rites, like the Roman Fontinalia, honoring nymphs of wells and fountains (Hope xiv). With Christianity, "hundreds of magical springs which dotted the country became 'holy wells,' associated with a saint, but . . . still employed for magical healing and for divining the future. Their water was sometimes even believed to be peculiarly suitable for use in baptism" (Thomas, *Religion* 54). Hundreds of holy wells existed in England when Long wrote in 1930, many associated with holy trees (for the tree/well conjunction, see also Cornish). In 1893 Robert Hope catalogued 450 wells in England alone; in 1902 Wood-Martin estimated there were more than 3,000 in Ireland (see also Logan); in 1954 Francis Jones studied 1,200 in Wales. Literature and myth often juxtapose trees and wells. The Redcrosse Knight revives after dragon fights by falling into the well of life and by the dripping balm from the tree of life (*Faerie Queene* I.xi.29–30, 46–48). Chrétien's Lancelot fights under a sycamore tree near a spring (358). In the Charybdis story, Ulysses escapes a (vaginal?) whirlpool by clinging to a (phallic?) fig tree, and his final rescue seems an assertion of phallic power: when his ship is sucked down, he is saved as its mast rises. Romulus and Remus are suckled beside a spring in an oak grove (Ovid 389). In the Bible, the trees of life and of the knowledge of good and evil are near a river's source (Gen. 2:9–17), and Moses creates a spring by smiting the earth with his rod (Exod. 17:6). Many holy wells supposedly sprang from a holy man's striking the earth with a staff—a version of the holy tree, as is clear in the legend of Glastonbury's well: when Joseph of Arimathea, on a pilgrimage to England, rested on his staff to pray, it rooted and grew into a tree; from his chalice, buried nearby, a spring gushed (Long 86–87), seemingly versions of Joseph's lance and chalice in the Grail legend (persisting as Tarot suits) which are probably pagan fertility symbols, male and female. During the civil war, Parliamentary troops chopped down the Glastonbury tree as a relic of paganism (Thomas, *Religion* 87).

George Long says wishing wells are relics of holy wells into which spirit-propitiating gifts were thrown, and haunted wells, with legends of drowned maidens, are equivalents of springs with a nymph or naiad—female because springs represent female power. Springs had been linked with female spirits in England since Celtic times; as rain was identified with the Sky God's semen, so terrestrial water sources were likened to breast milk; and though "many people visited holy wells seeking cures for ailments, women often resorted to them specifically to cure their barrenness" (Bord and Bord 93, 2, 98). Ancient association of springs with the female may linger behind Ophelia's extravagantly unrealistic death, reminiscent of virgin drownings in saints' legends:

> There is a willow grows askant the brook,
> That shows his hoar leaves in the glassy stream;
> Therewith fantastic garlands did she make
> Of crow-flowers, nettles, daisies, and long purples
> That liberal shepherds give a grosser name,
> But our cold maids do dead men's fingers call them.
> There on the pendent boughs her crownet weeds
> Clamb'ring to hang, an envious sliver broke,
> When down her weedy trophies and herself
> Fell in the weeping brook. Her clothes spread wide,
> And mermaid-like awhile they bore her up,
> Which time she chanted snatches of old lauds, . . .
> Like a creature native and indued
> Unto that element. But long it could not be
> Till that her garments, heavy with their drink,
> Pull'd the poor wretch from her melodious lay
> To muddy death.
> (*Ham* IV.vii.166–83)

Here is a tree near water, flower weaving as in well-dressing, a garland hung on a tree like tokens on branches near wells to propitiate spirits, a fertility symbol in the phallic "long purples" the shepherds naughtily nickname. Ophelia's hymn singing while she is adrift suggests a sacred rite. Like a naiad, she is "a creature native . . . / Unto that element." Her fate reverses the fig tree's rescue of Ulysses from the vaginal whirlpool: the male tree's breaking branch dooms her, as Hamlet's rejection and her father's death deprive this timid creature, so dependent on male support, of her wits and her life.

Desdemona too, dying at men's hands, thinks of trees and streams. Her Barbary, like Ophelia, was forsaken by a lover who "prov'd mad." Barbary's song has a tree beside a stream, and like Ophelia's death, willow-garland weaving: "The poor soul sat sighing by a sycamore tree. / . . . Fresh streams ran by her, . . . / Sing all a green willow must be my garland" (IV.iii.43–53).

As Western culture often links sacrificed females with water (e.g., Andromeda and the sea monster), it links sacrificed males with trees. Pentheus is pulled from a tree and killed in Euripides. Jesus' cross was called a tree—typologists linked it with Eden's tree of life, and it draws on an old symbol: the Cosmic Tree at earth's center, linking heaven and earth (Eliade, *Rites* 119–20). Jack's beanstock recalls such trees; true to trees' male symbolism, Freudians have not failed to find meaning in Jack's stiff stock rising in the night. The tragic hero sometimes evokes imagery of trees: defeated Antony fears becoming "branchless"; Macbeth's doom approaches as a moving forest.

This sexualized landscape of masculine trees and feminine pools is part of a semiotic system I will call the discourse of fertility. I hope the reader is gaining a sense of how pervasively that discourse operates in Shakespeare. In his day many relics of pagan fertility magic remained, and like the notion that the body is an image of society or that evil can be transferred to another, the discourse of fertility is an invisible mental structure providing shape to many scenes and sometimes whole plays. Magical thinking was still powerful in early modern England: Shakespeare was born the same year as Galileo, but the great soothsayer Nostradamus was still alive in that year, and so was the world of magic.

Caterpillar Charms and Night Battles: Historicizing Magic

In the Middle Ages, fertility magic saturated life. Saints were supposed capable of controlling the weather. Liturgical books offered rituals to cure sterility in animals or make the marriage bed fruitful. A water carrier took holy water around the parish so that people could sprinkle homes, fields, and animals for fertility. Church processions set out to cure "plague, bad harvests and foul weather"; a communicant might smuggle a wafer home and "sprinkle it over his garden as a charm against caterpillars." All this differs little from tribal magic: "the line between magic and religion is . . . impossible to draw in many primitive societies, . . . [and] in medieval England" (Thomas, *Religion* 28–57). Though heavily attacked in the Reformation, fertility magic persisted: people recited "set prayers when planting and grafting"; "the medieval practice of reading the gospels in the corn fields survived in some areas until the Civil War"; "'three parts at least of the people' were 'wedded to their old superstition still,' declared a Puritan document in 1584" (71, 73, 84). Seasonal magic permeates medieval romance, still popular in Shakespeare's day. Chrétien de Troyes's romances often begin with a seasonal feast. *Lancelot* opens with the feast of Ascension Day; Guinevere disappears, Proserpinalike, and it is hinted that when Lancelot's quest ends in finding her, spring will return and prisoners be released, like Christ's releasing humankind from death: "as soon as one succeeds in fairly escaping from this durance, then all the rest may go forth" (297). Contracts to return in a year (see *Gawain and the Green Knight* or *Lancelot*) suggest the agrarian "year story."

In early modern Europe, fertility rites were still being practiced; the degree to which such agrarian rites aimed at magically ensuring the race's survival by promoting crop growth or had ebbed into nonmagical festivity is still debatable. The most common are various kinds of combat. A hero representing summer and fertility combats an antagonist representing winter and spent fertility, sometimes an old versus a new king. The Swedish historian Olaus Magnus described in 1555 a traditional May 1 battle between cohorts representing summer and winter; a woodcut shows a joust wherein Summer—man and horse crowned with leaves and flanked by a leafy tree—pierces with a lance the horse of Winter, a man in a fur hat, flanked by a leafless tree (503). In the Isle of Man, a mock battle between forces of the Queen of May and the Queen of Winter (a man in furs) persisted through the early nineteenth century (Train 118–20). The tug-of-war was a common early modern rural sport (see Bord and Bord's account of late survivals in Shropshire and Radnorshire on Shrove Tuesday [195–97]); that it was vestigially a winter-summer combat is suggested by ethnographic evidence further afield:[7] an Inuit rite has two sides, "the ptarmigans . . . , those who were born in the winter, and the ducks . . . , or the children of summer. A large rope of sealskin is stretched out. One party takes one end of it and tries with all its might to drag the opposite party over to its side. The others hold fast to the rope. . . . If the ptarmigans give way the summer has won the game" and the winter will be mild (Boas 605). George Calderon likens to winter/summer mock battles the Ruthenian and Bulgarian pre-wedding-night mock battle: "this fighting [seems] to have a phallic significance, being intended to procure vigour for the male principle" (80). In a modern African fertility rite Victor Turner calls "the fruitful contest of the sexes" (*Ritual* 77), in which men and women hurl insults at each other, combat leads to fruition; Cornford notes similar male/female slanging matches, fertility rites of the ancient world (110–11). Such cross-cultural parallels should be pursued with caution: anthropologists apply the pejorative label "butterfly collecting" to the Frazerian habit of amassing examples out of context from many disparate cultures, and the most we can safely claim for some cultural resemblances, in societies as remote in time and place from Shakespeare's as are Turner's Ndembu, is probably analogy. But such analogies can indeed be suggestive; and much evidence of lingering fertility magic can be found in early modern Britain and northern Europe, without butterfly collecting in modern Africa.

In some rites, sterility is driven out: a killjoy is expelled or (in saturnalian rites) revelry-dampening authority figures are dethroned. Death's effigy may be carried out of town, and as a complement to expulsion, a tree or the Green Man (crowned Forest King) may be brought in.[8] Phillip Stubbes's description of the pulling of a maypole into English villages—by thirty or forty yoke of oxen with nosegays of flowers on their horns—is familiar to many readers. The Green Man may be represented in the "foliate head" with features of foliage, or foliage springing from its mouth, a carving on late-medieval churches (see Basford); some English pubs to this day are called the Green Man.

The May King and Queen recall rites of the Sky's union with Earth—rain and soil. British culture offered a palimpsest of Mother Earth beliefs. Pre-Roman Celts worshipped earth goddesses such as Rosmerta, related to Greek Maia, and a sky god, Taranis (see G. Webster). In pre-Christian Roman Britain these were worshipped alongside Cybele, Atys, Isis, and Syrian sky gods imported by Romans (Miranda Green 53–59). Ernst Curtius argues that throughout the Middle Ages, "the pagan Natura," or Mother Earth, "never entirely vanishes from consciousness"; in the twelfth-century writings of Bernard Silvestris on Natura, "as through an opened sluice, the fertility cult of the earliest ages flows . . . into the speculation of the Christian West" (108, 123; see also Deiterich; Gill;

Neumann, *Great Mother*). Mother Earth beliefs contributed to Mariolatry. Thomas Kuhn and others have shown that the history of science cannot be separated from that of magic: early modern science was often piggybacked on traditional beliefs, as when Copernicus spoke the language of Sky God/Mother Earth: "The Earth conceives by the sun and becomes pregnant with annual offspring" (1.10.50). The "earth that's nature's mother" came naturally to Shakespeare: "from her womb children of divers kind / We sucking on her natural bosom find" (*Rom* II.iii.9–12); the Earth is our "common mother, . . . / Whose womb unmeasurable and infinite breast / Teems and feeds all"(*Tim* IV.iii.177–79).

What seem to us simple social activities in Renaissance festivity often have magical antecedents: the verb *to wassail* had a meaning specifically drawn from fertility rites: "to drink to (fruit trees, cattle) in wassail, in order to ensure their thriving" (OED). Fertility is a discourse, comprising in early modern Europe a complex semiotic system whose signs include hero combat, seasonal personifications, processions with greenery, sacrifice, harvest, water, food, babies, tugs-of-war, slanging matches, health drinking. Early modern readers would likely have placed such signs much more readily than we do in the discourse of fertility.

Folk plays, mummings, and morris dances preserved some degree of ancient magic.[9] Shakespeare mentions Jack-a-Lent, mummers' plays, Whitsun/May Day morris dances and their hobby horse (see *Wiv* III.ii.22, V.v.127; *Cor* II.i.74; *MND* II.i.98; *AWW* II.ii.23; *H5* II.iv.25). The folk play's whiffler, whose sword or broom made space for players, is vestigial in Puck, clearing a way for newlyweds, "sent with broom before, / To sweep the dust behind the door"; (*MND* V.i.384–85; see Barber, *Shakespeare's Festive Comedy* 138–39); in *Henry V*, the sea "like a mighty whiffler 'fore the King / Seems to prepare his way" (V.Pro.12–13). The mummers' Rumour (Long 221) may survive as the Rumour who opens *2 Henry IV*; sometimes spelled "Roomer" in the mumming context, he may be related to the whiffler who "makes room." The mummer who boasts "In comes I, the Turkish Knight, / . . . Only me and seven more / Fought and killed eleven score" (Long 225) reminds us of Falstaff's boast of eleven buckram men; surely the mummers have as good a claim to have influenced Falstaff and other braggarts as has the *miles gloriosus*; Falstaff, like the Turkish knight, falls in battle and is "resurrected," a magical motif turned comic in both cases.

How much magic remained in vestigial fertility rites such as May games, Twelfth Night festivities, the mummer's play with its dying-and-reviving figures and ritual-linked Robin Hood? One link between such drama and high-culture drama is that like the "men's ceremonial" of mumming or sword dance, high drama was enacted by men; both Shakespeare's Viola and the mummers' "betty" were played by male actors. But were such rites possessed of any more real magic for Elizabethans than Halloween is for us? Some writers, like Robert Weimann, regard mummings and May games as ceremonies clung to for community cohesion, to keep in touch with the past in an age of great social change; magical meanings, they think, had been largely forgotten by the twelfth century. The anthropologist Jack Goody thinks all rituals lose meaning over time, through forgetting and the numbing of repetition, which makes response automatic and dulls meaning (32).[10] Others hold that right into the seventeenth century, popular observances were consciously understood as remnants of ancient religious rites. Hewitt reminds us that Puritans opposed mummings, May games, and morris dances in the belief that they were remnants of a pagan religion. An early twentieth-century theory that seventeenth-century witches were knowledgeable about ancient religions and practiced pagan fertility rites[11] received stunning support in Ginzburg's *Night Battles,* 1966 (in English, 1983), which draws on Inquisition archives to show the widespread existence until at least the late sixteenth century of *benandanti,* good witches, who as custodians of an ancient agrarian cult practiced fertility magic. They claimed that their spirits left their bodies by night during Ember Days (at solstices and equinoxes), to combat evil witches who harmed crops and children: "When the witches win, a great famine follows, and when the *benandanti* win, there is abundance" (103). After Ginzburg's Italian finds, *benandanti* were discovered across Europe; what he discovered "was only a small part of a phenomenon of European or even world dimensions" (Peter Burke 33). In England, "beliefs in black witches and cunning men were integrally connected. . . . Contemporaries rightly called them both 'witches': 'The one twineth; the other untwineth,' said a Hampshire man in 1532"; a woman hanged for witchcraft in 1582 "had protested that 'though she could unwitch, she could not witch,' while John Weemse later wrote that 'there are some witches which the common people call the loosing witches, who do no harm at all, but remove only that hurt which the binding witch lays on the sick person'" (Thomas, *Religion* 654).

Many Renaissance charges against "bad" witches cast them as figures of sterility. They harmed crops, livestock, and babies: witches, for example, took away nursing mothers' milk (Kittredge 166). They harmed human fertility by causing impotence. "Witches were characterized not in terms of crimes theologically defined, but rather in terms of the destruction they brought to the harvests and famine, and the sorcery they worked on children" (Ginzburg 27).[12]

Similarly, evil-eye beliefs are centrally concerned with sexuality, children, and food. In chapter 4 I will argue for a marked presence of evil-eye beliefs in the most prominent sexually oriented literature of the day, Petrarchan love poetry. Nearly every study of the evil eye I have seen, including documentation from many cultures, mentions that children are at greatest risk and shows that when a child falls ill, people cast about to see whether the child has been praised by a childless relative, whose sterile envy of the fertile mother produces the evil eye. Here is one of many examples: "Whenever a friendly gathering of mothers with children, in Italy, Latin America, or an Italian neighborhood in [the United States] suddenly breaks up as soon as a childless woman joins the group, the wise observer knows what has happened. The frightened mothers just take it for granted that the barren woman must envy their happiness and therefore cannot help casting the evil eye" (Schoeck 198). And the evil eye is so often connected with food that the psychoanalytic folklorist Geza Roheim argues that "the key to the whole evil eye belief [is] oral jealousy, oral aggression" (356). The evil eye dries up milk in nursing mothers and in dairy cows. The accusation of the evil eye, like that of witchcraft generally, often falls upon one who has been turned away after begging food, and the evil eye causes loss of appetite and the wasting away of the victim's flesh; in an age of condign punishment, it was fitting that one denied food should cause starvation. In the case of the evil eye and of witchcraft more generally, then, the early modern mind conceived of evil in terms of sterility and starvation.

Whether or not Renaissance people were conscious of lingering pagan fertility magic in folk plays and other popular observances or in witchcraft, similar material was accessible in Christianity. The Christian myth is of the same family as that of Dionysus or Osiris, a dying-and-reviving spring god restoring the earth, and Christian rites resemble other fertility rites. In medieval art, Jesus closely resembles a fertility god: in one painting a stalk of wheat and a grapevine grow from his body; in an altarpiece, Mary and the evangelists pour grain into a mill and crank out a wafer and the baby Jesus; in an embroidery, Christ is pressed under the crossbeam of a winepress, identified with the crucifixion cross; his blood is wine (Bynum, plates 4, 1, 5). The Easter liturgy recalls winter/summer combat: the atonement was "understood as an agon—a dramatic conflict between Christ and Satan culminating in the triumph of the Resurrection" (Hardison 82). Christ's death and descent into hell, ritualized in Holy Saturday liturgies dwelling on the harrowing of hell, recall Persephone's underworld descent and annual resurrection, ritualized in Eleusinian mystery rites. Ritual copulation, Sky wedding Earth, lingers in the notion of the church as Christ's bride, reflecting the Christian myth of divine father impregnating human mother, Jehovah fathering Jesus upon Mary as Zeus fathered Dionysus upon Semele. The spring god's death and revival appear in rites like the medieval Maundy Thursday *tenebrae* service, a death ceremony (Hardison 117) followed by the Easter announcement of Christ's resurrection. Ancient rites of theophagy, a sacrifice to renew humanity, survive in the communion service, especially central at Eastertime.

As Greek drama was acted at Dionysus's spring festival, medieval drama began in the Easter service's *Quem quaeritis,* and the spring religious festival was a time for plays: mystery cycles were acted at Corpus Christi. Shakespeare associates drama with Easter and Christmas: the end of Eastertide—Pentecost/Whitsuntide/Corpus Christi—is a time for plays (see *TGV* IV.iv.157–59; *WT* IV.iv.134); Christmas is in mind when players come to Elsinore (*Ham* I.i.158–64). Comedy is associated with Christmas (*LLL* V.ii.463; *Shr* Ind.ii.133–34).[13]

Renaissance culture was a delta mingling rivers of magic, Christian rites blending with half-understood pagan rites in mummings, sword dances, May games, spells, and charms. This mixture was infused with information on pagan religion from mythographers, Ovid's *Fasti,* and other classical works dear to Renaissance readers. Thomas suggests that much rural magical lore came from "classical sources, like Pliny's *Natural History*. . . . Sir Thomas Browne in the seventeenth century and William Cobbett in the early nineteenth, both of them acute observers, held the classical writers responsible for the bulk of English rural superstitions" (*Man* 77)— magical belief was piggybacked on Renaissance new learning itself. And Shakespeare harbors a good deal of this material.

Seasons, Colors, Numbers, and Human Fertility

Shakespeare heavily favors spring: he never refers to September, October, or November, and only once to February and twice to January, July, and August; but he refers ten times to March, eighteen to April, twenty-two to May, and four to June. The only nonspring month stressed is December; and six of seven references stress its cold barrenness, contrasted with spring or summer. Shakespeare's references to specific holidays cluster around spring fertility festivals: Shrovetide, before Lent; Good Friday; Easter; Whitsuntide; Pentecost; Ascension Day; St. David's and St. George's Days. As for pagan spring fertility festivals, he mentions the Lupercal and its thinly Christianized counterpart Valentine's Day, as well as May Day. Second most often mentioned is harvest season: Lammastide, consecrating loaves made from the first ripe corn; Bartholomew-tide, time of a great harvest fair; Holy-Rood Day; Michaelmas. Harvest feasts are mentioned—harvest home and a reapers' holiday—as are late-autumn feasting times: St. Martin's summer, and Martlemas, a time for feasting on fatted beef. Most other holiday references cluster about the winter solstice: Christmas; New Year; Twelfth Night.[14]

Shakespeare links trouble with winter: "The grisled north / Disgorges such a tempest" that Marina has a terrible birth at sea (*Per* III.Pro.47–48). A father blustering like the north wind blasts lovers: "like the tyrannous breathing of the north / Shakes all our buds from growing" (*Cym* I.iii.36–37). Enemies often issue from the north. History favored such symbolism—the Percies, *Henry IV* antagonists, were northern barons—but Shakespeare played it for all it was worth, harping on their northernness.[15] The default of Northumberland's troops, which turns the tide of war in both *Henry*

IV plays, is unexplained and may be symbolic: happily titled Northumberland is less a developed character than a northern sterility figure, whose iciness spells death even to his son, who vainly "threw many a northward look" waiting for his father (*2H4* II.iii.13–14). If Northumberland has touches of the Nordic ice giant defeated by the fertility god Thor, who was (as I argue in chapter 4) Santa's ancestor, Northumberland's natural opposite would be Santaesque Falstaff. But his true opponent is the thin man, Hal. In this play about civil wars following a royal assassination, semiotics suggest not fertility versus sterility, but one sterility emblem (winter) versus another (thinness, hunger)—one usurping family fending off another. Richard III too is let down by northern allies: "Cold friends to me! What do they in the north?" (IV.iv.484). Richard II's exile north after parting from his springlike wife begins with a possibly symbolic request: "Part us, Northumberland" (*R2* V.i.76). Northern lands Denmark and Scotland in *Hamlet* and *Macbeth* have been at war with an even more northerly land, Norway. Even England's southerly enemy in the histories, France, has a northern ally: Joan of Arc is aided by demons "under the lordly monarch of the north" (*1H6* V.iii.6)—the Devil himself is a northerner. Documenting a long tradition associating hell and the demonic with the north, T. M. Pearce cites references in *Beowulf,* Chaucer's Friar's Tale, King James's *Demonologie,* Burton's *Anatomy of Melancholy,* and elsewhere. The clear implication is that moral evil was associated with wintry sterility.

Love in Shakespeare usually goes with spring or summer: *Love's Labor's Lost* and *Cymbeline* are set in summer, *Dream* and *Twelfth Night* around May Day or Midsummer Day, the love tragedy *Romeo and Juliet* in late spring or midsummer.[16] Kate and Petruchio, oddly for a comedy, marry in winter—but this is fitting for a marriage so inauspicious in its beginnings.

Aptly for tragedy, when *Hamlet* opens "it is very cold" (I.iv.1). Among disruptions of nature attending Duncan's murder (the sun does not rise, horses eat each other) summer shifts to winter overnight: on arrival at Macbeth's castle, Duncan sees the martlet, "guest of summer"; by morning the Porter complains, "this place is too cold for hell."

Some plays make patterns of seasonal references. *As You Like It* begins with "the icy fang / And churlish chiding of the winter's wind"; "my age is as a lusty winter"; "winter and rough weather"; "Blow, blow, thou winter wind."[17] After a passage moving quickly from April to December to May (IV.i.140–41), the play welcomes spring in its last song: "sweet lovers love the spring" (V.iii.15–20). *Measure for Measure,* which makes fertility itself problematic, is all fall and winter (see II.i.124–27, III.i.72–75). The first tetralogy of histories, where many heirs come to grief, riots in images of summer cut off: "Short summers lightly have a forward spring," quips Richard, visiting a speedy winter on a precocious youth (*R3* III.i.94; cf. *2H6* II.iv.2–3; *3H6* II.iii.46–47).

Seasonal references in *Love's Labor's Lost* are in calendar order from spring of one year to Christmas of the next: "*spring* is near when green geese are a' breeding"; "first-born infants of the *spring*"; "proud *summer*"; "At *Christmas* I no more desire a rose / Than wish a snow in *May*'s new-fangled shows"; "Love, whose month is ever *May*"; "sweet roses in this *summer* air"; "*summer*-flies"; "a *Christmas* comedy."[18] The play's closing spring and winter songs underline its seasonal purposefulness. The references suggest an orderly round of eight seasons: spring, summer, (fall), winter, spring, summer, (fall), winter—with his usual aversion to the autumn months, Shakespeare omits mentioning fall in both years. The eight seasons echo the play's eight lovers; and a further year is specified (V.ii.793–94), a total of three years' cycles, nature's answer to the proposed three-year abstinence from women and food with which the play began.

Do the four sets of lovers represent the seasons? Were the women costumed like the seasonal personifications dear to court masque and civic pageant? Maria, winter, wears a white dress (II.i.197) and is given pearls; dark-complected Rosalind is a Mother Earth, summer figure, if Shakespeare's sonnets are anything to go by (see chapter 4). A sonnet about May is written for Katharine; her hair is amber (IV.iii.83), a reddish-gold that might have gone with a red costume. The princess, who is like "the golden sun" (IV.iii.23), may have worn gold. Except for Maria's pearls, the love tokens are vague (a glove, a jewel), but could have been color-coordinated with the costumes. The men might have worn white, black, red, and gold to match their ladies; the vizards have some distinguishing marks (V.ii.383). I will later argue that the sonnet mistress's complexion draws on red and white as ancient fertility colors; for now, I conjecture that *Love's Labor's Lost* might, in its early performances, have color-coded its seasonal symbolism to imply, with gentle irony, that the witty, artificial, scholarly court of Navarre is tied to nature's cycles and the drive toward procreation.

The romances offer timeless moments when all seasons are present. *The Winter's Tale*'s tragic movement is governed by the winter of the title, the comedic movement heralded by Autolycus's singing of two green seasons: "When daffodils begin to peer" and "summer songs for me and my aunts" (IV.iii.1, 11). But in the sheepshearing scene, all seasons mingle: Perdita, like "Flora / Peering in April's front," gives "flow'rs of winter"; she sets the action in autumn—"the year growing ancient, / Not yet on summer's death, nor on the birth / Of trembling winter," though sheepshearing takes place in spring. She then gives "flow'rs / Of middle summer," refers to "blasts of January," laments the lack of "flow'rs o' th' spring," wishes Proserpina could provide March daffodils, violets, primroses, oxlips, and lilies of spring, and mentions springtime Whitsun (IV.iv.2–134). Into this seasonal time warp comes Autolycus, whose song (218–24) suggests the seasons: he sings of wares white, black, amber, and golden—the same colors that seem to encode the women of *Love's Labor's Lost*. *The Tempest*'s masque too conflates seasons; August reapers appear with Ceres, the harvest goddess, who is however linked with "spongy April"; her blessing unites seasons: "Spring come to you at the farthest / In the very end of harvest!" (IV.i.65–134; "Prospero" is a partial anagram of "Proserpina").[19]

I sometimes suspect numeric symbolism encoding the four seasons or the year. Just as *Love's Labor's Lost* has four seasonally linked sets of lovers, so *As You Like It*, whose sources are in ritual-related material, weds four couples, one identified with winter (V.iv.134–35); *Much Ado,* which promotes fertility ("the world must be peopled" [II.iii.233–4]), like *Love's Labor's Lost,* stages a four-couple masked dance. *Titus* and *Julius Caesar* have links with fertility rites; and in each, four men seeking power over Rome divide into two groups of two, like a tug-of-war between winter and summer: brothers Saturninus and Bassianus versus brothers Titus and Marcus Andronicus; Brutus/Cassius versus Antony/Octavius. The annual cycle seems to lie behind men who sired a huge number of sons: Titus has twenty-five, "half of the number that King Priam had" (*Tit* I.i.83), and *Troilus and Cressida* I.ii.158–63 adds Priam himself and (apparently) his illegitimate son Margarelon to reach fifty-two (the number of weeks in the year; see chapter 4 on stylized winter/summer battles and on the magical meaning of the number fifty-two in playing cards).

The clownish aura of Shakespeare's comic rebirths tempts us to trace them to folk observances: the jumping-up of apparently dead Bottom and Falstaff remind C. L. Barber of the mummers' St. George, "alive again, after the miraculous cure, . . . [a] primitive resurrection motif" (*Shakespeare's Festive Comedy* 154, 205). And of course, Shakespeare offers serious rebirths as well: Thaïsa, Hermione.

Shakespeare's persistent linking of humanity with vegetation, pools, seasons, reveals a culture in touch with nature. We could add to this his pervasive semiotics of food, of fullness and hunger.[20] And no shaman could be more attentive to promoting human fertility. Even Charmian desires children: "Let me have a child at fifty. . . . How many boys and wenches must I have?—If . . . fertile every wish, a million" (*Ant* I.ii.29–42).[21] Hermia's alternatives—death or the convent—come to the same thing from her genes' point of view: a Shakespearean comedy may be a gene's way of making other genes. Stereotypically, women in Shakespeare are incomplete until they have a child; but as Coppélia Kahn shows, so are the men (*Man's Estate* 175). As among the African Yao "manhood is achieved through [the] wife's first pregnancy" (Vizedom 41), so in the *Tempest* and *Lear* "the King's ability to govern his state depend[s] on his ability to enact his ritual role as father" (Boose, "Father" 328). So integral is child-breeding to his idea of love that Shakespeare hardly speaks of love without a pregnancy image, even if it is love at first sight ("Heavens rain grace / On that which breeds between 'em!" [*Tmp* III.i.75–6]), even if it is lust ("She speaks, and . . . / my sense breeds with it" [Angelo, *MM* II.ii.146–47]), even if it is homosexual—on leaving Bassanio, Antonio's eye is "big with tears" (*MV* II.viii.46). No oath is stronger than vowing that something matters more than one's progeny (*Cor* III.iii.113–17; *WT* II.i.149–51). Lady Macbeth's readiness to kill her baby rather than break an oath draws power and horror from the sacredness surrounding fertility and hope for progeny.

The book of Genesis, where, as J. P. Fokkelman says, fertility and "survival through offspring are an urgent concern," must have reinforced Shakespeare's interest in fertility: God's commandment, "'Be fruitful, and multiply, and replenish the earth' (1:28), predominates.... God promises the patriarchs numerous offspring.... All three matriarchs, Sarah, Rebekah, and Rachel, are barren—an insurmountable obstacle to continuity," but God always opens "the womb of the barren woman" (42–43). Shakespeare may have seen in the Genesis "begats" the kind of generation-unto-generation continuity he invokes in his comedies.

Shakespeare usually cites classical fertility myths offhandedly—jests about Jove's amours, oaths by Jupiter or Isis lend local color in Roman or Egyptian plays—but the late romances deploy such allusions with greater force: his identifying Perdita with Proserpina (*WT* IV.iv.116) and his staging Ceres (*Tmp* IV.i) are crucial. His career-long devotion to fertility, to rebirth in a new generation, climaxed in his last plays. Richard Wincor compares the romances to mummers' plays "that celebrate the return of spring after a barren winter"; "resurrections" (Thaïsa, Imogen, Hermione) remind him of mummers' Mock Death and Cure; he traces figures like Cerimon to their reviving doctor (219–24).

Tragedy and the Discourse of Fertility

If male lovers evoke hawthorns and acorns in comedies, the sexualized landscape appears conspicuously in tragedy too, as we have seen with with the tree-and-pool complex associated with Ophelia and Desdemona and the trees associated with Macbeth and Antony. Theorists of fertility magic have often focused on tragedy. Murray wrote on *Hamlet; Macbeth* has attracted several such theorists: "a whole company . . . carrying green branches [such as the soldiers carrying boughs from Birnam Wood], was a familiar sight as a Maying procession, celebrating the triumph of new life over the sere and yellow leaf of winter" (Holloway 66; cf. Karl Simrock); at Macbeth's death, Norman Holland suggests, "the old and sterile king with all the accumulated sin of his year's reign is sacrificed and replaced by a new fertility" ("Macbeth" 38).

Scapegoat and fertility rites overlap in that sacrifice is part of the discourse of fertility, and when tragedy invokes the language of fertility, the same question arises as with scapegoating: does the hero's death bring symbolic fertility to the land? Is it redemptive? Does tragedy work like fertility magic, allaying our fears, assuring us that life will go on? In most cases, we must say no. Only one tragedy shows a consistent pattern of fertility secured by the sacrifice of the hero: *Titus Andronicus* seems to use human sacrifice and seasonal and sexual symbolism in a ritual pattern of renewal. But even *Titus* is very problematic, as a close look at the play will make clear.

The dominant stage image, a tomb that keeps swallowing Andronici, objectifies the moribund condition of the state, which through lack of a ruler is a headless corpse. Titus is to "help to set a head on headless Rome" (I.i.189). The state here is a magical dying/reviving figure; renewal of the state is described in terms recalling rituals of the land's renewal after winter. The new emperor Saturninus is no real cure for headlessness. Sterility lurks in his name: "Saturnine" then as now meant cold, sluggish, gloomy-tempered, governed by the planet Saturn in its sterile aspect (see chapter 5). Aaron has the same frosty disposition: he tells lustful Tamora, "Though Venus govern your desires, Saturn is dominator over mine." Contemporaries would have understood the disposition as not merely gloomy but natively evil: in the Renaissance magical practice of chiromancy, or palm reading, the middle finger was associated astrologically with the planet Saturn, and a certain configuration of lines was "a token of an evil . . . *Saturnine* nature" (Indagine [D9]). The evil in *Titus* is specifically assimilated to the discourse of fertility/sterility: the Saturninus/Tamora party are linked with winter (he hangs his head "as flowers with frost"), the Andronici with summer: "We'll follow where thou lead'st, / Like stinging bees in hottest summer's day"; summer meets winter in the passage where Titus depicts his daughter, to Tamora's sons who have raped her, as "this goodly summer with your winter mix'd" (II.iii.30–31; IV.iv.71; V.i.13–14, ii.171), an intriguing image of a kind of seasonal miscegenation, a mixing of kinds, a blurring of boundaries that according to Mary Douglas produces pollution. Andronici tears are fertilizing rain: Lucius, telling his son to "learn of us / To melt in showers" (V.iii.160–61), echoes Titus's earlier image:

> Let my tears stanch the earth's dry appetite; . . .
> O earth, I will befriend thee more with rain,

That shall distill from these two ancient urns,
Than youthful April shall with all his show'rs.
In summer's drought I'll drop upon thee still;
In winter with warm tears I'll melt the snow,
And keep eternal springtime on thy face.
(III.i.14–22)

Rain falling on dry earth is mythically in tune with the rape of Lavinia. Greek myths of a sky god raping a woman (Jove's rape of Europa, Leda, Danaë) seem mythic embodiments of rites promoting penetration of Earth by the Sky God's rain (for Danaë, Jove actually becomes a shower). Does Lavinia's rape ritually fertilize the land? Just before her rape, the tomb-dominated civic setting yields to a forest, not unlike the comedies' shift to Frye's green world. The suggestive juxtaposition of the rape with the tumbling of several male characters into a hole in the earth links Lavinia with Earth. Seven lines after the resolve to "deflow'r" Lavinia, Quintus finds the earthen hole and positively bludgeons us with a flower image: "What subtle hole is this, / Whose mouth is covered with rude-growing briers, / Upon whose leaves are drops of new-shed blood / As fresh as morning dew distill'd on flowers?" (II.iii.191–201). Rape seems a dubious force for political renewal; but then Lucrece's rape too rescues Rome. In *Titus,* spring's renewal of a winter-barren land is an analogue of Rome's political renewal; because Lavinia at one level represents the land, her rape, echoing restorative rapes of mythic and ritual Earth Mothers, can lead to political salvation. As we saw in chapter 1, the human body can serve as an image of society. As a violent act of sexuality, rape combines the world of sacrifice with that of fertility; here is another explanation for why women so often serve as scapegoats. As John Niles drily observes, "magic in general is not noted for its generosity" (53); magical thinking is often brutal, nasty, victimizing; and women are often its victims.

Are the rape, dismemberments, cannibalism, and blood sacrifice all linked with fertility? Beginning with Alarbus's lopped limbs, *Titus* multiplies mutilations: decapitation of Titus's sons, "trimming" of Lavinia's tongue and hands, severing of Titus's hand, dismemberment of Tamora's sons, their blood thriftily caught in a basin as if the recipe had specified "reserve the fluid." Like *sparagmos,* these dismemberments fertilize the land, renew the state. At the end, a once headless state has a new emperor, Lucius, who has been linked with summer: the restored state is a ruined harvest regathered, dismembered body reassembled, its pieces gathered up like those of the torn fertility god Osiris. One arresting passage stunningly combines the restored harvest with the gathered-up mutilated body: "Sons of Rome, / . . . let me teach you how to knit again / This scattered corn into one mutual sheaf, / These broken limbs again into one body" (V.iii.67–72).

Many hints combine to suggest that the Renaissance saw dismemberment as potentially regenerative. The blazon of love lyrics, analyzing a woman into a series of body parts, has seemed to feminists creepily akin to dismemberment; but as I will show in chapter 4, sonnets use some of the same semiotic systems as some tribal fertility rites, and their dismemberments—of male *and* female lovers—are often regenerative. As Bartlett Giamatti shows, the Renaissance saw its project of recovering the classics, damaged by time, as resurrection of a mutilated body: Petrarch calls a fragment of Quintilian "the dismembered limbs of a beautiful body" (Giamatti 18); when Poggio Bracciolini found a whole text, an associate wrote, "Quintilian, who used to be mangled and in pieces, will recover all his parts through you" (21–22). Poggio said that Cicero, too, lay "cut to pieces and scattered" (25). Boccaccio's collection of myth, *The Genealogy of the Gods,* resurrects into a body (*corpus*) the scattered "relics of the Gentile gods." Alluding to a favorite myth of the classics recoverers, Boccaccio says he will restore myth just as Aescalapius restored Hippolytus's dismembered body (29–30). The now unfashionable nineteenth-century term *Renaissance,* rebirth, was not false to the humanists' view of themselves as magical physicians raising to life dismembered bodies of the ancients. In my essay "Patchwork," I argue that such magical thinking underlies Renaissance writing habits—the breaking down of reading into small units in commonplace books to be resurrected into a new body when reassembled in a literary work drawn from many sources. The regenerative dismemberments of *Titus Andronicus,* so clearly linked with fertility magic—especially in that crucial passage "knit again / This scattered corn into one mutual sheaf, / These broken limbs again into one body"—are evidence of the existence of such magical thinking in the period.

The ritual import of *Titus*'s cannibal scene emerges from Titus's telling his victims he will "make two pasties of your shameful heads, / And bid that strumpet, your unhallowed dam, / Like to the earth swallow her own increase" (V.ii.189–91).[22] If Lavinia, by the brutal logic of rape/fruition myths, objectifies Mother Earth in her fructifying phase, cannibal Tamora is Autumnal Earth, devouring vegetation by absorbing it into herself as it decays. (The earthen pit into which Bassianus is thrown is called a "swallowing womb" [II.iii.239].) The Renaissance often sees the grave as a mouth, devouring corpses. To die is to be eaten, as many Renaissance texts show: in hell the damned are devoured; death is personified as a cannibal; Earth cannibalizes the dead (*R3* I.ii.63–66; *Rom* I.ii.15; *1H4* I.i.5–6). The Tamora who eats her sons, explicitly linked with Autumnal Earth eating the living things she gave birth to in spring, represents sterility, the play's analogue of political repression; she is the consort of tyrant Saturninus. Images of sacrifice, Earth as a cannibal, and the rape of Earth (the pit, that "swallowing womb") unite in one passage: Bassianus lies like "a slaughtered lamb, / In this detested, dark, blood-drinking pit" (II.iii.222–24).

The pattern of fertility magic is complete in *Titus:* society is saved. Titus is a rare tragic hero in being survived by a son and grandson. But the saving of society becomes problematic insofar as all the women in the play are killed—even the nurse—which hardly befits a semiotics of regeneration. Also highly problematic is that rape and dismemberment in *Titus* are not celebrated for promoting renewal but decried as evil.

I have said that *Titus* is the only tragedy to show a consistent pattern of fertility secured by the sacrifice of the hero, and that even here, the redemptive effect is seriously undermined. The two narrative poems, closely contemporary with *Titus,* also show signs of redemption through fertility magic, but in both these cases, too, the redemption is very problematic. *The Rape of Lucrece,* like *Titus,* makes political renewal contingent on the rape and death of a woman; and like *Titus,* it undermines the effect of this renewal by focusing on human suffering, the cost of renewal: as Heather Dubrow notes, *Lucrece*'s focus is not finally on the political renewal the argument stresses (an answer to the question "Why were the Tarquins banished?") but on suffering (an answer to the question "What happened to Lucrece?"; *Captive* 160). Comparing this text where the world of politics is overwhelmed by a private grief with a similar movement from politics to private life in *As You Like It* can act as a corrective to new historicist readings in which the political eclipses all other interests.

Venus and Adonis is an obvious locus for fertility magic: Adonis was the center of a major Greek fertility cult. Here again is a ritual pattern: Venus is linked with Earth (236–39); Earth is in love with Adonis (722); Venus urges him to feed the Earth with "thy increase" (170); he distills showers upon her (65–66). Adonis suffers *sparagmos,* torn by a boar; his death renews Earth as he becomes a flower, a common fertility symbol. As Clark Hulse suggests, Shakespeare may have known Boccaccio's allegorical interpretation in which "Adonis is the sun and Venus the earth; their love brings forth lush flowers, leaves, and ripe fruit. But winter is like the boar that slays the beautiful Adonis, for then the sun seems banished from our world, Venus mourns, the earth lies barren" (96). Awareness of fertility magic behind the source speaks even in the dedicatory epistle's metaphor: "If the first heir of my invention prove deform'd, I shall . . . never after ear so barren a land, for fear it yield me still so bad a harvest." But *Venus,* too, shows signs of the fertility magic's having been undercut by the poet's tendency to view the action as a merely human story. In a manner inappropriate to myth, the sexual drive belonging to fertility rites gets entangled with morality: in his prim distaste for lust, Adonis is more a first draft of Octavius Caesar than a human sacrifice in a fertility cult. Shakespeare handles magic playfully, even naughtily: the parallel between a stallion servicing a mare and the consummation Venus seeks with Adonis, a barnyard business startling in a mythic context, seems provokingly comic and works against a sober reading of the poem as being deeply involved in the redemptive sacrifice of slain gods.

Outside *Titus* and these two "tragic" narrative poems, the redemptive, fertilizing nature of tragedy is even more problematic. If a simple relation between drama and fertility magic obtained, as early "ritual" theorists maintained, the effects of comedy and tragedy would be broadly similar, comedy celebrating the survival of humanity by marriages and forecasting of "fair issue," tragedy securing, by human sacrifice, a more fertile future. But tragedy inverts rather than extends comedy's terms. The signifiers of fertile comedy are balanced almost algebraically by those in tragedy: change sides, change signs. Tragic semiotics, seemingly generated as the converse of comedy's vegetative fruition, include images of harvest ruined, plants frozen or blasted; unlike comedy's forests, fields, and orchards, tragedy's sets are barren: *Macbeth*'s dank castle and blasted heath; *Lear*'s heath— "for many miles about / There's scarce a bush" (II.iv.301–2). Brutus's orchard is a rare exception: tragic sets usually offer bleak, sparse vegetation or cold stone buildings—medieval castles in *Hamlet, Macbeth,* and *Lear,* solid civic buildings in the Roman plays. Elizabeth's coronation progress included a tableau resembling comic and tragic stage sets: "two artificial mountains, one 'cragged, barren and stony,' representing 'a decayed commonweal'; one 'fair, fresh, green, and beautiful,' representing 'a flourishing commonweal.' On the barren mountain there was a dead tree, an ill-dressed man slumped disconsolately beneath it; on the green one a flowering tree, a well-appointed man standing happily beside it" (C. Geertz, "Centers" 18). Elizabethan politics, as if tutored by the drama, often adopted the semiotics of fertility.

The implications of such semiotics are that tragedy represents not the redemptiveness of sacrifice but the triumph of sterility. Tragic heroes are sterile: Hamlet tells his potential bride to become a nun; Othello and Desdemona, Romeo and Juliet, Richard III, the Macbeths die childless; Lady Macbeth imagines infanticide; Macbeth has a "fruitless crown," a "barren scepter"; Lear curses his daughter with sterility and his line perishes. Since neither Romeo nor Juliet has siblings, the fact that their deaths end the feud is a Pyrrhic victory: death both reconciles the families and wipes them out. Old Capulet will not sire more heirs, and Romeo's mother dies the same night as her son. Her gratuitous last-minute demise seems part of a campaign to leave no women alive onstage at a tragedy's end. Except in some Roman plays, Shakespeare kills off every woman prominent enough to have appeared in a tragedy's last scene: Lavinia, Tamora, Portia, Ophelia, Gertrude, Desdemona, Emilia, Ladies Macbeth and Macduff, all three daughters in *Lear* (a play with no other women). Most of these deaths are ill-prepared for and thinly explained. Shakespeare identifies women with fertility (one reason their roles are central in comedy); his destroying them in tragedy stresses the triumph of sterility.

The Roman tragedies are less sterile—the women survive in *Coriolanus;* Titus, Antony, Cleopatra, and Coriolanus are survived by children—perhaps because the locale is southern (the southernmost,

Egypt, is the most fertile; even Cleopatra's death is teasingly fertile: "the fig is a universal symbol of fecundity; . . . a basket of figs is fertility and represents woman as goddess or mother" [Bord and Bord 200]). Wiped-out families, dead women, a pervasive icy atmosphere typify northern tragedies. The love tragedies' Italian settings suit their emotional temperature—warmer than the tragedies of ambition, revenge, or filial ingratitude; yet posterity and women are wiped out in *Romeo and Juliet* and *Othello* as in *Hamlet, Lear,* or *Macbeth,* and it won't do to argue that Verona and Venice are in northern Italy. The difference is only of degree.

In many tragedies, doomsday threatens. Of Duncan's intention to leave on the morrow, Lady Macbeth cries, "Never / Shall sun that morrow see!" Behind her primary meaning, that he will not live until morning, lurks an unintended meaning: tomorrow the sun will not rise. It happens: next morning, "darkness does the face of earth entomb, / When living light should kiss it." The old man's "'Tis unnatural" is understated: if the sun does not rise, the world ends, a threat that pervades *Macbeth.*[23] The state in tragedy often seems on the verge of collapse (see *Julius Caesar, Hamlet, Lear, Macbeth, Coriolanus*). The rich word *confusion* (e.g., *Cor* III.i.188) denoted both civil commotion and the universe's collapse into primordial chaos—in the Elizabethan imagination, the step from civil strife to obliterated universe was short and terrifyingly logical. Comedy banishes confusion: witness marriage-god Hymen's first line: "Peace, ho! I bar confusion" (*AYL* V.iv.124). But in tragedy universal dissolution remains a real threat. Frank Kermode thinks that tragic figures are exaggerating with such doomsday talk, caught up in apocalyptic thinking, the need to impose on shapeless reality the sense of an ending; doomsday paradoxically imposes order on history. Doomsday allusions may simply characterize the tragic hero at the moment of self-absorption so often heralding imminent death: the call for universal dissolution is a conventional tragic trope (see Clemen). Cleopatra's wish to take the world down with her (IV.xv.11–12), Macbeth's wish that the world were undone (V.v.50), might be simple selfish unwillingness, like the senex's, to let the world go on without them. But a high-ranking tragic hero is not an isolated individual: that hero embodies society. For Gloucester, Lear's agony provokes not a personal *memento mori* but a general *memento doomsday:* "This great world / Shall so wear out to nought" (IV.vi.134–35). Macduff responds the same way to Duncan's death (II.iii.77–78). Tragedy conjures the extinction of the human race.

Fertility magic is practiced out of intense anxiety, born of a belief that nature requires human help—if rites are not performed, crops will not grow nor seasons change, the sun will not rise, life will perish; and against a capricious nature and the malevolence of enemies even the most assiduous rituals will sometimes—often—fail. And because nature *is* capricious, life uncertain, and sterility lies all around us, even those who no longer believe in fertility rituals can still experience the anxiety. This primal anxiety, this helplessness before nature, tragedy invokes; but where fertility rites invoke anxiety to allay it, tragedy lets it stand. It focuses on the individual, for whom death means world's end; Shakespeare sometimes calls one death a doomsday.[24] And all will die at last: the race's death is simply spread out over history, a piecemeal doomsday.

Fertility magic is at odds with the tragic spirit: rites aim at controlling nature, allaying anxiety caused by nature's uncertainty; tragedy, confessing our helpless inability to avert disaster, only heightens anxiety. Fertility magic soothes; tragedy achieves only the calm of an audience flattered that it is tough enough to face the truth, only the selfish relief of an audience suddenly distanced from a hero whose agony it has shared, rising from theater seats with a sense of reprieve: I must die like Lear, but not yet.

Tragedy has dealt in sterility since Sophocles: in *Oedipus Tyrannus,* the "soil's produce now no longer springs; / Nor women from the labour / Of their child-births arise"; Oedipus's daughters will "wither, / Barren—unwed" (133, 172). Oedipus is like a "wintry Northern strand" (*Oedipus Coloneus* 295). Some tragedies alter the mythic patterns they inherit, to render them sterile: Hamlet, unique among heroes of his story group, dies without succeeding to the throne. Oddly, Gilbert Murray, though committed to a "fertility rite" reading of *Hamlet,* notes without comment this change that destroys the magical pattern: in what fertility rite does spring die without succeeding winter? It may be true, as Richard Wincor believes, that "fertility magic is the beginning of comedy; the winter mock-death of good things in life is the source of tragedy" (220); but tragic deaths are not "mock-deaths": tragedy focuses on a slain figure without admitting the renewal that is the point of ritual slaying. Shakespearean comedy, celebrating the race's survival, takes a long view of life—generation succeeding generation—in the spirit of fertility magic. Tragedy, focusing on death without rebirth, takes a short view: individuals are not reborn. Tragedy seems hostile to magical thinking: instead of belief in rituals making crops grow and preserving humanity, tragedy offers a clear-eyed vision of winter winning. It is as if tragedy, like a psychoanalyst, forces magical thinking to the surface of consciousness; as if comedy were the voice of the old magical thinking and tragedy the voice of the new rationality.

The trace of magic lingering even in tragedy, though, is that winning and losing, surviving or perishing, are articulated in a language of plants and seasons: tragedy *and* comedy cast goodness, happiness, triumph in terms of greenness, growth, fertility; both cast evil, misery, defeat in terms of sterility. Shakespearean tragedy pretends to no ritual efficacy; it repeatedly challenges the possibility of human control over events. But its language situates it within a discourse of fertility, casting what is desirable as organic, green, even explicitly rural. Such mental sets were bound to cause strain in an urbanizing culture.

Green Self-fashioning

But we cannot explain the bleak anxiety of Renaissance tragedy by adducing sterility as a generic hallmark of tragedy since the Greeks: tragedies were not being written through most of the intervening centuries. What early modern conditions favored the revival of this bleak genre and its language of sterility? Most obviously, the construction of the subject as an irreplaceable individual of marked interiority and autonomous will, an early modern phenomenon,[25] is an enabling condition of tragedy: only if the individual is irreplaceable is the death tragic, and the language of sterility makes sense only if we forget about the community whose life goes on, to focus on the individual who, like Cordelia, will come no more. But what if we stood this view on its head, arguing not that dying heroes become tragic because they are individualized, but that tragedy arose to check the threat of individuality? Shakespeare's most willful and self-actualizing characters are his outstanding villains (cf. Richard III's "I am myself alone") and the individualizing tendencies of the age were a source of anxiety to many writers—witness Donne's "Every man alone thinks he has got / To be a phoenix."[26] We are now skeptical of autonomous individuality, seeing the human subject as an overdetermined product of forces beyond his or her control. Some in the early modern period actively pursued autonomous individuality, fashioning their identities as Greenblatt has shown (*Renaissance Self-fashioning*); some questioned the possibility of autonomous individuality—Lear becomes acutely aware of the social construction of identity; some believed autonomous individuality existed and was dangerous to the community. In a period when new possibilities for self-fashioning sparked both exhilaration and anxiety, is it an accident that writers revived a genre that both celebrated the autonomous individual subject and killed him or her?

In this age of emergent individuality, many tragic figures, far from being ritualesque figures in a sacramental action, seem to use the trappings of fertility magic to further ideological purposes and aid their own self-fashioning. (I say "seem" because I want to problematize this idea presently.)

Julius Caesar opens at a fertility festival; Caesar's barren wife looks to Lupercal rites for a cure, and Caesar's falling sickness recalls Weston's theory that the king's illness that opens Grail romances was a symbolic impotence encoding his land's sterility. This Rome *is* a sterile land; the augurers' beast without a heart suits a nation without a heart, soon to be a headless state like *Titus*'s Rome. Ritual renewal is hinted: a dream "signifies that from [Caesar] great Rome shall suck / Reviving blood"; like slain gods and fisher kings, Caesar dies in spring, "the youthful season of the year." But death brings no fertilizing renewal; it unleashes chaos. (On the way that politics overwhelms festival in the play, see Liebler.) Ritual exists in conspirators' minds: *they* choose March 15, as in spring ritual slayings; Decius, a conspirator, gives the statue dream a ritual interpretation to ensure that Caesar will walk into the assassins' trap. Brutus uses ritual to mystify the coup d'etat: "Let's be sacrificers, but not butchers, . . . carve him as a dish fit for the gods" (II.ii.87–88, II.i.166–73). Whether calling assassination pious sacrifice is a program for later propaganda or a self-deception by Brutus, prettying up a thing whose ugliness he cannot confront, the play's ritual elements generally seem to expose rather than justify those who call murder sacrifice. In contrast to Brutus, Antony insists on "another sense of what has happened, repeatedly bringing the conceptualized, overformalized ritual of Brutus back to the bloody reality of the butchered Caesar" (De Gerenday 28).

Blood sacrifice is at least part of Brutus's culture; nothing suggests that Othello's African culture practiced human sacrifice, and he has converted to Christianity anyway—but when he murders his wife he calls it "sacrifice" (V.ii.66–68). For a Renaissance Christian like Othello to rationalize murder as sacrifice is the wild grasping of a desperate mind; the very cultural incongruity intensifies the desperation. Here is no sick and sterile society, and Desdemona's death is in no way redemptive: ritual allusion only reveals Othello's character.

At least so it appears to us, who have lived with centuries of literary subjects constructed as autonomous individuals and to whom the magical thinking of blood sacrifice is foreign enough that we cannot conceive of belief in it as other than rationalization or mystification. Shakespeare's plays are at once deeply embedded in the archaic discourse of fertility and (as products of a dawning rationalistic and anti-ritualistic age) shrewdly skeptical of old magical thinking, and it not always possible to tell when the plays are being rational and when magical. We often assume that Shakespeare saw through Brutus's or Othello's pronouncements on human sacrifice; but I hope I have problematized such assumptions by historicizing medieval and early modern magical thinking about fertility. Given the pervasive magical thinking in the early modern psyche, it is possible that Shakespeare himself thought of the assassination of Caesar or the murder of Desdemona in terms of ritual sacrifice.

Green Comedy

Comedy would seem more amenable than tragedy to "fertility" interpretations, since it celebrates human survival; but again we must correct by reference to history: though greener than tragedy, comedy is not necessarily more prone to magical thinking—if we find the magical premises of tragedy undermined by new ways of constructing the subject, we might expect to find historical pressures operating on whatever magic underpins comedy as well. The element of efficacy, which distinguishes a jewel from an amulet, divides all literature from magic,[27] but magical thinking widespread in a culture will often surface in literature, and comedy is an obvious surfacing point. In Shakespeare's comedies, though, we can often trace a reduction in fertility-magic thinking from a more generous presence in medieval sources.

As You Like It's ultimate source, the anonymous medieval *Tale of Gamelyn,* looks heavily influenced by the discourse of fertility, especially as found in popular rites. Gamelyn combats his elder brother to come into his inheritance, recalling rites pitting summer against winter. After initial triumph, Gamelyn revels, locking up his brother during a week's feasting, a killjoy expulsion like the fertility rite "carrying out Death." The brother, freed, ties up Gamelyn; abbots and priors mock him. Freeing himself, he knocks *them* about—as clerical administrators they are vulnerable to such saturnalian authority flouting. After beating the sheriff, Gamelyn drinks on, but threatened by police, moves to the forest, where he succeeds the outlaw chief (unnamed, but clearly Robin Hood) as master of the forest dwellers. As Forest King, the Green Man, he still buffets authority figures: the Robin Hood myth, in its authority-flouting, is essentially saturnalian. Returned to town to stand trial, he hangs the sheriff, judge, twelve jurors, and his brother. Vegetation spirit triumphant, he becomes Chief Justice of the Forest. At last he marries, adding human sexuality to his greenness.

Gamelyn means "the old one":[28] who older than the Green Man? The frequent epithet "young Gamelyn" hints at age magically rejuvenated. The brother, embodying not moral evil but sterility, must be hanged—Gamelyn does not regret it; nor would those attuned to seasonal rites. A moment's sadness in Gamelyn, an instant's nostalgia for days when he and his brother played in the nursery, would be a cardinal absurdity and spoil the story. Readers used to seasonal magic, accustomed to May games, morris dances, and mummers' plays know at some level of consciousness that here is no human sibling. He is Winter.

Centuries later Thomas Lodge, borrowing the plot, made the brother, Saladyne, behave like a human. *Gamelyn* echoes attempts to control nature by magic; it is literature, not magic, but its characters act like figures in a ritual. Lodge lived during an era of increased interiority in the literary subject, most prominent in tragedy but incipient in comedy and in prose fiction; his *Rosalynde* represents human behavior. Saladyne, who has at least a rudimentary interior life, is not hanged, but reconciled with his brother, as winter is never reconciled with summer. Where Gamelyn was a pate-cudgeling bone breaker, Lodge's hero is "courteous" (13); he fights only in self-defense. Gamelyn had been "good" as summer is good—by definition; but Lodge's hero needs our *moral* approval—must be courteous, must not exult in hangings, must forgive.

In *As You Like It,* Shakespeare patched several new plots onto this literary heirloom and tinkered with those already there. Additions like the quadruple wedding extend the fertility theme, and teasing mementos of Gamelyn's Forest King role glimmer about Orlando: he sits "under a tree, like a dropp'd acorn" (III.ii.231–32), carves "Rosalind" on trees and hangs odes on the hawthorn, that emblem of spring; he finds his brother under an oak; and Shakespeare named him De Boys—"of the forest." However, where Lodge had forgiven the brother and killed another wintry figure, the usurping duke he had introduced into the tale, Shakespeare forgives the brother, now named Oliver, and his version of Lodge's substitute, Duke Frederick. R. G. Hunter traces Shakespeare's heavy emphasis on forgiveness to medieval mystery, miracle, and morality plays. But Shakespeare can be more forgiving than his medieval sources. Medieval Gamelyn, with little Christian charity, gleefully hangs his brother; Renaissance Orlando forgives his. The change was not a matter of religion but of how early modern subjects were constructed in an age when magic was ebbing. Though comedy operates within a discourse of fertility, Renaissance literary subjects were constructed as people, not seasons. Oliver is *eligible* for forgiveness as Gamelyn's brother is not: one can forgive the worst of men, but one cannot forgive winter.

Like a fertilizing blood sacrifice, Robin Hood died (on May Day) when his blood was drained out; he figured in ritual mummer's plays, and Robin Hood and Maid Marian were often the May King and Queen. Robin made his literary debut in *The Tale of Gamelyn,* and *As You Like It*'s outlaws live "like the old Robin Hood" (I.i.112); but Shakespeare handles them with indifference to magical meanings. In *The Two Gentlemen of Verona,* Valentine, like Gamelyn, becomes outlaw chief; but since he is no Green Man but a developed human subject, the improbable election must be rationalized. Myth appearing in realistic work, Northrop Frye says, poses problems of plausibility; he calls devices for solving such problems "displacement" (*Anatomy* 136). Shakespeare displaces himself out of joint trying to make Valentine's leadership plausible. Interviewing the candidate for bandit chief, outlaws inquire into his qualifications, stopping just short of demanding a curriculum vitae. They decide, "by the bare scalp of Robin Hood's fat friar, / This fellow were a king for our wild faction," on grounds that he is "beautified" and "by [his] own report / A linguist" (IV.i.33–57). Green Men behave in a variety of ways, but they are never short-listed for administrative posts. Even in comedy, the magic is starting to melt.

In other comedies, magic evaporates like a mirage as we approach. Spens thinks the proposed decking of a hunter in deer horns and hide (*AYL* IV.ii) is a ritual remnant (37); but it has no magical import, and a song reduces it to a horn joke. Kissing through a hole in a stone is an old fertility rite (Bord and Bord 33–34), but the accidental bawdry of *Dream*'s "I kiss the wall's hole, not your lips at all" (V.i.199) is not sacramental but funny. *Eastward Ho* reduces to a cuckold joke the dawn elevation of ox horns on St. Luke's Day—a ceremony with the appearance of ancient ritual. The *Merchant*'s pound of flesh hints at human sacrifice; Antonio, "a figure to be mutilated, . . . resembles the mythical figures of Osiris, Attis, Adonis—the dying gods" (Holland, *Psychoanalysis* 233). But here no whiff of ritual remains. We are in a courtroom, not before a pagan altar. Frye sees in *Merry Wives* "an elaborate ritual of the defeat of winter known to folklorists as 'carrying out Death.' . . . Falstaff must have felt that, after being thrown into the water, dressed up as a witch and beaten out of a house with curses, and finally supplied with a beast's head and singed with candles, he had done about all that could reasonably be asked of any fertility spirit" (*Anatomy* 183).[29] Magical elements seem present; yet in a play concerning a cynical attempt to make money through seducing urban wives, magic supports the theme only by contrast: the agrarian world where sympathetic magic makes crops grow is not the *Merry Wives*'s world. If he is using fertility magic here at all, Shakespeare is flippantly exploiting its inappropriateness to modern (and especially town) life.

While it lasted, the countryside comedy, despite the loosening hold on it of archaic fertility magic, remained the most magical of genres, partly because it owed much to pastoral, whose links with fertility magic are clear. In that widespread genre the pastoral debate, as Steven Marx shows, winter images attach to an old debater, summer to a young; close links with ritual winter/summer combat appear in the first surviving medieval eclogue, Alcuin's *Conflictus Veris et Heimis,* eighth century, a summer/winter combat written by a man with a deep belief in such ancient magical notions as the king as a guarantor of crop fertility, as is seen in Alcuin's letter to King Athelred in 793: "In the king's righteousness is the prosperity of the whole folk, victory of the army, mildness of the seasons, abundance of the land, the blessing of sons, the health of the people" (Opland 33). Over many centuries, pastoral debates in literature addressed such diverse topics as hetero- versus homosexuality, thrift versus generosity, even lentil soup versus lentil puree, but the commonest topics were youth versus age and spring versus winter (Marx 153–54). Such a youth/age combat in a green world is clearly the war that paradoxically brings fertility, as in the ritual tug-of-war or the mummers' rivalry between young and old suitor. The Renaissance recognized the ancient, tribal nature of the pastoral debate: Scaliger "saw in this bucolic convention a literary imitation of the verse debates of primitive peoples" (Marx 151–52). Sexual conflict is central to the imagery of Renaissance epithalamia too, appropriate to a genre of marriage and fertility, and the Renaissance genre was strongly influenced by an epithalamium of Catullus, cast as a debate: "The maidens are contradicted by the youths, virginity is pitted against marriage" (Dubrow, *Happier Eden* 47). *As You Like It,* alongside its vestigial winter/summer combats in Oliver/ Orlando and the two dukes, features debates in a pastoral setting: among them, an old shepherd and a young shepherd (Corin and Silvius) and a man and a woman (Orlando and Rosalind) debate about women and love. The footprints of fertility magic are nowhere clearer than this.

Sometimes the old magic was nakedly co-opted by modern political and financial interests. Royally sponsored pastorals, pretending to what Empson calls "a beautiful relation between rich and poor" (11–12) justified autocratic Tudor rule by casting England as a rural utopia, glossing over the brutal realities of unemployment, rural depopulation, enclosures, shepherds who never owned their sheep (see Montrose, "Eliza"). Such pastorals, written by courtiers not shepherds, were ideological tracts fostering a pseudo-magical thinking wherein modern poverty and disenfranchisement became a life of timeless rural happiness. Country-house poems cast as a timeless rural way of life the regime of manorial estates which were actually founded by new money in the dawning capitalist age (see R. Williams). In a Quaint Olde England campaign as blatantly manipulative as any modern advertising promotion, King James officially fostered rural sports and feasts to co-opt any rebelliousness among the poor.

Rural idylls of Jonson, Herrick, and Spenser are positively sycophantic toward land-owning classes; Shakespeare never produced an ideological idyll on the order of "To Penshurst" or Herrick's *Hesperides,* but he does employ the "I wish I were a happy shepherd rather than a miserable king" trope: Henry VI and the doomed heir apparent Arthur wish specifically to be shepherds (*3H6* II.v; *Jn* IV.i); less specifically rural are Henry IV's envy of "my poorest subjects" in their hovels and Henry V's envy of those who do "profitable labor" (*2H4* III.i.4; *H5* IV.i.294). On this trope, readers like Greenblatt and Montrose have heaped scorn, judging such pronouncements necessarily insincere—a king praises country life so that peasants will stay down on the farm and leave the life of power to him; peasants accept the king's power because he assures them it makes him miserable and he would rather be a shepherd. The presumption of hypocrisy here rests on the assumption that a retired rural life is by definition less desirable than a public, civic life of political power.

New historicists, making such assumptions, share the values of Renaissance literary theorists such as Sidney, who placed pastoral at the bottom of his hierarchy of genres. Such unexamined contempt for country life and private life involves significant losses: through the ages pastoral has often done what new historicists try to do—expose the ugliness, brutality, and emptiness of power and public life—sometimes the court, sometimes the city. Royally sponsored pastorals are far from being the whole genre: pastoral has long offered what feminist criticism and postcolonial theory now offer—a view of the center from the periphery. Our decentering post-structuralist age has labored to shift the focus from center to periphery, to value the people who live in and the authors who write from and about the margins; but country people and pastoral writers inhabit one of the last undefended margins. Criticism has erased them, defined them as a spectral presence, an Other created in binary opposition to the "real" world, having no existence except as ideological mystifications perpetrated by a cynical ruling class. But Shakespeare knew people who lived in the country: one still sees cows grazing by the path from Stratford to Shottery that he must have walked. Of course pastoral was among the most conventional of literary genres; but conventions can express human feelings, and pastoral expresses among others the feeling that a life close to nature, though harsh, has value in itself and is capable of giving pleasure and satisfaction; that thinking about such a life (even when one does not live it) can raise serious questions—not only affected or hypocritical questions—about the value of the cutthroat strivings of civic and public life.

In Shakespeare's premier countryside comedy, *As You Like It,* the perspective of a retired rural life throws into relief the corruption of the court. The play alludes to an important early modern socioeconomic issue, the power shift from manorial estates to the city, where old landed wealth was translated into what Barthes calls "the fashion system" ("the city-woman bears / The cost of princes on unworthy shoulders" [II.vii.75–76]). The play does patronize its country folk, unsophisticated rustics greatly outshone in wit by woods-slumming courtiers; but it does not assume that the pastoral alternative is by definition unworthy or impossible. The court jester feels out of place, finding country residence "a very vile life" (III.ii.11), yet he marries into it; most courtiers go home to the court at the end, yet the fact that several choose to stay in the country shows that to "[throw] into neglect the pompous court" (V.iv.189) and "live and die a shepherd" (V.ii.14) is not inconceivable, despite Montrose's claim that "for the great, the material reality of a peasant's life can hardly have been a desirable option" ("Eliza" 156). While we cannot be sure how seriously Shakespeare and his contemporaries took the pastoral option, the thrust of the pervasive semiotics of fertility and sterility in Shakespeare is that what is desirable is what is growing and green.

As You Like It problematizes the question of the place of human beings in green nature. It demystifies—not by showing green nature as only an ideological construct invoked to justify a conservative view of social relations, but by showing that humans exploit nature, that however desirable a life close to nature might be, in practice humans cannot approach nature without destroying it. "Shall we go and kill us venison?" asks the Duke; "and yet it irks me the poor dappled fools, / Being native burghers of this desert city, / Should in their own confines with forked heads / Have their round haunches gor'd" (II.i.21–25). "Irks" connotes a small emotion, an irritation—that twinge that some animal rights advocates feel when eating steak—we cannot let it become larger than a twinge and go on being carnivores. This emotion differs from what Jaques feels: he "grieves."

> The melancholy Jaques grieves at that,
> And . . . swears you do more usurp
> Than doth your brother that hath banish'd you.
> Today my Lord of Amiens and myself
> Did steal behind him as he lay along
> Under an oak whose antique root peeps out
> Upon the brook that brawls along this wood,
> To the which place a poor sequest'red stag,
> That from the hunter's aim had ta'en a hurt,
> Did come to languish; and indeed, my lord,
> The wretched animal heav'd forth such groans
> That their discharge did stretch his leathern coat
> Almost to bursting, and the big round tears
> Cours'd one another down his innocent nose
> In piteous chase; and thus the hairy fool,
> Much marked of the melancholy Jaques,
> Stood on th' extremest verge of the swift brook,
> Augmenting it with tears.
>   (II.i.26–43)

Here our old conjunction of oak tree and brook creates a sacred venue that makes this death a martyrdom. As "grieves" goes farther than "irks," so Jaques' views are more politically advanced than the Duke's; killing deer "in their own confines" had troubled the Duke as a breach of hospitality—in itself a serious enough matter, as texts from *Macbeth* to *Timon of Athens* testify; to Jaques it is even more serious—a usurpation, an abuse of political power like Duke Frederick's. Here are the seeds of an animal rights argument: abusing animals brutalizes us, makes us capable of abusing humans, habituates us to power abuse, enlarges our capacity for political crime. The lord who reports the episode attributes such sentiments toward animals to Jaques' humor, twice calling him "the melancholy Jaques"; yet the lord's language shows him moved by animal suffering. Should he smile indulgently, reporting that Jaques "swears you do more usurp / Than doth your brother," as if obvious overstatement typifies the "humors" figure, or should an actor speak this as if half persuaded of its truth? The Duke asks for elaboration, perhaps smiling in anticipation of Jaques' predictable behavior—but a circumspect smile would not be out of order. The lord continues:

> For his weeping into the needless stream:
> "Poor deer," quoth he, "thou mak'st a testament
> As worldlings do, giving thy sum of more
> To that which had too much." . . .
> Anon a careless herd,
> Full of the pasture, jumps along by him
> And never stays to greet him. "Ay," quoth Jaques,
> "Sweep on, you fat and greasy citizens;
> 'Tis just the fashion. Wherefore do you look
> Upon that poor and broken bankrupt there?"
> Thus most invectively he pierceth through
> The body of the country, city, court,
> Yea, and of this our life, swearing that we
> Are mere usurpers, tyrants, and what's worse,
> To fright the animals and to kill them up
> In their assign'd and native dwelling-place.
>   (II.i.45–63)

Is Jaques' speech mere affectation? Is sympathy for the deer emotional opportunism, a pretext to display melancholy wit? Does he relish the deer's arrival as he relishes Touchstone's, as occasions to exercise his humor—he who sucks melancholy from a song as a weasel sucks eggs? Perhaps; but affectations are for display, and this is a soliloquy. (He seems not to know he is overheard.) And he is still bitter about deer killing two acts later. This is part affectation, part real feeling; he is both "humors" character and serious thinker. The Duke, also complex, loves to meet Jaques "in these sullen fits, / For then he's full of matter"; he indulgently appreciates affectation ("you're so cute when you're melancholy") but sincerely wants to be edified. Even the lord is fairly complex. He knows the Duke is magnanimous enough to be told that Jaques called him a usurper; yet he chooses a story he knows the Duke will like and cautiously avoids offering his own views on Jaques or on animal suffering. The interiority of the subject, so visible in tragedy, appears in this comedy too, in a complex interplay of character: a melancholy Jaques testing the line between affectation and emotion; a Duke who has repressed scruples, courting a lecture on animal rights, tempting Fate to turn him into a vegetarian.

Much in this scene looks beyond a retired country life to the more pressured and hectic life of politics (usurpation), economics (testaments and bankruptcy), the city ("fat and greasy citizens"). Yet I strongly resist the tendency of so much New Historical writing to value literature only for its public and political moments. *As You Like It*'s remarkable conversation about the pitiable death of a deer in the midst of green nature is of value and of interest not only because it talks about usurpation, bankruptcy, and citizens; it is of value and interest because it talks about a deer and green nature. Ecology may be political, but it is not only political.

There is a gender issue here. I have shown that fertility magic flickers throughout *As You Like It,* and the green-world setting is vital to that sense of pervasive natural magic. Though some ancient cultures associated fertility with male deities, many others worshipped female fertility gods, and true to its Celtic heritage, Shakespeare's culture often linked fertility with the female principle. It is no accident that the magician who brings about four weddings at the end of *As You Like It* is a woman, Rosalind. Yet of all our century's many "ritual" approaches to literature, it is fertility ritual that is thoroughly out of fashion. Studies of ritual stratify along gender lines: "male" rites like ceremonies of political power, male initiation, war, and ceremonies of international diplomacy draw most theorists' attention, while "female" rites promoting human and agrarian fertility now languish in neglect, after a period of virulent scholarly attacks. Those who write of political power are seldom attacked for their mere choice of subject matter as are those who opt for fertility; anything to do mainly with women and rustics is automatically suspect. The exclusion of fertility from serious attention, the defining of ritual as rites of power, the subjugation of the green world to the political world is the preference of a male-dominated society.

As You Like It was both an apogee and a swan song: high countryside comedy was in its last days. The belief that the world of rural folkways has disappeared within living memory is perennial: Raymond Williams traces it through modern literary critics, longing for the organic society, through nineteenth-century novelists, eighteenth-century poets, seventeenth- and sixteenth-century dramatists, medieval moralists—finally all the way back to Hesiod, eighth century B.C. But Shakespeare's generation—witnessing urbanization, deforestation, enclosures, capitalism invading the countryside—had good enough grounds for the belief. This age saw, in Thomas's phrase, "the decline of magic." Urbanization proceeded even faster in the eyes of English writers than in the eyes of the nation at large—stationed as the writers were mainly in London. Even in a comedy of forest and field such as *As You Like It,* the magic is starting to bleach out of the landscape. And this kind of comedy soon disappeared. The comedies best interpretable by allusion to seasonal rites—what Barber calls festive comedies—are green-world comedies, rural in at least some of their settings; *Measure for Measure* and other Jacobean city comedies are *not* congenial to "seasonal" readings. Urbanization made the world of rural folkways seem remote, sentimentalized. Shakespeare kept his rural world viable by letting "greasy Joans" and a skeptical Touchstone and Jaques subvert sentimentality by taking a non-utopian look at its churlish landlords and its deer slayers. But the blandishments of city life helped destroy rural comedy; though the organic, green semiotics of happiness made it hard to write about cities in anything but a satiric voice, city comedy relished even as it denounced city living. "The town," Thomas says, "was the home of learning, manners, taste and sophistication, the arena of human fulfilment. Adam had been placed in a garden, and Paradise was associated with flowers and fountains;" but heaven was "envisaged as a city, a new Jerusalem" (*Man* 243).

Still, if green nature was retreating from comedy, human fruition remained, and I persist in believing that fruition, rather than politics, is what Shakespearean comedy is mainly about. We might see Shakespeare's career as a generic battleground where tragedy and comedy wage war, like the ritual tug-of-war between winter's sterile and summer's fertile forces: in these generic night battles, to adapt Carlo Ginzburg, "when the witches win [i.e., tragedy], a great famine follows, and when the *benandanti* win [i.e., comedy], there is abundance." The late tragicomedies stage within each play the struggle between tragic witches and comedic *benandanti*. In this view, one satisfaction of Shakespeare's career is that it ends comedically: the *benandanti* win. Yet this binary opposition is deconstructed by that medial genre the history play, wherein the earlier tetralogy ends "tragically" with the hero's death, the later tetralogy "comically" with the hero's impending marriage. Here is a genre that truly *is* mainly about politics; and yet among scepters and crowns, green nature still sprouts.

Magical History Plays

The history plays often speak the language of seasonal magic. In *Richard III*'s opening, strife between Lancaster and York, each with its own king, is a winter/summer battle, "the winter of our discontent / Made glorious summer by this sun of York" (I.i.1–2). In the *Henry VI* plays, two sides pull at the crown, like spring and winter in tug-of-war fertility rites (the red and white roses are also a legacy of fertility magic: see chapter 4).

Richard II is a force of sterility: his tears and sighs "shall lodge [beat down] the summer corn, / And make a dearth" (III.iii.162–63); gardeners lament his land's metaphorical ruined vegetation (III.iv.43–49); he is linked with winter and feels like a snowman (IV.i.259–63); his rival is identified with spring and sunshine (V.ii.46–50). Richard's death is a human sacrifice renewing vegetation: his successor says Richard's blood has sprinkled him to make him grow (V.vi.45–46). Bolingbroke's imagery hints at a new sky god, come to inseminate Earth: he will "lay the summer's dust with show'rs"; "on the earth I rain / My waters" (III.iii.42–60). Rites of carrying out Death and bringing in the Green Man peep through the scene where London welcomes Bolingbroke's procession and expels Richard: "Rude misgovern'd hands from windows' tops / Threw dust and rubbish on King Richard's head" (V.ii.5–6). Several passages recall *sparagmos,* dismemberment and sprinkling the earth with blood for fertility: "Ten thousand bloody crowns /

... [shall] bedew / Her pastures' grass with faithful English blood"
(III.iii.96–100); "The blood of English shall manure the ground"
(IV.i.138). Aumerle, a young man unnaturally old, is renewed like
Aristophanes' old men rejuvenated: "Come, my old son. I pray God
make thee new" (V.iii.146). When Richard is sent north, his leaving his wife is like vegetation leaving earth in winter: "I towards
the north, / Where shivering cold and sickness pines the clime; /
My wife to France, from whence . . . / She came adorned hither like
sweet May, / Sent back like Hallowmas or short'st of day [the winter solstice]." She puts a curse of sterility on vegetation:
"Gard'ner, . . . pray God the plants thou graft'st may never grow"
(V.i.40–80, III.iv.101–2). In an age that believed in ritual cursing,
curses of sterility on plants or people (*Lr* I.iv.268–72; *3H6*
III.ii.125–26; *R3* I.ii.21) had great dramatic force. Especially in
Catholic countries, curses still worked: in 1628, "theft of church
silver provoked the Bishop of Barcelona into putting a curse on the
land . . . , and the subsequent crops were ruined" (Thomas, *Religion* 600). Whether it suggests a Catholic connection or is merely
literary convention, curses in Shakespeare nearly always work.

Nevertheless, such eruptions of magical thinking sit oddly in a
sophisticated genre exploring power politics, and magical meanings
that tease us throughout *Richard II* are constantly subverted. If
Richard is sacrificial victim, king slain to restore the land's fertility, the magic doesn't work: the blood manuring the ground is an
image of civil war. Far from redemptive, the king's death brings a
curse on England, decades of war and debilitation. If the queen symbolizes Mother Earth, she remains fixed at winter, moving from May
to the winter solstice rather than the other way around ("she came
adorned hither like sweet May, / Sent back like Hallowmas or
short'st of day"), a movement into winter seen in some sonnet cycles (see chapter 4). The arrested cycle—the earth that cannot revive, the victim whose sacrifice brings no renewal—reminds us that
if Bolingbroke's story ends like a comedy, Richard's ends like a tragedy. As tragedy frustrates fertility by focusing on the hero's death
without allowing the renewal that is the aim of ritual slaying, *Richard II*'s quasi-tragic plot and prototragic hero are out of step with
fertility magic. Again, the interiority of the subject absorbs magical meanings.

The play's ritual imagery is often simply part of Richard's self-fashioning. The prime exponent of Richard as Christ-figure is Richard: it is mainly he who compares himself with Christ, his enemies with Judas or Pilate. Character issues in rhetoric: self-comparison with Christ exposes his blasphemously inflated view of himself, his evasion of responsibility for the realm's ills by luxuriating in martyrdom's divine inevitability, his self-justification through casting opponents as archetypal betrayers. He hides, behind a hedge of ritual, from the truth about himself. Opening scenes brilliantly establish his use of ceremony as sedative, the pomp of public ritual anesthetizing a cankered private heart. Later, empty ritual comforts him again: "Not all the water in the rough rude sea / Can wash the balm off from an anointed king" (III.ii.54–56). When Richard is deposed, after this declaration of divine support, god's omnipotence is not besmirched: the theology was not Shakespeare's but Richard's. Magical thinking about anointment spares him the effort of acting to defend his throne. No slain god, Richard does not figure in a ritual; ritual figures in him. Richard the rationalizing, self-dramatizing, self-pitying deceiver of himself, capable of flashes of shrewdness, moments of courage; Richard the vacillator among roles—arbitrary tyrant, fatuous courtly titterer, languishing connoisseur of martyrdom, outraged protester against injustice: here is a complex self-fashioning. Surrounded by allusions to fertility rites, taking part in an action dripping with seasonal ritual, the king absorbs all this magic into his own personality.

One problem with the "discontinuous subject" theory propounded by Belsey and others, the difficulty of distinguishing between discontinuity and complexity, in part involves applying new terms to an old problem: when we encounter a quicksilver personality like Richard's, should we damn Shakespeare for inconsistency or praise him for complexity? If Belsey is correct in arguing that the early modern period did not yet possess a concept of the unified subject and that after a long period of belief in the unified subject we are now coming to disbelieve in it, we should soon be arriving back at something approximating Shakespeare's own mind-set on this issue. My position is, however, that Shakespeare lived on the cusp with regard to subject unity—he could still create "splits" and project parts of a personality onto other characters, as I showed in the last chapter, but he was also starting to create complex characters who contained internal inconsistencies and acted multiple and shifting roles, quite in the manner of subjects we meet in the extraliterary world. Richard II is a relatively early example of such a character. This is the kind of subject whose developed interiority is constantly pulling against magical modes of thinking—and the tension becomes acute with the intricately realized subjects who are protagonists (and even villains) of tragedy.

When the gardeners speak of a weed-choked kingdom, they do not envision ritual king slaying to restore fertility; they are criticizing Richard's neglectful political gardening. The play enacts the bewildering difficulty of moral judgment in the real world: Richard's confrontation with Bolingbroke—confiscator versus usurper—exists in a grey area. The English history play is without simple villains, acted not on a timeless sacramental plane but in a historical, political world; its *Realpolitik* shatters its ritual framework. In history plays, fertility magic often leaps from the page; witness Falstaff's parody of the young king restoring fertility to the old king's sterile land: "the cold blood [Hal] did naturally inherit of his father, he hath, like lean, sterile, and bare land, manur'd, husbanded and till'd with excellent endeavor of drinking good and good store of fertile sherris" (*2H4* IV.iii.116–20). But Shakespeare often sets up such patterns only to work against them.

A semiotics of human sacrifice, a king's body feeding his subjects, permeates *Henry IV*. To woo the populace, Henry was seldom seen: "my state, / Seldom but sumptuous, show'd like a feast"; his rival fed the populace to gluttonous surfeit: "daily swallowed by men's eyes, / They surfeited with honey and began / To loathe the taste of sweetness, / . . . Being with his presence glutted, gorg'd, and full" [*1H4* III.ii.57–84]). When Henry paints the people as ravenous feeders "starving for a time / Of pellmell havoc," rebels have their own politico-culinary views:

> Being fed by us you us'd us so
> As . . . the cuckoo's bird,
> Useth the sparrow; . . .
> Grew by our feeding to so great a bulk
> That [we dared] not come near your sight
> For fear of swallowing.
>   (V.i.59–82)

Henry has shifted from feast-for-my-people to devouring cuckoo. In the archbishop's bulimic tirade, Henry's position in the food chain comes full cycle:

> Their over-greedy love hath surfeited. . . .
> O thou fond many, with what loud applause
> Didst thou beat heaven with blessing Bolingbroke. . . . [And now]
> Thou, beastly feeder, art so full of him
> That thou provok'st thyself to cast him up.
> So, so, thou common dog, didst thou disgorge
> Thy glutton bosom of the royal Richard.
> (*2H4* I.iii.88–98)

Here is some sense of cyclical history, the people feeding on a succession of sacrificed kings; but context denies the ritual aura. These speeches are manipulative oratory: Henry tries to burden Hal with guilt or outdo the rebels in war oratory; the archbishop, a rebel, speaks to lash his party into action. Henry's scorn for Richard who "grew a companion to the common streets, / Enfeoff'd himself to popularity" bears the politician's telling stamp of absolute falsehood: we never saw Richard behaving thus; it was *Henry* who courted the masses (*R2* I.iv.31). In the history plays, seemingly ritual elements often turn out to be rhetorical ploys, manipulated by cynical politicians; it is precisely their sacramental air, seeming to raise them above the sordid world of politics, that makes them so useful as rhetorical ploys. Since gorging and gluttony images are often thus manipulated, we should not too quickly accept attempts to shift the realm's evils onto the shoulders of the chief glutton, Falstaff. And since leanness can signal sedition—*Henry V*'s conspirators, like *Julius Caesar*'s, are "spare in diet" (II.ii.131) and rebel Jack Cade is starved (*2H6* IV.x)—one wonders about Hal. Maybe only compared with Falstaff is he a "starveling," but peace-relishing fat man confronting warrior thin man may point to the usurping Lancastrians as a sterilizing force. If so, sterility wins in the Henriad—quite at odds with ritual. (R. J. Dorius, discussing fatness and thinness in the histories, tends to accept the Lancastrians at their own estimate ["responsible men . . . are thin" (15)], but does allow Falstaff's modifying perspective.)

Henry VIII inverts a familiar ritual pattern. In place of a Mother Earth passively accepting a series of divine spring bridegrooms, much-married Henry accepts the first two of a series of brides. Like Mother Earth, he remains fairly passive through cycles of change, one wife declining into winter, another blowing in like spring, one overbearing clerical advisor (Wolsey) arousing the ire of all the king's men, succeeded by another overbearing clerical advisor (Gardiner) doing the same. Queens and clerics wax and wane, Henry goes on and on; the play, ending in a new generation's birth, has the rhythms of nature. Henry, historically dynamic and headstrong, is here cast in a more typically "feminine" fertility role, his masculinity defined by begetting a child: "Thou hast made me now a man! Never, before / This happy child, did I get anything" (V.v.65–66).

Some of the clash between *Realpolitik* and magic is a by-product of new ways of constructing the subject in all its interiority. But the fertility materials are deeply functional. In the histories the discourses of fertility, divine kingship, and chivalry create a golden world located vaguely in the Middle Ages, a world always already gone against which modernity defines itself. The golden world *seems* to pass in *Richard II,* where usurpation shatters divine kingship, where chivalric justice (trial by combat) yields to squeaky-wheel modern justice (Aumerle's treason pardoned because of his mother's noisy pleas). But golden and modern worlds are juxtaposed again in *Henry IV:* a world of businesslike politics defines itself against chivalric Hotspur and a figure from the discourse of fertility, Falstaff. Though Hotspur dies, Henry V revives chivalric talk; his "the fewer men, the greater share of honor" (*H5* IV.iii.23) is indistinguishable from Hotspur's avowal that his small army "lends a lustre and more great opinion, / A larger dare to our great enterprise" (*1H4* IV.i.77–78); and throughout its world of modern politics and war, *Henry V* interlaces seasonal imagery.

Golden ages are useful ideological tools: our political right cherishes rural visions like *The Waltons* or *Little House on the Prairie,* idealizing self-sufficiency, traditional morals, father at the head of a close-knit family. The political right in early modern England used the same tactics: "A 'timeless' past, structured only by the rhythms of the festive year, is central to the depoliticized politics of Robert Herrick's *Hesperides.* . . . [It is] an essential part of a mythical genealogy which founds an 'uncontroversial' Englishness in 'custom,' 'rural life,' 'popular festivity'" (Stallybrass, "'Wee Feaste'" 244).[30] As

Raymond Williams says, idealizing the past against "the crudeness of a new moneyed order, often serves as a critique of the capitalism of our own day"—which might appeal to the political Left, except that it is an evasion: frontier self-sufficiency is not open to many today, and to valorize "a pre-capitalist and therefore irrecoverable world" (R. Williams 36) is to avoid confronting present ills; a typical move is to blame modern ills on the decline of the Walton-style family and hence on some scapegoat like feminism. The Left is not attracted, either, to critiques of capitalism that offer feudalism as an alternative. Shakespeare's characters often conjure golden worlds, rural and feudal: where does *he* stand ideologically?

Williams says the best antidote to ideologically mystified golden worlds is a clear look at the past; and Shakespeare takes that look. The histories recurrently allude to a lost, Edenic world; but it is endlessly deferred into the past, its goldenness always already tarnished. *Richard II*'s opening, predating the shattering of sacred kingship by usurpation, already shows chivalry and sacred kingship a sham; it implicates the king in misuse of funds and in murder. In the plays' ecology, golden and modern are mutually modifying: the posited golden world—sacred kings, chivalrous knights, oneness with nature—throws into relief the tawdriness of the real political world; the gritty, brutal complexity and sheer human interest of the real political world expose the impossibility, perhaps undesirability, of the golden. Against the histories' *Realpolitik,* the discourse of fertility functions like Howard Felperin's "endomimesis," a technique in which Shakespeare embeds highly conventional scenes like *Hamlet*'s mousetrap or Edgar's stagy madness in *Lear* to make other scenes lifelike by contrast. In the green endomimesis of the history plays, Shakespeare constructs a ghostly organic society, and out of the shadows of a hazy golden world step shrewd and worldly kings, like flesh and blood.

The Emerald City

I have said that Shakespeare's misty golden world is compounded of the discourses of fertility, chivalry, and sacred kingship. Of the three, only the discourse of fertility really has a life of its own outside politics and outside the ruling class. The ubiquity of fertility and sterility in the plays' language, the many plots and characters seemingly drawn from ancient fertility material via popular rites, mummings, and tales, show Shakespeare's plays steeped in the discourse of fertility, counting on the mentality of a populace accustomed for centuries to shaping experience in terms of battles between seasons, divine impregnations of Mother Earth, ritual rebirths, processions with greenery. Though Shakespearean literature of all genres—even comedy, whose "fertility" themes are the most affirmative—repeatedly works against such magical patterns, they continue to underlie it and to give it shape. The sterility of the tragic hero; tragedy's language of evil—wintry, sterile, hungry; the history plays' casting of civil war as seasonal combat and playing off of political against pastoral worlds; and the world-peopling greenness of Shakespearean comedy—all these form a strong and rather touching link between a naive folk consciousness and that great theatrical Green Room, Shakespearean drama.

Our politicians still conjure agrarian utopias, but much of the old consciousness is gone. Woodland pools aren't haunted by nymphs any more, and oaks retain little aura of sacredness or fertile masculinity. The sexual semiotics of nature, so long available to literature, has faded away; the phallicism of trees, once taken for granted by the peasantry, is kept alive only in the iron lung of Freudian criticism. The loss of the sexualized landscape is as momentous to English literature as the loss of grammatical gender to the English language.

Shakespeare grew up in a little farming town in days when England's vast woods were being pushed back and its great city was mushrooming. That he left Stratford for the city, but at last returned to town and countryside, echoes the hovering, undecided place green nature and the archaic world of fertility magic occupy in his works. Protestantism and nascent rationalism were driving back magical thinking: no Puritan countenanced communion wafers as caterpillar charms, and holy processions to promote crop fertility were dying out. In literature, interiority of character was displacing emblematic modes of representation in which human figures might represent winter or the Green Man; and genres like rural comedy, steeped in the green world, were giving way to city comedy with its usurers, bawds, bankrupts, gamesters, and other urban denizens. But happily in Shakespeare's day the process was incomplete; his works occupy a liminal zone where nature and fertility retained their power though a world of modern politics and city life was being born. In the centuries after he wrote, Shakespeare became beloved of both inveterate Londoners like Sam Johnson and back-to-nature Romantics like Keats and Coleridge. His work deconstructs the opposition between civilization and nature, between modern rationality and medieval magic, partly because he lived in an age both exhilarated by nascent modernity and enchanted by lingering magic. The greatest haunter of London he ever created, worldly patron of the great city's taverns and its whores, died babbling of green fields.[31]

Notes

1. Attempts to locate in ancient fertility rituals the origins and structure of literary forms, especially tragedy and comedy, began with classicists—Jane Harrison, Gilbert Murray, Francis Macdonald Cornford—and spread rapidly to the modern literatures (Murray himself made the leap from Orestes to Hamlet) where, thanks to the prestige of theorists like Northrop Frye, the theory enjoyed a considerable vogue long after its complete demise among classicists. For an account of "ritual" approaches in our century, see the introduction to Woodbridge and Berry's *True Rites and Maimed Rites*. For the case against Harrison, Murray, and Cornford, see Pickard-Cambridge, Else, and Dover; for that against Frazer, see Fontenrose, Lang, Lyall, and Douglas, *Purity* 24, 28. Richard Hardin provides a useful overview of this question ("'Ritual'").

2. Difficult, but not impossible: the Lupercal, whose festivities appear in *Julius Caesar,* was a fertility rite, as Shakespeare would have known from Plutarch; see Naomi Liebler's essay "'Thou Bleeding Piece of Earth.'"

3. Cf. also *WT* III.i.1–2; *Luc* 107; *H5* V.ii.36–37; *2H6* I.i.236; *Ant* II.vii.21–23. The reign of Elizabeth is to resemble happiness as imagined by Aristophanes: "Every man shall eat in safety / Under his own vine what he plants, and sing / The merry songs of peace to all his neighbors" (*H8* V.v.34–36).

4. Cf. also *MM* I.iv.41–44; *MND* II.ii.117–18; *1H4* I.iii.34–35; *Ant* II.ii.237–38; *AYL* III.v.100–103.

5. Raymond Williams shows that celebrations of a rural order in Jonson's "To Penshurst" and Carew's "To Saxham" involve a "magical extraction of the curse of labour, . . . by a simple extraction of the existence of labourers. The actual men and women who rear the animals and drive them to the house and kill them and prepare them for meat; who trap the

pheasants and partridges and catch the fish; who plant and manure and prune and harvest the fruit trees . . . are not present; their work is all done for them by a natural order" (32).

6. *Cym* III.iii.60–61, IV.ii.354–55, V.iv.140–43, v.266–67. See also *3H6* II.vi.47–51, V.ii.9–11; *Lr* IV.ii.35–36; *Luc* 1167–69; *2H4* II.iv.330.

7. But not so far afield as to render cultural contact impossible: some evidence suggests that Arctic beliefs and rites influenced Scandinavia and other parts of northern Europe via Iceland; Nordic invasions of England during the early Middle Ages are a possible channel of transmission for a custom such as the tug-of-war representing the seasons (see Kieckhefer 52).

8. In Russia a rag figure was thrown into the river (Calderon 80); at Eisenach a straw man representing Death was burned, a ribbon-decked tree brought in (Witzschel 192ff).

9. For the connection of these forms with fertility magic, see Dean-Smith; Tiddy; Chambers, *English Folk-Play*; Speirs; Helm; Baskervill, "Dramatic Aspects"; Brody; and Cawte, Helm, and Peacock. For dissenting views, see Pettitt, and Kirby's two essays. Julia Dietrich and Harry B. Caldwell provide useful bibliographies on the folk play. For more on this topic, see chapter 4.

10. Elsewhere, Jack Goody and Ian Watt show that oral tradition, by which such rituals are transmitted from generation to generation, subtly modifies what it transmits, tailoring it to present needs; however anciently rooted, the folk festivities were adaptable to early modern needs. However, if in this case the need, occasioned by social upheaval, was primarily for a sense of stability, one would expect a period of fossilizing folk forms, clung to (as Weimann suggests) precisely because of a need for social cohesion.

11. E.g., Margaret Murray 172–85, on witches' rainmaking/fertility rites. Some of Murray's theories on witchcraft as the remnants of pagan religions, wildly speculative, have quite rightly been discredited; but some of her theories receive support from Ginzburg's recent work. The implications for weather magic and crop growth are especially interesting. The assumption that witchcraft is always malevolent has led commentators to interpret rainmaking as mischief causing floods or marine catastrophes; Ginzburg's work opens the possibility of seeing witches' rainmaking as promotion of crop growth. (For a 1489 woodcut in which witches with a snake, cock, and cauldron produce rain, see Bord and Bord 117). For a comparison of early modern witchcraft as reported by inquisitors with sorcery beliefs in modern tribal Africa, see Runeberg 49–59.

12. This tradition has a long history: "A sixth-century code of the Visigoths . . . refers to sorcerers who travel about and get paid by peasants for putting curses on their enemies' crops and animals. The same law code refers to sorcerers who arouse destructive tempests" (Kieckhefer 177).

13. However, "Harbage has drawn attention to the extraordinary 'expansion of the Elizabethan theatrical 'season'; . . . companies were playing six days a week and ten months a year. . . . The great increase in professional playing must have weakened the age-old ties between the occasions of dramatic performance and the annual communal cycle" (Montrose, "Purpose" 68), another example of the weakening sway of the agrarian calendar and its fertility festivals.

14. See *2H4* V.iii.35; *AWW* II.ii.23; *Jn* I.i.235; *1H4* I.ii.113; *Rom* III.i.27; *H5* II.iv.25; *WT* IV.iv.133–34; *TGV* IV.iv.157–59; *Err* IV.i.1; *Rom* I.v.37; *Jn* IV.ii.152, V.i.22–25; *1H6* I.i.154; *H5* IV.i.55; *JC* Act I; *MND* IV.i.138; *Ham* IV.v.48; *MND* title, I.i.167, IV.i.132—and Helena is called a maypole, III.ii.296; *AWW* II.ii.23; *H5* I.ii.120; *H8* V.iv.14; *Rom* I.iii.16; *H5* V.ii.308–9; *1H4* I.i.52; *Wiv* I.i.189; *1H4* II.iv.54; *Wiv* I.i.264; *1H4* I.iii.35; *Tmp* IV.i.134–36; *1H6* I.ii.131; *2H4* II.ii.96; *LLL* V.ii.463; *Shr* Ind.ii.133–34; *Ham* I.i.158–64; *Wiv* III.v.8. François Laroque's *Shakespeare's Festive World* gathers together a good deal of information on these holidays and on the Elizabethan festive calendar; though mention of "French scholarship" on its dust jacket seems to promise something at the cutting edge of theory, the book does not seem to me to improve significantly on older work on the festive calendar, by George Long and others, and Laroque's applications of festive customs to Shakespeare's plays are mostly unconvincing and sometimes bizarre.

15. See *1H4* I.i.50–51, II.iv.101–2, 33, III.ii.145; *2H4* II.iv.356; *1H6* II.v.67.

16. See *LLL* V.ii.294; *Cym* IV.ii.219; *MND* title, V.i.131–32; *TN* III.iv.58, 144—though the *TN* references may not be literal—the title suggests winter; *Rom* I.iii.16, v.37. On greenness in early tragedies, see the essay by Forker.

17. *AYL* II.i.6–7, iii.52, v.8, vii.173; see also III.ii.103, iv.15–16.

18. I.i.97–106; IV.iii.98; V.ii.294, 409, 463; emphasis mine.

19. It is a perfect anagram of "Proserpo"; Abraham Fraunce had derived "Proserpina" from "the Latin word Proserpo, which is to creep forwards, because the roots creep along in the body of the earth" (Sig. G4ᵛ).

20. Many comedies end with feast plans, and in metaphor, love is a feast, valor a feast, education a gourmet treat; need for food unites humankind (see *MM* II.ii.183–84; *AYL* III.iv.55; *Mac* I.iv.54–56; *Shr* I.i.28; *LLL* IV.ii.24–25; *AWW* V.ii.54–55; *MV* III.i.57–60). Hunger images attend the "anticomic theme" that opens comedies (N. Frye, *Natural Perspective* 74): Petrarchan lovers fast out of love sickness, and separated lovers hunger for each other's sight (see *TGV* II.i.23, iv.127–29, vii.15–17; *MND* I.i.222–23; *Err* II.i.87–90; *Shr* IV.i.161, 179, iii.9; cf. in tragedy *Rom* I.ii.55; *Ham* II.ii.147). Against comic feasting, tragedy has eating perversions. In-

stead of wholesome food, tragedy has poison, cannibalism, fire swallowing. Instead of plenty, it offers starvation: Lear pities hungry people and meets an unfed man; *Coriolanus*'s poor suffer famine. Comedies sometimes begin with a hunger image; but tragedy also ends in hunger: "I will eat no meat, I'll not drink"; "No more / The juice of Egypt's grape shall moist this lip" (*Ant* V.ii.48, 281–82; see also *Rom* V.iii.39; *Oth* V.ii.371). Characters eat horrid things: frogs, toads, tadpoles, newts, cow-dung, rats, ditch-dogs, urine, puddle scum (*Lr* III.iv.128–33; *Ant* I.iv.62–69). Tragedy is full of thin men: "spare Cassius" has "a lean and hungry look"; Brutus cannot eat; illness leaves Ligarius "lean" (*JC* I.ii.194–201, ii.113). A thin man in a comedy can herald fullness: Dr. Pinch in *Errors* ("a hungry lean-fac'd villain, / . . . A needy, hollow-eye'd, sharp-looking wretch, / A living dead man" [V.i.238–41]) recalls the mummers' shamanesque doctor who revives the dead (the play's confusions thwart the efforts of this figure of popular drama to perform his revival). Pinch's skeletonesque thinness suggests a figure in a liminal zone between life and death ("a living dead man") with a shaman's ability to revive from death or madness. A similar figure points up hunger's triumph in tragedy: as Romeo resolves on suicide, a near-allegorical figure—Starvation? Death?—appears: "Misery had worn him to the bones. / . . . Famine is in thy cheeks, / Need and oppression starveth in thy eyes" (V.i.40–70).

21. See also *Per* I.ii.73–74; *Tmp* IV.i.24, 105; *AWW* I.i.128–29, iii.24–26; *Ado* II.iii.233; *MND* V.i.399–409.

22. Anthropological sources on cannibalism include Eli Sagan's *Cannibalism: Human Aggression and Cultural Form* and F. J. P. Poole's "Cannibals, Tricksters, and Witches." Jan Kott's *The Eating of the Gods* connects Greek myths of *sparagmos* and cannibalism with Greek tragedy. Maggie Kilgour's *From Communion to Cannibalism* discusses metaphors of incorporation in literature. Joseph Lowenstein applies ideas about cannibalism to Renaissance writing habits.

23. *Mac* I.v.60–61, II.iv.9–11, iii.5–9, III.ii.17, V.v.49–50. See also *Rom* III.ii.65–67; *JC* III.i.97–98; *Ham* I.i.118–20, II.ii.237–38, III.iv.49–51, V.i.60, 229–30; *Oth* V.ii.103–5; *Lr* IV.vi.134–35, V.iii.267–68.

24. E.g., *Rom* V.iii.233–34. Phillipe Ariès discusses representations of a soul on its deathbed in a personal Last Judgment, with the Trinity, Virgin, and heavenly court on one side, Satan and demons on the other (106–10).

25. I disagree with Catherine Belsey's placing of this development in the late seventeenth century; late sixteenth- and early seventeenth-century tragic heroes—not only Shakespeare's but others from Dr. Faustus to the Duchess of Malfi—show many signs of being constructed in just this way.

26. Terry Eagleton's thesis that the rise of the autonomous subject attended the rise of capitalism, with the new interiority as a kind of *laissez*

faire of the soul (*Ideology,* chap. 1) is interesting in light of the fact that the language of sterility belongs both to the tragic hero's destiny and to the early modern discourse of money: "When did friendship take / A breed for barren metal of his friend?" (*MV* I.iii.135).

27. As on all points connected with magic, there is disagreement on this point—some argue that to distinguish religion from magic on grounds of efficacy in manipulating the material world is ideological complicity in the downgrading of magic compared with religion. I take Keith Thomas's point, however, that though he claims "no universality for a distinction between magic and religion, [he does] suggest that in European history, at least, it *is* analytically useful to distinguish those religions which, like medieval Catholicism, credited their rituals with physical efficacy from those which, like eighteenth-century deism, did not" (97); the former, he argues, have more of a magical component, and I agree.

28. *Gamelyn* viii–ix.

29. Frye's "fertility spirit" here is vague; he perhaps means a scapegoat. For more precision on Falstaff's ritual role, see Jeanne Roberts's three works, and also Bryant—although he at times exemplifies the literal-minded Frazerism that has brought "fertility" readings into disrepute ("Frazer records no observance in which laundry, as such, is used as part of a ceremony" [297]).

30. It is precisely François Laroque's slighting issues like this that makes his *Shakespeare's Festive World* so disappointing: in his old-fashioned (and rather gushy) enthusiasm for "the joyful domain of youthful celebrations" (64), Laroque, ignoring the political mystification of rural festivity, goes to the opposite extreme from those who refuse to see in rural festivity anything *but* political mystification. I have tried to steer a middle course between these two extremes.

31. Theobald's inspired emendation of *H5* II.iii.16 makes as much sense as anyone has made of the Folio's "a table of green fields"; what seems significant to me, whether Falstaff babbles or not, is that green fields appear in conjunction with this great Londoner's death.

4

Black and White and Red All Over: The Sonnet Mistress amongst the Ndembu

I must advance the colors of my love.
—*The Merry Wives of Windsor*

Among terminally ill figures of speech, the cliché of rosy cheeks, ruby lips, and snow-white skin may be counted downright deceased. In Renaissance love poetry, roses in the cheeks, lips like cherries, skin like ivory, lilies, or snow were stiffly conventional: freshness of complexion prompted no freshness of metaphor. The mistress's red-and-white face was relentlessly emblazoned, and "red and white" became shorthand for female beauty: "With lilies white / And roses bright / Doth strive thy colour fair" (Wyatt 65); "Thou art not fair for all thy red and white" (Campion 264). In Jonson's *Masque of Beauty,* the first "element of beauty" carries a red and a white rose. Male lovers waxed "pale with anguish, red with fear" (Daniel 20). Not for lack of inventiveness did writers thus stylize love and beauty: the red-and-white scheme is part of a semiotic code visible through long periods of history, worldwide, encoding seasonal fertility magic and personal rites of passage.

In his classic 1967 "Color Classification in Ndembu Ritual," Victor Turner cited African tribal cultures that link red and white with sexuality and with fertility rites, human and agrarian. In many ritual contexts, "red is associated with masculinity . . . and white with femininity; [but in] at least an equal number of ritual occasions, . . . white represent[s] masculinity and red femininity. . . . Red and white may be situationally specified to represent the opposition of the sexes" (61). Each color, "multivocal" in meaning, has a "fan" of referents; but "when they are paired in ritual, white may stand for one alleged polarity of life, such as masculinity or vegetable food, while red may represent its opposite, such as femininity or meat" (89). Black often completes a triad, but "sex-linking of white and red in the Ndembu theory of procreation leads inevitably to a consideration of these colors as a pair, as a binary system. For black is very often the neglected member of the triad, because of its symbolic ties with death, sterility, and witchcraft" (89). Red and white stand for life fluids—blood, milk, semen; black represents "body leavings, body dirt, and the fluids of putrefaction" (80). But all three are necessary in rites; at Ndembu puberty rites, initiates are taught the mystery of red and white rivers linked with male and female sexuality (the white, bisexual, representing semen and milk), a black river linked with death (65). Surveying anthropological studies, Turner finds the tricolor code in many African, Australian, and North American rites, such as the Bemba girls' puberty rites, where pottery emblems are painted white, black, and red, and black mud and red dye applied to whitewashed novices (67).

Many others have noted the same three colors in a number of cultures. Among the Australian Yuin, male initiates are smeared with red ocher, female with white clay; Tierra del Fuegans have red-and-white painted initiators; Dyaks of Borneo isolate a white-clothed pubescent girl in a white cabin, feeding her white foods and red blood (Eliade, *Rites* 44). Of symbolism in a Ugandan cult, Abrahams thinks white means ash and red means fire, linking the binary oppositions coolness and heat ("Spirit" 127). The catalogue of a 1982 Smithsonian exhibition of ritual objects includes red-white-and-black masks—a masked Hindu statue of Jagannatha, a Korean Pongsan mask, a Zairean initiation mask, and a New Guinean harvest festival mask (*Celebration* 19, 100f, 122, 230a).

The resemblance between a pubescent Dyak and Daniel's Delia or Sidney's Stella may elude us; but Renaissance beauties do come in red and white, and the color scheme of Renaissance love poetry is red, white, and black.

Stella in Sidney's *Astrophil and Stella* has a forehead of alabaster, lips of "red Porphir" with pearl teeth, cheeks of "marble mixt red and white"; her lips, "blushing red," are like roses and rubies, her teeth like pearls; her beauty is that of lilies and roses (9, 43, 100, tenth song). Cupid uses her face as a heraldic device, "roses gules are borne in silver field" (13)—in heraldic terms, "gules" is red, "silver" white. But her eyes are black: sonnet 7 explores the paradox of black beauty. Images of blackness permeate the cycle: the lover courts with "troops of saddest words" marching under a "black banner"; thought and night have "one livery, / Both sadly black, both blackly darkened" (55, 96). In Surrey's sonnets, the male lover's cheeks vary "from deadly pale to flaming red"; the lady wears a black cornet (15, 22). Davison's lady has black eyes, cherry lips, "snow-white breast" (3).

Deliberately destabilizing the conventional heterosexuality of the sonnet-mistress scenario, Shakespeare immortalizes the red-and-white beauty of a young man, who has roses in his cheeks (see 67, 98, 99). Blackness in this sonnet cycle belongs to the female mistress: "In the old age, black was not counted fair, / . . . But now is black beauty's successive heir" (127). Her blackness mocks the red-and-white convention: "Coral is far more red than her lips' red; / If snow be white, why then her breasts are dun; / If hairs be wires, black wires grow on her head. / I have seen roses damask'd, red and white, / But no such roses see I in her cheeks," but Shakespeare also calls on black's link with night and death: mention of "swart-complexion'd night" forecasts his "woman color'd ill"; "black night . . . , / Death's second self" prepares us for self-loathing in his relationship with her (130, 28, 144, 73). Early thoughts of the youth making "black night beauteous" prepare for the lover torn between red-and-white man and black woman; color imagery prepares for his rejection of the woman "as black as hell" (28, 147).

The tricolor imagery saturates Shakespeare's early poems. *Venus and Adonis* and *Lucrece* treat sexual antagonism, female lusting after unwilling male in one, male after unwilling female in the other; both end in death. A poem on Venus, goddess of love and beauty, and Adonis, center of an ancient fertility cult, cries out for "fertility" colors; and red and white abound. As in the sonnets, Shakespeare flouts convention by attaching the red-and-white semiotics of beauty to a male; but unlike the sonnets, the female is also here emblazoned with red and white. Adonis, "more white and red than doves or roses," is asked for short and long kisses, "making [his lips] red and pale with fresh variety" (10, 21). Venus is "red and

hot as coals of glowing fire," Adonis red for shame, white for anger; "being red, she loves him best; and being white, / Her best is
better'd" (76–78). We see "the fighting conflict of her hue, / How
white and red each other did destroy" (345–46). Red and white
become sinister in the boar, "frothy mouth, bepainted all with red,
/ Like milk and blood" (891–92). As in crucifixion poems (see below), red and white attend the fertility figure's sacrifice, blood staining Adonis's "lily white" (1052–53). The purple-and-white violet,
resembling Adonis's "pale cheeks and the blood / Which . . . upon
their whiteness stood" (1168–69) hints rebirth against black's seeming ascendancy—"black chaos comes again" (1020).

Lucrece's beauty is "unmatched red and white"; fear makes her
"red as roses . . . then white as lawn" (11, 25). As rites and games
offer ritualized combats between white and red forces (see below),
in "beauty" poetry red and white often war within a complexion,
as in the "fighting conflict of [Venus's] hue" (*Ven* 345); Lucrece's
complexion, in a heraldic conceit, is scene of a "silent war of lilies
and of roses" (52–77). Underlying this trope, I think, is a structure
of magical thinking wherein ritual combat between the sexes is paradoxically fructifying—it is what Victor Turner, as we saw in chapter 3, called the "fruitful contest of the sexes." Military metaphors
in amorous contexts, such as the siege of a woman's heart that I
explored in chapter 1, are a residuum of such magical thinking.
When Lucrece asks Tarquin "under what color [i.e., pretext] he
commits this ill," he takes it in its military sense, as "colors" under which troops rally: "the color in thy face, / That even for anger makes the lily pale, / And the red rose blush" (476–79).

As we saw in chapter 1, Lucrece sheds red and black blood: "Some
of her blood still pure and red remain'd, / And some look'd black,
and that false Tarquin stain'd" (1742–43); this makes more sense in
light of Turner's findings that when appearing in the ritual triad, black
represents pollution and has specifically sexual connections.

In all Shakespeare's major nondramatic works, red and white
have a fan of meanings centering on sexuality, and black represents
death and lust. The sonnets' black-haired lady inspires lust; Tarquin's lust stains blood black; Adonis resists Venus's lust as a thing
of blackness ("black-fac'd night, desire's foul nurse" [773]).[1]

Though not so prominent as in the poems, the ritual colors surface in Shakespeare's plays as well, especially in contexts of male/
female love and conflict, such as *Othello*'s love/death scene (see Boose,

"Othello's 'Chrysolite'" 428).[2] In the tragicomedic *Winter's Tale,* black precedes red/white. Doomed Mamillius admires black-browed beauty; Leontes thinks his own deeds black (II.i.8–11, III.ii.172). The play's comedic half begins with a song about lovers tumbling in the hay: "When daffodils begin to peer, / . . . the red blood reigns in the winter's pale" (IV.iii.1–4), an image heralding an insistence on red faces: "Let's be red with mirth"; "something / That makes her blood look on 't"; "I'll blush you thanks" (IV.iv.54, 60–61, 67, 159–60, 586). In ritual fashion, red-and-white imagery is linked with love, sexuality, the return of spring, resurrection: the last white face turning red ("who was most marble there chang'd color" [V.ii.91]) prefigures the resurrection of the "marble" Hermione.

Taken in pairs, our colors are central in Shakespeare: in passages where he names two colors together, he twice mentions green/yellow, green/gold, red/gold, and red/blue; three times white/purple and black/red; but he mentions black/white fourteen times, and red/white or red/pale forty times; all other combinations occur only once each. Philip Bock notes that red, white, and black are the most prominent colors in Shakespeare (and in Donne).

The color scheme links beauty with language and writing: black ink on white paper memorializes red-and-white beauty. The beauty of Shakespeare's red-and-white youth will be seen in "black lines"—a "miracle" that "in black ink my love may still shine bright" (63, 65). When he wins Stella's heart, Astrophil vows to paint joy "in black and white"; when she is sick, her paleness is white paper on which to write with "beauty's reddest ink" (70, 102).

Love poetry's color conventions seem to have influenced real-life fashions. White complexions were so much in vogue that ladies wore masks to prevent sunburn or tan. In Sidney's sonnet 22, Stella is the only woman who dares go out with bare face—the sun, in love with her, kisses her gently. Cosmetics created a chalk-white face with bright red cheeks, a pierrot effect: the Elizabethan beauty could have stepped out of the pages of *Astrophil and Stella.*

Love Poetry and Fertility Rituals

But colors may, after all, only be colors. Is there any other evidence in Renaissance love poetry of an orientation toward fertility magic? Let us suppose for the moment that the sonnet mistress is a version of Mother Earth, the lover (usually a first-person speaker) of the male fertility principle—the Sky God, the Green Man, King of the May, Spring. Suppose that sublimated in the imagery are classic ritual actions—the hero combating wintry sterility to fertilize the earth; the hero wounded or slain by sterility; the hero reviving (like plants in spring) and feasting to celebrate victory. Far-fetched, perhaps. But much love poetry fits this pattern remarkably.

Images of geographic immensity paint the sonnet mistress more as earth goddess than ordinary girlfriend: "My love doth in her selfe containe / All this worlds riches that may farre be found" (Spenser, *Amoretti* 15). Donne's lady is "both the Indias of spice and mine" (p. 11). The mistress's physical charms are often the fruits of mines—sapphires, rubies, gold—she has all the depth of earth.

Love is a changing season, at a Janus-guarded threshold:

> New yeare forth looking out of Janus gate,
>> Doth seeme to promise hope of new delight:
>> And bidding th'old Adieu, his passed date
>> Bids all old thoughts to die in dumpish spright.
> And calling forth out of sad Winters night,
>> Fresh love, that long hath slept in cheerlesse bower:
>> Wils him awake . . .
> For lusty spring now in his timely howre,
>> Is ready to come forth him to receive:
>> And warnes the Earth with divers colord flowre,
>> To decke hir self, and her faire mantle weave.
> Then you faire flowre, in whom fresh youth doth raine,
>> Prepare your selfe new love to entertaine.
>
>   (*Amoretti* 4)

Like a forest king, Spenser's persona, married on the summer solstice, exults "The woods shall to me answer and my Eccho ring" (*Epithalamion* 18, 271). Shakespeare's persona urges a reluctant Green Man to become a fertility spirit: he is "herald to the gaudy spring"; poetry will keep him "green" (1, 63).

Struggle against sterility may be the sonnet cycle's main action. "Fruitless," a key word, is almost a pun in a ritual context. Wyatt's persona woos "in fruitless hope"; Spenser's undergoes "fruitless" labor before attaining "her paps like early fruit in May" (33, 76) and laboring to beget "fruitfull progeny" (*Epithalamion* 403). Hunger, one of sterility's forces, plagues the lover: "For hunger still I starve" (Wyatt p. 214).[3] Hunger is abroad in the land because winter has come: the mistress's cruel disdain. The sonneteer hopes by sighs' heat to thaw the frigid mistress: "Ice . . . hath congealed her heart" (Daniel 49).[4] Winter images abound: "Boreas' reign, / Where hoary frosts the fruits do bite" (Surrey 19).[5] Hunger and winter unite in the frequent word *starve*, meaning to die of hunger or to freeze: "In fruitless hope (alas) [I] starve" (Wyatt p. 245).

Summer's battle with Winter appears, new king versus old: "summer took in hand the winter to assail / with force of might and virtue great, his stormy blasts to quail, / And . . . clothed fair the earth about with green" (Surrey 23). If the dark lady is a version of Earth, welcoming (like mythic Gaia or Rhea) a succession of lovers, each a Spring supplanting his predecessor Winter, Shakespeare's fresh touch is to view the battle through Winter's eyes: "beated and chopped with tanned antiquity," his verse "barren" and "decayed," the speaker is supplanted by a youth who "o'ergreens" him in the affections of his Earth Goddess, whose coloring suggests good rich loam (62, 76, 79, 112).

Lovers receive desperate wounds: "In deep wide wound the deadly stroke doth turn" (Wyatt p. 83); "Beauty made this mortal wound" (Surrey 14). Like Christ's spear wound, Petrarchan wounds often have a sacred aura: "Miraculous love's wounding." Ritual wounding is part of initiation rites—scarification, circumcision— and the "thigh" wound of fertility figure Adonis is likely a euphemism. The icy Petrarchan mistress, like Cybele, castrates devotees.

The lover expiring from a mistress's frowns became a figure of fun in his own day; but the motif has the contours of ritual. Astrophil cries, "my death-wound is already got, / Dear killer" (48).[6] Sacrificial diction abounds: "Heart sacrificed unto the fairest" (Daniel 8); it will "do your heart such good / To see me bathe in blood" (Wyatt p. 54).[7] Shakespeare envisions his young man's blood drained (62). Immolation is common: "I to her . . . / Will builde an altar to appease her ire: / And on the same my hart will sacrifise, / Burning in flames" (*Amoretti* 22); "Whilst I burn, she sings. . . . These smokes that from affliction rise, / Serve as an incense to a cruel dame: / A sacrifice thrice-grateful to her eyes" (Daniel 47). Visions of lover as whole burnt offering join winter images in "freezing fires" oxymorons: "Of cold I me bewail, / And raked am in burning fire" (Wyatt p. 26). Contemporaries denounced love poets' blasphemy, thinking that talk of altars and sacrifice parodied Christianity, making earthly love its rival. But most poems' generic ritual language is as near the cult of Adonis or Tammuz as the cult of Jesus.

Dismemberment images recall the fertilizing scattered pieces of slain gods like Osiris in *sparagmos* rites: "Piecemeal in pieces . . . I be torn" (Wyatt p. 4); we recall the seemingly regenerative dismemberments in *Titus Andronicus* (see chapter 3). Images of hearts torn out are not in this period dead metaphors like "my heart goes out to you," but remain vivid: "My heart was torn out of his place" (Wyatt p. 202). Wyatt's lady holds the excised heart in her hand, and mention of her small white fingers makes the image gruesome. She mutilates his heart, voodoo-like: "[She] wished each stitch, as she did sit and sew, / Had pricked mine heart. . . . As she thought this is his heart indeed, / She pricked hard" (pp. 65, 32).

Amoretti's "piteous passion of his dying smart" (48) is not the only passage to suggest both amorous emotion and Christ's Passion. The lover, as literary fertility god, ideally did not suffer and die pointlessly: his passion was supposed to restore greenness, thaw the winter under which the Earth Goddess lay frozen. Spenser places Petrarchan sufferings in the Christian context of sacrificial atonement, death restoring spiritual greenness. The first of his *Foure Hymns* examines Petrarchan love, the second, heavenly love: parallel passages describe the lover's "sharp sorrowes" and Jesus' "sharpe assayes" in very similar terms. In the first, poet/lover complains of Cupid's mistreating

> me thy vassall, whose yet *bleeding hart,*
> With thousand wounds thou *mangled* hast so sore
> That whole remaines scarse any little part,
> Yet to augment the anguish of my smart,
> Thou hast enfrosen her disdainefull brest,
> That no one drop of *pitie* there doth rest.
> (142–47; emphasis mine)

The second deals with the crucifixion:

> Then let thy flinty *hart* that feeles no paine,
> Empierced by with *pitifull* remorse,

> And let thy bowels *bleede* in every vaine,
> At sight of his most sacred heavenly corse,
> So torne and *mangled* with malicious forse.
> (246–50; emphasis mine)

One mangled fertility god parallels another. The Earth Goddess's "disdainefull brest" needs to thaw, come to life again through the poet-god's mangling and death, just as the sinner's "flinty hart" must experience remorse, achieve spiritual regeneration as a result of Christ's sacrificial atonement.

And the slain god is reborn: one lover whose "heart was torn out" hopes that "her help to health [will] me restore" (Wyatt pp. 202–23).[8] A "leach that would apply / fit medicines" tries to revive a wounded lover (*Amoretti* 50), recalling mummers' doctors, vestigial shamans who revive the dead. Spenser's gustatory sonnets 76 and 77 present celebratory feasting, the mistress's chest a table spread with delicacies on which the lover's thoughts feed—appropriate if the mistress is fruitful earth in harvest, though rather an eyebrow raiser as a plain simile. The two mouth-watering apples in both poems are her breasts: the lover's longing to feed on them casts him as her baby as well as her impregnator, an arresting image of rebirth, of a man fathering himself.

As other clichés seem ritual remnants—bleeding heart, love's wounds, burning lover, freezing mistress—so the tears-as-rain image suggests Father Sky fertilizing Mother Earth with the semen of rain. Some references are vague—"O tears, no tears, but rain" (Sidney 100)—but many retain a startling ritual force. The lover's tears penetrate the mistress's dry ground to bring forth fruit: "My tears . . . wet her barren heart, / . . . So in her stony heart / My plaints at length shall grave, . . . / May bring to me some fruit" (Wyatt pp. 171–72). The verb "grave" for rain's penetration of earth suggests rebirth: paradoxically, the grave gives birth, as in myth the slain god's burial suggests earth insemination. The conceit's sexual suggestiveness recalls sympathetic magic between human and vegetable fertility that caused (or rationalized) May Day gown-greening. "Making their tomb the womb" (Shakespeare 86) is a common paradox (see Parfitt), which ritual can decode like a riddle: grave is womb because woman is earth. The sexual slang "die" reeks of ritual: the dying/reviving god lurks behind Donne's "we kill ourselves to propagate our kind." Hints of vaginal penetration are frequent: Surrey's "Love . . . doth me drive into a deep dark hell" (22) may allude to Boccaccio's tale of phallic devil and vaginal hell (the variant "dark, deep well," though less allusive, is no less suggestive), as may Shakespeare's "I guess one angel in another's Hell" (144). Astrophil wants to "pierce" Stella's soul; his "piercing phrases" "invade her ears" (recall the frequent image of ear penetration as vaginal penetration, discussed in chapter 1); sex is a "fray, where blows both wound and heal, / The pretty death" (57, 58, 61, 79).

Sidney also calls sex "breakfast of love." Petrarchan gastronomy has a ritual aura: hunger accords with sterility; a sexual thaw is celebrated by feasting. Once she gives in, Stella is begged not to be niggardly with the viands: "Nymph, which keeps the cherry tree, / . . . Do not alas / From coming near those cherries banish me" (82). Spenser's lady, his soul's "long lacked foode" (*Amoretti* 1), he sees with "hungry eyes" (35),[9] subsisting on a low-calorie diet of the odd cheerful glance ("More sweet than Nectar or Ambrosiall meat, / Seemed every bit [of glance] . . . I did eat," 39). Yet he feasts on apples at last, as Astrophil feasts on cherries.

Several ladies relent in spring: "As when, rough winter spent, / The pleasant spring straight draweth in ure, / So after raging storms of care, / Joyful at length may be my fare" (Surrey 13); when Stella relents, "Gone is the winter of my misery: / My spring appears" (69). In sonnet 67, *Amoretti*'s lady is won; the next sonnet, set on Easter, compares Christ's love with hers.

How conscious were sonneteers of these underlying contours of fertility magic? The ubiquity and consistency of seasonal references is the clearest sign of consciously manipulated magical material. And fertility deities are often conjured: Sky God/Earth Mother,[10] or the dying/reviving god.[11] Such allusions mingle with Christian allusion: did authors suspect that Mary, god-impregnated mortal, was a version of Mother Earth like Leda or Maia or see slain Jesus as a mythic cousin of Adonis? Spenser, at least, knew of the syncretism of Ficino, Pico, and Bruno, who saw all religions as at base the same. Syncretic theorizing has gone on by fits and starts from the first century A.D., when scoffers saw Christianity as a theft from Greek myth (Allen chap. 1), to students of myth in our own time. For Renaissance love poets to dabble in comparative religion is not strange. We should not count out the possibility of conscious manipulation of semiotic systems related to ancient weather magic. However, as I have argued throughout this study, such invisible mental structures often give shape to Renaissance works and seem as capable of welling up from the unconscious as belonging to a conscious artistic program. They also to a certain extent arrived prepackaged in the form of literary conventions.

Courtly love stories of medieval romance were probably one channel by which fertility magic flowed from medieval popular rites to Renaissance sonnet. Weston's theory of the ritual affinities of romance's Grail legend, though old now, is persuasive in its main outlines; the love stories, too, look ritualesque. Their adultery recalls Mother Earth's seasonal fickleness: the lady turns from wintry old king (Arthur, Mark) to embrace a new lover, Spring (Lancelot, Tristan), as the woman in the mummers' Wooing Ceremony rejects one suitor in favor of another, often an old man in favor of a young.

Love Poetry and Eye Magic

The color triad comprises a visual encoding of beauty. Hints of oral delivery or song attend many Renaissance lyrics—Donne's poems were entitled *Songs and Sonnets,* and many lyrics of the period were set to music by Campion, Byrd, and others. However, representation of the sonnet mistress was aggressively visual. She is typically a silent woman. Sidney's Stella is one of the few sonnet mistresses occasionally allowed to say something, and even then it is not much; in one song she asks who is complaining under her window and tells him to "begone" and "come no more, lest I get anger"; in another she is limited to repeating the same line nine times, once at the end of each sexual proposition by the sonnet speaker; her lines mostly consist of repeating the same word four times, and the word thus reiterated thirty-six times is a conversation-dampening "no."[12] Petrarch's love poems make a fetish of silence; in their hushed, mournful sufferings, silence grows almost palpable. With the sonnet mistress, the visual overwhelms the aural. Tellingly, Sidney connects Stella's beauty with ink on paper (102). The sonnet mistress was a creation well suited to the early days of print culture: fixed and frozen upon a page, represented by a visual color code, her beauty appealed not to the ear but to the eye.

Marshall McLuhan's theory that with the coming of print, an eye-oriented culture replaced an ear-oriented culture helps make sense of the obsessively visual orientation of Renaissance love poetry. Their red-white-and-black semiotics is a nonverbal, possibly pre-verbal communicative system appealing mainly to eye rather than ear; this system that had for centuries existed in both oral and writing cultures took an instant hold in the early world of print culture where verbal communication was visual. The Renaissance obsession with the visual appears in the passionate attention to eyeballs and sight in texts from *Macbeth* and *Lear* to Milton's hymn to light; in the obsession with light and with minute visual detail in paintings of the Dutch masters; in the development in painting of perspective, chiaroscuro, foreshortening, and other illusionistic visual devices; in Kepler's stunning breakthrough in the science of optics. According to the statistics of the word frequency list in Marvin Spevack's concordance, "eyes" is among the dozen or so most frequent nouns in the Shakespeare canon. (I say "dozen or so" out of a superstitious dread of reporting that it is the thirteenth most frequent.) Renaissance love poetry, with its silent woman and its intensely visual representation of beauty by color-coding, found a hospitable environment in the age that gave Europeans, in McLuhan's phrase, "an eye for an ear."

The pervasive eye imagery of Renaissance love poetry often has a magical aura. The early age of print culture, obsessed with eyes and the visual, was ripe for evil-eye beliefs. Indeed, John M. Roberts shows that evil-eye beliefs are commonest in cultures that possess writing—magical beliefs about vision, we might infer, thrive in the visual orientation of a writing culture. (Small scripts in writing or print are commonly worn as amulets against the evil eye.)

As noted in chapter 1, the evil eye was often attributed to envy, and chapter 5 will discuss evil-eye beliefs as socially specialized to situations of family conflict. Eye magic was also intimately connected with love. Bacon, in "Of Envy," recognizes a connection between envy and love: using the word *fascinate,* the technical term for casting of the evil eye, he writes, "None of the affections . . . have been noted to fascinate, or bewitch, but love and envy. They both have vehement wishes; they frame themselves readily into imaginations, and suggestions; and they come easily into the eye; especially upon the presence of the objects which are the points that conduce to fascination. . . . Scripture calleth envy an evil eye" (27). The sexuality always latent in the idea of evil-eye bewitchment is suggested by the fact that the Latin *fascinum,* "bewitchment," came to refer to the penis (OED); the phallus was often represented on amulets against the evil eye. That we still apply magical terms such as *fascinate, charm,* and *bewitch* to the act of inspiring amorous devotion hints at magical belief submerged in our conceptions of sexual attraction.

The evil eye could cause illness and death, or it could freeze into immobility by a kind of hypnotism, irresistibly attracting even while terrifying; one definition of *to fascinate* in the OED is "to deprive of the power of escape or resistance, as serpents are said to do through the terror produced by their look." The two effects are related by the fact that illness caused by the evil eye was typically not abrupt and dramatic but prolonged and wasting—headache, loss of appetite, languishing in bed—an immobility similar to that caused by hypnotic fascination. I think Petrarchist poetry presents love in terms of such eye mesmerism and such wasting. This is apt for a visually oriented age; McLuhan defines hypnosis as "the filling of attention by one sense only" and argues that the Renaissance was hypnotized by one sense—sight (17).

Eyes are among the most prominent images of Renaissance love poetry. Petrarch uses the phrase *begli occhi* (occasionally *belli occhi*), meaning "beautiful eyes," sixty-six times in his love lyrics, along with *occhi chiari* (eyes full of light), *occhi sereni* (serene, clear eyes), *occhi languidi* (languid eyes), *occhi lucenti* (luminous eyes) and many more—the prominence of the eye in Petrarch is overwhelming, and other love poets followed suit. Shakespeare uses *eye* and its derivatives 101 times in 154 sonnets, and the frequency in Sidney's sonnets is comparable—Sidney devotes much energy to interpreting Stella's "eyes-speech" (198). A good deal of lingering magic animates the operation of this semiotic system.

In a specialized form of the amorous-combat trope, the mistress's eyes shoot deadly rays: in Laura's "gaze," the "rays of love are so hot that they kill me" (Petrarch 37). The male lover's eyes are vulnerable orifices, like the mouths, vaginas, and ears I discussed in chapter 1: he often takes a mortal wound by the rays his mistress shoots directly through his eyes, as archers at the Battle of Agincourt killed knights by shooting arrows through the eyeholes of their armor. "Thorough mine eye the stroke from hers did slide, / Directly down unto my heart," Wyatt's persona gasps (17); an eye may "slay, / And strike more deep than weapon long" (Wyatt 31).[13] Astrophil demands, "Stella, whence doth these new assaults arise, / A conquer'd yielding ransackt heart to win, / Whereto long since, through my long-battered eyes, / Whole armies of thy beauties entered in?" (36). The mistress's deadly eye rays are seen as weapons: "Blessed eyes, from whom I received that blow against which no helm or shield availed"; "As soon as he has released the string, a good archer discerns from afar which shot . . . will strike the intended target; thus you, Lady, felt the shot from your eyes pass straight into my inward parts" (Petrarch 95, 87); "One day as I unwarily did gaze / On those fair eyes, . . . in her glauncing sight, / Legions of loves with little wings did fly, / Darting their deadly arrowes, fiery bright, / At every rash beholder" (*Amoretti* 16).[14]

Weapons are usually configured masculine, and this semiotics of female eye-darted weapons is part of the reversal of "normal" gender dominance so common in Renaissance love poetry—as the mistress is dominant, her male lover groveling, so in the imagery she pierces him with the phallic weaponry of eye arrows, through his vaginally dilated vulnerable eye. To Patricia Parker's scheme connecting sexual with rhetorical dilation, we might add the dilation of the pupil of the eye, in a vulnerable sonnet speaker whose cycles of verse often grew to such enormously dilated length. As Parker shows, dilation was usually encoded female—another instance of the feminized posture of the male sonnet speaker, to which we can add that *his* eyes respond to the aggressive ray penetrations with that always "feminine" fluid, tears.[15]

The image of eye weaponry is more normatively applied to a male when we hear that Coriolanus "is able to pierce a corslet [body armor] with his eye" (*Cor* V.iv.20), or when Queen Isabella describes Henry V's warlike gaze; his aggressive gaze modulates into a gaze of "love"—the sort of love that goes with political domination:

> We are now glad to behold your eyes;
> Your eyes, which hitherto have borne in them
> Against the French, that met them in their bent,

> The fatal balls of murdering basilisks:
> The venom of such looks, we fairly hope,
> Have lost their quality, and that this day
> Shall change all griefs and quarrels into love.

Her reference to "fatal balls" suggests that "basilisks" means the cannons of that name, which harks back to Henry's earlier image of the eye as cannon: "When the blast of war blows in our ears, / ... Then lend the eye a terrible aspect; / Let it pry through the portage [i.e., porthole] of the head / Like the brass cannon" (*H5* V.ii.14–20, III.i.511)—the proper response to an invaded ear is an aggressive, weaponlike eye. But Isabella's reference to "venom" suggests that she has in mind also the fabulous basilisk whose sight poisons the beholder (see below).

The mistress's deadly, wounding eye was as much a stock feature of Petrarchist love poetry as her red and white complexion, and both are highly visual. Shakespeare's sonnet mistress's eyes "dart their injuries," and the speaker implores, "since I am near slain, / Kill me outright with looks, and rid my pain" (139). Phoebe denies that "eyes can wound," or that her "eyes are murderers"; she assures Silvius that "mine eyes, / Which I have darted at thee, hurt thee not." Silvius disagrees; and Orlando says his own heart has been "wounded ... with the eyes of a lady" (*AYL* III.v.10–19, V.ii.25–27).[16]

The deadly ray's effect is very similar to that of the classic evil eye—it causes the victim to waste away in emaciation. (As Rosalind reminds us in *As You Like It,* the "lean cheek" was a lover's hallmark.) Petrarch's persona speaks of consuming himself (237); Wyatt's persona reports that love "left my face both pale and wan" (Wyatt 17); "Lo, see, mine eyes swell with continual tears; / The body still away sleepless it wears; / My food nothing my fainting strength repairs, / Nor doth my limbs sustain" (Wyatt 21). As Tobin Siebers says, "The most common symptoms of fascination are identical to those of amorous infatuation. Throughout love poetry, the natural effect of the lover's consuming gaze is the ebbing away of energy and vitality" (67).

Against an evil eye, magical protection is needed; typically, such protection turned back the magical gaze on itself, often by amulets with a reflecting capacity, either mirrors or images of the eye (see

Elworthy). Petrarch's persona repels the mistress's lethal glance with his own eyes, significantly associating this self-protective measure with a myth connected with evil-eye beliefs—Medusa's petrifying gaze: "Wherever she angrily turns her eyes, who hopes to deprive my life of light, I show her mine full of such true humility that she necessarily draws back all her anger. And if that were not so, I would not go to see her otherwise than to see the face of Medusa, which made people become marble" (179).[17]

And we might well think of the poetry itself as protection against the mistress's baleful eye. A sonnet sequence's series of pictures of the lady, including the itemized blazon, turned a mirror on her, reflecting her gaze back on herself as did evil-eye amulets. "The dread of being pictured," Elworthy noted, "is found all over the world"; in the late nineteenth century, he "often heard Somerset people object to having their likenesses taken on the ground that it is unlucky, and that so and so was 'a-tookt,' but soon afterwards she was 'took bad and died'" (86). As I mentioned in chapter 1, praise was often thought to attract the evil eye, and sonnet sequences involve extended, lavish praise—what better way to turn back the mistress's scorching gaze upon herself? The proud sonnet mistress, incapable of loving another (or so her sonneteer often charges), is a prime example of narcissism, and "Narcissus was thought to have *fascinated* himself, and hence his untimely fate, for it has always been held that too much praise or admiration of any person or object, . . . even by himself, would bring upon him the curse of fascination" (Elworthy 12). Of Narcissus, object of the unrequited love of the Boeotian youths, Siebers writes, "The accusation that the beloved has fallen in love with himself represents the lover's spiteful attempt to place him beyond the reach of other potential lovers, and to reciprocate his rejection by finding fault with his character" (73; one thinks of the accusation that Shakespeare's young man is "contracted to [his] own bright eyes" [1]). Similarly, the sonneteer protects himself against the mistress's wounding eye by directing her eye rays back upon herself. His malicious praise is revenge.

The gaze of the mistress is replete with "masculine" dominance and weaponry while that of her male lover is "feminine" in its openness and vulnerability, but the aggressive gaze of a mistress can ricochet off a sonnet and rebound upon her. At one point Spenser locates narcissism in the male lover rather than the mistress: "My hungry eyes, through greedy covetize / Still to behold the object of their paine, / . . . In their amazement like Narcissus vaine, / Whose eyes him starv'd" (*Amoretti* 35), a hint that the charge of narcissism against the mistress may be a projection of the lover's own character. Some of this reflexivity, reversal, and general confusion is built into magical eye beliefs themselves, where it is often difficult to know whether it is being looked upon or looking which is perilous. In evil-eye beliefs, it is the eye looking at the victim that kills. In the case of Medusa, it is the victim looking at Medusa that kills.[18] In the case of the fabulous basilisk or cockatrice, it is the basilisk looking at the victim while the victim is looking at the basilisk that kills, and this complex reciprocal gaze seems closest to the situation in love poetry of the Petrarchan tradition.

This fabled animal fascinator crops up often in Shakespeare, and its lore illuminates eye magic. Henry VI says to Suffolk, "Look not upon me, for thine eyes are wounding: / Yet do not go away: come, basilisk, / And kill the innocent gazer with thy sight" (*2H6* III.ii.51–53)—here it is both gazing upon and being gazed upon by the basilisk that wound and kill. Suffolk wishes on his enemies that "their chiefest prospect [shall be] murdering basilisks" (III.ii.324); if their prospect, or view, is to be basilisks, the suggestion is that looking as well as being looked upon will murder them. Richard Duke of Gloucester plans to "slay more gazers than the basilisk" (*3H6* III.ii.187)—his danger is specifically to *gazers*.[19] Like the evil eye, the basilisk gaze can operate without its possessor's will: Camillo tells Polixenes that he, though well, is making others ill; Polixenes answers: "Make me not sighted like the basilisk: / I have look'd on thousands, who have sped the better / By my regard, but kill'd none so" (I.ii.388–90); the basilisk-sighted, well himself though making others sick, is a sort of magical Typhoid Mary. When Sir Toby laughs at the challenges issued to Sir Andrew and Viola, his jest turns partly on the ambiguity of whether cockatrices kill by looking or being looked upon: "This will so fright them both that they will kill one another by the look, like cockatrices" (*TN* III.iv.213–15)—since both are more frightened than frightening, they will perhaps die by looking upon rather than kill by looking.[20]

Witches were often credited with the evil eye, and this power made them seem basilisk-like; as Sir George Mackenzie wrote in

1674: "Witches may kill by their looks, which looks being full of venomous spirits, may infect the person upon whom they look. . . . I know there are [those] who think all kinds of fascination by the eyes, either an effect of fancy in the person affected, or else think it is a mere illusion of the Devil . . . ; whereas others contend that by the received opinion of all historians men have been found to be injured by the looks of witches: and why may not witches poison this way as well as the Basilisk doth?" (102).

With the basilisk, a weaponlike gaze penetrates the orifices of another's eyes—the basilisk is in a masculine, penetrative position, the hapless gazer feminine and penetrated.[21] This is exactly like the sonnet mistress, who (in a gender reversal) pierces her lover, and it is fitting that the basilisk confuses gender: it was said to be born from a cock's egg. It was also a confusion of kinds, part serpent, part bird; like all such boundary crossers, it gathers power and danger from its hybridity. And it was a body invader; in Pliny it darts down the throat of a sleeping crocodile and kills it by gnawing through its stomach (8.24.35). In chapter 1 I discussed Shakespearean poisonings through the ear; the basilisk's gaze is a poisoning through the eye: Phillip Stubbes wrote in 1583 of cockatrices or basilicocks, "which slay . . . men with the poison of their sight" (Sig. Iᵛ).[22] This threatening body penetration goes along with others I spoke of in chapter 1 as an anxiety of the palisaded Elizabethan age. That horrific body penetrator the black plague was often seen to operate like the lethal glance of the evil eye or the basilisk: "It was . . . believed in England at the time of the Black Death, that even a glance from the sick man's distorted eyes was sufficient to give the infection to those on whom it fell" (Elworthy 34), and Shakespeare connects this evil-eye/plague belief with falling in love: "Write 'Lord have mercy on us' on those three; / They are infected; in their hearts it lies; / They have the plague, and caught it of your eyes" (*LLL* V.ii.420–22). That magical emblem of falling in love, Puck's love juice, is an invasion through the eyes—Puck drops it in lovers' eyes with the words "upon thy eyes I throw / All the power this charm doth owe" (*MND* II.ii.78–79).

At its least threatening, Petrarchan love involved an ocular mutuality, the benign interchange of eye-beams Donne imagines: "our eye-beams twisted, and did thread / Our eyes upon one double string" ("The Ecstasy"); as Prospero reports of Ferdinand and Miranda, "At the first sight, / They have changed eyes" (*Tmp* I.ii.441). Confronting his love's "powrefull eies," Spenser posits two possible gazes, one benign and one malign: "Fair eyes, . . . / When ye mildly looke with lovely hew, / Then is my soule with life and love inspired: / But when ye lowre, or looke on me askew, / Then doe I die, as one with lightning fired" (*Amoretti* 9, 7). Sidney too posits a dual gaze: after Stella has relented (a moment when Astrophil tellingly cries, "Envy, put out thine eyes" [69]), Astrophil sees the destructive "rays" of her eyes changing to "beams" (76). The darkness of Stella's eyes, a saving grace, makes them "beamy"; if they were lighter in hue, "they sunlike [would] more dazzle than delight" (7). Petrarch associates Laura's destructive "rays" (*raggi*) with the sun but sometimes endows her with a milder gaze. That rays are usually of sunlight while beams suggest moonbeams fits the sun/male, moon/female schema common in European semiotic systems, and it is interesting in light of sonnets' unstable gender configurations that the sonnet mistress's magical gaze contains, in potential, both rays and beams.

Exchange of eyebeams could be mutual and benign. But at its most threatening, Petrarchan love was more akin to the wasting away of spirit and flesh symptomatic of evil-eye assaults. Many of the deep cultural anxieties I have already discussed, the sort that call up reserves of superstition even in rational thinkers, surface in Petrarchan love: fear of saturnalian topsy-turviness (the woman on top), fear of pollution through mixing of kinds ("male" and "female" behavior confused), fear of body invasion through vulnerable orifices (rays shooting through the eyes), fear of the plague, fear that a neighbor-enemy (the mistress) might be able to kill from afar by magical missiles projected from her eyes. The sonnet mistress, whose gaze was magical, a "mighty charm" (*Amoretti* 47), was that most feared of mythical monsters, the cockatrice:[23]

> Fair cruell, why are ye so fierce and cruell?
> Is it because your eyes have powre to kill? . . .
> . . . Bend your force against your enemies.
> Let them feele th'utmost of your cruelties,
> And kill with looks, as cockatrices doo:

But him that at your footstoole humbled lies,
With mercifull regard, give mercy too.

(Amoretti 49)

The hypnotic quality of Petrarch's love poetry reproduces stylistically the condition of wasting away through the evil eye. Perhaps it is no coincidence that this poet, able to reproduce so vividly the sensation of having been malevolently "overlooked," hailed from Italy, a kind of world capital of evil-eye superstitions and amulet manufacture right through the nineteenth century, if Elworthy's account is accurate. Petrarch's ritualistic repetition of words is mesmeric—*Laura, l'aura, lauro, dolce, begli occhi*—as is the sonorousness of vowels and liquid consonants, the languishing tone, the falling accents of unvarying feminine endings, the silence so often spoken of, broken only by the soft murmurs of birds or breezes, the infinitely quiet trickle of tears. The spare, emblematic images—snow, roses, rivers—create a minimalist landscape with little to distract attention from the mistress's mesmeric gaze. The reader becomes hypnotized by the narcotic repetition of moods and images and sighings, and the sheer length of it all—years and decades pass, and Laura remains remote, and her lover worships and weeps. Laura is a kind of belle dame sans merci, and the poems to her chronicle a hopeless, wasting illness to which one is perpetually a languishing, lobotomized slave. Like a wasting victim of the evil eye, the lover of Laura is in thrall to a witch. The atmosphere is similar to that of Spenser's Bower of Bliss (on whose gate is inscribed the story of the enchantress Medea), where among roses and soft sounds young Verdant languishes in the power of the witch Acrasia who, staring at him with "false eyes," sucks his soul out through his eyes; he has been blinded by a "horrible enchantment" (*Faerie Queene* 2.12.73, 2.12.80.9). Such poetry of amorous bewitchment has a distinctive mesmeric air, perfectly captured in the saccharine hypnotism of Elizabethan madrigals.

The charmed immobility of the victim of fascination suggests sexual impotence, and the enchanted male of Renaissance love mesmerism, in thrall to a woman, seems to embody anxiety about impotence. "Since phallic gestures like the *fica* were used to ward off the evil eye, and since males often touched their genitals upon seeing a priest or other individual thought to have the evil eye, then it is not unreasonable to assume that the evil eye threatened to make men impotent" (Dundes 164). Johann Weyer's sixteenth-century compilation of witchcraft beliefs, *De Praestigiis Daemonum,* advises that "the bridegroom should urinate through the wedding ring to be free from the evil eye and from sexual impotence" (393).

For all of Petrarch's influence on them, none of the English sonneteers recreates perfectly Petrarch's mesmeric, bewitched atmosphere—Wyatt comes closest to Petrarch's narcotic effect of endlessly repetitious suffering, but his edge of spite and revenge is often so sharp as to break the spell; one feels that Wyatt's self-protective magic would be all too effective against the evil eye of nearly any mistress. Sidney fosters too boisterous a sense of good health—perhaps it is the horsiness that breaks the spell in *Astrophil and Stella.* Shakespeare's sonnets lack Petrarch's sense of hopeless thraldom, though the first half of his sequence approaches nearer than most other sequences to Petrarch's hushed stillness. *Amoretti* at times achieves the drugged, wasting effect of the truly bewitched love experience (under the mistress's gaze, "My soule was ravisht quite, as in a traunce" [39]), though Spenser achieves it even more strongly in parts of *The Faerie Queene*—among the most interesting is the gender reversal that finds Amoret in such a languishing, love-drugged state in book 3.

Though it seldom achieved a truly Petrarchan zombie air, however, Renaissance love mesmerism was a common literary state of mind, which I think was residually magical, owing much to evil-eye and allied beliefs that held some eyes to be supernaturally powerful and others dangerously vulnerable. The way that the public gaze constitutes a ruler is a whole other topic; but that it had links with love's eye magic appears when the Prince of Navarre falls in love and becomes (according to Boyet) all eyes: "All senses to that sense did make their repair"; then "all eyes saw his eyes enchanted with gazes" (II.i.238–40). In an infinite regress of gazes, the prince, object of everyone's gaze, finds his own gaze captivated by a woman's gaze.

In its seasonal symbolism, its semiotics of fertility, sterility, and human sacrifice, its language of sacrificial dismemberment and other sacramental vocabulary, and finally in its aura of bewitchment and magical eyesight beliefs, Renaissance love poetry seems to encode magical thinking. The obsessive, hypnotically visual quality of this love poetry is hospitable to semiotics perceptible only to sight, especially the sign system of color. And the other magical associations of the love poetry make predictable the fact that its colors are the magical triad red, white, and black.

Basic Color Terms

In 1967, Turner wrote that black, white, and red are the only colors "for which the Ndembu possess primary terms. Terms for other colors are either derivatives from these . . . or consist of descriptive and metaphorical phrases. . . . Colors that we would distinguish from white, red, and black are by Ndembu linguistically identified with them. Blue cloth . . . is described as 'black' cloth, and yellow or orange objects are lumped together as 'red' ("Color Classification" 74, 60).

Two years later, Brent Berlin and Paul Kay's *Basic Color Terms* radically extended this perception; surveying England, Lebanon, Bulgaria, Spain, China, the Americas, Israel, Hungary, Nigeria, Indonesia, Japan, Korea, the Philippines, India, Thailand, Mexico, Vietnam—languages from Arabic to Swahili to Amerindian tongues—they found that all languages have terms for white and black; a language with three terms has a term for red; four, green or yellow; five, green and yellow; six, blue; seven, brown; eight or more purple, pink, orange, grey (2–3). Positing "a fixed sequence of evolutionary changes through which a language must pass, Berlin and Kay concluded that for a language to gain . . . color terms it must do so in the order specified" (14–15). They found a rough correlation "between general cultural complexity . . . and complexity of color vocabulary" (16); three-term languages were extant in tribal societies (25). They reported with chagrin discovering (after completing field research) similar studies from the nineteenth century— one a survey of missionaries and colonial officials on sixteen American, twenty-five African, fifteen Asian, three Australian, and two European languages. The earlier studies occasionally disagree with Berlin and Kay on yellow, green, or blue; but all agree that languages' basic colors are white, black, and red.

Besides this prevalence in modern languages, historical records and artifacts also reveal the color triad in ancient civilizations. In the Ziggurat of Ur, 2300–2180 B.C., a red story atop a black story rose from a white court (Fabri 62). (A blue shrine surmounts the Ziggurat; throughout this chapter, note that when a fourth color occurs with the triad in a ritual context, it is usually green or blue. Since these are the colors of plants, sky, and water, one might posit a complementary relationship: red, white, and black as colors of humanity, green and blue as colors of nature.) In the Song of Solomon, the beloved is "white and ruddy"; his locks are "black as a raven" (5:10–14). The Bible specializes in colored horse visions. Zechariah sees a man on a red horse; behind are "red horses, speckled, and white" (1:8); in another vision are chariots with horses red, black, white, and grisled (6:1–3); here, as often, a fourth item of vague color joins the triad, perhaps to complete the square valued in many symbolic schemes or suggest the seasons. Revelation 6 has a vision of horses white, red, black, and "pale"—another vague fourth. In the Hindu *Upanishads,* seventh or eighth century B.C., "Whatever they thought looked red, they knew was the color of fire. Whatever they thought looked white, they knew was the color of water. Whatever they thought looked black, they knew was the color of earth. Whatever they thought was altogether unknown, they knew was some combination of these three" (Birren 16)—another amorphous fourth. Turner thinks that the color scheme is pre–Indo-European; archeologists have found it in Stone Age burials; in Paleolithic cave art the color triad "is always prominent" ("Color Classification" 86–87).

Human races have long been conceptualized by the ritual triad: visually scrutinized, the Negro races may be dark brown, American Indians light brown, Caucasians peach, but as in "basic color terms" they are called black, red, and white. The use of "black" for "non-European races, little darker than many Europeans" (OED) goes back to Old English; Middle English dubbed Saracens, for example, "black." "White" for Caucasians and "red" for New World Indians are first recorded in the seventeenth century; I suspect they are older. The only other color term applied to a race, "yellow," a late-developing color term in Berlin and Kay's scheme, is not recorded before the midnineteenth century. Golding's 1587 translation of de Mornay categorizes the races by the tricolor-plus-vague-fourth-color scheme: "some folks white, some black, some red, and some tawny" (OED).

Why are these colors basic to many cultures? One would think that in tribal life attuned to nature, green might have attracted more attention. Berlin and Kay offer no explanation. Marshall Sahlins calls on optics: "Red is to the human eye the most salient of color experiences. At normal light levels, red stands out in relation to all other hues by virtue of a reciprocal heightening effect between saturation and brightness. . . . Red not only 'stands out,' it stands closer: a direct spatial effect known as 'chromatic aberration,' which brings red surfaces subjectively nearer to the observer than objects of other hue situated at an equal distance" (168). Sahlins posits "not a simple order of three equivalent terms but a mediated opposition, i.e., of black and white by red, . . . because of [red's] ability to maintain saturation over a wide range of brightness values. . . . Red is especially like black in opposition to white, but occasionally like white in opposition to black" (176), a theory close to Turner's: "In abstraction from social and ritual contexts, Ndembu think of white and black as the supreme antitheses in their scheme of reality. Yet . . . in rite after rite white and red appear in conjunction and black is seldom directly expressed. In abstraction from actual situations, red seems to share the qualities of both white and black; but in action contexts red is regularly paired with white" ("Color Classification" 74).

Turner explains the triad through bodily fluids and leavings—blood, milk, semen, excretia: "the human physiological component is seldom absent whenever reliable native exegesis is available" (88). As the Renaissance based a "humors" psychology on red, white, and black bodily fluids (red blood, white phlegm and yellow-white choler, black bile),[24] so Turner bases a psychology on bodily essences: the colors stand for "basic human experiences of the body . . . gratification of libido, hunger, aggressive and excretory drives, . . . fear, anxiety"—in short, "primordial psychobiological experience" (89–90). This is rather odd, in an anthropologist noted for his elegant analysis and "thick description" of one specific culture, the Ndembu, in all its particularity: it seems dangerously universalistic, ahistorical, almost essentialist in its assumptions about culture. Turner argues that "since the experiences the three colors represent are common to all mankind, we do not have to invoke diffusion to explain their wide distribution" (90), but I think we should invoke diffusion as a much more reasonable explanation than "primordial psychobiological experience," Jungian notions of collective memory, or other pieces of mysticism. There are a few instances of cultural items having spread nearly all over the world by diffusion from a single origin—the bow and arrow is just one example—and it is at least possible that the magical color triad is another. At any rate, it is possible to trace it through various cultures that had contact with each other, and I propose to do that here, moving back from English Renaissance literature into the early Middle Ages, along routes that persistently cross paths with rites of sexual maturity and fertility. In following such routes rather than tracing medieval-Renaissance color theory (like Dolce on color symbolism or Agrippa's theory relating colors to planets—black to Saturn, red to Mars), I take what Turner dubs the "operational" approach to cultural symbols, observing how a culture uses symbols, rather than the "exegetical method" of accepting explanations of its "informants" (*Forest* 50–51). Others—Moshe Barasch for example—have examined what the Renaissance *says* about its color symbolism; my quarry is what it *does* with such symbolism.

Mircea Eliade's work on initiation supports Turner's observation that "among societies that make ritual use of all three colors, the critical situation in which these appear together is initiation" ("Color Classification" 88). (Other rites of passage make some use—the black-and-white of bride/groom/priest, white of baptism, black of funerals, at least in Europe.) Initiation rites are deeply, though not solely, concerned with sexual maturity: that Renaissance literary use of the triad occurs mainly in love poetry suggests that such poetry, exquisitely artificial and elegant, has roots in tribal rites of sexual maturity—that its delicate sighs and lovely languishings are somehow linked with circumcisions, animal masks, and red ochre body smearing.

I will take time to trace the colors historically to document, for one case of magical thinking, a transmission route: a rather large historical gap separates the English who performed initiation and fertility rites with bloodlettings and clay daubings from the English who penned Petrarchan love ditties. Approaches to literature through ritual and magic are often dismissed precisely because they fail to confront the problem of transmission: how did archaic materials find their way into civilized cultures' sophisticated literature? Throughout this study I have tried to anchor Renaissance magical thinking in medieval (and earlier) magical belief; I will do that more extensively here than I have earlier, in the hope that tracing lines of transmission will be persuasive enough to generalize to other modes of magical thinking and help exorcize the skepticism of readers resistant to magical interpretations.

Ritual Colors: The Literary Heritage

As to direct literary influence, the colors are in Petrarch: Laura's eyebrows are ebony, her complexion like "scarlet roses . . . amid the snow," (157, 131). Chaucer avoids red-and-white imagery for bumptious adulterous fabliau wives, reserving it for that sexual coming of age, the courtship and marriage of a virgin. In the Knight's Tale, Emelye, first seen on May Day, wears a garland of red and white flowers; Arcite competes for her love under Mars's red banner, Palamon under Venus's white banner; Emelye worships Diana, whose oratory is of red coral and white alabaster. (Chaucerian red and white attach to a spectrum of courtship relations from willing nubility to determined virginity.) In the Second Nun's Tale, an angel gives newlyweds crowns of lilies and roses, "snow white and rose reed."[25] Black enters love poetry when the lady is a widow: in *Troilus and Criseyde* an April rite is observed, and red-and-white flowers are blossoming, but Criseyde wears a black widow's habit (158, 170), suggesting black's associations with death and with mature sexuality.[26]

Medieval courtly and popular love poetry employs red-and-white imagery, sometimes black. The lady may be a flower "with colors fresh ennewed, white and red" (Robbins, *Secular Lyrics* 186); she has strawberry lips, cheeks of red roses, a neck "as white as whale's bone" (126-27). Five poems in Robbins's *Secular Lyrics of the Fourteenth and Fifteenth Centuries* praise red-and-white complexions. Two parodies skew the colors, one praising yellow skin, grey lips, red eyebrows: the parody depends on readers knowing the right colors (220–23). One poem, previewing Sidney and Shakespeare, defends black beauty:

> Black is a color that is good—
> So say I and many mo;
> Black is my hat, black is my hood,

Black is all that [be]longest thereto.
Black will do as good a need
As the white at board and bed.
(30)

The poet charmingly adds that black doesn't show the dirt.

Such poems might simply be influenced by Chaucer or Petrarch; but these secular lyrics exist side by side in the fourteenth century with religious lyrics in a similar style, also using red-and-white (sometimes black) imagery, and these form a continuum with thirteenth-century lyrics, predating Petrarch and Chaucer. They center on a prominent fertility myth, the springtime sacrificial death of Jesus. In one crucifixion poem, "White was his naked breast and red of blood his side" (C. Brown, *Fourteenth Century* 1); in another, "thy body was . . . wan and red" (C. Brown, *Thirteenth Century* 140). Jesus' mother cries white and red tears (C. Brown, *Fifteenth Century* 175). Because Jesus shed "his blood that was so red," communion bread is white outside and red inside (*Fifteenth* 180–81), a seeming reference to transubstantiation, a mystery hinted in a riddle-like carol on the body's inseparability from blood: "This bread giveth eternal life / . . . It seemeth white, yet it is red" (R. L. Greene 194). In "A Rose Hath Borne a Lily White" (R. L. Greene 116–18), the rose is Mary, the lily Jesus. The allegorical red rose, goal of the quest in *The Romance of the Rose,* is at times the virginal lady, at times her sex organ, ripe to be plucked. Courtly love's veneration of woman was entwined with veneration of the Virgin; that both traditions involve the sexual colors red and white is more intelligible if both are linked with fertility myths, including the death of Jesus.

The triad is central to Arthurian romance. Lady Bercilak in *Gawain and the Green Knight* has a red-and-white face and wears "bright red"; Morgan le Faye, with "black brows," is "swathed all in white" (1206, 952–61). The *Morte D'Arthur* riots in white knights, black knights, red knights, white palfreys, red cities; the poem features eighteen red shields, fourteen white, twenty-seven black, eleven red and white, three black and white, three silver, and two black and silver (heraldic "silver" means white). The only other colors are in five green shields and one gold: red, white, and black heavily predominate. (Green is a distant but important fourth in

Malory. Like the Gawain poet, he has a green knight.) Lance and Grail may descend from male/female symbols in fertility rites, and Malory's Grail quest colors fit: the quest begins in a white abbey, a monk offering to the world's best knight a white shield with red cross; black knights of unconfessed sin face white knights of virginity. In Chrétien de Troyes, Enide with face like a lily, "its delicate pallor . . . suffused with a fresh crimson," is "the damsel with the white raiment"; later she wears scarlet ("Erec et Enide," *Arthurian Romances* 6–18). The hero of Chrétien's "Cligés," echoing biblical horse visions, enters a tournament with four horses, black, white, "fallow red," and reddish (sorrel) (146).

Red/white imagery occurs in sexual contexts in classical literature (and sometimes black/white: moly, which helps Odysseus approach Circe, has a white flower and a black root). "Throughout the *Metamorphoses* Ovid draws special attention to the colors red and white," notes Catherine Rhorer. "White is associated with innocence and chastity, with the frigid absence of sexual feeling, . . . [red with] shame that afflicts the innocent whose eyes have just been opened to erotic reality, and with . . . the violence of rape" (79). Sexually oriented red/white occurs in the tales of Pygmalion, Narcissus, Hermaphroditus, and Atlanta; *Pyramus and Thisbe* is framed with a mulberry tree, whose ripening berries turn from white to red to black. (So *that's* why Shakespeare got a mulberry tree rather than an oak.) In *Amores,* beauty is white suffused with red.

Ritual Colors in Popular Seasonal Observances

A direct link with fertility rites occurs in popular forms still alive in Shakespeare's time, and vestigial even in ours: mumming, morris dancing, and May games. That these are survivals of ancient pagan fertility rituals is accepted by all major authorities—Tiddy, Cornford, Helm, Chambers, Brody. As Helm writes (1981), even modern actors "are performing what is left of an ancient ritual. Although the original purpose of what they are doing may be unknown to them, they are nevertheless basically enacting the life-cycle drama, so that fertility of crops, animals, and people can be ensured after the dead period of Winter" (6). Puritan opponents of

May games, mumming, and morris dancing cited their pagan origins (Hewitt 10–23; Alford, *Sword Dance* 214).

Some nine hundred versions of the mummers' plays are known (Alford, *Sword Dance* 50); associated with Christmas and the solstice, sometimes Eastertide, they are of two types. In the Hero Combat, St. George (or another hero) fights the Turkish Knight (or other foes); the dead are revived by a doctor—a remnant of resurrection rites encouraging post-solstice renewal of the year, with the doctor a vestigial shaman. In the Wooing Ceremony a young woman's wooer, rejected in favor of a fool, enlists in the army—its enactment on Plough Monday and its actors being called plowboys link it with ritual plow plays across Europe and unite human fertility (the mate selection) with that of newly planted crops.

Shakespeare often has a love triangle of a woman and two men, one a fool figure—Costard (*LLL*), Thurio (*TGV*), Gremio (*Shr*), Touchstone (*AYL*), Aguecheek (*TN*), Cloten (*Cym*), Roderigo (*Oth*), perhaps even Stephano and Caliban (*Tmp*): do such lover-fools owe anything to the Wooing Ceremony? Though his fools (unlike their mumming analogues) usually lose as suitors, the light-hearted irresponsible sexiness of fools like Touchstone or Launcelot Gobbo suggests the ancient fool of fertility rites (see Welsford, *Fool*; chap. 5 of E. Berry). Sonnet cycles with their rival suitors (cf. Shakespeare's woman and two men) are all about wooing; like the Wooing Ceremony they may link human and crop fertility.

The mummers' doctor usually wears a black costume and often whites his face. Most other figures black their faces or raddle (redden) them with ochre. In the accounts Helm collected, a nineteenth-century mumming troupe wore black, red, or white beards; fools had crimson tattered robes or one red and one white sleeve; a modern Cheshire group wears white shirts and pants, red ribbons and handkerchiefs, "in the style of Morris dancers" (39–42). The Turkish Knight is often a black figure, sometimes named the Black Prince. The recruiting sergeant in a 1913 Wooing Ceremony wore a red uniform, the doctor a white waistcoat and white beard (11).[27] Britain's first colony, Newfoundland, visited in 1497 and claimed in 1583, preserves in modern Christmas mumming the ritual triad: faces are often black, sometimes white or red; veils or masks are black or white. Some dress as ghosts, faces whited; recalling the Wooing Ceremony; bride/groom pairs are common, in black with red-white-and-blue decorations (Widdowson and Halpert 149–61). Mummers enact the Hero Combat in towns like the happily named St. George's.

Turning from mumming to morris dances, one type, the bean dance, is agricultural (Long 106). The sword dance is a ritual killing, "a concerted act by a group against an individual" (Helm 21). In the Hero Combat "one champion must die for the benefit of his community"; in the sword dance one "dies" in what resembles a scapegoating or other fertility-bestowing sacrifice. The victim may be resurrected: in Ampleforth, "the Clown stretches the dead man's legs apart, draws his sword down the body from throat to groin, and the dead man springs to life" (Helm 17, 26). "Meaningless" to Helm, this resembles a Ndembu funeral rite: "a line is drawn in white clay from the middle of the chest down to the navel, [promoting] . . . reincarnation" (Turner, "Color Classification" 66).

Morris dancing, like other fertility rites, occurs at the winter solstice (sword dancing) and in spring (other kinds of morris), especially from May Day on. Dancers typically wear red sashes across white costumes and black their faces (Ickis 85; Palmer and Lloyd 21). In her survey of European sword dances, Alford uses historical records and modern observation of costumes: given the influences, corruptions, discontinuations and revivals affecting the dance over many centuries, the color triad's persistence is remarkable. Alford very occasionally notes, say, blue stockings, but only rarely finds colors other than red, white, and black in the costumes. Across Europe, this color scheme typifies an all-purpose holiday costume: "White shirts and trousers with a coloured waist-sash and béret is the gala dress for men across an immense area of Mediterranean coast, in France as far north as the Dauphiné Alps, in Spain also." Ancient forerunners of sword dancers, the Roman Salian dancers, wore red tunics (*Sword Dance* 26–208).

"Morris" comes from "Moorish," but Chambers thinks "faces were not blackened because the dancers represented Moors, but . . . dancers were thought to represent Moors, because their faces were blackened" (*Elizabethan Stage* 214–16). Blackface, or faces reddened or whited, in mumming, the morris, and May games (and in the Roman Saturnalia [Palmer and Lloyd 94]) is often dismissed as a reveler's device to prevent recognition by friends; but the frequency of face painting in tribal fertility and life-crisis rites seems to link it with ritual. Recognition prevention is itself more than holiday fun: evil spirits must not see one's face as they must not know one's name. Painted faces can also cast rite participants as gods or spirits; and they help participants and spectators shift gears from everyday reality and well-known faces into ritual's spiritual realm. Sidney's sonnet cycle opens and closes with a personified "Woe" in blackface, like a mummers' presenter: "fit words to paint the blackest face of woe" (1); "black horrors of the silent night, / Paint woe's black face" (98).

Can blackface stem from humanity's earliest cultural efforts? Miners' faces become blackened; and mining, a godlike earth penetration redolent of underworld journeys, has always had its rites and superstitions (see Fish); miners often have a mysterious, sinister air in folk tales, which tend to be suspicious of iron. Another ancient technology, writing, blackens adepts, and the Renaissance knew those black-faced technicians, printer's devils. Agriculture, especially plowing, can blacken. Black, one of culture's colors (as against nature's green and blue), suggests dabbling in technology, with its ancient points of contact with the "black arts." The black face may be culture's badge.

The maypole, that phallic symbol, is related to the sacred tree linked in myth and ritual with dying male fertility figures (see above). Its stripes are usually red and white. A very old red and white maypole, beside a London church, "was so tall that the church became known as St. Andrew Undershaft" (Palmer and Lloyd 17). The May Queen wears white; May celebrants often black their faces (Helm 55). In an eighteenth-century May game, white-clothed girls danced with black-clothed, blackfaced chimney sweeps; Burland likens this to Godiva processions, a black hag with sooty imps expelled in favor of Godiva—a winter/summer combat (53). In a modern May festival at the Cornish village Padstow, a very old rite is enacted around a maypole: participants in white with red sashes dance about a black hobbyhorse in a tarred skirt (formerly a stallion's skin) and "ancient, . . . voodoolike mask" of black, red, and white; he mimes dying and reviving (Marian Green 12). "Perhaps the colours echo old Celtic symbols," Green muses; "black for death, red for life, and white for the sun."

As Helm notes, it is not always easy to distinguish among mummers, morris dancers, plowboys, May celebrants. Often the same actors take part in several. One sword dance troupe wears the words "God speed the plough" (Alford, *Sword Dance* 40). And the same figures keep cropping up: the May King and Queen are often called Robin Hood and Maid Marian, who are also morris characters; Robin may replace St. George in the Hero Combat mumming. Father Christmas often appears, as does Beelzebub, who carries a club and a frying pan, "symbols of the male and female principles," Helm thinks (30).[28] Very widespread is the hobbyhorse, a dying/reviving figure in the Padstow May game, the doctor's mount in some mummings, a dancer in the morris, a drawer of plows in the Plough Monday Wooing Ceremony (Helm 19). Most rites have a fool, a betty or "female" figure, and a sweeper dispersing ill luck with a broom (May Day chimney sweeps, the mummers' Besom Betty or Broom Betty and Little Devil Doubt, prototype of Puck who ends *A Midsummer Night's Dream* sweeping with his broom).

The broom is an old emblem of domesticity and domesticated sexuality. Jumping over a broom into a house was a form of common-law marriage, jumping over a broom out of a house a common-law divorce. Here the broom represents both sexuality (Samuel Menefee thinks the broom jump was once a magical chastity test) and household protection: it forms a threshold, barring strangers, magically turning stranger into husband as he jumps. The broom also sweeps away evil spirits. The chimney sweeps in May games hint at a link between chimneys and fertility rites. In folk belief, a sweep invited to a wedding would bring the couple luck (E. Porter 26). A sweep's thrusting a broom into a chimney, that household orifice, is sexually suggestive; the broom's connection with housework links it with the female principle, but as chimney scourer it seems to represent the male principle. It was the perfect Janus-faced emblem for the hermaphroditic, cross-dressing "betty" who wielded it in popular rites.

Elsewhere in Europe, folk observances are also clearly linked with fertility rites, and the red-white-and-black scheme again is prominent. In a Basque festival, two troupes called Les Rouges and Les Noirs dance around a glass of red wine. In a Rumanian ceremony filmed in 1939, a procession led by a figure in white with a red cummerbund met an antagonist in red rags; in another filmed rite, a figure in an animal mask, carrying a wooden phallus and a crook with a red binding, performed a kind of sword dance (Helm 47–48).

Folk remnants of fertility rites clustered around the winter solstice and vernal equinox. A few more rites at each season use the triad. In Scottish "first footing," good luck comes to a house whose first guest January 1 is a dark man with a lump of coal; he is given red wine and white bread. In the Lincolnshire Plough Monday hood game, red-clothed villagers scramble for red hoods; a clown wears blackface (Palmer and Lloyd 118–19). St. George's Day honors a mythic hero, often the mummers' hero, whose dragon fight is a winter/summer combat. His red-crossed white shield or tabard became England's flag; Spenser's Red Crosse Knight, modeled on St. George, uses the emblem. Red-and-white Valentine's Day, observed since the third century A.D., is a thinly Christianized fertility feast, the Roman mid-February Feast of Lupercal (Spicer 36).

The triad's strong seasonal ties with Christian spring holidays appear in church vestments. To the standard black cassock and white surplice, a priest adds red vestments at Pentecost. The first colored vestments—tenth century—were white with touches of red and black (Addis and Arnold 832). Monastic habits tended toward the triad: a medieval satire notes a worldly friar's large wardrobe of habits, in "russet, black, and white" (Robbins, *Historical Poems* 167).

The Colors of Christmas

As one of the two most important ritual seasons of the year, the winter-solstice/Christmas season was noted for its saturnalian topsy-turviness and was marked, predictably, by the ritual color triad. Our modern Santa with white-fur-trimmed red tunic and pants, white beard, red cheeks, black belt and boots has an older ritual ancestry than his commercial ambience might suggest. Santa is an American invention, exported to England and grafted onto Father Christmas after the publication of Clement Clarke Moore's 1823 "A Visit from St. Nicholas." Moore's Santa, mummerlike, has a kind of animal costume ("all in fur from his head to his foot"); the earliest of Thomas Nast's illustrations, which popularized Santa, show a small figure in skins. The face seems adapted from Petrarchism: "His cheeks were like roses, his nose like a cherry! . . . The beard of his chin was as white as the snow."

Moore, an ordained minister, might have been influenced in color symbolism by vestments' red, white, and black. (The colors appear in the poem, though Moore does not specify the color of Santa's clothes: their vivid red-and-whiteness in the later popular tradition is a tribute to the pervasiveness of the triad in the popular mind.) And Moore was a New Yorker, as was Washington Irving, whose *Knickerbocker History of New York* had in 1809 pictured St. Nicholas flying in a wagon, a probable influence on Moore; *The Children's Friend,* which two years before Moore's poem had published colored engravings of Santa, also emanated from New York (Barnett 26–27). This matters because it was to New Amsterdam that the seventeenth-century Dutch had imported their St. Nicholas, whose celebrations became a feature of New York life (Palmer and Lloyd 108). From the Middle Ages to the present, Dutch St. Nicholas has had a white horse, red robe, and servant Black Peter. Elsewhere in Europe too the Christmas gift giver has a black companion, face blacked or wearing a devil mask—Ruprecht, Krampus, Hans Trapp, Klaubauf, Rumpanz (O. M. Spencer 247–51), recalling the blackface so common in popular rites. Moore did not create Santa so much as he "crystalized popular notions of the visit of the gift bringer" (Barnett 27); he took over ritual colors, probably from the Dutch, whose St. Nicholas, like his, comes down the chimney, and added touches of white and black: "His clothes were all tarnished with ashes and soot."

Given the familiarity of the color triad, soot is a predictable symbol, its blackness completing a triad with fire's red and ash's white. (Fire and smoke have been crucial to fertility rites from Hebrew and Greek burnt sacrifices through the smoke directed over cornfields at English May celebrations [Bord and Bord 124–29].) Santa's chimney descent supports the theory identifying Santa with the Norse god Thor, with his long white beard. Thor's color was red, his element fire, into which he descended through chimneys; white goats drew his chariot. This Yule god battled giants of ice and snow; he lived in the north among icebergs (Weiser 113; Odin, who rode a white horse or drove reindeer, may also have contributed to Santa). Moore's St. Nick is a fire spirit at least in his pipe smoking. Professor of Hebrew and Oriental languages at a theological college (Pimlott 115), Moore had the education to know of mythic antecedents of the Christmas figure he assembled. In 1872, O. M.

Spencer placed Santa and Thor in the context of seasonal fertility rites: Thor battling the ice giant is spring's conflict with winter. The ritual colors attending St. Nicholas are apt for a figure rooted deeply in such seasonal rites.

Among other red-and-white Christmas images, candy canes are striped like maypoles; a common northern European decoration is a little white church on white cotton, red lights showing through its windows (Ickis 139). A medieval Twelfth Night poem links Jesus with red and white blossoms (C. Brown, *Thirteenth Century* 41). Red apples have belonged to Christmas since medieval times (Palmer and Lloyd 112–13): the guild cycle paradise play had a fir tree hung with red apples, probable origin of the Christmas tree. In Germany, white wafers were added to signify the Host, eventually cut into bells, stars, angels: these first Christmas tree ornaments were thus red and white (D. J. Foley 41). Ben Jonson uses the triad for winter: in *The Masque of Beauty* January has a white mantle, north wind Boreas a russet-and-white mantle; another wind is in blackface.

Christmas has always been a time of fertility. Recalling Druid tree magic, we still have our erect Christmas tree, the male principle, and encircling wreath, the female. The wreath's position on the door symbolizes the sexual receptiveness, as it were, of the house. Adapting Mary Douglas's terms, the house is an image of the body; and at Christmas its normally sealed-up chastity is unlocked, orifices thrown open: a spirit comes down the chimney; strangers (from carolers to charity solicitors) are welcomed through doors, as in the original myth three foreign kings were welcomed into Jesus' country. Category boundaries break down. Bringing in a tree breaks the outdoor/indoor boundary. The human/animal boundary was transgressed with the baby born in a manger; at midnight on Christmas Eve, animals talk. Mary deconstructs the boundary between virgin and mother, Jesus the boundary between human and divine. At Christmas gender lines are crossed in the transvestism of popular rites; saturnalian rites rupture class boundaries. Boundary violation, dangerous and powerful, provides for our culture's central ritual season an image of openness, readable in body/society symbolism as sexual openness, appropriate to the human fertility which our culture, for all its technological sophistication, still needs. Christmas is aptly colored red, white, and black.

The Mystery Cycles

Mummers' plays were at Christmas, those belonging to morris dances and May games in spring—the two seasons during which most fertility rites were enacted. As if adhering to this tradition, mystery plays were enacted at Whitsuntide or Pentecost,[29] or a few days later at Corpus Christi, still a favorite time, in present-day Europe, for the sword dance and its plays (Alford, *Sword Dance* 201). Christmas was play season throughout the Renaissance, a time for court masques and "Christmas comedies" (*LLL* V.ii.463).

Since mystery cycles took place during the same seasons as ritual-based folk plays and enacted a divine sacrifice/resurrection, it is natural to find the color triad in the guild plays. The Paradise Tree had red apples. According to the costume expenditure records examined by M. L. Spencer, Jesus had a white leather coat, one of the Marys a "crimson gown" (217), angels white mantels, Annas a scarlet hood, Caiphas a red tabard furred with white. Devils wore black. Six souls often appeared, three saved souls in white, three damned souls in black with blacked faces; in one play Herod was in blackface. Jesus' tormentors wore black or red and black. Judas had red hair and a red beard. Knights in two cycles wore white armor (217–46). Colors other than white, red, and black rarely occur; the fourth color is almost always green or blue. The Chester Cycle stages Zechariah's vision, with horses red, white, black, and "of divers hue" (Lumiansky 60–117).

The Ritual Triad in Games

The color triad emerges, too, in some ancient, ritually oriented games: chess, checkers, playing cards, and archery. Chess as we know it is some fifteen hundred years old; the first indisputable reference to it is in a Sanskrit text, sixth or seventh century; its forerunner chaturanga appears in the Hindu *Upanishads* (Golombek 1–14). From medieval to modern times, boards have been checkered black/white, red/white, or red/black; pieces are black versus white, black versus red, red versus white. Though in recent centuries chess has been a male preserve, in medieval illustrations a woman often plays a man; and chess has long been a literary metaphor for tension between the sexes. In one medieval carol a chess metaphor expresses a shrewish woman's combativeness (Richard Greene 237); another casts as a chess game a marital battle (243). In a sonnet by Surrey, a lover's pursuit and mistress's coyness are like a chess game (12); in *The Shepheardes Calendar* (*December*), a shepherd is checkmated by love; a chess game parallels a seduction in Middleton's *Women Beware Women*. As the wooer must win the struggle between the sexes for new life to be conceived, so chess offers a metaphor for life struggling against death: "Death knocked at my gate, / And . . . said to me, checkmate" (C. Brown, *Fifteenth Century* 236). A medieval carol envisions a solstitial fertility combat as a chess game: welcoming feasting-time Christmas, the caroler reviles hungry Advent, accusing this death dealer, "with us thou playest checkmate" (Richard Greene 2). The Middle Ages and Renaissance linked chess with the struggle for fertility: in a fifteenth-century drawing a green tree grows out of a chessboard on which a king and queen play (Kott, *Bottom Translation* 105).

A much older red/black (occasionally white) game, checkers was mentioned by Plato; Homer shows Penelope's suitors playing the game; in the Egyptian afterlife, the dead play a board game with animal-head pieces on red and black squares (Falkener 20). A board from an Egyptian tomb dates to 1600 B.C.—its pieces are lions and goats; in a papyrus, a lion plays checkers with a goat (Falkener 22, 14). The animal emblems suggest totemism, a tension between two moieties each with an animal symbol. Lévi-Strauss reports "sexual totemism" in some societies, each sex with its totem animal: fierce antagonism erupts if a member of one sex injures the totem animal of the other (*Totemism* 37–38). Is checkers, like chess, imbued with the spirit of sexual tension? In some of the earliest (Egyptian) depictions of checkers, a woman plays a man, and checkers is in at least two languages the Game of Women: *Les Dames* in French, *Damespiel* in German. One Egyptian version has six pieces per side, probably on a twelve-by-twelve board (Falkener 19, 44); this suggests six months versus the other six, winter/summer combat, like fertile combat between the sexes. The goal of a fertility rite that Turner calls "the fruitful contest of the sexes," wherein the sexes hurl insults at each other, is "the arousal of sexual desire by stressing the difference between [the sexes] in the form of antagonistic behavior" (*Ritual Process* 77). Could checkers offer a ludic allusion to such a sexual-combat rite? Literary images of chess as sexual combat support the idea. Agonistic games were a common feature of ancient festivals; Fontenrose thinks spring/summer battles are more like games than like Frazer's "combat fought for a real divine kingship" (49). But such games were serious—combat might be to the death—and to transmute fertility rites into games like chess or checkers need not reduce them to recreation. Homo ludens tends to play for keeps.

Most playing card decks have white cards with red and black suits. Cards' likeness to chess is often noted—both have king, queen, jack (knight or valet), and the likeness to chess's forerunner is striking: chaturanga, a four-sided game, had four kings, four divisions of the "army." The suspicion that the chess/checkers battle represents sexual or seasonal fertility combat intensifies with the playing deck. That its suits represent the seasons is suggested by the fifty-two cards, like the year's fifty-two weeks. (This is fairly standard; decks with more than fifty-two usually add several one-of-a-kind picture cards to four thirteen-card suits.) And the suits, though varying across Europe, have a combat/fertility pattern. Black suits, suggesting combat, are weapons: clubs or batons (cudgels in Spanish decks) and spades or swords (Italian *spada* = sword). Red, bespeaking food and wealth—fruits of fertility—are vessels, jewels, or money: hearts/cups, diamonds/coins. In the tarot deck, a relative (either offspring or ancestor) of the playing deck, the "weapon" suits may be phallic symbols, the "vessel" suits vaginal symbols, as the Grail lance and cup represent, in Weston's theory, the male and female principles celebrated in fertility cults. One remembers the mummers' Beelzebub with his club and frying pan. In Glastonbury legend, the staff of Joseph of Arimathea (of the Grail stories), grew into a tree; many "sacred tree" legends involve a holy staff of phallic import (Long 85–88). "Leaves," a German suit, pictures a stafflike tree shading two lovers—a dovetailing of weapons with fruition. (The German suit "acorns" reflects the sacredness of oaks.) Condensing some complexities, a pattern emerges, black suits representing the male, red suits the female principle; cards seem related to sexual-combat fertility rites.

Leaving aside other red-and-black indoor games like roulette or rouge-et-noir, I offer an outdoor example. When the first undisputed references to competitive archery's concentric-ring target appear in the seventeenth century, its rings are white, black, white, and red, with a gold center; a blue ring later replaced the inner white. The ritual colors fit the sexual connotations of arrow wounds, from the myth of erotic archer Cupid to the many images of love striking like an arrow, as in the complaint of Peele's "Enamoured Shepherd": "Thou makest my heart, / A bloody mark, / With piercing shot to bleed; . . . too keen / Thy arrows been" (85). Cupid's arrow became delightfully entangled with the Renaissance eye-beam theory: light shooting from the eye illuminates objects, and light from the sonnet mistress's beautiful eyes affects the lover like Cupid's arrow. Sidney's Cupid hides in Stella's black lashes to shoot a fateful arrow (20). When eye-beam theory was tinged with evil-eye belief, the mistress's shooting of her deadly rays became a kind of magical archery. Book 3 of the *Faerie Queene,* which anatomizes relations between the sexes, is full of sexually charged arrow wounds, sometimes evoking red-and-white imagery, as when an arrow wound stains with red Britomart's "lilly smock" (1.65.9). England's greatest archer, Robin Hood, has his links with fertility gods.

That the archery bull's-eye was originally gold rather than red does not spoil the triad: gold, the color of sonnet mistresses' hair as well as of archery bull's-eyes, was often identified with red in the Middle Ages and Renaissance—gold and silver coins, for example, were called red and white money. Alchemical manuals prescribed use of a white stone for production of silver and a red stone for production of gold (Kieckhefer 138). Often red/gold images were linked with the sun, white/silver with the moon, again suggesting the male/female opposition, both mythologically (the sun is male—Apollo; the moon female—Diana), and physiologically (women were thought governed by the moon).

Mummers' plays, morris and sword dances, May games, chess, checkers, playing cards, Christmas, archery, and Arthurian romance are extensively interconnected, suggesting their mutual links with fertility rites.

Chess is entwined with chivalric romance. Thomas Wright notes chess games in many medieval romances. Charlemagne stakes his kingdom on a chess game; his son kills Ogier's son by hitting him with a chessboard; foes are brained with chess pieces, which were then large and heavy enough for this purpose (195ff.). Combat in

Malory often resembles a chess game: forays are made against the Red Knight of the Red Lands (who lives in a white tower). Symbolic colors abet stylized, chesslike action: "They came to a black land, and there was a black hawthorn, and thereon hung a banner, and . . . a black shield, and by it stood a black spear, . . . and a great black horse. . . . Also there sat a knight all armed in black harness, and his name was called the Knight of the Black Lands" (book 7, 302–3). Mummers' figures resemble chess pieces, Father Christmas the king, the betty/old woman the queen, the hobbyhorse the knight, the Combat Hero the rook (a champion in early Arab chess [T. Wright 205]). Morris and mummers' animal disguises recall ancient animal-headed checkers.

Playing cards, whose spread in Europe coincided with that of courtly love poetry, have links with many red-and-white games and rites. The French call the diamond suit *carreau,* paving tile, recalling the pavement effect of chess- or checkerboard. In sixteenth-century decks, the queen wears a black-and-white chessboard ruff (see photos in Benham), which persists in stylized form in modern decks. The bells of German and central European decks are the sort worn by morris and sword dancers, to ward off demons. In Rowlands's *Knave of Hearts,* 1613, the knave complains of the out-of-date fashions on cards, "which we have worn / Hundreds of years," adding, "my sleeves are like some Morris-dancing fellow" (10). The mummers' dying/reviving figure is often named Jack, like the face card: "Here Jack! Take a lick out of my bottle, / And if thou be not quite slain, / Rise, Jack! and fight again" (Helm 2), recalling bottle-revivable Falstaff, who "dies" and revives at Shrewsbury and is called "Jack." In some old French decks, king and jack of clubs are black men (Benham 115), like the ubiquitous blackfaced figures in mumming, morris and sword dances, and May games; the fool of such dances and plays recalls the cards' cap-and-bells joker. Chivalric romance too has playing-card links. Italian and Spanish decks have knights on horses as knave/jacks. The French deck gives names to face cards, as did the English as late as 1576 (Beal 55), often from romance: the knave of diamonds was Roland, king of clubs Alexander, king of hearts Charlemagne, knave of spades Ogier, knave of clubs Lancelot (Benham 122–57); Charlemagne and Ogier are also chess players in the romances. The French call the knave of spades "Black Peter" (Benham 155)—compare the Dutch name for St. Nicholas's servant; and cards were long a Christmas game—in early modern England, only at Christmas was card playing lawful for working classes (Benham 26). Reiterating the card suits' weapons motif and dovetailing with archery, the French deck's Ogier and Lancelot are archers (Benham 122–23). And archery has links with sword dancing: a Swiss dance featured an archer, and low country sword dances emerged from archers' guilds (Alford, *Sword Dance* 80, 99).

In these traditions, horses are everywhere. The horse (knight) is an old chess piece, going back to chaturanga (Golombek 15–16). The Italian and Spanish playing-card knight is horsed; the card is called *caballo* in Spain, cradle of card playing. Hobby horses attending mumming, morris dances, and May games, black in Padstow, white in Wales or the Isle of Man, were recorded as early as 395 A.D. (Alford, *Sword Dance* 70, 24; cf. Cawte). St. George, English patron saint and mummers' hero, rides a white horse, as does St. James, Spain's patron saint, in processions attending sword dances. Dutch St. Nicholas and Norse Odin ride white horses. The prehistoric white stone horses on English hillsides are fertility oriented, to judge by the impressive phallus of their related white giant. Three of Revelation's four horsemen, with their red, white, and black horses, seem keyed to card suits, especially French face cards: two are warlike, a swordsman and an archer; the third offers food and plenty—oil, wheat, barley, and wine (6:2–6). The equine archetype lay behind the favorite horse of my youth: Walter Farley's black stallion races a red horse, Cyclone, and a white horse, Sun Raider. The film version extended the color scheme: the red-haired boy with his black horse meets a black man with a white horse.

Love and War

Mummers and morris dancers often wear military uniforms, which happily come in the right hues: European uniforms of recent centuries, especially those of officers, are preponderantly of our three colors. Students of mumming and the morris decry such uniforms as a late corruption. It is certainly late—full-blown military uniforms were not in general use before the late seventeenth century. But is it necessarily a corruption or is it consistent with the rites' ancient meanings? Is Alford, who makes a strong case against war-dance origins for the sword dance, justified in denying *any* connection between war and these rites? Combat is prominent in folk forms: one kind of mummers' play is a Hero Combat; in the other, a rejected suitor joins the army, and a recruiting sergeant tries "to enlist all that follows horse cart or plough" (Helm 11). Most legends on chess's origin feature a war; chaturanga was in origin a war game (Golombek 14), based on the Indian army's four divisions, with war elephants among its pieces. Archery domesticates for competition a weapon of war. Seasonal rites often have a winter/summer combat, just as in myth, Thor battles the Ice God; human fertility may involve Turner's "fruitful contest of the sexes."

Red and white are the colors of war and peace, a red flag signaling imminent battle, a white, truce. Chaucer's warlike Theseus has a white banner with a red statue of Mars (Knight's Tale 975–76). Tamburlaine signals by colors the shift from possible treaty (tents decorated with white streamers) to imminent war (red streamers) to certain death for all in a besieged town (black streamers; *Part One* IV.ii). "From the seventeenth century white has been specially associated with royalist and legitimist causes (e.g., the white flag of the Bourbons), and . . . constitutional or anti-revolutionary parties," a contrast with anarchistic, revolutionary red (OED).

Shakespeare envisions the conflict between red-rosed Lancaster and white-rosed York as the winter/summer battle, as in *Richard III*'s "Now is the winter of our discontent / Made glorious summer by this sun of York." Under Richard II, a curse of sterility withers England; Richmond's war restores fruition: "reap the harvest of perpetual peace / By this one bloody trial of sharp war" (*R3* V.ii.15–16). Fruitful war restores the land's fertility, and Richmond weds Elizabeth of York to unite red rose with white. Richard II's horse roan Barbary—a roan is red with intermingled white—passes to his enemy Bolingbroke, who then himself acquires a foe with a roan horse, Hotspur; the death of a black villain on a white horse (Richard III on White Surrey) unites red and white. Recalling the Lancaster-York union, red and white became the Tudor colors. During her coronation procession, Elizabeth encountered a tableau on the Lancaster-York union:

> an arch spanning the street, covered with red and white roses. . . . On the lowest [level sat] two children, representing Henry VII, enclosed in a rose of red roses, and his wife Elizabeth,

enclosed in one of white. . . . On the middle level there were two more children, representing Henry VIII and Ann Boleyn, the bank of red roses rising from the Lancaster side and the bank of white ones from the York. . . . And at the top, amid mingled red and white, perched a single child, . . . Elizabeth. (C. Geertz, "Centers" 17)

Mars was in one aspect the war god, in another, a fertility god: he was a suitor in the Roman spring festival Anna Perenna (probably "the perennial year"), which Brody connects with the Wooing Ceremony. The red/white/black triad has in European culture Turner's "fan of referents," a volatile compound of war, courtship, sexual conflict, and fertility, and Renaissance love poetry displays exactly this fan. War imagery is its staple—the woman besieged—and sexual conflict lies at its heart: the love poems place lovers in an adversarial position, woman scorning and refusing, man alternately languishing under a crushing load of frowns and spiritedly accusing the beloved of cruel pride. The love poetry rejoices in many of fertility magic's central elements.

From Raddle to Riddle

One last folk form in which conflict conduces to fertility is the riddle, with its conflict between poser and solver. Riddlers are often women or others not in authority who make authority figures look foolish; riddling is a natural tool for sexual combat. Folklorists have found links in many cultures between riddling and marriage (see Maranda, Abrahams, Dundes, Gorfain's three essays), and in folk tales and folk-influenced literature, riddling is often a marriage test. A very common riddle answer with obvious "fertility" associations is "egg" (M. Bryant includes ten examples). Some very ancient riddles deal with pregnancy, breastfeeding, and embryos (see M. Bryant, queen of Sheba's riddles, 570, 571). An overwhelming number of riddles are teasingly sexual: "Stiff standing in the bed, / First it's white, an' then it's red. / There's not a lady in the land, / That would not take it in her hand." Answer: radish (Taylor 1572a).

The colors in riddles are very often our triad. "What's black and white and red all over?" seems modern (newspapers are only two centuries old) and linguistically limited (the red/read pun works only in English); yet the color scheme is ancient and widespread in riddles. The triad's link with fire/soot/ash symbolism, already noted in several folk forms, occurs again in riddles: "Black within, white without, / Fo' corner roun' about" (answer: chimney; Taylor 1531, 1530c). Pots and fire are often the answer to red/black riddles (Taylor 1542–43). One black/white riddle about smoke and fire is as old as the Greek Anthology (see M. Bryant). Riddles often consider eggs red and white: "What is red an' white inside, an' white outside?" (answer: egg; Taylor 1505a–c). In line with fertility, food abounds: "Red outside, / White inside" (answer: apple); "who is white at the age of a baby lamb, red at the age of a lamb, and black at the age of a sheep?" (answer: blackberry; Taylor 1512, 1561).

Some riddles suggest year-story rites; these are typically black/white, with six black or dark daughters versus six white or fair—the two halves of the year warring in winter/summer battle; for such riddles, answered "the year," see Cleobulus, ca. 600 B.C., and two Renaissance riddles (M. Bryant 359, 644, 704). Here, then, is another folk form dealing in "the fruitful contest of the sexes" in its personal and year-story versions, with the ritual colors.

Against Ritual

That an "aristocratic" genre like courtly love poetry should be influenced by rites of the peasantry and urban working class is not so surprising. One of the best love poets hailed from a small country town and married a farmer's daughter; and popular ballads as well as courtly poetry offer rosy cheeks, pearly teeth, and sexual frustration—magical remnants appear in love poetry of every social class. And not all magical survivals were as rustic as maypoles and morris dances: chess and cards were aristocratic; lower-class access to cards was restricted by law. But what may be surprising is the way that poets, having set up a magical pattern, worked against it, swam upstream against the magic. This reflects both the historical decline of magic and the irreducible gulf between magic and literature.

A salient twisting of ritual is a skewed order of seasons. In fertility rites, spring or summer triumphantly succeeds winter, and this is Sidney's pattern and Spenser's. *Amoretti* begins at New Year, moves to another New Year, and thaws the lady the second Easter, when "fresh spring" is dispatched to awaken Earth: "Goe to my love . . . / yet in her winters bowre not well awake" (4, 62, 76–77); *Epithalamion,* with its solstitial wedding, suggests the year story in 365 long lines (see Hieatt). In book 7 of the *Faerie Queene,* Mutabilitie summons seasons and months in an order climaxing in winter to show that change and decay rule; but nature refutes her: permanence reigns, for the seasonal cycle will begin again. The year interests Spenser obsessively (*The Shepheardes Calendar* too proceeds through twelve months, with much winter/summer combat), and he often renders it in order from winter sterility to summer fruition. But with almost all other love poets, as with tragedians, winter keeps the upper hand, as it does of course in *The Shepheardes Calendar* itself.

Tudor poems arrest nature at winter: the lady never thaws. The year's spring leaves the lover behind. Wyatt's persona finds himself a paradoxically impotent May King (p. 73). For Surrey, "The winter's hurt recovers with the warm" but nothing can "restore / My fresh green years" (11). In a series of old-turned-young images, his persona laments not sharing the seasonal rebirth:

> Summer is come, for every spray now springs,
> The hart hath hung his old head on the pale;
> The buck in brake his winter coat he flings;
> The fishes float with new repaired scale;
> The adder all her slough away she slings . . .
> Winter is worn, that was the flowers' bale . . .
> Each care decays, and yet my sorrow springs.
> (2)

This mode occasionally recurs late in the century (see Daniel p. 259; Spenser sonnet 19). But Elizabethans and Jacobeans more typically set the seasons up a peg: instead of progressing triumphally toward spring, or being arrested at winter, poems begin in spring and contemplate winter's inevitable onset.

The lover's situation in Wyatt's generation, fixated in winter, is summed up in his "To wish and want and not obtain" (p. 43); in Shakespeare's generation, spring overcast by gathering winter clouds, the lover "weep[s] to have that which [he] fears to lose"

(64).[30] Winter's shadow darkens Shakespeare's cycle: "When forty winters shall besiege thy brow"; "Never-resting time leads summer on / To hideous winter"; "Let not winter's ragged hand deface / In thee thy summer"; "Summer's green all girded up in sheaves, / Borne on the bier with white and bristly beard" (2, 5, 6, 12). Spenser's spring overcomes winter; Shakespeare dwells on winter that dooms summer: "Everything that grows / Holds in perfection but a little moment / . . . Men as plants increase, / . . . Vaunt in their youthful sap, at height decrease"; "Three winters cold / Have from the forests shook three summers' pride, / Three beauteous springs to yellow autumn turned" (15, 104).

Earlier sonneteers occasionally foresee the mistress's winter (see Wyatt p. 49; Surrey 7). But it was the high Renaissance that obsessively beheld love and beauty in terms of summer under winter's death sentence. Though in Jacobean love poems diurnal imagery began replacing seasonal, the carpe diem theme often kept the perspective of spring/summer anticipating winter: "Gather ye rosebuds while ye may, / Old time is still a flying: / And this same flower that smiles today / Tomorrow will be dying" (Herrick 84). A foretaste of winter sours May Day: "We shall grow old apace, and die. / . . . Then while time serves, and we are but decaying, / Come, . . . let's go a-Maying" (Herrick 69).

This is not the way of fertility magic. Winter, in ritual, is prelude to spring; much Renaissance love poetry has it the other way around. Except for Spenser's and perhaps Sidney's, the love poetry is less like comedy's summer than tragedy's winter. It does not, with comedy, celebrate humanity's generational cycle in a long view of the race; but with tragedy, it focuses on the mortal individual. Though the lover is like a fertility god in death and dismemberment, the poet may rule out resurrection: "Though I starve, and to my death still mourn, / And piecemeal in pieces though I be torn, / And though I die, . . . / Shall never thing again make me return" (Wyatt p. 4). Shakespeare, believing in his beloved's uniqueness, entertains a cyclical view of life reluctantly—"If there be nothing new, but that which is / Hath been before, how are our brains beguiled!" (59). He gradually abandons a view of immortality as rebirth in posterity in favor of a linear view of individual immortality.

Cyclical and *linear* are Harold Watts's terms: "Comedy is a representation of life that asserts cycle (as does the bulk of myth), and tragedy is that representation of life that asserts the linear, the non-cyclic. The laughter [associated] with comedy is . . . testimony to the fact that we have cause to rejoice when we contemplate the totality of existence as cycle; the tears that we shed for tragedy . . . [are] a natural by-product of the perception that total existence is not cyclic at all—at least, not cyclic when it concerns us most intimately" (162). Rooted in cyclic ritual, the love poetry slivers and disbranches from ritual's material sap through a "linear" recognition: the individual is irreplaceable. Shakespeare retreats from ritual in shifting from fruition to art, "distillation"—summer's flowers, artificially preserved, perfuming winter:

> For never-resting time leads summer on
> To hideous winter and confounds him there,
> Sap checked with frost and lusty leaves quite gone,
> Beauty o'ersnowed and bareness everywhere . . .
> But flowers distilled, though they with winter meet,
> Leese but their show. Their substance still lives sweet.
>
> (5)

In the fruition sonnets, distillation can mean cyclical regeneration (see 6). But by sonnet 54, it means poetic immortality: "Of [roses'] sweet deaths are sweetest odors made. / And so of you beauteous and lovely youth, / When that shall fade, by verse distills your truth"; thereafter, cyclical rebirth appears no more. The transition lies in sonnet 17: "Were some child of yours alive . . . / You should live twice, in it and in my rhyme." One rebirth of "live twice" is in the generational cycle; the other is immortality through art. In sonnet 18, indestructible art triumphs over yearly destroyed nature: "Rough winds do shake the darling buds of May, / And summer's lease hath all too short a date. / . . . But thy eternal summer shall not fade. / . . . So long as men can breathe, or eyes can see, / So long lives this, and this gives life to thee."

Undoing ritual, focusing on individual life rather than natural process, reflected impersonative thinking: though figures may have had homologues in ritual, the poems now regard them as mimicked humans, even figures drawn from the life. Was the dark lady a ritualesque figure, imagined as human? Does ritual explain her behavior, a Mother Earth welcoming a succession of lovers, like ritual figures of Spring? If so, her casual fickleness, condonable in Earth, excites horror in a woman: the shift from magical thinking creates a moral climate that makes logical the speaker's revulsion from her. Sidney rejects the fertility myths of Europa, Leda, and Danaë, to speak what he feels for one real woman (6), and rejects Petrarchan convention to call for poetry modeled on the living (15).

Poets more and more treated mistress and lover as people. Wyatt preserves a ritual impersonality—"She hath no name: / It doth suffice she doth me wrong" (p. 224)—but Surrey details his mistress's pedigree and gives her name (29);[31] Sidney establishes Stella as Penelope Rich; Spenser's lady is named Elizabeth (74). By embedding in the cycles references to their craft as poets, writers conflated speaker and poet. To model the lady and the lover on named people is to eschew ritual representation, which is impersonal: readers are invited to view them not only as people who might exist but as portraits of the artist and his friends. Readers have accepted the invitation: that the dark lady might be a literary construct with no living model is scarcely entertainable by the many questers for her identity.

John Buxton identifies "the principal question to be decided if we are truly to appreciate *Astrophel and Stella*: is it, or is it not, autobiography?" (271). But how can we decide? Stella might easily have hailed from ritual: married to an old king, she accepts a lover, who in spring becomes new king: "My spring appears, / . . . For *Stella* hath . . . / Of her high heart giv'n me the monarchy" (69). This adulterous love might stem from adulterous medieval romances out of which Petrarchism grew, related to rituals wherein Earth accepts a series of lovers. Stella needed no living prototype: but she had one. Penelope Rich was real, was married. Was the dark lady real? Married? Convention and life lie tangled, epitomizing an era of transition: literature was moving toward figures who invite confusion with life. Biographical readings have not been foisted on us solely by Romantics: Renaissance anti-Petrarchists, citing poets' girlfriends or even wives, called the poets liars: "He term[s] his dirty ill-faced bride, / Lady, and queen, and virgin deified: / Be she all sooty black or berry-brown, / She's white as morrow's milk" (Hall I.vii). Many readers, doubting that "the poet nothing affirmeth, and therefore never lieth," viewed poetry as the autobiography of liars: "The poets of our age . . . extol their whores, which they call mistresses, with heavenly praises. . . . Many that would seem serious, have dedicated grave works to ladies toothless, hollow eyed, their hair shedding, purplefaced, their nails apparently coming off; and the bridges of their noses broken down; and have called them the choice handiworks of nature, the patterns of perfection, and the wonderment of women" (Beaumont and Fletcher Sig. [F4]).

The Renaissance worked against the ritual patterns it set up because it realized that the individual's death blunts any celebration of seasonal regeneration and the race's continuance and because the shock effect of violating ritual with roots deep in European culture creates the dynamic tensions on which art thrives, as varied metrical feet play against a poem's basic beat. Since love poetry frustrates its magical heritage, sawing off the branch it sits on, we may scoff at ritual readings: we cannot picture Penelope Rich with a face raddled in ochre. But ignoring the pervasive magical elements, which generate so much of the poetry's power, diminishes it greatly. Authors drew on a well of readers' unconscious or partly conscious ritual understanding, not seeping through mysterious channels of racial memory but surrounding them daily in popular rites, ritual-linked games, evil-eye superstitions. Since the red/white/black triad is so widespread and persistent, a sensitive author can tap this reservoir today, as does Toni Morrison in *Tar Baby*'s pattern of black and white people, its beautiful woman of white skin and red hair, a Valentine face (236), outshone by a more beautiful black high-fashion model: "now is black beauty's successive heir." Good writing can still draw power from magic that lurks even in modern life; and that magic comes in red, white, and black.

"To Hear with Eyes": Eros Visually Encoded

In Renaissance representations of love, little is straightforward or simple. Sonnets, continuing the conventions of high courtly love, involved a female-dominated relationship where the male brimmed with frustrated desire and the female radiated scorn; and then artists such as Shakespeare in his romantic comedies and Spenser in *Fowre Hymns* and *The Faerie Queene* illogically linked this female-dominant tradition with the male-dominant institution of marriage. Sonnets present us with the strange spectacle of an erotic relationship thriving on mutual antagonism, its abusive power relations seeming only to enhance desire. Shakespeare's sonnet sequence, the most complicated of them all, features a bisexual love triangle, or love/hate triangle.

Sonnet relationships are enriched and bedeviled by complexities and emotional contortions distant from the everyday world, and sonnets handle all this in a peculiarly abstract manner. One need only compare the representation of any sonnet mistress with that of Rosalind in *As You Like It* to notice what elements of everyday sexuality and humanity are suppressed in the sonnet mistress: there is in the sonnet relationship no playfulness, no sense of humor, no affectionate teasing, no griping about a beau who is late for a date, no great sparks of sexual electricity between lovers; above all, the sonnet mistress never shares in Rosalind's voluble, witty, incessant talking. As a boy actor playing a woman dressed as a boy who at times plays the part of a woman, the Rosalind role cannot be declared a piece of novelistic realism; yet Rosalind seems positively lifelike compared with the sonnet mistress.

Sonnets ritualize sexuality: the unmoving sonnet mistress is like the queen on a playing card. She is a flat surface, all symbol. The medieval and Renaissance discourse of sexuality and fertility had elaborated a semiotics of visual signs: the checkerboard pattern, vessels and weapons, arrows, horses, brooms, vegetation symbols from roses to Christmas trees, and above all a color code of red, white, and black. A few items in this complex symbolic system are auditory: the mummer crying "In comes I, the Turkish knight," the melody of a Christmas carol; but for the most part, the ritualized sexuality/fertility system is pervasively visual, a system of *signs* in the truest sense. Since the semiotics of red, white, and black is found in many *oral* cultures, past and present, its intense visual orientation makes problematic a theory such as McLuhan's, that oral cultures are all ear.

Why sexual semiotics should have developed into so one-sidedly visual an affair is perhaps attributable to a connection with coming-of-age rites: as Victor Turner and others have shown, silence is often an aspect of the liminal phase of such rites. Another explanation is that sexual semiotics is connected with women, who have so often been enjoined to silence. Generations of Christian preachers harped on the text "silence is the ornament of a woman." The Philomela story, a variant of which appears in *Titus Andronicus,* gives mythic treatment to a social reality: women, silenced, expressed themselves in visual art: when her tongue is cut out to prevent her telling who has raped her, Philomela weaves the story into a tapestry. As Ann Bergren points out, "The semiotic activity peculiar to women throughout Greek tradition is not linguistic. Greek women do not speak, they weave. Semiotic woman is a weaver. Penelope is, of course, the paradigm" (71). In sonnets, women's traditional silence is transformed into scornful indifference, a displacement from the ideologically valorized silence of the marriage preachers or the brutalized silence of the raped woman; but the conjunction of female silence with a highly visual form of representation remains.

If it is true, as McLuhan maintains, that with the introduction of print Western culture became visually oriented, to the exclusion of the ear, one can easily see why the new technology was so hospitable to such love poetry, why, in England's first century of print culture, so many sonnet sequences were printed. The sonnet's focus on the visual, to the exclusion of the aural, declares itself everywhere in Shakespeare's sonnets.

References to eyes, to sight, seeing, looking, gazing, beholding, watching occur in no fewer than 83 of Shakespeare's 154 sonnets; the word *eye* and its derivatives occur 101 times. References to eyes, sight, or view occur in almost every line of sonnet 148, and sonnet 104 draws attention to the pervasiveness of eyes by its absurdly punning palate tormentor "when first thy eye I ey'd." The sonnets are heavily committed to the visual arts: painting and drawing are adduced in ten sonnets,[32] including a conceit based on perspective and framing in sonnet 24. Forty of the sonnets speak of beauty, an attribute with obvious visual appeal.

Sound, by contrast, is downgraded and suppressed. Voluminous references to sight enormously outweigh the scanty references to sound. Oral speech is represented as wrongheaded or malicious, as in the scorned old men who speak with "less truth than tongue" (17), the purveyors of "hearsay" (21) and of slander (69, 70, 95, 112, 140). Writing about a loved one is ennobling, but talking about one is cheapening: "That love is merchandiz'd whose rich esteeming / The owner's tongue doth publish everywhere" [102]. (Wariness about publishing the merits of the beloved is reminiscent of evil-eye beliefs; one recalls that Collatine brought disaster on his wife Lucrece by being the "publisher" of her excellence [*Luc* 33].) The poems' chief emotional sound effects are moans and groans (71, 131, 133). Other sounds are melancholy and deathlike: "the surly sullen bell" that gives "warning to the world that I am fled / From this vile world, with vilest worms to dwell" (71); the hushed natural world when the loved one is absent: "thou away, the very birds are mute; / Or, if they sing, 'tis with so dull a cheer / That leaves look pale, dreading the winter's near" (97). The speaker thinks that music should, by the example of its harmony, suggest to the young man the value of marriage and propagation, but instead it only makes him sad (8).

The lady, identified with lust and betrayal, is tellingly connected with sound; the first thing we hear about her is that she is dark and that "every *tongue* says beauty should look so" (127) and the second is that she plays a stringed instrument and is called "my music." The speaker informs us that "I love to hear her speak, yet well I know / That music hath a far more pleasing sound" (130), and later denies even that he loves to hear her speak: "Nor are mine ears with [her] tongue's tune delighted" (141). Like a mother pursued by her neglected child, she provokes her lover to "loud crying" (143).

The downgrading of sound appears in a number of images of tongue-tying. The thought that a rival poet will outdo him renders the speaker "tongue-tied, speaking of your fame" (80). His muse is "tongue-tied," consigning him to "dumb thoughts" (85). If the lover is displeased with his praise, "in my tongue / Thy sweet beloved name no more shall dwell" (89), although he later reminds himself, "Because he needs no praise, wilt thou be dumb? / Excuse not silence so" (101). He warns the lady, "do not press / My tongue-tied patience with too much disdain" (140).

A number of sonnets stage a confrontation between sight and sound, and eye invariably triumphs over tongue: the eye even appropriates the function of the tongue. The young man's eye-astounding beauty relegates the tongue to silence: we "have eyes to wonder, but lack tongues to praise" (106). The tongue's power is less devastating than the eye's: "Wound me not with thine eye but with thy tongue" (139). Appropriately for a writer whose theatrical works were heavily oriented toward sound (oral delivery, sennets and alarums, thunder made by cannons), when Shakespeare treats

the topic of the inadequacy of speech for conveying love, the supe-
riority of printed love poetry, he uses the image of an actor silenced
by forgetting his lines:

> As an unperfect actor on the stage
> Who with his fear is put besides his part,
> Or some fierce thing replete with too much rage,
> Whose strength's abundance weakens his own heart,
> So I, for fear of trust, forget to say
> The perfect ceremony of love's rite,
> And in mine own love's strength seem to decay,
> O'ercharg'd with burden of mine own love's might.
> O, let my books be then the eloquence
> And dumb presagers of my speaking breast,
> Who plead for love and look for recompense
> More than that tongue that more hath more express'd.
>   O, learn to read what silent love hath writ.
>   To hear with eyes belongs to love's fine wit.
>
>   (23)

Oral facility has failed: silenced through loss of memory (that
mainstay of oral performance), the actor is equated syntactically
with an inarticulate roaring beast. As in so many other sonnets, the
"speaker" (conventionally so designated) is here no speaker at all,
having grown tongue-tied. The "books," like the forgetful actor, are
dumb; but unlike the actor or the poet as speaking subject, they
can communicate without benefit of sound waves. Shakespeare underlines the visual efficacy of bookish communication by using visual diction, "look for" to mean "expect." Only in oral communication is silence meaningless: for a writing poet, silence can speak
volumes as long as the addressee can read. "To hear with eyes"
belongs not only to love's fine wit but to a visually oriented writ-
ing/reading culture. Shakespeare personifies the books, imagining
them as "dumb presagers," or presenters, silent emissaries to his
beloved. One has only to recall an emissary sent with an *oral* mes-
sage to a beloved to be struck by the difference between Orsino's
dispatching the saucy chatterbox "Cesario" with love messages to
Olivia and Shakespeare's sonnet speaker sending books of poems
to the beloved.

So complete is sight's ascendancy over hearing that the lover's
eyes have taught the dumb to sing (78). Even when he alludes to

the Sirens, Shakespeare mentions not their famous song but the tears that issue from their eyes (119). Crystalizing the speaker's self-portrayal, one sonnet shows him sitting in complete silence, remembering dead friends and the youth's beauty: "When to the sessions of sweet silent thought / I summon up remembrance of things past" (30). The image is of a courtroom ("sessions"), ordinarily a place of noisy orality and combative discourse, to which plaintiffs and defendants are summoned; but the sessions imagined here are sweetly silent. The process of thinking, reading, and writing was not typically a silent one before the age of print: in medieval manuscript culture, people read aloud; a scriptorium full of scribes was a noisy place, since transcription proceeded through one monk's reading a manuscript aloud to the scribe who was copying it. The image of a poet sitting alone, mulling over his loves and his sorrows and silently writing about them belongs to the early modern interiorization of subjectivity. Sonnets' valorizing of silence, of sight without sound, heralds an age when face-to-face communication was less necessary than ever before.

Shakespeare occasionally refers metonymically to his verse as "rhyme," an acoustic term; but more typically he envisions it as "lines," written or printed black lines on white paper. These lines construct the beloved: "His beauty shall in these black lines be seen" (63); "in black ink my love may still shine bright" (65). Poetic lines are set against the "lines of life," or lineage, the young man may establish through progeny (16); they are juxtaposed with the lines drawn by a portrait artist, which become, in one conceit, the lines of aging drawn in the beloved's skin by time (19). One cannot help feeling that the young man is being absorbed into the paper, that ink on paper comprises his whole existence. His earthly immortality consists not of the biological propagation of a line of young Mr. W. H.'s, but in the technological multiplication, via print, of millions of copies of Shakespeare's sonnets.

The sonnet tradition, to an extraordinary degree, appeals to the eye: it comprises the manipulation of visualizable symbols upon a visible page, and it suppresses sound. Magnifying the power of the eye, it opens the door to fear of bewitchment by and through the eye, which it articulates obsessively. And its most important semiotic code is available only to the eye—color symbolism in red, white, and black.

A remarkable moment in Shakespeare's sonnets is his identification, in sonnet 102, with Philomela. In a rare representation of his literary art as oral (his tongue publishes his love, he sings "lays"), the speaker is concerned to justify his occasional silence, his abstinence from song. This he does by reference to a second silencing of Philomela: eliding altogether the main part of her story, wherein she is raped, has her tongue torn out, and silently speaks through weaving, the speaker focuses only on her metamorphosis into a nightingale, which restored her voice but without language. Even this bird voice, however, grows silent in late summer, and "therefore like her I sometime hold my tongue, / Because I would not dull you with my song." Philomela's silence is thus reconfigured as a self-silencing, a self-initiated restraint rather than brutalization by another. She is even seen as silencing others: "her mournful hymns did hush the night." The reconfiguring of this myth reproduces the Renaissance sonnet sequence's reinterpretation of woman's silence, from oppressed dumbness to dominating scorn: both grant women an agency they lacked in myth and in life. And the male sonnet speaker identifies with Philomela—an unvictimized Philomela, in control of her own song.[33] The stilling of song, the stilling of the voice, is here not tragic loss but gain, just as Renaissance love poetry suppressed the ear only to delight the eye.

Sonnets quite literally delighted the eye. Since fourteen lines is approximately as long as iambic pentameter is wide, sonnets on a page form sets of squares, not unlike a checkerboard. Two of the three ritual colors are there for the eye to see—black ink on white paper, recalling the two fundamental color terms that are common to all languages. And sonnets delighted the mind's eye as well: the mind had to supply the red on its own, had to imagine the red-and-white beauty, the roses and other visual symbols conjured by a sonnet text.[34] Sonnet readers brought with them a vast visual semiotics of sexuality and fertility and learned to apply it to the visual and imaginative experience of silent reading. The very exercise must have enhanced the powers of the eye, an already potent and magically dangerous organ. When sonnets were printed, ancient fertility magic met modern technology, and their mutual ocularity multiplied their visual impact. A bridge between the ancient discourse of fertility and the new culture of widespread literacy, Renaissance love poetry, even when it subverted the discourse of fertility, preserved and propagated the familiar magic of its red, white, and black beauties, while teaching contemporaries a whole new way to read: "learn to read what silent love hath writ; / To hear with eyes."

Notes

This chapter is a significantly revised version of "Black and White and Red All Over: The Sonnet Mistress amongst the Ndembu," which appeared in *Renaissance Quarterly* 40 (1987): 247–97.

1. In a Ndembu context, however, black can also be "connected with licit love and in several contexts represents marriage," as in the wedding night (Turner, "Color Classification" 73), and we see the same thing in Juliet's wedding-night invocation, "Come, civil night, / Thou sober-suited matron, all in black" (III.ii.10–11), or night wrapping newlyweds in "sable mantle" (Spenser, *Epithalamion* 321); sable is the heraldic term for black.

2. Boose links this imagery with the Song of Solomon's "epithalamic motif, its red, white and black color symbolism" (428); but possible influences on the scene's color symbolism are much wider flung.

3. Cf. "Mine eye is famished" (Shakespeare 47).

4. Cf. "She doth friese with faint desire" (*Amoretti* 55).

5. Cf. "My galley . . . / Thorough sharp seas in winter nights doth pass" (Wyatt p. 21); "Winter . . . / Makes summer's welcome thrice more wished, more rare" (Shakespeare 56).

6. In other examples, Wyatt's persona is "slain outright," dies "unknown, dazed with dreadful face" (pp. 54, 240); Surrey declares, "Sweet is the death that taketh end by love" (4); Shakespeare's persona is "near slain" (139).

7. A priestess/mistress may perform the slaying, "in bloody bath / of such poore thralls her cruell hands embrew"; "She kills with cruell pryde, / And feeds at pleasure on the wretched pray: / Yet even whilst her bloody hands them slay, / Her eyes . . . upon them smile" (*Amoretti* 31, 47).

8. Cf. Shakespeare's young man, "new-made when thou art old, / And see thy blood warm when thou feel'st it cold" (2); in Spenser, the lover tries to renew his forces, that he may "dying live" (14); in Surrey, it is in spring that "Mine heart gan new revive, and changed blood did stir / Me to withdraw my winter woe" (Surrey 23).

9. Shakespeare too speaks of "hungry eyes" (56).

10. Sidney alludes to Zeus's impregnation of Europa, Leda, and Danaë (6), Spenser to Maia and Alcmena (*Epithalamion* 307–29).

11. Shakespeare's young man is like Adonis (53); the dead planted in the Garden of Adonis "grow afresh, as they had never seene / Fleshly cor-

ruption" (*Faerie Queene* III.vi.30, 33); the dying/reviving Bacchus is crowned at *Epithalamion*'s wedding feast (248–55).

12. Emphasizing the rare orality of the poems in which Stella speaks, they tend to be called songs rather than sonnets.

13. There is something horribly fitting about the fact that Marlowe, the poet who penned the line "Whoever loved that loved not at first sight?" should have died by being stabbed with a dagger through the eye.

14. The image appears in plays too: Bertram goes to war, away "from the sportive court, where thou / Wast shot at with fair eyes, to be the mark / Of smoky muskets" (*AWW* III.ii.109–11).

15. In the science of optics from the Greeks through the Middle Ages and into the pre-Kepler Renaissance, vision was explained by two main concepts: the "extramission" concept of rays shooting out from the eyes to illuminate the world and the "intromission" concept of emanations or even particles shooting off objects and into the eye. Metaphors of projectiles, especially arrows, were common (see Lindberg).

16. Spenser writes of "the huge massacres which her eyes do make"; love is war: "I sought with her hart-thrilling eies / To make a truce, and termes to entertaine" but he was ambushed by rays breaking forth from her "guilefull eyen," which "me captiving streight with rigorous wrong, / Have ever since me kept in cruell bands" (*Amoretti* 10, 12).

17. In other identifications of Laura with Medusa, Petrarch writes, "Her very shadow turns my heart to ice and tinges my face with white fear, but her eyes have the power to turn it to marble" (197), and "those lovely eyes that turn hearts to stone . . . —by these magicians was I transformed" (213).

18. However, Medusa was sometimes conceived of as affecting the eyes of a gazer: Macduff says on the discovery of Duncan's body, "Approach the chamber and destroy your sight / With a new Gorgon" (*Mac* II.iv.76–77)—looking on the Gorgon (Medusa) in myth turned the whole body to stone; but here it is specifically a destruction of sight.

19. In other examples, Posthumus says that Imogen's ring "is a basilisk unto mine eye, / Kills me to look on 't" (*Cym* II.iv.106–7)—looking on the evil-eyed creature is what kills. Anne, who experiences the evil sight damaging the looker ("Out of my sight! thou dost infect my eyes"), wishes her eyes could adopt the more aggressive magical role: "Would they were basilisks, to strike thee dead!" (*R3* I.ii.149–51).

20. Spenser, too, insists on the gaze of both basilisk and victim: "the basiliske . . . from powrefull eyes close venim doth convay / Into the lookers hart, and killeth farre away" (*FQ* 4.8.39.7–9).

21. That the eye seems feminine has often occurred to psychoanalysts: "the pupil represents[s] the vagina, the lids the labia, and the lashes the pubic hair" (Tourney and Plazak 489).

22. Other examples of the basilisk gaze as a poisoning: Chaucer, Parson's Tale, "That sleeth right as the Basilicok sleeth folk by the venym of his sighte" (778); "O, that it were the basilisk's fell eye / To poison thee" (H. Porter xiii.45–46).

23. Just as other Petrarchan terms became sexually debased over time (*mistress* becoming a kept woman, *servant* the illicit lover of a citizen's wife), so *cockatrice* became a slang term for prostitute (see Jonson, *Cynthia's Revels* II.ii.100–101, IV.iii.223–24, IV.iv.15, V.iv.22; Fletcher, *Love's Cure* III.iv.112).

24. And Renaissance slang linked red and white with bodily fluids, those of female sexuality: "the reds" meant the menses, "the whites" leucorrhea.

25. The phrase recalls the title of a folk tale; the triad is very common in folk tales ("skin as white as snow, lips as red as blood, and hair as black as ebony"). Eliade may go too far in claiming that "the ordeals and adventures of [folk-tale] heroes and heroines are almost always translatable into initiatory terms" (*Rites* 126), but the ritual colors' presence is suggestive.

26. In other Chaucerian examples, Blanche in the *Book of the Duchess*—called White—in youth had white hands, and red nails; her suitor waxed "pale and red" (955, 1215). Venus in *The House of Fame* has a garland of red and white roses. The speaker of *The Legend of Good Women* rhapsodizes on May and on daisies, given white color by Cybele, red by Mars (531–34).

27. Other British examples: all Marshfield Paper Boys except the black-clad doctor wear costumes of white paper strips and black boots. Brody, who thinks this is the oldest mummers' costume, compares it with those of Bavarian Wild Men and African medicine men (23). In Chambers's accounts, Cornish mummers in 1846 had a doctor with a red-and-white face; Beelzebub wore a black hat, and the fool a red mask; one character called attention to his "face red as fire" (*English Folk-Play* 83, 85, 33)—could Bardolph memorialize such figures?

28. Anticipating my next chapter, I note here that kitchen implements often substitute for weapons in carnival. In Breughel's painting *The Battle of Carnival and Lent*, "Carnival rides on a wine barrel instead of a horse, and the combatants brandish cooking utensils instead of weapons" (Bristol 67). Folengo's *Orlandino* has a "carnivalesque description of a tournament. . . . [Knights] carry baskets instead of shields and kitchen utensils, pails, pots and pans, on their heads instead of helmets" (Bakhtin 210). A long history of folk symbolism identifies weapons with the male, vessels (like cooking pots) with the female principle. Archeology shows that even in Iron Age Britain, weapons and cauldrons were the commonest votive offerings (Merrifield 24).

29. Shakespeare speaks of Whitsun morris dances (*H5* II.iv.25) and Whitsun pastorals (*WT* IV.iv.134).

30. Astrophil laments, "If now the May of my years much decline, / What can be hoped my harvest time will be?" (21). *Delia's* lover, spending "the April of my years in grief," foresees his mistress "winter-withered"; since "no April can revive thy withered flowers," he counsels carpe diem: "Love whilst that thou mayst be loved again, / Now whilst thy May hath filled thy lap with flowers; / . . . Now use the summer smiles, ere Winter lowers" (32, 38–42).

31. She is only partially emancipated, however, from ritual impersonality: "Geraldine" seems to have been nine years old when the poem was composed.

32. Sonnets 16, 20, 21, 24, 53, 62, 67, 82, 83, and 146.

33. On the way that male narrative and lyric seem, in various cultures, to occupy the same conceptual space occupied by female spinning and weaving, see Edwards and Sienkewicz (162–66), Rowe (52–60), and my essay "Patchwork."

34. When sonnets were read silently, the mind's ear had to supply sound effects, to appreciate the alliteration in "sessions of sweet silent thought," so that orality too turned inward; but Shakespeare's sonnets are not heavily alliterative, nor nearly as replete with sound effects as with visual effects.

5

Shakespeare and the Carnival of Time

Tempus edax rerum.
—Ovid, *Metamorphoses*

Julius Caesar, which enacts revolt against authority, pays great attention to people's relative ages. The Senators are older than Caesar; Antony is older than Octavius; Cassius is older than Brutus; a poet is older than Cassius or Brutus; Cicero is older than all the conspirators. Relatively young Caesar has usurped authority from the venerable Senate; when he is overthrown, he is succeeded by a set of young men—not necessarily younger than he is, but encoded "young" as he is not ("young Octavius" is repeated as if the epithet were part of the name; Antony is an athlete and reveler). Onto political strife has been mapped the issue of age. In *Antony and Cleopatra*, by some artistic alchemy Octavius is still "the young man" but Antony has aged into an "old ruffian"—perhaps through dissolute living, perhaps because Shakespeare again wants to present political conflict as youth/age conflict. (In the arena of sexual strife, a Cleopatra "wrinkled deep in time" demands to know the age of her rival Octavia.) Why all the concern with age in plays of political conflict? How does the political topsy-turviness of Caesar overpowering the Senate or conspirators toppling Caesar invite an atmosphere of generational conflict?

Such conflict is rife in Shakespeare. Adults mock youth's impotent callowness: "How green you are and fresh in this old world!" (*Jn* III.iv.145); but the youth at whom an adult sneers "So wise so young, they say, do never live long" (*R3* III.i.79) may grow up to turn the tables on the tormentor. The little prince threatens Richard's ambitions, perhaps his manhood: "Would you have my weapon, little lord?" (*R3* III.i.122). When time gives children adult weapons—of war, wit, virility—the children may turn these weapons on their elders, mocking their weakness as the elders had mocked youth's: "the faint defects of age / Must be the scene of mirth" (*Tro* I.iii.172); "old men have grey beards, . . . their faces are wrinkled, their eyes purging thick amber and plum-tree gum, . . . they have a plentiful lack of wit, together with most weak hams" (*Ham* II.ii.197–201). The old in Shakespeare are often under the tutelage or leadership of the young. Armado is rebuked as a "negligent student" by Moth, whose "true wit" is "offer'd by a child to an old man" (*LLL* III.i.33, V.i.58–59).[1] Posthumus is "a child that guided dotards" (*Cym* I.i.46–50); Hal and Hotspur are youths who lead armies and dominate followers much older than themselves.

Reverses in the generational power struggle typify the topsy-turviness of Renaissance literature, which riots in inversions of class, gender, and age group. Class inversions range from Prince Hal's turning highway robber while Falstaff plays king to fools and jesters tutoring countesses and kings. Gender inversion may be of sonneteers groveling at the feet of disdainful mistresses who are addressed in the language of political hierarchy ("my sovereign"); of milksop husbands dominated by shrews; of *The Faerie Queen*'s female knight Britomart terrifying the male coward Braggadocio, or Radigund forcing captive males to spin; of the warlike, "mankind" women of history plays (Joan la Pucelle, Margaret), a world where "ladies and pale-visag'd maids / Like Amazons come tripping after drums, / Their thimbles into armed gauntlets change, / Their needles to lances" (*Jn* V.ii.154–57). And inversion of age group gives us an aged Falstaff following a teenaged Hal, a Hotspur dominating his elders, a legion of young folks outmaneuvering their elders to marry according to their choice—the stuff of comedy. Such inversions, I think, were especially widespread in late medieval and early modern literature. Chaucer's Alice of Bath, inverting gender, age, and class expectations by gaining the upper hand in marriage, marrying a man twenty years her junior, and giving a lecture on marriage to a crowd including many social superiors, set the tone for literary successors.

If literature witnessed inversions, so did history. It was an age of class strife—the Cade rebellion of 1450; the German peasant revolt of 1525 in which "knights in rags were compelled to serve their vassals at table; the peasants dressed themselves in knightly raiment and mimicked knightly rituals" (Kunzle 64); the English civil war, in which the middle classes and some proletarian sects gained the upper hand over royalty and aristocracy. Gender was inverted too: women adopted male attire on the London streets, courtiers were said to be effeminate in dress, men dressed as women in corn riots and enclosure disturbances (Davis, "Women on Top" 175–76), boy actors cross-dressed. And age groups were inverted: London apprentices were involved in anti-establishment revolts (S. Smith 157); students locked out masters and took over schools in widespread barring-out rebellions—boys held Manchester Grammar School for two weeks, "supplied with food and firearms by the townsmen"; in other barrings-out, ushers were shot at and masters burned with hot pokers or "hit in the eye when they peered through the keyhole" (Thomas, *Rule and Misrule* 4, 20–26). As Christopher Hill shows, the civil war witnessed both generational and class conflict: "We think of refusal of 'hat honour' and the use of 'thou' by Quakers as gestures of social protest, and so they were. But they also marked a refusal of deference from the young to the old, from sons to fathers" (152). As in more recent radical movements pitting youth against age, such as China's Cultural Revolution or our 1960s counterculture, older people seemed icons of traditional ideas. Most leaders of the English revolution were young: "It was a young man's world while it lasted" (Hill 296).

Linking inversion with social crises, Victor Turner suggests that when authorities, through dissensions over "segmented interests," have brought disaster on the community, "it is for structural inferiors . . . to set things right again, . . . by symbolically usurping for a short while the weapons, dress, accouterments, and behavioral style of structural superiors" (*Ritual Process* 184). In literature, the world of the *Henry VI* plays that called forth Joan of Arc and Margaret seems to be in such a crisis, full of "dissensions over segmented interests"—war abroad, civil strife at home. And in history, the civil war was not the only social crisis that might have provoked topsy-turvy behavior: one thinks also of the decay of feudalism, the rise of a nation state with a powerful and often repressive central government, the Reformation with its attendant wars and persecutions, realignments in the class system, urbanization, protocapitalism, the coming of print culture, the dawning scientific revolution, proliferating witch-hunts,[2] the plague—these large upheavals destabilizing traditional life could surely be called social crisis.

In many areas of culture the early modern period witnessed generational strife. Louis Montrose thinks primogeniture intensified the sibling rivalry to whose ubiquity folk tales attest, "block[ing] the generational passage of the younger brother. . . . The conflict of elder and younger brothers also projects an oedipal struggle between father and son" ("'The Place'" 36–37). Walter Ong ascribes some early modern devaluing of elders to the advent of print culture, which diminished oral cultures' dependence on knowledge-conserving elders (*Orality* 41). Keith Thomas thinks nascent intellectual revolution added to generational tensions: intellectuals' "growing assumption . . . that knowledge was to be advanced rather than hoarded . . . was to make inherited wisdom obsolete. The new science . . . [produced] the dogma that only the young could make intellectual discoveries" ("Age" 246–47). In the realm of politics, Anthony Esler thinks that the Elizabeth/Burleigh "older generation" hardened ideologically, closing out a talented younger generation.

Fueling both literature and life in this age of crisis was some ancient magical thinking embodied in topsy-turvy festive rites. Among rituals seeking magical control over nature and circumstance are rites belonging to holidays of the saturnalia type. Celebrated from ancient times near solstices and equinoxes, they included fertility-god worship, they invoked spirits of the dead, and they turned the world topsy-turvy, masters serving slaves and slaves enjoying a time of license. Saturnalia itself, the great festival of the Roman year just before the winter solstice, celebrated Saturn, god of seed; the dead were honored and slaves did as they liked. On Feralia, or Parentalia, in February, ghosts were propitiated. At Matronalia, in March, mothers brought flowers to Juno, goddess of marriage; mistresses feasted their maids. At the Greek Cronia, a harvest feast, slaves were honored; at Anthesteria, Dionysus was honored, the dead walked, slaves were feasted (see Bourboule for an account of rites of the Saturnalia type in the ancient Mediterranean world).

The odd conjunction of solstitial observance and social inversion suggests that fear of social crisis (slaves rising against masters) has been mapped onto more nature-oriented anxieties (fear that the seeds will not germinate or that the crops will fail). The coupling of seedtime and harvest rites with rites dealing in servant/master relations hints at one of those "invisible mental structures" Keith Thomas postulated: the tilled earth is being constructed as an unwilling servant, and both earth and servants are ritually propitiated as a way of reconciling them to their state of exploitation, as in hunting rites a hunter will sometimes ask pardon of the animal before killing it. The magical, ritual means by which archaic societies sought control over an unruly and often disobedient nature seem here to have entered the magical unconscious in the form of a belief that unruly and disobedient subordinated social classes can be magically managed too, by calendric rituals that both express and contain the fear of class revolt. It is significant that Saturn, god of Saturnalia, was both the god of seedtime and harvest and the mythic figure who presided over a golden age of social harmony, when no social classes (and hence no class-based tensions) existed. The festival seems to be transferring magical rites of an agrarian society onto the social relations of a more complexly organized society.

Suggesting this mental link between magical control of seasons and crops and magical control of social relations, medieval and Renaissance versions of Saturnalia in Europe, with their ritualized status and age inversions, clustered near the winter solstice: Twelfth Night with a Lord of Misrule from Christmas to January 5 or 6, the Feast of Fools and the Boy Bishop at Holy Innocents, December 28. The link with ancient fertility rites was direct: Christmas grew out of Saturnalia and a Roman holiday, "Birthday of the Unconquered Sun," celebrating the strengthening of sunlight after the solstice. Romans brought Saturnalia to Britain; a sixth-century pope approved the converting of Saturnalia to Christmas in Britain. Puritans disliked Christmas's link with paganism: Prynne wrote, "our Bacchanalian Christmases and New-year's tides" share a date with "Saturnalia and feasts of *Janus*"; both include "dancing, drinking, stage-plays, masques, and carnal pomp" (Macey 38–39, 116, 117). In 1689 John Selden noted, "*Christmas* succeeds the *Saturnalia,* the same time, the same number of holy days, then the master waited upon the servant like the Lord of *Misrule*" (33). Boy Bishop festivities were sometimes earlier, at feasts in November—a season associated with festivals of the dead from Greek antiquity to Remembrance Day and Veterans Day.[3] Spring festivals could also be saturnalian—Shrove Tuesday, an apprentice holiday, involved hooliganism and other class and age-group topsy-turviness; pre-Lent carnival, across Europe, incarnated the saturnalian spirit.

All these festive inversions involve lower-class celebrants taking the places of their social betters or festively rebelling against authority, and many involve gender inversion;[4] but age inversion is very prominent too. The text "He hath put down the mighty from their seat, and hath exalted the humble" (Luke 1:52) was prominent at the Feast of the Innocents, with its custom of electing a Boy Bishop and allowing boys to sit in their elders' seats and conduct some divine offices. The festival, "more common [in England] than anywhere else in Europe," combined two ideas, "the humble overthrowing the mighty; the young overthrowing the old" (Kolve 156–57). College and inns-of-court students elected Christmas princes who burlesqued authority. "The universities had their licensed buffoons: the Terrae Filius at Oxford and the Prevaricator at Cambridge, young MAs appointed annually to make a speech at the chief academic ceremony of the year, [full of] outspoken jests and insults directed at the morals and private lives of the vice-chancellor, heads of houses and other dignitaries" (Thomas, "Place of Laughter" 78).

Some festivity seems to us more conflict than inversion, but the Renaissance often saw in conflict an effect of inversion. Sexual conflict, which we might see as egalitarian, to an early modern eye meant inversion of "normal" dominance, because the sexual hierarchy placed males on top. When obedience is expected of inferior orders such as women or youth, conflict (with males or with elders) becomes by definition an inversion of the "natural" order.

The workings of the carnival spirit can again be understood by recourse to Mary Douglas's idea of the body as an image of society, discussed in chapter 1. In *Rabelais and His World*, Bakhtin interprets carnival's obsession with what he calls the "lower bodily stratum"—with overeating, sexual excess, grotesque births—by invoking an analogy between the physical body and society. In carnival time the lower half of the body (belly, digestive tract, genitals) are given preeminence over the upper half (heart and head, emotion and intellect) echoing the lower-class ascendancy over the ruling class that is characteristic of saturnalian festivals. The anonymous *The Passion-*

ate Morris, 1593, describes the overwhelming of intellect by sexual desire in terms of saturnalian festivity, specifically the misrule of Christmas: "Liking will not be long a-doing, and love that follows is but little, whereby he brings no great harm; but all the mischief comes with desire, which swells the affections, and predominates over love and liking; he makes the misrule, and keeps the open Christmas" (97). Here a topsy-turnivess in which the lower half of the body (sexual desire) lords it over the upper half (liking and love—more intellectual operations) is mapped onto the inverted social class relations of saturnalian festivity.

In Marlowe's *Dr. Faustus,* the hero's "lower bodily stratum" continually overwhelms his intellect—he has a yen for "princely delicates" (I.i.86), is "wanton and lascivious" (II.i.142), lusts for Helen, and sells his soul in exchange for twenty-four years of living in "all voluptuousness" (I.iii.96). Intellectual matters are spoken of in appetitive terms: Faustus is "glutted . . . with learning's golden gifts" and "surfeits upon cursèd necromancy"; "How I am glutted with conceit of this!" he cries (I.Cho.24–25, I.i.79). In the terms I introduced in chapter 1, Faustus is the antitype of the sealed-up virgin or the careful observer of food taboos: in his gluttonous insatiability and sexual incontinence, he is no defender of boundaries. He takes in the outside world through his mouth, allows his soul to be sucked out through his mouth, and blurs the human/demon boundary by intercourse with the devilish Helen. Inevitably, he ultimately fails to preserve the distinction between himself and the outside world, a loss of difference and identity symbolized by his being torn limb from limb and sent to a hell where the bodies of the damned are roasted and devoured. If the body is an image of society, it is significant that this text too, like the closely contemporary *Rape of Lucrece* and *Titus Andronicus* that also involve bodily violations, mutilations, and dismemberments (see chapter 1), belongs to the immediately post-Armada era. The dismembered Faustus is an apt signifier for a land that went in fear for its territorial integrity. And carnival's carnality could border on the demonic.

Festive inversion and misrule may have provided for life and literature Gombrich's schemata, familiar structures by which to make sense of new experience. In the wake of the Cade rebellion, black-faced farmers broke into the duke of Buckingham's park and stole his deer, and corn riots were often led by women or men dressed as women, often in blackface (Davis, "Women on Top" 179, 156); blackface is a hallmark of popular rites (see chapter 4). To Davis, transvestism in popular uprisings is a signifier suggesting that real-world revolt was modeled on festive topsy-turviness. Participants in a 1612 riot in Dean were called "Robin Hoods" (Underdown, *Revel* 110). Sandra Billington shows that popular uprisings were sometimes understood by reference to the class topsy-turviness of the Robin Hood tradition, with its robbing the rich and giving to the poor (13–15), and that the notion of the Lord of Misrule came into people's minds when kings misbehaved: "In the eyes of satirists a mock king was not necessarily an untitled man pretending to be king, but could also be a real one whose title did not match the reality" (87). Christopher Hill has shown that the world-upside-down trope came into people's minds during the civil war. Margaret Ranald shows that when in degradation rites the officials were of such status that they could be degraded only by inferiors, the saturnalian impulse to thumb one's nose at authority sometimes erupted, as when Bishop Bonner, officiating at Archbishop Cranmer's degradation, "behaved in a rude and arrogant manner to his erstwhile superior" (187); this must have lent Bonner the air of a Lord of Misrule, imparting a whiff of temporariness to his authority. In Shakespeare, Bolingbroke, degrader of his superior Richard, is also in the Lord of Misrule position, a posture of temporariness from which his regime never wholly recovers.[5]

In considering the relation of festive misrule to actual revolt, we should bear in mind that the conjunction of festive misrule with rituals designed to manipulate nature and ensure the food supply suggests that such misrule was in its remote origins a ritual designed to prevent magically (or quasi-magically) the disaster of social crisis and real revolt, just as solstitial rites were to prevent magically the disaster of prolonged winter and crop failure.

A good deal has been written on inversions of class and gender; I will focus in this chapter on the relatively neglected inversion of age groups, which I think was the granddaddy of all inversions.

The Saturnalia of Time

In Renaissance literature, elders seek control: alive, they try to control property and family (Gloucester is horrified at the idea of his son's managing his revenue); and to make sure property descends to the right heir, they must choose children's spouses, prevent wives from producing uncertain heirs through cuckoldry, and discourage widows from remarrying. These aims generate many a Renaissance plot. The difficulty of exercising control during life, let alone after death, sparks much anxiety, and this drives many plays. Anxiety gives birth to paranoia: the old go in perpetual fear that the young are merely waiting their chance to seize control.

A paradigm of elders' suspicion of the young is the biblical story of Herod, who killed all the land's male babies when a prophecy said one would be king of the Jews, seemingly supplanting him; Jesus, hidden, escaped the massacre. The mystery plays still acted in Shakespeare's youth dramatized Herod's massacre (it was in the Towneley, York, and Digby cycles); Hamlet mentions their Herod, a man who put the "rant" in "tyrant." The Boy Bishop feast, saturnalian in its youth/age inversion, was on Holy Innocents Day, commemorating Herod's massacre. Renaissance literature abounds in Herods. Cambyses vows to kill his brother for fear of supplanting. In *Lear* Gloucester fears that his son is plotting against him: like Zeus in the Cronus myth, Edgar hides in hovels from his father's wrath. Timon calls on a mythic pattern when exhorting a sacker of cities: "Spare not the babe. . . . / Think it a bastard, whom the oracle / Hath doubtfully pronounc'd thy throat shall cut, / And mince it sans remorse" (*Tim* IV.iii.121–25).

Henry IV needs no prophecy to fear supplanting; knowing Hal as we do, can we blame him? *Part 1* hints at the murderous-father motif: Hotspur quips, "But that I think [Hal's] father loves him not / And would be glad he met with some mischance, / I would have him poisoned with a pot of ale" (I.iii.231–33); but Henry has as yet no great fear of Hal, who is pretending to harmless irresponsibility. It is *Part 2,* where old age is prominent, that baldly articulates his fear: he first fears leaving the realm to Hal's irresponsible governance, dreading "th' unguided days / . . . that you shall look upon / When I am sleeping with my ancestors," and then, when Hal makes off with his crown, begins to fear supplanting before death: "Dost thou so hunger for mine empty chair / That thou wilt needs invest thee with my honors / Before thy hour be ripe?" (IV.iv.58–61, v.94–96). Hal's rather thinly motivated lower-class sojourn recalls the mythic pattern of figures who escape tyrants' murderous suspicion by hiding in hovels until old enough to stand up to the tyrant; his feigned irresponsibility resembles the feigned madness by which Hamlet or the mythic Brutus escape tyrants' wrath until strong enough to strike back. Only after Hal emerges as strong and responsible does Henry's fear of him become overt.

Generational strife is especially rich in Shakespeare, who is even more concerned than his contemporaries with family life. But the early modern world in general was age obsessed: generations comprised a basic organizing principle of society. "In modern Western societies," Thomas says, "age is a less decisive determinant of man's fortunes than at simpler stages of economic life"; early modern England was still "gerontocratic: the young were to serve and the old were to rule." At church, generations were segregated, the young consigned to the back; "in 1617 a girl was presented to the church court for sitting in the same pew as her mother, to the great offence of many reverent women. . . . In rural games and calendar customs age-differences were fundamental" ("Age" 205–11). Early marriage was opposed because it meant "undue propinquity of years between parents and children, thus diminishing deference." In politics, "men in their forties and fifties . . . ruled." As Thomas notes, the age system justified by analogy "the whole social order; for the lower classes at home, like the savages abroad [and, I might add, like women], were often seen as 'childish' creatures, living in a state of arrested development, needing the mature rule of their superiors" ("Age" 226)—another reason the saturnalian behavior of classes, genders, and age groups was similar.

In the history of letters, Ernst Curtius says, the war of generations "appears as the battle of the 'moderns' against the ancients" (98; cf. Eisenstadt 33).[6] Shakespeare and his contemporaries felt they were contending against a world of overshadowing ancestors: they wrote in an age when those upstart youths the vernacular languages were doing battle against the ancient patriarchy of Latin and when modern authors were striving to come into their own against the almost deified shades of the Greek and Roman classics.

In the end, the old are perfectly right to feel paranoid about youth's desire for control. Rituals of age inversion mimic a fact of life: the young do grow up to take over the world. Rites of passage such as initiations, designed to ease youth into the elders' shoes, often express conflict between generations: ordeals that elders inflict on initiands in tribal coming-of-age rites may subliminally express the older generation's resistance to the younger's assumption of power (see Vizedom 47). Age-group ideology is inherently conflictive, expressing the rival interests of two groups desiring power.

The magical thinking behind all this resides in the fact that ancient Saturnalia was a fertility rite, and Time's saturnalia, humbling the strong generation and elevating the weak, promotes the continuance of the race. "Time's the king of men, / He's both their parent, and he is their grave" (*Per* II.iii.47–48); as in scapegoating, the health of one generation demands the sickness of the other. This paradox—that the old must lose their power struggle with the young for life to go on—explains some of the internal tension that destabilizes myths attached to Saturnalia's god, the complex Saturn.

The Renaissance inherited from the Romans a conflation of Roman Saturnus with Greek Cronus or Kronos. Saturnus, like Greek Ceres, was god of seedtime and harvest, a fertility god, his emblem the scythe, symbol of harvest. Cronus too was associated with a reaping tool: the sickle with which he castrated his father. Saturnus embodied fecundity, new generations; Cronus (almost a sterility god) embodied lethal tension between generations, a struggle of young seizing power from old, then trying to stave off their own children's power seizure. Upon a prophecy that Cronus would be deposed by one of his children, he ate them all at birth—a version of the story of Herod, who killed babies because it was foretold that one would replace him. (Infant Zeus, hidden from Cronus as Jesus was hidden from Herod, did grow up to depose him.) Suggesting wintry sterility, the Greeks called the Arctic Ocean the Cronian Sea.

But Cronus was already ambiguous for the Greeks. Like Saturnus, he had presided over a golden age without social classes, when labor was unnecessary. Cronus's eventual vomiting up of his children is an image of rebirth; and one of them was harvest goddess Ceres. The Cronia, a harvest feast, was in his honor. The sickle that myth explained as a castrating tool was possibly a remnant of an earlier Cronus, more clearly a fertility god, with a harvest tool. In uniting Cronus and Saturnus, Romans only intensified the ambiguity already present in Cronus, whose internal contradictions appeared in very ancient times: Hesiod (eighth century B.C.) stresses Cronus's treacherous patricide and his presiding over the golden age (Macey 24). Recognizing his contradictory nature, two myths endowed Saturnus with different wives: Ops, a goddess of plenty, and Lua, a goddess of barrenness. Saturn combined elements of fertility (harvest, plenty, childbirth) and sterility (winter, dearth, war, child murder). Saturn as Saturnus and Cronus, scythe symbolizing harvest and murder, was the sort of figure that appealed to the Renaissance, a union of contraries, like that other favored emblem the hermaphrodite.

Allegorically, Cronus represented Time,[7] his eating his young signifying that children, devoured by Time, die out of childhood by growing up. Iconography derived a figure of Time from Cronus, an old man with a scythe (see Panofsky). (During Elizabeth's coronation procession, a man "representing Father Time, complete with scythe," emerged from a cave [C. Geertz, "Centers" 18].) Death the Grim Reaper also belongs to the Time icon: as Time kills us by aging us, we are the harvest Death reaps. Antony wants to contend with Death's "pestilent scythe" (*Ant* III.xiii.195–96). Astrologically the planet Saturn governed old age; Hal mocks Falstaff's geriatric amours: "Saturn and Venus this year in conjunction!" (*2H4* II.iv.262). Shakespeare's portrayal of Time is often Cronian. Like Cronus, Time is the "eater of youth" (*Luc* 927; cf. *Tro* III.iii.145–50; sonnet 19). In *Love's Labor's Lost,* Time is a Cronian devourer with a scythe: "devouring Time" threatens with his "scythe's keen edge" (I.i.4–6).

Though the inversions practiced in saturnalian festivals in the ancient world were usually of social class—servants lording it over masters or at least enjoying a period of license—the god of Saturnalia is one whose myth has mainly to do with age inversion, the younger generation striving to seize power from the old. Age inversion in the myth has been translated into class inversion in the rite. In drama contemporary with ancient Saturnalia, Roman new comedy, class inversion appears in the service of age inversion: the clever servant, often brighter than the master, directs the action (Mosca and Jeeves are descendants); but this class inversion directs action toward the main goal, the young man outdoing the old— his father. Gail Paster summarizes the typical plot: "a young man, blocked in his erotic pursuits by parental disapproval, financial difficulty, or other disabling obligation, enlists his slave in a successful scheme to win the girl. In the joint triumph of *adolescens* and *servus,* normative social values topple" (52). In both Saturnalia and new comedy, class inversion subserves age inversion: in the festival, class inversion points to the god of age inversion; in the comedies, class inversion helps effect age inversion. And fertility magic drives both: the triumph of the younger generation promotes the continuance of the race.

The translation from age inversion in the Saturn myth to class inversion in the Saturnalia rite resembles the process of displacement that Freud says takes place in dreaming: something threatening (the permanent loss of one's power to the younger generation) is displaced onto something relatively trivial and unthreatening (a temporary, festive loss of power to servants). A primal fear is repressed and disguised as controllable festive merriment. Just as in Thomas's formulation the age system justified by analogy the whole social order, I think the deep structure of *all* saturnalian topsy-turviness—inversions of class, gender, age—derives from inverting generations through the action of Time, that "true hero of every feast, uncrowning the old and crowning the new" (Bakhtin 219). In life's saturnalia, society's weakest members—children—grow up to rule the world, while its strongest members—adults—decline into feeble age: Time makes "the child a man, the man a child" (*Luc* 954). This pattern of life animates ancient rituals of saturnalian inversion as it puts its stamp on oral tales and on literature: many folk tales explore "the battleground of home" (Brewer 33); in Greek tragedy Oedipus, who kills his father, is driven out by his sons. Ancient myths as well as modern case studies led Freud to place the family power struggle at the center of life's drama. And a basic Shakespearean plot device is the generational inversion I will call the saturnalia of Time.

My belief that age inversion is the model for all saturnalian inversions finds support in Natalie Davis's research into the origins of European organized misrule. England had Lords of Misrule; France had Abbots of Misrule called the Abbot of Gaiety, Prince of Pleasure, Prince of Fools, Prince of Youth; Rouen had a Prince of Improvidence, Cardinal of Bad Measure, Bishop Flat-Purse, Duke Kickass, and the Grand Patriarch of Syphilitics; Lyon had a Judge of Misrule with a Bench of Bad Advice ("Reasons" 43–44). What Davis discovered, to her surprise, was that "The Abbey of Misrule was in its inception a youth group!" (50). The Lord of Misrule tradition seems to have sprung from societies of *varlets à marier,* young bachelors; youth abbeys existed all over medieval France. Members performed charivaris and jumping dances for crop fertility; their ringing bells for the village's dead ancestors recalls festivals of the dead so often part of saturnalian holidays, as does their disruptive behavior at second marriages—Davis thinks that among other functions, such rites placated the dead spouse's spirit (51–53). A period in a youth abbey resembled a rite of passage (55), and Victor Turner's description of liminal phases fits these groups with their social egalitarianism, age topsy-turviness, and occasional transvestism. The rural Abbeys of Misrule moved into cities during the Renaissance—the sixteenth-century Lyon printers' journeymen, charmingly, had a Lord of Misprint (Davis, "Reason" 59–60). Davis found similar abbeys in Switzerland, Germany, Italy, Hungary, and Rumania, and evidence was later found of their existence in England.[8] Across Europe, then, saturnalian misrule was firmly linked to institutionalized youth/age conflict.

Here again is the two-edged scythe of Saturn, murderous weapon of generational strife and fruitful harvesting tool: the youth abbey promoted crop growth and fruitful marriage not despite of but because of its rebelliousness and usurpation of adult authority. The continuance of humanity depends on the young displacing the old. The ethos of the youth abbey—generational conflict and promotion of fertility—surfaces in literature in that set piece the youth/age debate, which has traceable links to fertility magic.

In dialogues of this genre, an old man is hostile or indifferent to love and women, and a young man defends them (e.g., February of *The Shepheardes Calender*; Newman's *Short Dialogue of a Woman's Properties, between an Old Man and a Young*). High Renaissance debates retain a fertility link in the theme of women and love, and earlier prototypes are explicitly seasonal: the early Tudor *Debates or Strifes between Summer and Winter* casts Winter as an old man, Summer a young man (see Barber, *Shakespeare's Festive Comedy* 116). Steven Marx traces the youth/age debate back through the Middle Ages, to eighth-century Alcuin's debate between Summer and Winter. In *The Shepheardes Calender*, "youth vs. age appears in some guise in every one of the twelve months" (Marx 203). Shakespeare taps this genre when Rosalind spies "a young man and an old in solemn talk," which concerns love: "Being old, thou canst not guess, / Though in thy youth thou wast as true a lover / As ever sigh'd upon a midnight pillow" (*AYL* II.iv.19–25).

Literature often read youth and age in terms of fertile summer and sterile winter, as *The Passionate Pilgrim* shows: "Youth like summer morn, age like winter weather; / Youth like summer brave, age like winter bare" (12). Such thinking sheds light on why the January-May marriage seldom thrives in literature: youthful love and marriage were connected with fertility, and charivaris against January-May marriages express both a community's wish for human fertility and the opposition between youth and age that had become encoded in a seasonal vocabulary. (In Chaucer's tale of an aged man cuckolded, the Merchant's Tale, the husband is actually named Januarie, the wife Mayus.) Winter/summer combat, a common form of fertility rite, translated easily into generational strife when youth was linked with summer, age with winter. The tensions of a January-May marriage actuate *Othello* and probably contribute to our unease at Isabella's marrying the "old" Duke (*MM* IV.iii.156). That common literary figure the aged cuckold combines powerful archaic fears—men's fear of women and age's fear of youth. Bakhtin views cuckoldry as a carnivalesque uncrowning and does not forget that Saturnalia was a fertility festival: in "the uncrowning of the old husband and a new act of procreation with the new husband, . . . the cuckolded husband assumes the role of uncrowned old age, of the old year, and the receding winter" (241).

The Senex

That old age was ambiguously valued appears in the commonest Shakespearean terms for the old—"grave," "graveness," and "gravity": from the Latin *grave* ("heavy"), they import a weighty dignity. Shakespeare uses them to denote age in general: "reverend and grave elders" (*Cor* II.ii.46); the clothing of "settled age" imports "graveness" (*Ham* IV.vii.80–81). Gravity also means wisdom, especially in governing: he refers to "an opinion of wisdom, gravity" (*MV* I.i.92); a land can be "famously enrich'd / With politic grave counsel" (*R3* III.iii.20).[9] Shakespeare also uses *gravity* in regard to possession of political power, which for Elizabethans was the prerogative of age: "Most potent, grave, and reverend signiors" (*Oth* I.iii.76), "grave tribunes" (*Tit* III.i.31), "grave wrinkled senate" (*Tim* IV.i.5). Yet that which is heavy sinks, obeying the law of *gravity,* and the Latin adjective *grave* often sinks toward the Anglo-

Saxon noun *grave,* as in Mercutio's "Ask for me tomorrow and you will find me a grave man" (*Rom* III.i.102)—a bilingual pun with a carnivalesque effect allowing the word's Latin sense to be overwhelmed and displaced by the vernacular, English sense. Cicero's fate is foreshadowed in the conspirators' image of burying in gravity: "Our youths and wildness shall no whit appear, / But all be buried in his gravity" (*JC* II.i.149–50); since he meets his death before the end of the play, the gravity/grave ambiguity grows sinister in hindsight. The aged man whose gravity means power, then, also has one foot in the grave. There is something deathlike about political power in Shakespeare: nearly everyone who becomes a king in Shakespeare dies during the course of the action, as if supreme power itself were the kiss of death. The seemingly magical basilisk capacity of power to kill those within its compass is, I think, a product of the automatic linking in Elizabethan minds of political power with great age, of the deep subliminal association between gravity and the grave.

The rebellious wish to push gravity more quickly into the grave, animating what I call the saturnalia of Time, lies behind one of literature's longest serving figures, the senex: the old man who must be outwitted that the younger generation may come into its own.

A paradigm of child cheating parent of power over dependents and inheritance, the tale of Jacob defrauding his blind father and stealing his brother's birthright is echoed in *The Merchant of Venice:* Launcelot jokingly tricks his blind father, begging his blessing. In this play one father posthumously controls his fortune and his daughter's marital choice; another is robbed by his daughter and fails to control her marital choice. Portia is more typical of Shakespeare than is Jessica: parents' anxiety is usually out of proportion to the child's actual behavior. Children who really abuse their parents are very rare in Shakespeare. Coriolanus threatens to let his mother die, as if he were "author of himself / And knew no other kin" (V.iii.35–37), but face to face with her, he cannot go through with it. His "hysteria" at the age inversion of Volumnia's kneeling to him, Janet Adelman argues, suggests a forbidden wish, a mutiny against her; his horror of the mutinous people projects "mutinous forces within himself" (141–42). Goneril, Regan, and Edmund make *Lear* unique in Shakespeare: nowhere else do children openly abuse their parents. The shock impact of their brutality in an age deeply concerned with parental authority must have been very great. It is still very great.

Often in Shakespeare, parents' fear of their offspring is unwarranted.[10] Even Hal is innocent of the loveless ambition his father suspects—or his explanation of the prematurely grasped crown almost persuades us that he is.[11] The unfocused anxiety Time's saturnalia produces in parents, who find themselves growing weaker, their children stronger, may be displaced onto the children: the child seems to be robbing the parent of power, though the true thief is Time. Such displacement, a magical thinking akin to scapegoating, appears in a tale like *Snow White*, where the queen's fear of losing her beauty with age is displaced onto her stepdaughter, whom she views as a kind of sexual rival. Displacement helps explain the ubiquity of the *senex iratus,* angry old man, usually a father, irate because his child wants to marry against his wishes. Shakespearean examples include the fathers of Juliet, Hermia, Silvia, Anne Page, Jessica, Florizel. Not all fathers are old, but literary senexes (as the term *senex* itself suggests) usually are old: I think they are irate because the child's marriageability reminds them how old they are. A child's attempt to marry without parental blessing is an act on which a parent can displace all his or her primal Cronian anxiety about the younger generation's taking over. The wish to marry seems only human; Solanio is surprised at Shylock's extreme reaction to Jessica's elopement, since "it is the complexion of them all to leave the dam." Shylock cries, "She is damn'd for it," shocked that "my own flesh and blood [could] rebel!" (III.i.28–32). Jessica did not overtly rebel, challenging her father's authority, but eloped, an evasive action; Shylock's "rebel" suggests aggression more than evasion, an attempt to usurp authority. His reaction to Jessica's thefts is not simple materialism, but anxiety at a loss of power over property that has defined his authority. And Solanio, impishly misconstruing "my own flesh and blood" as Shylock's body, suggests that Shylock's anxiety is prompted by aged sexual impotence: "Old carrion! Rebels it at these years?" (III.i.33), which calls on a trope like one we have seen before—where *The Passionate Morris* describes the overwhelming of intellect by sexual desire in terms of saturnalian festivity, Solanio puts this revolt of the lower bodily stratum against the intellect in terms of political revolt.

When a son absents himself without explanation in Shakespeare, the father may well suspect secret love. When Romeo's father worries about his absence, Romeo is mooning over Rosaline. When Polixenes inquires, "When saw'st thou the Prince Florizel, my son? Kings are no less unhappy, their issue not being gracious, than they are in losing them," Camillo tactfully reports, "It is three days since I saw the Prince. What his happier affairs may be are to me unknown; but I have missingly noted he is of late much retir'd from court" (*WT* IV.ii.25–32). The passage closely resembles Henry IV's query, "Can no man tell me of my unthrifty son? / 'Tis full three months since I did see him last," except that in that case Percy tactlessly (maliciously?) reports, "Some two days since I saw the Prince, / And told him of those triumphs. . . . His answer was, he would unto the stews, / And from the common'st creature pluck a glove, / And wear it as a favor." This strangely reassures Henry; canny Hal has ensured that his father will hear he is merely sowing wild oats with prostitutes, not planning an unauthorized marriage, as Florizel is doing during *his* absence. Relieved of playing the senex, Henry leaves Hal to his own devices with a perfunctory moralization: "As dissolute as desperate! Yet through both / I see some sparks of better hope, which elder years / May happily bring forth" (*R2* V.iii.1–22).

Comedies from Terence through *Tom Jones* foil the senex and let the children marry: "To beguile the old folks, how the young folks lay their heads together!" (*Shr* I.ii.136–37). Parents are not much abused by this: the child's chosen mate is nearly always worthier than the parent's nominee. (Boose explains the senex's poor taste as near-incestuous possessiveness: he insists "on someone she does not want, lest a desired husband usurp the father's primary position" ["Father" 331].) A son's chosen slave girl turns out to be a citizen, a foundling is a princess, an illegitimate child is heiress to millions. Once the senex is outwitted, his fortune is safe after all. But time still passes him by, and senexes from Egeus to Shylock are shuffled quickly offstage during the happy ending, lest we contemplate their feelings. The parent's fulminations about a suitor's inferior social class seem an emotional smokescreen: what parents really cannot face is the next generation taking over. Here again, in the frequent intrusion of social class or lack of money as a pretext for opposing a marriage, we see a translation from matters of age and generation to matters of class, just as age inversion in the Saturn myth is translated into social class inversion in the

Saturnalia. The behavior of the senex exposes the mechanisms through which magical thinking about age operates: generational anxieties are driven into the unconscious and displaced onto less frightening concerns. Even social class, a serious enough issue, seems less threatening than generational conflict.

The senex is a figure of sterility and winter: Imogen cries at her husband's banishment, "comes in my father, / And like the tyrannous breathing of the north / Shakes all our buds from growing" (*Cym* I.iii.36–37). The senex drags his feet at the prospect of life going on without him. Comedy's long view of life minimizes the individual; the senex strives against being discarded as humanity marches on. Time's saturnalia robs him of his central position and bestows it on those weaklings, the young, rushing to blossom: "What talk we of fathers, when there is such a man as Orlando?" (*AYL* III.iv.36–37); "I think not on my father. / . . . What was he like? / I have forgot him. My imagination / Carries no favor in 't but Bertram's" (*AWW* I.i.81–85). Lear exposes what lies in the senex's heart when he curses Goneril with sterility. Faced with his own annihilation, the senex tries to take the human race down with him.

The parameters of Shakespearean comedy and tragedy can almost be defined generationally: the topsy-turviness of youth's triumph in comedy seems right side up, since comedy takes a youth's-eye view, or at least a humanity's-eye view that recognizes that youth must triumph. Many tragedies—*Antony and Cleopatra, King Lear, Macbeth*—give us an elders'-eye view, which either sees the triumph of youth as a world having stayed topsy-turvy or simply refuses to take much consolation in the fact that the human race is carrying on. What happens to generations is crucial to both genres. In tragedy, families perish. And the new generation's escape in comedy is narrow: in fifteen of Shakespeare's sixteen comedies, one or more of the romantic leads is an only child. If the senex succeeded in blocking his child's marriage, his lineage would be wiped out.

Lear is the only Shakespearean character who willingly hands over political power to his heirs before his death; the unhappy consequences appear too grossly. Alonso wishes he could abdicate in favor of his son, but he talks that way only while he thinks his son is dead (*Tmp* V.i.149–53). Some characters anticipate nursing by their offspring: "I thought the remnant of mine age / Should have been cherish'd by her child-like duty" (*TGV* III.i.73–74); "I lov'd

her most, and thought to set my rest / On her kind nursery" (*Lr*
I.i.123–24). Being nursed by one's children is less bleak than the
childless pensioner's fate ("unregarded age in corners thrown"), but
it is humiliating too, and "second childishness" *can* be "mere obliv-
ion" (*AYL* II.ii.38–42, vii.164).

A Jacobean preacher spoke of a man living with his son: soon
the father, "by his coughing or spitting or testiness or some . . . un-
towardness or other become[s] troublesome either to his own son
or to his nice daughter-in-law, . . . or to the children, with taking
up their room at the fire or at the table, or to the servants, while
his slow eating doth scant their reversions" (Thomas, "Age" 238).
This is *Lear*'s world. *Lear* makes brutally explicit what is latent in
other texts: "thou mad'st thy daughters thy mothers; . . . thou gav'st
them the rod, and put'st down thine own breeches"; "Dear daughter, I confess that I am old; / Age is unnecessary. On my knees I
beg / That you'll vouchsafe me raiment, bed, and food" (I.iv.169–
71, II.iv.152–54). The daughters' grosser abuses go unnoticed: Lear
never seeks to reenter Regan's house, never knows that she has
locked the doors against him or that his daughters have plotted to
kill him. The humiliation of becoming their child, rebuked like a
boy, is enough to drive him mad: it is not open abuse that prompts
his "O heavens, / If you do love old men, / . . . if you yourselves
are old, / . . . take my part!"; it is Regan's "O, sir, you are old; /
Nature in you stands on the very verge / Of his confine" (II.iv.144–
91). Time's saturnalia has let his child declare his redundancy. Part
of the play's greatness is that it wrests redemptive moments out of
the terrors of generational inversion, as when Lear plans to kneel
to ask Cordelia's blessing (V.vii.84–85), not in an embittered his-
trionic gesture like his earlier kneeling to Regan, but in earnest. Such
moments raise large questions about the age hierarchy: "Kneeling
to ask blessing was a common gesture of respect from child to parent, a symbol of generational hierarchy. In Lear's vision, parent
kneels to child. The need for forgiveness reverses hierarchies of both
age and sex, and suggests their limitations" (Novy 288).

The Empire Strikes Back

The saturnalian inversion of Falstaff and Hal, old man as follow-
er of young man, departs from allegorical sources: in plays like *The*

Interlude of Youth, figures like Riot are not old; prodigals' companions are typically young. Falstaff speaks more truly than he knows when he jocularly claims, contrary to the expected pattern, that he is the misled party ("Before I knew thee, Hal, I knew nothing; and now am I . . . little better than one of the wicked" [*1H4* I.ii.91–94]; a similar dramatic irony informs an exchange in *Part 2: Justice:* "You have misled the youthful Prince." *Falstaff:* "The young Prince hath misled me" [I.ii.143–44]). The age inversion of Falstaff under Hal's leadership echoes the political/military action, especially in *Part 1,* where two young men strive to come into their own. As Hal is ringleader of old tavern reprobates, so he leads the army at Shrewsbury, while older heads follow. Hotspur dominates his father, uncle, and older allies; he is called "Mars in swathling clothes," "infant warrior" (*1H4* III.ii.112–13). The play thus thrice repeats the youth-leading-age pattern. Does age, though, take its revenge? Dying Hotspur says Hal has robbed him of his youth, but he also dies because his father's troops defaulted. Hotspur's wife accuses Northumberland of abandoning his son to death: Hotspur futilely "threw many a northward look to see his father / Bring up his powers" (*2H4* II.iii.10–14). In this play where generational tension is strong, one of the fathers of these two precocious sons steps back and lets the younger generation take a fatal fall. A callous joke is Northumberland's reaction to his only son's death—he says Hotspur is now Coldspur—and grief strangely makes a new man of him: his limbs, "enrag'd with grief, / Are thrice themselves"; he throws away his nightcap and crutch (*2H4* I.i.48–50, 138–47). The image of an old man turned young at his ambitious son's death speaks louder than his averral that grief gives a man strange energies.

War allows the older generation to strike back: Shakespeare's political leaders, not unlike some in our day, are often war-mongering old men eager to send young men to their deaths on foreign shores; in a kind of revenge for the young men's superior virility, the old wield political power as a substitute for virility, as in myth, Romulus "divided the people into two parts according to their years; . . . the one age advised war, the other waged it" (Ovid 325). Coriolanus and his wife and son seem the sole members of the Roman younger generation: everyone else is old—Volumnia, Menenius, Cominius, the tribunes. It is "our best elders" who send Coriolanus to war.

The drama's ubiquitous child-killing parents suggest a general cultural anxiety. Curtius thinks "the opposition of generations" is "one of the conflicts of all tempestuous periods" (98), and this was a tempestuous period. Tamburlaine kills his son, Titus Andronicus his son and daughter; Tamora orders her infant killed; Leontes threatens to dash his baby's brains out and then exposes her on a seashore, like fathers in myth who expose babies (*WT* II.iii.140–41, III.ii.191). Menenius sees in the plot to kill Coriolanus that Rome is "an unnatural dam" eating her child (III.i.290–94), a sinister simile in light of Coriolanus's mother's behavior. Lady Macbeth imagines infanticide, and the witches speak of drabs and their "birth-strangled babes" (I.vii.57–59, IV.i.32). With no children of his own to fear, Macbeth seeks to kill Banquo's son—because of a prophecy (properly mythic) that Banquo's offspring will succeed him.

Elders also strike back through disinheritance, the converse of comedy's happy transfer of property to an heir. Lear disinherits Cordelia, and Gloucester, Edgar; Henry VI bars his only son from the succession; Capulet threatens Juliet, "Graze where you will, you shall not house with me" (III.v.189).

Saturnalia's god, Cronus/Saturn, is an apt symbol of child murder. Diodorus Sicilus records one sacrifice of two hundred noble children to Cronus: "There was in [Carthage] a bronze image of Cronus, extending its hands, palms up and sloping toward the ground, so that each of the children when placed thereon rolled down and fell into a sort of gaping pit filled with fire. . . . [The] ancient myth that Cronus did away with his own children appears to have been kept in mind among the Carthaginians through this observance" (5.365).

Emotional Effects: Ritual, Literature, Life

If inversion of strong and weak is central to Renaissance drama, it is partly because that drama arose in a culture dominated by a religion that inverts strong and weak: "the last shall be first"; the master washes disciples' feet; to enter heaven one must become as a little child; wise men kneel to a baby. Turner has termed Christianity a religion of liminality.[12] As Billington notes, "Christ features throughout medieval drama as the apparent mock, fool king, whose greater kingdom, not of this world, is misunderstood by men conscious only of their worldly power, and it would seem from the crown of thorns that this was how he was treated in his own time" (93). But baby Jesus grew up to be a king and came into his inheritance as a true king in heaven; even Christian liminality is not permanent.

The classic saturnalia inverting social classes is resolutely temporary. The exhilaration lower classes feel, released from duty and constraining authority, is tempered by their being accountable next week to authorities they flout during the holiday; the chagrin of abused authority is softened by anticipated resumption of power. Ideally, lower-class celebrants will carry through the year the sense of worth they felt during saturnalia, and authority figures behave with humility, recalling what it was like to submit to authority; but saturnalia's strongest effects are temporary, ceasing with the festive season. The fact of the limit makes safe the granting of the license.

Unlike festival saturnalias, Time's saturnalia is permanent: once the younger generation has taken over, power is not restored to the aged. If age saturnalia was the model for ritual inversions, if rites of class topsy-turviness mimicked age-inversion myths that mimicked a rhythm of life, the temporariness of festive inversions might anesthetize elders to the permanence of what was to be their condition, tricking their consciousness into believing such conditions temporary—a mode of magical thinking. Since authority figures are not forced to tolerate saturnalian abuse—they have the power to prevent it—presumably such festivities perform a useful function for them; indeed, schoolboy barrings-out, Thomas shows, were promoted by *adults* (*Rule and Misrule* 33). An obvious function is to co-opt potential rebelliousness in subordinates; a less obvious, more magical function is to create the illusion that their nightmare loss of power and prestige in the festival, inferiors insulting and patronizing them, is a temporary dream from which they will awaken. The fertility rites in which such topsy-turviness was deeply involved were satisfying because they gave a sense of human control over nature and social relations—a mind fearing loss of control to the younger generation might naturally reach back for that comforting, magical sense of control.

But despite such ritual anaesthesia, saturnalias like all fertility rites aim ultimately at handing over the world to the next generation. In the basically saturnalian configuration of much comedy, too, the old are outwitted and the world handed over to the young. And in tragedy, where the vision of fertility fails, the tragic ending is expressed not only in terms of sterility and posterity cut off (see chapter 3) but at times also in terms of a younger generation that doesn't measure up.

Matters of Age in *Julius Caesar* and *Antony and Cleopatra*

That elder statesmen should exercise power *Julius Caesar*'s conspirators acknowledge as they consider recruiting Cicero: "His silver hairs / Will purchase us a good opinion . . . / It shall be said his judgment rul'd our hands; / Our youths and wildness shall no whit appear, / But all be buried in his gravity" (II.i.144–49). Caesar, historically in his fifties but (as the play presents him) not yet in the silver-haired league, should acknowledge his junior position: his arrogant remark about Senators—he is not "afeard to tell graybeards the truth"—creates a saturnalian scenario, younger man lording it over elders. The inversion has made people nervous: three instances of age trying to pull rank on youth suggest a desire to return to society's old ways. "Octavius, I have seen more days than you," says Antony; "I am a soldier, I, / Older in practice, abler than yourself," Cassius tells Brutus; and a poet lectures Cassius and Brutus: "Love and be friends, as two such men should be; / For I have seen more years, I'm sure, than ye" (II.ii.67; IV.i.18, iii.30–32, 130–31). Conspirators feel they are restoring order after a misgoverned period: they view Caesar as a kind of Lord of Misrule,[13] an identification strengthened by the fact that Caesar's plebeian adherents celebrate in his honor what is called a "holiday" three times in the play's first scene; the clown/cobbler effects a carnivalesque inversion by rather making an ass of Flavius.

But the misgoverned interval proves permanent. Silver-haired Cicero is executed in a bloodbath of seventy to a hundred venerable Senators, and Rome falls into young men's hands—Octavius is thrice called "young Octavius" (III.i.297, IV.iii.152, 167), and Antony is a young athlete and reveler. The play offers neither the security of a political world returned to the elders' control nor the exhilarating hope of a new regime in competent, energetic young hands. One segment of the younger generation—Caesar's assassins— is eventually closed out entirely, and the triumph of other young men offers nothing like comedy's sense of a younger generation coming into its own. We don't trust them—Antony's shifty ruthlessness comes to the fore soon after Caesar's funeral, as does Octavius's inflexible willfulness—and they don't trust each other. The last lines depict an unsettled society: "Let's away, / To part the glories of this happy day" forecasts the conflict to come. The radical excision of the older generation, like the death of a patriarch whose children are minors, leaves little prospect but sibling rivalry; the age-based Elizabethan polity might well have felt uneasy about a nation governed by squabbling youngsters.

And this was, of course, Rome: as we saw in chapter 1, "the ancient world was the setting for one third of the Shakespeare canon" (Velz 1) and Shakespeare's age was intensely preoccupied with things Roman. England's deep cultural identification with Rome must have combined with the age's deep veneration of Latin and of classical Roman writers to render profoundly distressing to the English this vision of Rome racked by generational strife and governed by a set of rebellious youths. The aged, venerable Cicero who is executed during the play was perhaps the single most influential Roman writer in terms of Renaissance *imitatio*. Seventeenth-century rebellions against his literary authority took the form of setting up Seneca as a rival model; sixteenth-century rebellions seldom went further than arguing that Cicero was not the sole acceptable literary model on the planet (see Scott, White). Julius Caesar himself was much admired and studied as a literary stylist in Shakespeare's time. The very idea of rebellion against venerable authority in Rome—a prominent theme of *Julius Caesar*—must have had complicated resonances in the Renaissance psyche; were not those who wrote in the vernacular and struggled to come into their own against the overwhelming authority of Roman writers rather in the position of *Julius Caesar*'s conspirators? Writing *Julius Caesar* in English, inscribing a crucial piece of Roman history within a vernacular language, allowing only three words of Latin to be spoken in the entire play and then by a dying man, was itself a kind of literary sedition, a rebellion against the father.[14]

From the conspirators' point of view, the action amounts to a generation closed out. As in a saturnalian festival, the dead return;

before Caesar's death, "gliding ghosts" are seen, "graves have yawn'd and yielded up their dead / . . . And ghosts did shriek and squeal about the streets" (I.iii.63, II.ii.18–24); the world of the dead broods over the play. In Act I, Caesar has come fresh from triumph over Pompey; yet he dies under Pompey's statue, as if his dead rival has triumphed. That Brutus's ancestor Brutus ousted the tyrant Tarquin, Cassius and Brutus recall; the legend has been impressed on them by their fathers (I.ii.158–59, II.i.53–54). Portia's father Cato (Brutus's uncle as well as father-in-law) opposed tyranny too—he died supporting Pompey against Caesar. His memory is invoked by Portia, Brutus, and Cato's son young Cato, who dies in battle shouting "I am the son of Marcus Cato, ho! / A foe to tyrants" (II.i.295–97, V.i.101–2, V.iv.4–5). Caesar is murdered specifically in emulation of these tyrant-opposing ancestors; but given the paternal associations attending Caesar, the murder carries Freud's double sense of emulation—imitating and competing with the father. The ancestral presence is suffocating; ancestors enjoy a civic immortality the present generation will never attain. This generation does not measure up: "Rome, thou hast lost the breed of noble bloods! / When went there by an age, since the great flood, / But it was fam'd with more than with one man?"; "Romans now / Have thews and limbs like to their ancestors; / But . . . our fathers' minds are dead" (I.ii.152, iii.80–82). The generation sits "groaning underneath this age's yoke," suffering the "hard conditions" of "this time" (I.ii.61, ii.174).

The young have the air of a group of former schoolmates: Brutus remembers Casca at school and reminds Volumnius "we two went to school together"; he numbers Cassius among his "good friends"; Cassius calls Titinius "my best friend." Antony is a perennial type, that hard-drinking but athletic jock who will find fraternity connections useful in political life; Octavius, somewhat younger, is called a "peevish schoolboy" (I.ii.296; V.v.26; I.ii.43–44; V.iii.35, i.61).

Looming over this male-bonded younger generation is the oppressive world of the ancestors, omnipresent in statuary. Brutus lives under the shadow of the statue of ancestor Brutus; he seems to visit it often—Cassius sticks one of his forged messages on the statue with wax, expecting Brutus to find it soon. Caesar dies on the pedestal supporting Pompey's statue. Brutus's only triumphant moment in the play is when a plebeian cries, "Give him a statue with his ancestors," but it is not to be: Caesar is the only one to join the ancestral statuary world while still alive. Commoners deck his "images" in the play's first scene, and a statue has been raised to him, of which his wife dreams. This rankles with the conspirators: Caesar, who once seemed another schoolmate in his competitive sports and dares—the swimming contest with Cassius—now has "a statue with his ancestors," has become the largest of all statues, the Colossus, "and we petty men / Walk under his huge legs and peep about" (I.iii.146; III.i.115, ii.187–88, ii.50; I.ii.135–37).

Of what generation is Caesar? He seems a young power usurper when he dismisses the venerable Senate as "greybeards" (historical Caesar, of the people's party, was sometimes at odds with the aristocratic Senate; the play's stress on his plebeian following gives a tincture of class conflict to his relations with the Senate). But to the conspirators he is tyrant/father, and Antony defers extravagantly to him ("When Caesar says, 'Do this,' it is perform'd" [I.ii.10]). I will soon argue that the Renaissance lacked a concept of middle age, and Caesar seems less a middle generation than a magically liminal figure, possessing youth's rebellious energy and age's weighty authority at the same moment. His power seems magical to conspirators. Brutus thinks his own fear of Caesar is irrational, which seems odd: since Caesar does behave like an absolute monarch, we may be puzzled that Brutus thinks absolute power might "change his nature" or that "the quarrel / Will bear no color for the thing he is" (II.i.13–29)—the thing he is looks fairly autocratic to us, dangerous in a supposed republic. Yet Brutus fears not what Caesar is, but his mysterious potential: he is an adder waiting for sunshine, "a serpent's egg" (II.i.13–32). Caesar is a young/old figure, a schoolmate who can turn statue.

The ancestors are ambiguous: as venerated forebears, they are the world of the father, before whose monumental image the present generation adopts postures of deference. Yet Lucius Brutus and Cato are venerated not only as ancestors but as rebels against authority; one can imitate them by revolting against present authority. Caesar comes to represent the world of the father, the monumental image, the ancestors. Sonship flickers in images attaching to those who support him—"were you, Antony, the son of Caesar, you should be satisfied" (III.i.226–27); Octavius is Caesar's adopted son.

One of Cassius's earliest images of Caesar, too, casts him as his father: "As Aeneas, our great ancestor, / Did from the flames of Troy upon his shoulder / The old Anchises bear, so from the waves of Tiber / Did I the tired Caesar" (I.ii.112–15)—Caesar is metamorphosing in Cassius's psyche from swimming buddy to father and patriarch of the Roman nation. One venerates rebellious ancestors by rebelling; one imitates the father by killing him: Freudian emulation indeed.

Caesar, who had one foot in the statuary realm while still alive, consolidates his hold on the ancestral world after death. Uncannily, Brutus saw it coming: "We all stand up against the spirit of Caesar, / And in the spirit of men there is no blood" (II.i.167–68). Images of saintly canonization and relic veneration surround Caesar's death: "great men shall press / For tinctures, stains, relics"; "they would go and kiss dead Caesar's wounds / And dip their napkins in his sacred blood, / Yea, beg a hair of him for memory, / And, dying, mention it within their wills" (II.ii.88–89, 134–37). All this is rhetoric; but Caesar makes good his claim on the ancestral world by returning as a spirit, as ghosts walk at Saturnalia, to take a decisive part in human affairs: "O Julius Caesar, thou art mighty yet! / Thy spirit walks abroad, and turns our swords / In our own proper entrails" (V.iii.94–96). Brutus does not see himself as defeated by Antony and Octavius—an intragenerational sibling rivalry—but as having failed in his attempt to overcome the father.

The conspirators never measure up to the illustrious forebears whose shadows haunt the play. Brutus has a vague try at immortalizing Cassius—"It is impossible that ever Rome / Should breed thy fellow" (V.iii.100–101)—but Cassius's own hopes for immortality, not in monumental statuary but onstage ("How many ages hence / Shall this our lofty scene be acted over / In states unborn and accents yet unknown!" [III.i.112–14]), seem dashed: the end of this play's lofty scene dismisses him as having acted only "in envy of great Caesar" (V.v.70). Brutus fares better in the eulogy; but Caesar has defeated him too.

To return to a question with which this chapter began: why all the concern with age in plays of political conflict? Elizabethans naturally conceived political revolution in terms of oedipal struggle within the family, because their system of political power was based on age and seniority and because they were heirs to a long tradition of festive behavior in which inversions of many kinds of public power—lord of the manor/Lord of Misrule, bishop/Boy Bishop, masters running the school/boys taking over the school—were intimately associated with ritual age inversions such as those of the youth abbeys. *Julius Caesar's* revolution causes to happen quickly and prematurely what in the ordinary course of events would happen gradually, mediated by rituals: the inversion of generations that passes power from old to young. Like a premature baby, the infant regime gasps for breath. As the play ends, we are uncertain whether the fatherless child so untimely ripped (by Caesarean, shall we say?) will maintain its precarious hold on life.

Julius Caesar's sequel offers a very different political scenario. In *Antony and Cleopatra,* the world of the father has virtually disappeared. Octavius never mentions his adoptive father Julius Caesar as imperial conqueror or ruler of Rome. In *Julius Caesar* the great man had appeared as competitor of Pompey, young-man-against-Senate, military hero, absolute monarch, and figuratively as Anchises, father of Rome's founder; in *Antony and Cleopatra* he is remembered almost exclusively in a role entirely absent from *Julius Caesar*—as Cleopatra's lover. His earlier world-shaking public role here yields to a private, sexual role. Even the two brief references to him as Octavius's father (III.vi.6, xiii.83) occur in the context of his relationship with Cleopatra.

The world of dead ancestors appears otherwise only in the person of Pompey the Great; however, his son's claim to be opposing Octavius and Antony because they defeated Brutus and Cassius, who were avenging Julius Caesar's defeat of Pompey, takes some liberties with history. Young Pompey's settling quickly for a couple of provinces shows his father-avenging a mere pretext for wars of acquisition. He does not measure up—"Thy father, Pompey, would ne'er have made this treaty," Menas mutters (II.vi.82–83)—but people have stopped caring much about that. No ghosts haunt the play, and nobody worries about not living up to Rome's heroic heritage. The main thread tying current luminaries to dead heroes is the fact that the three great Roman military geniuses, Pompey, Julius Caesar, and Antony, were all lovers of Cleopatra. She does make comparisons of their powers; but usually Antony measures up, leaving no oppressive presence of overshadowing (even sexually overshadowing) ancestors.

One lightener of the stifling atmosphere of Roman history is simply the absence of Rome. Of forty-two scenes, twenty-six are set in Egypt, ten in other parts of the empire, and only six in Rome (and two of these are questionable). Only minimalist signs tell us we are in Rome: *Caesar:* "Welcome to Rome." *Antony:* "Thank you" (II.ii.29–30). In *Julius Caesar,* Rome is a real presence, with streets, walls, battlements, towers, windows, chimneytops, a multichanneled Tiber, the Capitol, Senate house, marketplace, scarf-bedecked images, the porch of Pompey's theater, pulpits for public oratory, and above all statues (I.i.37–63, I.ii.252–86, III.ii.20–27, I.iii.147–53, II.ii.52). Here is a tangible city, civic and imperial history standing about it in massive monuments to a glorious past. Rome in *Antony and Cleopatra* has no substance at all: its heroes are forgotten, except (in Pompey's case) as occasions for nourished grudges. It has no material reality—no streets, no Capitol, no pulpits, no heroic statuary. The only monument the play mentions is in Egypt. The world of Roman ancestors seems dead.

The difference befits a political scene changed from revolution against a ripening dictator to competition amongst power sharers. Renaissance politics spoke the language of the family battleground, and we would expect here less language of youth's revolt against a patriarch and more language of sibling rivalry. Yet the youth-against-age pattern persists: "old ruffian" Antony with his "grizzled head" loses to his young competitor and "must / To the young man send humble treaties" (IV.i.4; III.xiii.17, xi.61–62). Octavius is "scarce-bearded Caesar," "the boy Caesar," "novice," "the young Roman boy" (I.i.21, III.xiii.17, IV.i.i). Shakespeare warped nature to achieve this pattern—Antony ages greatly while Caesar seems not to age at all. Youth/age conflict seems unnecessary to a play of intragenerational strife; that Shakespeare emphasized youth/age conflict, even at the cost of age consistency, testifies to how fundamental to political thinking were age groups and seniority.

Turning Antony and Cleopatra into an older generation allows Shakespeare to convey, in the absence of brooding ancestral spirits, a sense of the younger generation's not measuring up. The soothsayer believes that though Antony is less lucky in worldly affairs, his spirit is greater than Caesar's: "Thy daemon, that thy spirit which keeps thee, is / Noble, courageous, high, unmatchable, / Where Caesar's is not" (II.iii.19–21), and I agree: the world in the hands of prim, efficient Octavius is a diminished place that has irrecoverably lost something that was grand even in its excess. The young Caesar who rules the world at play's end is one of Shakespeare's least attractive figures. If he cares about Rome—its history, its glory, its people—he never mentions it. If he takes pride in his ancestors or his illustrious adoptive father, he doesn't express it. If he has theories on good government, we don't hear about them. If he loves power, he doesn't say so. He dislikes drinking and partying. He has no sex life or love life, no interest in music or poetry, no sense of humor, no friends. The one thing he anticipates with pleasure is dragging his defeated enemies in a humiliating triumph through the streets of Rome. Only one thing matters to Octavius Caesar: winning.

His first utterance in this play is "It is not Caesar's natural vice to hate / Our great competitor" (I.iv.2–3); "competitor" meant both partner and rival, but he emphasizes rivalry. Hatred would be more human: Caesar's lack of "natural vices" is among his vices. He directs every action not toward governing or defending Rome, extending or consolidating empire, but solely toward triumphing over competitors—minor league Lepidus and Pompey, major league Antony. War is not a matter of state but of personal rivalry: "Your wife and brother," he tells Antony, "made wars upon me, and their contestation / Was theme for you—you were the word of war" (II.ii.47–49). War is an extension of the competitive sports and games at which Octavius always beats Antony:

> The very dice obey him,
> And in our sports my better cunning faints
> Under his chance. If we draw lots, he speeds;
> His cocks do win the battle still of mine,
> . . . and his quails ever
> Beat mine.
> (II.iii.33–38)

Though Caesar's move to break the treaty with Pompey and unseat Lepidus is one of those crucial decisions (like Bolingbroke's decision to return from exile) which Shakespeare maddeningly leaves offstage, Antony interprets it as a deliberate provocation to him. Can we believe Octavius's final protestation "how hardly I was drawn into this war, / How calm and gentle I proceeded still / In all my writings" (V.i.74–76)? He pretty clearly went looking for a contest with Antony and found it.

The key word of Cleopatra's eulogy to Antony is "his": "his face," "his legs," "his voice," "his bounty," "his delights"; the key word of Caesar's eulogy to Antony is "my": "my brother, my competitor / . . . my mate in empire, / Friend and companion in the front of war, / The arm of mine own body" (V.ii.75–99, i.35–47). When Cleopatra's eulogy to Antony is interrupted by a Roman, she shouts him down and finishes it; when Caesar's eulogy to Antony is interrupted by an Egyptian, he postpones it. Cleopatra's eulogy expands Antony to a magical giant striding the planet; Caesar's reduces him to a subordinate limb of his own body. As in the beginning, so in the end, Caesar calls Antony "my competitor," but he now shrinks him down to size. That is what winning means.

He does win, at least in his own terms. Cleopatra thinks that in his failing to lead her in triumph, Caesar's fabled luck has changed: she mocks "the luck of Caesar"; and Caesar's usual near-magical speed does fail him at the end: "too slow a messenger," exults Charmian (V.ii.285–321). It undercuts Caesar's triumph, too, that in the play's last line he gives a command to Dolabella, who has just betrayed his interests by tipping off Cleopatra. But the emptiness of youth's triumph lies most in what Caesar is: all that mattered to him on earth was winning, and now his last competitor on earth is gone.

Competition, Male and Female

Looking at competitiveness in *Antony and Cleopatra* reminds us that the saturnalia of Time is at base competitive, involving bitter competition between generations. Just as ritual combat between the sexes can paradoxically promote fruition, as we saw in chapter 3 (Victor Turner's "fruitful contest of the sexes"), so murderous competition between generations ultimately promotes the continuance of the human race. Arnold Van Gennep says that cultures often regard newborn babies, like all strangers entering one's territory, with suspicion and fear that demands ritual, which brings us back to the world of protective magic. Myths of a parent killing or exposing a baby because a prophecy says it will grow up to kill or supplant the mother or father hint that parents suspect and fear babies, suffering early intimations of what I call Time's saturnalia. Elizabethans did abandon babies, mostly out of poverty: in early modern times "between 10 and 40 per cent of urban children were abandoned" (Thomas, "Fateful Exposures" 913); they could be sold or pawned to creditors (see Boswell). Literary baptisms retain a sense that the ceremony ends a time of real danger for the baby; and the danger often resides in the parents. Baptism's public nature reminds parents that society has a stake in a baby's welfare. When Leontes resolves to expose his infant, a member of society unrelated to him, Emilia, stands up for the baby's rights; another nonrelative, Antigonus, preserves the baby's identity. The nurse in Phillip's *Patient and Meek Grissill* defends a baby against its father's death threats.

Most mythic baby exposers are fathers,[15] but mothers can play a curiously complicit role: babies have something to fear from them too. Hermione is offstage when Leontes orders her baby exposed; Griselde does not defend her baby because of "patience" with her husband's cruelty. Yet suggestively, both these baby girls grow up to be their mothers' sexual competitors: Leontes retains traces of the incestuous passion for his daughter overt in the source; Griselde's adult daughter is presented as the new bride of Griselde's estranged husband—her father. Successive tellers of these ancient tales have spun a comforting cocoon of explanations around their frightening implications. Keeping Hermione offstage simply avoids the issue of complicity in the baby's exposure, and Leontes' incestuous urges are softened. The Griselde tales encoat the tale with moralizing on cruelty and patience. Fairy-tale analogue *Snow White* mutes the fearful meaning by making the mother a stepmother. But shrouded within these tales is the idea that just as mythic fathers expose male babies for fear the boys will one day seize political power, so mythic mothers fear female babies as future sexual rivals. In some corner of their hearts, complicity in infanticide is preferable to the mirror's "Snow White is fairer far than you." Literature, myth, and tale reflect a world where male power is political, female power sexual; fathers fear political usurpation, mothers sexual usurpation. Society opposes father-daughter incest partly because it exposes the girl to her mother's jealousy. Such themes, now out in the open (in Toni Morrison's *The Bluest Eye,* a child raped by her father is beaten nearly to death by her jealous mother), were sublimated in Renaissance texts—for example, *Pericles'* incestuous daughter is imagined as cannibalizing her mother (I.i.65–66).

Baptism, a rite of lustration, is a purification rite with analogues in many cultures; inherited guilt (in this case original sin) is washed away with the symbolic water. If baptism's religious operation resembles the magical function of purification from pollution, baptism's social operation resembles the magical function of bodily protection. An important protective rite, baptism eases tension between generations and reminds parents that a child is not their property, to be disposed of as they wish, but an official member of the community, which will stand up for it against parental abuse. Child beating in our time has spawned laws requiring citizens to report child abuse; baptism was an earlier, ritual way of impressing on community members their duty as the child's advocates against the parents. Godparents were an earlier version of the modern child advocate.

In this context we can appreciate the social usefulness of evil-eye beliefs. I noted in chapter 3 that young children are thought particularly vulnerable to attack by the evil eye; I cited Schoeck's account of how in ethnic Mediterranean neighborhoods a meeting of women will suddenly break up "as soon as a childless woman joins the group. . . . The frightened mothers just take it for granted that the barren woman must envy their happiness and therefore cannot help casting the evil eye" (198). I would argue that evil-eye beliefs themselves play an important role in ensuring that "mothers just take it for granted that the barren woman must envy their happiness": such beliefs help construct motherhood as an enviable state by the workings of something like René Girard's mimetic desire—if a childless woman envies a mother, motherhood must be highly desirable. As I will soon argue, seemingly destructive civil wars can have the constructive result of reinforcing centralized government by making sovereignty seem desirable; similarly, the seemingly destructive scenario of evil-eye accusations can have the constructive effect of making parenthood seem desirable. (Constructive, that is, from society's point of view, if not always from the individual's.) With or without evil-eye beliefs, constructing the desirability of parenthood still goes on: young married women still experience pressure from society—from relatives, church groups, other women—to desire babies and to take pleasure in having and rear-ing them. This programmatic construction of desire, into which considerable cultural work has always gone, attests to the fact that nature itself cannot be counted on to do the whole job—to have to tell a young woman that desire for a baby is "natural" is itself a confession that nature alone, without culture's promptings, will not be persuasive enough. Young women in early modern times had many reasons for approaching motherhood with ambivalence. Times were hard. Male laborers' wages were designed to support one person: wife and children were expected to shift for themselves by spinning, selling eggs, and so forth. It was hard for women to find work: new statutes were barring women from many trades they had once practiced. Crop failures, enclosures, and depressions in the textile industry caused great hardship (see Sharp). Contraception was rare and unreliable, and many women died in childbirth. Motherhood was not necessarily a joyful prospect, and given the fact that 10 to 40 percent of urban children were abandoned, it might seem odd if mothers "took it for granted that the barren woman must envy their happiness." Society had many ways of persuading women to have and rear babies: charivaris punished childless couples; the childless couple was a feature of many folk tales, which always remedied the situation, even if only with the birth of a little Tom Thumb, and the resolution into parenthood was always presented as a joyful one. Evil-eye belief, declaring parenthood so enviable as to inspire fearful malice in those deprived of its joys, belongs to this cultural effort.

Evil-eye belief also allows any qualms a woman feels about motherhood to be projected onto the childless evil-eyed: it is not the mother who wishes her children dead—it is that malicious childless one. The mother projects her own evil eye, as it were, onto another. As Howard Stein puts it, "thoughts and feelings intolerable for the maintenance of self-esteem and which may be felt as endangering one's very survival are projected outward as ego-alien and become transformed into threats from without" (31; see also Dundes 265)—a process analogous to *Henry V*'s configuring the threat to England as external, which I discussed in chapter 2. We ourselves are so heavily socialized to believe that desire for children is "natural" and parenthood "naturally" an enviable state that even the vast amount of child abuse now coming to light is insufficient to shake such beliefs.

Freudian interpreters have emphasized the effect on a child of the seeming rejections and harshnesses involved in weaning and toilet training; but I think insufficient attention has been paid to the traumatic shock of becoming a mother—the sudden, cataclysmic cessation of freedom of action, the round-the-clock responsibility, and the heavy drain on material resources induce enough psychic strain to explain many a child beating and to explain why society has to invest so much energy in persuading women how joyful it all is. Folk tales, though involved in persuading childless couples how miserable they are, have long recognized the horrors of parenthood, especially in hard times: when food is short, Hansel and Gretel's mother abandons them in the forest.

Folk tales typically soften such insights so they are not unbearably painful, by splitting the parent into Good Mother/Bad Mother (Cinderella's fairy godmother versus her stepmother), or simply by making a rejecting parent a stepmother rather than a biological mother, and Shakespeare too displaces parental rejection onto stepparents or foster parents, as when *Cymbeline*'s queen tries to murder her stepdaughter. Though she is a folk-tale wicked stepmother clearly modeled on *Snow White*'s queen, *Cymbeline*'s queen's opening words in the play are "Be assured you shall not find me, daughter, / After the slander of most stepmothers, / Evil-eyed unto you" (I.i.69–71). Though Shakespeare does not ascribe the evil eye to natural parents, he here bestows one on a stepmother. He further sanitizes child hatred by making it an aspect of the surrogate parent's jealousy on a biological child's behalf. Thus Dionyza wants to murder Marina because she outshines her own daughter; Duke Frederick banishes Rosalind partly because she outshines his daughter; Cymbeline's queen hates Imogen because she will not marry her son. Such plots, even as they display cruelty to a child, can preserve society's cherished belief in the naturalness of parental affection: cruelty is possible only when nature is absent—a stepchild is not a biological offspring; and the naturalness of parental affection is affirmed in that the Dionyzas and Fredericks hate their foster children only out of love for their natural children.

That conflict between generations is an intimate part of evil-eye belief is suggested by Stein's findings among contemporary Slovak Americans, who attribute evil-eye belief to troubles at the time of weaning:[16] in this culture, weaning is a sudden, severe rejection—the breast is withheld and the child left to cry for several days until it drinks from a cup. If the mother cracks from the crying and reoffers the breast, the child will grow up to have the evil eye. In the moment when she is struggling to come to terms with a crying, rejected baby we can see crystallizing all the mother's guilt over her resentment of motherhood, her periodic mental rejection of the baby; she feels cruel, unnatural, rejecting, and the fact that it is the child who grows up to have the evil eye suggests that she projects her feelings of unnaturalness onto the child. The situation is strikingly like that in the commonest witch-accusation scenario, the accusation that an old woman to whom one has denied alms is a witch. In both, one person denies food to another and then attributes evil wishes to her: since I have harmed you, you must wish me ill; but the fact that you are so malicious as to wish me ill relieves me of responsibility for harming you. Evil-eye beliefs affecting children seem a kind of witchcraft belief specialized to the tensions of family life, the conflict between generations that was so central to the literature of this period. The competition between generations that often manifests itself as competition for power between an old man and a young, or sexual rivalry between a middle-aged woman and a young, appears in the mother/infant relation as a zero-sum struggle for survival. The baby, utterly dependent, struggles to survive against the mother's impulse to abuse, neglect, or abandon it; the mother struggles against the suckling infant's metaphorically sucking her dry—taking up all her time, energy, and resources. In creating a mutual love strong enough to blunt the competitive edges of this struggle, nature plays a part, but so does culture.

Competition between generations, then, is severe enough to call forth ritual protections and magical beliefs such as that of the evil eye, and it affects both sexes. As Shakespeare presents competitiveness in general, however, it much more frequently afflicts men than women. If women are socialized to desire babies, men are socialized to desire power, which suggests that desire for power is no more natural than desire for babies: that culture needs to pressure women and men respectively to desire babies and power suggests that cultures have an urgent need for reproduction and leadership and that neither of these is, for individuals, a natural desideratum, despite everything that has been said in favor of power by new historicists. These constructed desires affect the two sexes differently—although baby desire may result in competition between generations, it promotes cooperation within a single age group—the other young women who are saying how wonderful motherhood is; power desire sets members of different generations *and* the same generation against each other. When Shakespeare presents little knots of women together, they are usually cooperating; similar small groups of men are more often competing.

One cannot help feeling that one reason King Lear's family life has a cutthroat quality is that (perhaps because it lacks a mother) it lacks the strategies that women have evolved—including evil-eye beliefs—for coping with the natural conflicts of family life without allowing them to erupt into open competition and even war. Lear seems incapable of imagining family life as other than competition: Cordelia has, over the years, won the competition for his love, and now he launches a new competition to determine once and for all which daughter loves him most. In *Hamlet,* we see at Ophelia's funeral that one acceptable male way to deal with that embarrassingly "female" behavior, expression of emotion, is to turn it into a competition: Hamlet and Laertes compete to establish who is grieving the most.[17] In some crucial Shakespearean texts—*Antony and Cleopatra, As You Like It*—competitive sport is an emblem of such masculine competition. But the world of competition, as we clearly see in the futile triumphs of Octavius Caesar, is a world of sterility.

A Carnival of Language

At several points in this chapter I have spoken of the struggle of upstart young English to come into its own against the patriarch, Latin, and I have suggested that Shakespeare's inscribing Roman history and Latin sources within the English language was itself an inversion, a carnivalesque gesture. Another kind of carnivalization of Latin occurs, as François Laroque suggests, when clowns in Renaissance literature misunderstand Latin in such a way as to suggest Bakhtin's "lower bodily stratum": in Nicholas Udall's *Respublica* a clown hears the Latin *respublica* as "rice pudding cake" (3.3.636–37; 4.1.1007; 5.7.1612); in *Love's Labor's Lost* a clown hears *ad unguem* as "ad dunghill" (5.1.84) (43). Linguistically, English has here risen up and overwhelmed Latin; bodily, the lower-body associations of puddings and dunghills have risen up and over-whelmed the intellectual associations of *respublica,* a political entity, and *ad unguem,* a phrase concluding a scholastic exercise. In the plots of plays, the clown's exuberant liberties with language rise up and overwhelm the stuffy pedantries of an "intellectual" such as Holofernes, whose defeat is manifest when his very objection to the clown's linguistic carnivalizations, "I smell false Latin," is couched in the language of the senses. The best example of carnivalized Latin, however, is in Mrs. Quickly's clownlike role in *Merry Wives'* Latin lesson, where *hic, haec, hoc* becomes "'hang-hog' is Latin for bacon" and "genitive,—horum, harum, horum" provokes "vengeance of Jenny's case! fie on her! never name her, child, if she be a whore" (IV.i.42–65). It is no accident that malapropism belongs both to clowns and other lower-caste figures and to women, like Mrs. Quickly and later Mrs. Malaprop herself and a host of other female malaprops. Both belong to society's equivalent of the lower bodily stratum. (Latin itself was a jealously guarded male language to which most women had no access.) Their misuse of fancy, intellectual words is a revolt of the uneducated against the erudite, and if the world of erudition takes its revenge by the ridicule it heaps on a malaprop for making errors, some small part of the language abuser's perspective remains in our minds, qualifying our respect for all those who intimidate ordinary folk by using big words.

Clownish malapropism is a kind of absurd translation; some of its carnivalesque implications can be seen in serious translation. That this was a great age of translation, from learned languages into vernaculars, is of a piece with the age's other saturnalian revolts, from class uprisings to Protestantism: to bring the Bible down to the level of the people's language is to let the people rise. *Translatio linguarum* formed the basis of the whole Renaissance educational system; but despite its being one of society's intellectual foundations, there are at least some indications that translation was fraught with obscure anxieties: John Florio's dictum "all translations are reputed females" and are therefore "defective" (Sig. A2), suggests that translation comprises the dragging down of a master language into a vernacular, tantamount to a male's becoming a female. When translation thus becomes a kind of transvestism, the world of carnival has erupted: lower overwhelms higher. "Translation" partook of magical thinking—in Shakespeare's time the word had several magical and magico-religious senses ("translate" meant to move the dead body of a saint or hero from one place to another, to convey to heaven without death), and translation resembled some of the more frightening kinds of magic, such as shape-shifting: when Bottom is turned into an ass, Quince cries, "Bless thee! thou art translated" (*MND* III.i.122). Like printing, translation bordered obscurely on the diabolical—it allowed one to usurp the power of an illustrious dead culture hero by appropriating his language, magically replacing it with one's own, like folkloric demons who take over someone's body. This magic was a kind of revolt, a translator rising from the underclass to usurp the language of an author—a saturnalian task.

Other uses of language, too, have a saturnalian dimension. Riddles, linked with fertility rites (see chapter 4), have a saturnalian side: "Folklorists note the popularity which riddles hold in many cultures for women and children, who pose riddles and thereby assume the kind of authoritarian roles they do not normally fill. . . . The riddler enjoys the superior power of the interrogator" (Gorfain, "Riddles and Reconciliation" 272). And ritual cursing was topsy-turvy by nature: "It was only if the injured party was too weak to avenge himself in any more obvious way that he had recourse to the substitute of calling down supernatural vengeance. Curses were employed by the weak against the strong, never the other way around. It was when children had outgrown normal means of parental control that the dreadful weapon of the father's curse was invoked" (Thomas, *Religion* 607–8). King Lear's cursing is an index of how far authority has been inverted—while he still possessed royal authority, he had no need to curse. As verbal magic enabling the weak to overcome the strong, curses resemble riddles, and along with Lear's curses go the riddles of the Fool, whose foolish wisdom expresses in this saturnalian language the uncrowning of conventional wisdom, in a topsy-turvy *Lear* world in which categories of reason and folly, sanity and madness, are inverted, where Lear learns more in one night of madness than he had learned in eighty years of sanity.

The World Upside Down

Renaissance plays often imagine permanent saturnalia, a chaos where social hierarchies disappear and nature's laws are inverted: "Monarchs turn to beggars; beggars creep into the nests of princes, masters serve their prentices: ladies their servingmen, men turn to women . . . And women turn to men" (Dekker and Middleton, *1 Honest Whore* IV.iii.130–35);

> Are . . . women now transform'd to men?
> Why do you not as well our battles fight,
> And wear our armour? suffer this, and then
> Let all the world be topsy turved quite.
> Let fishes graze, beasts, swine, and birds descend,
> Let fire burn downwards whilst the earth aspires:
> Let winter's heat and summer's cold offend.
>   (Cary, *Mariam* Sig. [B4]ᵛ–C)

Vincentio compares his failure to enforce laws with chaos-spawning abdication of paternal authority: "In time the rod / Becomes more mock'd than fear'd; so our decrees, / Dead to infliction, to themselves are dead, / And liberty plucks justice by the nose; / The baby beats the nurse" (*MM* I.iii.23–30). He tries to cure this with more topsy-turviness: in a reverse saturnalia, an older man's lawless, licentious reign is interrupted by a perverse holiday—rigid law and sexual repression presided over by a young man (a pattern closely resembling that in *Antony and Cleopatra*). Angelo, a kind of public senex opposed to sexuality, ushers in an era previewing that historical reverse saturnalia, the Puritan interregnum. Pitting one topsy-turviness against another backfires; the play ends in a sense of nothing's having been resolved, of a society whose moral chaos may be permanent.

The world-upside-down literary topos (which first appeared, says Curtius, in a work of Archilochus, 648 B.C.), had a counterpart in broadsheet woodcuts of the world-upside-down type—a very saturnalian genre; among many inversions (male/female, master/servant, human/animal), age inversions are the most prominent, with infants beating fathers or feeding mothers, aged couples playing with toys, children bigger than adults (Kunzle 50). Such topoi spring from

the upside-down semiotics of festivity, which also provided schemata for making sense of real-life happenings: the literary world-
upside-down topos was often applied to that real-life inversion, the
civil war (see Hill). The English Renaissance, torn by religious upheavals, disoriented by dizzying social, economic, and technological change and racked by civil war, adapted the world-upside-down
topos to suit its own sense of impending chaos.

In other literary world-upside-down set pieces, Ulysses argues that
without hierarchy water would overwhelm land, strength "be lord
of imbecility, / And the rude son should strike his father dead" (*Tro*
I.iii.109–15). Timon utters a saturnalian curse:

> Obedience fail in children! Slaves and fools,
> Pluck the grave wrinkled Senate from the bench,
> And minister in their steads! . . .
> Son of sixteen,
> Pluck the lin'd crutch from thy old limping sire,
> With it beat out his brains!
> (IV.i.4–15)

In an astrological piece of magical thinking, Gloucester attributes
to "these late eclipses of the sun and moon" a number of world-
upside-down phenomena: "in cities, mutinies; in countries, discord;
in palaces, treason; and the bond crack'd 'twixt son and father"
(*Lr* I.ii.106–12). Such visions hardly suggest the festive release
thought an emotional effect of saturnalia. Plays employing this topos often disturbingly lack closure: unlike Chaucer or Henryson,
Shakespeare does not kill Troilus or give Cressida leprosy—the play
peters out in a limbo of cynicism; Timon, dying without the heightened passion or redeeming self-knowledge of other tragic heroes,
is buried in that liminal zone, the shore. Saturnalia's cathartic effect is absent; these plays leave us in inverted worlds, Alices stranded
on the wrong side of the looking glass. Shakespeare often truncates
saturnalian patterns before the moment of restoration. If these plays
do not openly challenge the magical thinking that legitimates the
status quo by correcting a frightening inversion, they do seem deeply
uneasy with such thinking and subvert it by leaving the world upside down.

Youth's ascendancy in the Henriad gives us less the comedic sense
of a world handed over to a new generation than the sense of a

truncated saturnalian ritual that leaves the world upside down. In *1 Henry IV,* one youth triumphs but the other dies, abandoned by his father. Images of age and debility haunt *Part 2.* An old man hobbling from sickbed on a crutch opens the play. Falstaff's amorousness is derided: "Is it not strange that desire should so many years outlive performance?" (II.iv.259–60). Shallow laments, "How many of my old acquaintance are dead!"; "Jesu, dead! A' drew a good bow; and dead? A' shot a fine shoot. . . . Dead?" (III.ii.34–46). Of Jane Nightwork, Falstaff reports, "Old, old." Shallow muses, "Nay, she must be old. . . . Certain she's old, and had Robin Nightwork by old Nightwork before I came to Clement's Inn." He is reminded, "That's fifty-five years ago." The Falstaff who elsewhere proclaims "they hate us youth" here includes himself among the aged: "How subject we old men are to this vice of lying!" (III.ii.205–10, 302–3). When the old order dies with Hal's aged father, youth sweeps into power; Hal's rejection of Falstaff is specifically youth's discarding of age: "I know thee not, old man . . . / How ill white hairs become a fool and jester! / I have long dreamt of such a kind of man, / So surfeit-swell'd, so old, and so profane, / But, being awak'd, I do despise my dream" (V.v.47–51). An audience undisturbed by this as an answer to "God save thee, my sweet boy!" will not be unsettled by Hal's saturnalia of Time, where the young and healthy pack the old and decrepit off to prison, out of sight, out of mind. But a history of indignation over Hal's brutal rejection shows that audiences *do* feel unsettled. If he began as a Lord of Misrule, Falstaff has become a human being with whom we sympathize. And if he represents old age, the dying year swept away by new year, a new generation, he also embodies life-affirming elements of comedy's world—food, plenty, holiday, escape from the workaday landscape of order and duty.

And Hal's greatest triumph, in *Henry V,* imaged as youth and spring sweeping over corrupt, debilitated France, ends more upside down than any of Hal's plays: the epilogue reminds us that Henry V will die young, leaving England in a dangerously saturnalian, "Boy Bishop" state, governed by a child: "Henry the Sixth, in infant bands crown'd King" will lose France and make England bleed.

Shakespeare's work riots in saturnalian situations; but plays exploit such vestigial magical rites mainly in working against them. Ritual soothes; its annual repetitions reassure us that after upheavals

the world will revert to normal, generations and genders and social classes resume "normal" hierarchies. But Shakespeare often
tears the veils from such mystifications, bids us face the truth that
Time's saturnalia is permanent and our children will displace us for
good, face the possibility that they may not measure up even to us,
may preside over a worse world than this one, more chaotic, more
venal, smaller in spirit. Even comedies, which ask us to accept
Time's saturnalia and rejoice at youth's triumph, leave moments of
terrible doubt—the crushing of Shylock, Vincentio's dubious marriage to a would-be nun, the younger generation of *All's Well,* so
unattractive we wish the world could remain in the hands of the
old. As Freud believes one can "undo dream-displacement by means
of analysis" ("On Dreams" 655), so Shakespeare sometimes undoes
magical thinking, decoding cunning displacements, forcing anxieties
up to the surface of consciousness.

The world upside down is rendered in magical terms in Marlowe's *Dr. Faustus,* where Faustus's bargain with the devil—you be
my servant for twenty-four years and then I will be your servant
for the rest of eternity—resembles saturnalian feasts wherein the
master/servant roles are reversed for an agreed-upon period of time,
after which they revert to the "normal" hierarchy. Perhaps the comforting familiarity of the saturnalia schema is part of Faustus's characteristic self-delusion, for a moment's reflection will show that there
is nothing "normal" about situating oneself as a servant of the devil.
We recall the way witchcraft was mapped onto political sedition,
as the demonic pact was read as a treasonable transfer of allegiance
from a rightful lord to a wrongful one. In making himself servant
to a rebel, Faustus becomes both rebellious (against God) and servile (to the rebel against God), the paradox visible in *Julius Caesar*
where rebels against the political father position themselves as paying homage to their (rebellious) ancestors. Faustus has his own servant, Wagner, who rebelliously makes unauthorized use of Faustus's
magic books, and Wagner enlists unemployed Robin to be his servant, and then Robin rebelliously makes use of the books and begins to lord it over Dick, and they call up Mephistophilis to be their
servant, in an infinite regress of master/servant relationships, like
the self-similar "scaling" effect discovered by modern scientific students of chaos. Here chaos indeed threatens, for there is instability
at every step: Mephistophilis informs Faustus, "I am servant to great

Lucifer / And may not follow thee without his leave" (I.iii.42–43), and Dick reminds Robin that he is not his servant—"You had best leave your foolery, for an my master come, he'll conjure you, faith" (II.iii.13–14). Small passages such as these are chinks through which we view a larger topsy-turviness: it is not clear at any point just who is serving whom. The supposed servant Mephistophilis casually refuses to comply with several of Faustus's demands, and it is pretty clear that the devil, far from waiting his turn to play master, is never under Faustus's control throughout the twenty-four earthly years—the fearsome bullying Faustus undergoes at the hands of Lucifer, Beelzebub, and Mephistophilis is hardly the scenario that Faustus had in mind when he imagined the wonders he would "make my servile spirits to invent" (I.i.98). The radical instability of master/servant relationships in the play could be referred to early modern social conditions, where class structures were shifting and tensions between classes were building.

Magical Thinking and the World of Misrule

Principles of magical thinking underlying the discourse of rule and misrule are imbued with principles of magical thinking underlying discourses of protection, scapegoating, fertility, and power that I have discussed. We could see the world of misrule as an orientalized rule, misrule being rule's cultural contestant as (in Said's formulation) the Orient has been Europe's. If in the Europe of rule we find adults, the ruling class, males, humans, and intellectuality, in the Orient of misrule we find children, the lower classes, females, animals, and the lower bodily stratum.[18] The Europe of rule speaks Latin, writes epics, and polishes its blank verse; the Orient of misrule speaks the vernacular, writes pastorals, poses riddles, and utters curses. Just as chaos is a special kind of order, Sandra Billington suggests that "misrule was thought to be allied to rule as an interrelated opposite" and that "just as one cannot understand daylight, white, and happiness without the contrast of night, black, and sorrow, so too the boundaries of rule were defined by the existence of its opposite, and it could be said that one did not exist without the other" (1, 3). Misrule can then be understood by the rules of enemy formation that I discussed in the chapter on scapegoating.

One constructs enemies because one needs an Other against which to define oneself; as Billington suggests, misrule was necessary to define the boundaries of rule. Enemies are mirror images of oneself because one projects onto them one's own disowned qualities—the world of misrule with its mock kings and court-mimicking ceremonies is a mirror image of the world of rule, and the frequency with which actual rulers were denounced as Lords of Misrule (see Billington) suggests that Lords of Misrule were constructed out of projections of actual rulers' misbehavior in the first place. The creation of the world of misrule depends on principles of detachability and transference that belong to the discourse of scapegoating.

The world of misrule, the carnival world, is the world of the lower bodily stratum described by Bakhtin; rule and misrule depend on the body as an image of society in Mary Douglas's terms, discussed in chapter 1. Douglas's interest in the threat of bodily pollution involved her in the contemplation of dirt, of which she concluded, "Dirt is essentially disorder. There is no such thing as absolute dirt: it exists in the eye of the beholder. Dirt offends against order" (*Purity* 2). Such a definition suggests a correlation between pollution and misrule: if cleanness consists of order, dirt of disorder, then purity is to pollution as rule is to misrule. Denizens of the Orient of misrule are often thought of as dirty—children are called snotty-nosed and said to delight in sandlot grubbiness and to resist washing behind their ears; women are seen as unclean—many cultures consider menstruation a pollution; and as for animals, I have known owners of immaculately clean cats who have insisted on washing the cat's dishes separately from the humans' dishes.

The boundary-protection magic I discussed in chapter 1 is not unrelated to the policing of the boundaries of rule by exiling to certain calendric ghettoes the licensed periods of misrule. And that the holiday periods of misrule often coincide with holidays devoted to fertility rites reflects the fact that misrule holidays often double with fertility festivals, since their purposes overlap—the triumph of youth over age brings fertility to the world. It is no accident that Robin Hood has connections both with fertility rites (he was often King of May) and with saturnalian revolt, robbing the rich to give to the poor.

Misrule is also intimately related to fertility in the recurring cultural subtext that holds that conflict is fructifying. Early modern thinking was entrenchedly hierarchical, and nearly every conflict could be seen as misrule rising against rule. Such unruliness conduced ultimately to fertility: this invisible mental structure seems operative in popular fertility rites such as hero combat, ritual tugs-of-war, and other seeming representations of the battle between summer and winter; in ritualized male/female conflict such as occurred on St. Distaff's Day and Hock Tuesday; in ritually connected games such as checkers, chess, and cards; and in the male/female and old/young debates in pastoral.

Steam Valve or Tinderbox?

The saturnalia that inverts social classes has long been a site of fierce debate: does carnival contain class tensions by providing a regular outlet, harmless because understood to be temporary (anthropologists call this theory *Ventilsitten,* steam valve), or foster a mentality conducive to actual revolt? Jonathan Dollimore dubs this disagreement the "subversion-containment debate" (12).[19] This debate is at the heart of the new historicist/cultural materialist praxis; though it is sometimes difficult to sort out who is on which side, in general the American new historicists tend to lean more toward containment and the British cultural materialists toward subversion. My quarrel with the containment faction is that they grant the ruling class—and often the monarch as a single person—near omnipotence and omniscience in the practice of social control. I have sometimes argued on the subversionist side of the debate; but with regard to saturnalia and carnival misrule, I incline toward the containment view, not granting the ruling class too much credit for consciousness in the matter of social control, but recognizing the complicity of oppressed groups in any hierarchical authority structure. They are indoctrinated to stay in their place, true; but also, the human desire for stability and predictability—even of an oppressive situation—creates inertia against major social change. Bristol is right that "holiday, or holy-day, Carnival and misrule are not isolated episodes in a uniform continuum of regularly scheduled real-life: the experience of holiday pervades the year and defines its rhythm" (201); this very fact shows how holiday misrule is co-opted, given a place in an annual cycle, which licenses it on condition that it remain temporary, isolated in calendric ghettoes. That carnival must give way to "laws and customs which subordinated plebeian to patrician" is "implicit in the very notion of a festive *calendar*" (Stallybrass, "'Wee Feaste'" 234).

Mapping subversion/containment onto age saturnalia, we see that school misrule had prescribed seasons: "the approach of Christmas, . . . Shrove Tuesday, Royal Oak Day, . . . St. Andrew's Day or the day of the mayoral election [were] traditional times of misrule" (Thomas, *Rule and Misrule* 29), just as 1960s university antiwar demonstrators favored the final exam period. Thomas concludes, "like other forms of misrule, barring-out [was] essentially an alternative to political activity rather than a positive agent of change" (34).

Davis shows that the charivari, "a noisy, masked demonstration to humiliate some wrong-doer," worked "in the service of the village community, clarifying the responsibilities that the youth would have when they were married men and fathers, helping to maintain proper order within marriage" ("Reasons" 42, 54). Here again, misrule was a kind of rule. And "apprentice rioters did not indiscriminately run amok; they pulled down brothels" (Thomas, *Rule and Misrule* 32)—another "unruly" enforcement of conservative community standards.

Thomas says charivaris expressed "a harshly intolerant popular culture, hostile to privacy and eccentricity, and relying on the sanction not of reason but of ridicule," adding of carnival abuse, "shocking though it seemed, the main drift of this laughter of burlesque and inversion was conventional. . . . It reinforced accepted morality by mocking superiors by standards which they themselves upheld" ("Place of Laughter" 78). The conservatism of festive abuse is too seldom granted; many regard nose thumbing at authority as tending naturally toward left-wing politics. Barber's hearing in the "satire of the period" the tone of "a Lord of Misrule's vaunting and abuse" (*Shakespeare's Festive Comedy* 52) ignores the overwhelming conservatism of Renaissance satire, whose targets were not obnoxious authority or repressive convention but fops, usurers, outlandishly dressed women, smokers, lying travelers—those who failed to conform to repressive convention. Paradoxically, early modern organized rebelliousness was a tool of social continuity. In its triumph, the younger generation ultimately became indistinguishable from the generation it supplanted.

The civil war abetted the waning, during the seventeenth century, of the "carnival forms of folk culture, which became small and trivial" (Bakhtin 236). The Puritan attack on all forms of "pagan" saturnalian expression had long been growing—Boy Bishop festivities were abolished in 1541, and Puritans attacked Lords of Misrule, court jesters, barrings-out, the Oxford Terrae Filius; a cleric fumed of this last that it was "one of the grossest immoralities" that youths should "boldly and openly reproach, vilify, name and point at their superiors." Throughout the Stuart period "the university authorities struggled to silence this licensed buffoon. They tried persuasion, threats, even bribery. One vice-chancellor called the troops in; another pulled the orator down with his own hands" (Thomas, "Place of Laughter" 79). The "vices" Puritans attacked were largely elements of youth culture: holidays when youth were free from adult supervision, resorts of young people such as theaters, alehouses, and dances, and "all the annual rites of misrule when youth temporarily inverted the social order" (Thomas, "Age" 221).

Thomas sees prewar unrest as a cause of antisaturnalianism: "Religious and political discord made mockery and affront appear a threat to the social order, rather than a means of symbolic reinforcement. . . . So long as the social hierarchy itself went unchallenged, the rites of inversion could be safely tolerated. . . . But once men had begun to question the principles of that hierarchy, then an annual ritual which emphasized its arbitrary nature came to seem positively dangerous" ("Place of Laughter" 79)

Again, tinderbox and steam valve compromise: saturnalian rites can spark revolutionary impulses, but revolution destroys saturnalia. Gluckman's findings about the Zulu translate well into a Renaissance context: saturnalian "ritual rebellions proceed within an established and sacred traditional system, in which there is dispute about particular distributions of power, and not about the structure of the system itself. This allows for instituted protest, and in complex ways renews the unity of the system" ("Rituals" 112). "Instituted protest" is protest encouraged by the authorities, "seemingly against the established order, yet [aiming] to bless that order to achieve prosperity" (114)—like the schoolboy barrings-out under adult sponsorship. Because calendric saturnalian rites occur "within an established and unchallenged social order," these African rites can "express, freely and openly, fundamental social conflicts" (126–27). In Zulu civil wars, "contenders for power against established authority sought only to acquire the same positions of authority for themselves" (127), a situation like the Wars of the Roses. Saturnalian rites can exist here, as the age saturnalia of Hal and Falstaff befits the Wars of the Roses, because such wars actually strengthen a centralized government. In the multitribe Zulu nation, as in the Wars of the Roses when feudalism was giving birth to a nation state, the greatest danger is tribal secession and national disintegration: "Periodic civil wars thus strengthened the system by canalizing tendencies to segment, and by stating that the main goal of leaders was the sacred kingship itself" (130–31). The Puritan civil war, however, differed fundamentally in replacing not monarch but monarchy; such a threat to the established order made saturnalian rites too dangerous to maintain. "'Ritual rebellion' can be enjoyed by tradition, as a social blessing, in repetitive social systems, but not in systems where revolution is possible" (Gluckman 135).

Looking back from the vantage point of the civil war, sixteenth- and early seventeenth-century Puritan opposition to rites of age inversion looks like another example of ritual opposed because it hits too close to real life; for despite Puritans' horror at age-inversion rites like the Boy Bishop, the Terrae Filius, or barrings-out, when it came time for the Puritans to rebel against the established political order, it largely was a case of young men rebelling against old, as Christopher Hill has shown.

Saturnalian rites were gradually disabled in England during the sixteenth and seventeenth centuries: Puritans dismantled ritual forms; political authorities co-opted what had not been dismantled; and revolutionary impulses sparked by saturnalian rites abetted a war whose chaos caused all classes to lose their taste for saturnalian rites. The rise of the middle classes damaged saturnalia, too, because as Thomas notes, saturnalia as a class inverter works best in a two-class system: waning of such rites "reflected the growth of a more complex social structure. Lords and servants could ex-

change places, but for the middle classes, who had no polar opposite, role-reversal was impossible" ("Place of Laughter" 79). The
same kind of deconstruction was bound to happen someday to the
age-inversion rites still intact in the Renaissance.

I have tried to some extent to separate from each other different
kinds of age inversion: the *ritual* inversions of saturnalian rites, carnivalesque forms like youth abbeys, charivaris, Boy Bishop feasts,
anti-authoritarian buffoonery in inns of court or universities, school
barrings-out, Shrove Tuesday rites; the *historical* inversions of class-
based wars, or opposition between political generations; the *natural,* biological inversion that time effects in the power relations of
human generations; and *literary* age inversions and generational
strife. These cannot strictly be separated but spill over into each
other, not least because festive behavior often provides schemata
for real life or for literature. But I want now to suggest a grouping
of these phenomena with the ritual and historical on one side and
the natural and the literary on the other. Temporariness is essential
to saturnalian festivities: reinversion, turning things right side up
again, is vital. And in history, when the civil war ended, its inversion of classes and age groups was reversed, the world turned right
side up with a vengeance: "At seventy-one Sir Robert Foster was
the oldest man in three centuries to be appointed Lord Chief Justice, while the new archbishops . . . were respectively seventy-two
and seventy-eight" (Thomas, "Age" 212–13).[20] Is this any less a
kind of magical thinking than that of the reinversion of a saturnalian rite? Both are cultural constructions, designed, like so many
of culture's fabrications, to prevent human beings from taking a
clear look at the devastating nothingness of their own mortality—
an old man regaining power usurped by the young must feel an almost magical sense of immortality. Culturally simulated inversions
are usually righted again if at all possible as a way of tricking our
consciousness into forgetting that nature's inversions cannot be: the
saturnalia of Time can never be undone. Curiously, that great cultural production Renaissance literature is often on the side of nature rather than culture on this issue. By resisting the magical closure of reinversion at which history and ritual conspire, the
literature shakes us awake to our condition, a cultural product itself piercing the veils of culture.

Hybrids

When Renaissance literary theory stressed decorum of types, age and youth were often exemplars: "Youth no less becomes / The light and careless livery that it wears / Than settled age his sables and his weeds, / Importing health and graveness" (*Ham* IV.vii.78–81)— one sign that the Renaissance lacked a concept of middle age, just as many of its political theorists ignored the middle classes. Pastoral figures are young or old: "one rarely finds a shepherd of middle age" (Marx 8). Jaques' seven ages of man speech elides middle age, leaping from young lover and soldier to a justice whose postprandial inertia is a short step from the "slipper'd pantaloon" of old age. "One can be either master or servant in *The Tempest*, either parent or child; middle ground scarcely exists" (Sundelson 33). The rhetorical figure of antithesis, with its contrasting extremes, is basic to Renaissance literary style. The unmediated binary oppositions that make Renaissance literature so deconstructible are at their clearest in youth versus age, and it was inevitable that someday middle age would come into its own and the generational strife so often giving shape to Renaissance literature would lose its stark and naked outlines.

One potential step toward that deconstruction is what Stallybrass and White call "hybridization," a festive alternative to inversion. Where inversion "shares with demonization the acceptance of the existing binary categories of high and low," hybridization deconstructs such oppositions. All three kinds of saturnalia produce hybrids as well as inversions: gender saturnalia produces the hermaphrodite symbol and cross-dressing (see my *Women,* part 2); class saturnalia produces figures like Robin Hood, outlawed aristocrat identifying with the poor; and age saturnalia produces the aged mother, the aged virgin, the *puer senex,* and that one-man saturnalia, the old man turned young.

That Scripture sets such store by the aged woman rendered fertile by supernatural aid (from Sarah to Elisabeth) suggests the magical potency of a child born to an aged mother—Isaac or John the Baptist. If active fertility belongs to the image of the young woman, so does conspicuous virginity: to transfer these qualities to an *old* woman without risking laughter requires magical mediation.

As Queen Elizabeth matured into an aged virgin, she could have deemphasized her virginity, which could all too easily have been read as sterility, but she took the risk of continuing to emphasize it, perhaps recognizing as Scripture had that the sexualized body persisting in old age could have a magical aura. She had previously used a rhetoric of gender hybridization in occasionally referring to herself in male terms; her aged-virgin image may have been a deliberate attempt to capitalize on the power, as well as the danger, of the boundary-crossing hybrid—like figures of the loathly lady tradition including the crone in the Wife of Bath's Tale, she cultivated the air of an old woman who could turn young and sexy at will. This late Elizabethan old/young queen paved the way for the hybrid-loving Jacobean age.

In the *puer senex* topos dating to the second century A.D., a boy is praised for having the wisdom and maturity of an old man (Curtius 99). Posthumus is "a child that guided dotards" (*Cym* I.i.46–50); of Portia it is said, "I never knew so young a body with so old a head" (*MV* IV.i.162–63). Such figures are no mere rhetorical constructs; there is something downright magical about them—they share their old/young faces with gods. Cupid is a little boy who leads grown men by the nose; Berowne, who makes him sound like Jaques' schoolboy—"this wimpled, whining, purblind, wayward boy, / This senior-junior, giant-dwarf, Dan Cupid"—is chagrined to find himself serving under this "great general" (*LLL* III.i.177–85). Cupid was not the only old/young god: early Christians pictured Jehovah "as a hoary old man with snow-white hair and a youthful countenance"; and in Buddhism, and Etruscan and pre-Islamic Arab religions, "saviors are characterized by the combination of childhood and age" (Curtius 101).

If the *puer senex* or the old-turned-young figures were potential deconstructors of the age/youth opposition, the deconstruction was a long time coming, for both figures are ancient. Aristophanes is full of old men turning young. Aged Demos in *The Knights* is cooked until young, an image of restored vigor in the state. *The Wasps*'s hero, submitting to his son's tutelage, an age inversion, rejects age's "frugal habits" for youthful feasting and drunken disorder; he proclaims, "I am very young," and the chorus quite approves (73, 68). Another chorus cries, "I sing and laugh more than if I had lost my old age, as a serpent does its skin" (*Peace* 170). Again, though Aristophanes handles the metamorphoses playfully, there is much magical thinking in them.

Images of rejuvenated age cluster in comedies, where the old grow figuratively young: "A wither'd hermit, five-score winters worn, / Might shake off fifty, looking in her eye" (*LLL* IV.iii.238–39). Child Mamillius "makes old hearts fresh"; love of Florizel renews Polixenes: "his varying childness cures in me / Thoughts that would thick my blood" (*WT* I.i.39–40, I.ii.170–71), diction reversing the imagery of a Lady Macbeth who would dash her child's brains out— "Make thick my blood" (*Mac* I.v.43). Jessica's treatment of her father troubles us, and Shakespeare perhaps tries to soften this by having Jessica speak of a mythic daughter who renews her father-in-law: "Medea gathered the enchanted herbs / That did renew old Aeson" (V.i.13–14).

In Shakespeare, most old men trying to turn young are lovers, votaries of Cupid, the oldest and youngest god: "Abraham Cupid" (*Rom* II.i.14), "five thousand years a boy" (*LLL* V.ii.11). Some are beaten out by younger suitors: Armado in *Love's Labor's Lost,* Slender and Caius in *Merry Wives,* Gremio in *Shrew.* But some older men, like Petruchio or Antony, succeed. Older couples—Hippolita and Theseus, Paulina and Camillo—sometimes marry at a comedy's end.

One of many daring strokes in an expectation-dashing play, sexuality and fertility in *Antony and Cleopatra* attach to the "aged" couple and its youth is a killjoy, almost (in his opposing the union of Antony and Cleopatra) a young senex. Antony and Cleopatra are magical old-turned-young figures. Physically he is an old lion, old ruffian (III.xiii.96, IV.i.4), she a "blown rose"; she has a "wan'd lip" and is "wrinkled deep in time" (III.xiii.39, II.i.21, I.v.30). Antony confesses of both of them, "grey / [Does] something mingle with our younger brown" (IV.viii.20–21). His "dotage," decried in the play's first line, hints at senility as well as amorous besottedness (he is later a "doting mallard" and his brown hairs accuse his white of "fear and doting" [I.i.i; III.x.20, xi.15]). But like a young soldier with a teddy bear, Antony takes his schoolmaster on campaigns (III.xi–xii); and the couple's outrageous sexuality bespeaks youth, as does Cleopatra's irrepressible playfulness, her hopping forty paces through the street, and her practical jokes on fishing trips. Something magical in her eternal youth enchants her austerest critics even today; age indeed "cannot wither her" (II.ii.245). But her old/young magic suffers as do the golden worlds conjured in history plays: the world of *Realpolitik* is inhospitable to magic.

The old/young hybrid failed to deconstruct the bipolar youth/age opposition or spawn a concept of middle age, because its very magical air insulated it from life, because the figure's effectiveness depends on its startling juxtaposition of two extremes we are meant to recognize as extremes—here is no blurring of distinctions or hint of a median state; and because the old/young figure, like the transvestite, is safe when confined to the zoo of magical thinking, but dangerous if loosed into life or realistic literature.

Like the hermaphrodite, the old/young figure is viewed favorably as pure symbol, but with suspicion when actualized in a fully developed figure. Hermaphrodism "is at the two poles of sacred things. Pure concept, . . . it appears adorned with the highest qualities. But once made real in a being of flesh and blood, it is a monstrosity" (Delcourt 45); the same is true of the old turned young. A real old man turned lover is not easily a joyous symbol of renewal: his behavior is dogged by doubts and complexities. Among tragedy's fully realized characters, a jealous Antony rages impotently; a Cleopatra resorts to demeaning feminine wiles, insecure because "wrinkled deep in time"; a Gertrude finds her son disgusted that a middle-aged woman could have sexual desires (*Ham* III.iv.83–84). When a January-May marriage, often the subject of farce, is treated tragically, an Othello fears his wife's affections will desert him because he is "declin'd / Into the vale of years" (III.iii.271–72). And the line dividing the joyous ritual old/young figure from the old man turned childish by senility—"an old man is twice a child" (*Ham* II.ii.385)—is blurred when the figure is fully developed.

Even comedy's characters, less complex than tragedy's, are often too fully realized to be treated magically. When in *Much Ado* aged Leonato joins in young-hearted playacting to trick Benedick into realizing he loves Beatrice, we are charmed; Benedick falls for it because he assumes old men don't get up to such high jinks: "I should think this a gull, but that the white-bearded fellow speaks it. Knavery cannot, sure, hide himself in such reverence." But Leonato's charm sours when he readily believes slanders against Hero: we are even more indignant with his behavior because he has seemed youthful than we would have been if he had behaved like a stock senex. Later, it is painful to see the old brothers Leonato and Antonio pathetically striving to become young bloods and challenge Claudio to a duel—he shrugs it off, snickering about having his nose "snapp'd off with two old men without teeth," while they impotently bluster (II.iii.118–20, 32–33). The play's attitude toward old men behaving as if young varies from delight to indignation to pity, attitudes more appropriate to life's mingled characters than to magical figures.

The greatest old man to behave like a youth, Falstaff, shamelessly casts the Gad's Hill robbery as starving youth's revolt against fat, aged authority ("Bacon-fed knaves! They hate us youth. . . . Young men must live. You are grandjurors, are ye?" [*1H4* II.ii.84–91]); his white hair and corpulence make the starving youth role hard to carry off. Hal, recognizing the magic of this old/young figure, calls Falstaff "latter spring . . . All-hallown summer" (I.ii.154–55), and the chief justice, though armed with that favorite descriptor of age, "gravity," fails to persuade Falstaff he is old:

> *Chief Justice.* There is not a white hair on your face but should have his effect of gravity.
> *Falstaff.* His effect of gravy, gravy, gravy. . . . You that are old consider not the capacities of us that are young; you do measure the heat of our livers with the bitterness of your galls. And we that are in the vaward of our youth, . . . are wags too.
> *Justice.* Do you set down your name in the scroll of youth, that are written down old with all the characters of age? Have you not . . . a white beard, a decreasing leg, an increasing belly? Is not your voice broken, your wind short, your chin double, your wit single, and every part about you blasted with antiquity? And will you yet call yourself young? Fie, fie, fie, Sir John!
> *Falstaff.* My lord, I was born about three of the clock in the afternoon, with a white head and something of a round belly. For my voice, I have lost it with halloing and singing of anthems. (*2H4* I.ii.159–88)

The transmutation of "gravity" into "gravy" is perhaps the happiest example in Shakespeare of the carnivalesque overwhelming of dignified Latin by lower-bodily-stratum English. Falstaff's pretense to youth affects people in different ways. When I hear "gravy, gravy, gravy," I want to cheer; other readers wax censorious about such gluttony and lying. However we regard it morally, though, it is clear that it *is* a pretense. When he is drinking with a whore who babies him ("You sweet little rogue, you!") and fondly advises him to "patch up thine old body for heaven," while Hal stands by making jests about geriatric sex, Falstaff knows he isn't young:

Falstaff. Thou dost give me flattering busses.
Doll. By my troth, I kiss thee with a most constant heart.
Falstaff. I am old, I am old.
Doll. I love thee better than I love e'er a scurvy young boy . . .
Falstaff. What stuff wilt have a kirtle of? I shall receive money
    o' Thursday. . . . A merry song, come. It grows late; we'll to
    bed. Thou 'lt forget me when I am gone. (*2H4* II.iv.267–76)

Falstaff in this scene is no symbolic figure; all remnants of magical meaning come rattling out of him like rusty nails, and he is a very real old man, drinking with a whore to forget.

Falstaff owes much to a magical tradition where a rejuvenated old man represents renewal of the human race, but here the effect is not only slightly altered but stood on its head, because early modern literature was moving toward more fully impersonated characters, and because this old/young figure has strayed out of comedy's more magical world into the chillier air of the history play, where he is just an old man pretending to youth. The pretense may be regarded with admiration for the dashing bravado of refusing to give in to age, contempt for a failure to mature into respectability, pity for the human condition that reduces a man to pathetic self-deceptions, worry about a man unable to face his own mortality—with any number of responses or a mixture of many. Such a figure invites and demands complex response, as the symbolic figures spawned by magical wish fulfillment do not.

Walkers and Watchers

On saturnalian holidays, ghosts walked. Shakespeare understood ancestral ghosts: there is something positively tribal in his notion that spirits of the dead maintain surveillance over the living: "the spirits of the wise sit in the clouds and mock us" (*2H4* II.ii.135). "When I am in heaven," Henry VIII says of baby Elizabeth, "I shall desire / To see what this child does" (V.iv.68–69). Asked "what wert thou, if the King of Naples heard thee?" Ferdinand replies, "He does hear me" (*Tmp* I.ii.434–36)—death has increased his father's sensory perception; he can now hear his son at any time. Jacques Le Goff writes of the medieval sense of constant surveillance by angels and demons (a sense *Macbeth* too conveys); did Elizabethans also have an archaic sense of surveillance by dead ancestors? The dead often take a lively part in plays—the fathers of Hamlet, Portia, Helena; Posthumus's ancestors. The spirit of Woodstock hovers over *Richard II,* the spirits of the old Romans (and later of Caesar himself) over *Julius Caesar.* Did the Renaissance have a sense, which we have lost, that the ancestors were watching? Were the dead an audience for the living?

Why do the dead walk at saturnalian festivals? Why should recalling the ancestors go hand in hand with topsy-turviness? The dead walk because the saturnalia deepest in our hearts is that which took the world away from our parents and gave it to us. The ancestors come back to remind us that their case will someday be our own. Carnival rites reassure: the dead will return to the grave; inversions will right themselves. But life is not so magical. In a world where the dead father's return restores Denmark but kills Hamlet, we must regard with other than festival eyes, with other than magical eyes, the tragedy of each human life.

Notes

1. In the "world upside down" broadsheets (see below), "the pupil or apprentice beats his teacher or master, . . . the child lectures his elders and betters (there is some resemblance here to compositions showing the boy Jesus teaching the elders in the temple, in which painters often exaggerated the youth of the former and the wizened crabbiness of the latter)" (Kunzle 50).

2. Witch-hunts involved the language both of the *mundus inversus* of ritualized play and of political sedition: demonologists "concentrated on the systematic reversal of traditional priorities, symbolised by the contrariness which made witches do things back-to-front or left-to-right," and preachers portrayed witches as traitors and rebels for renouncing God as king: "the political implications of witchcraft could not have been stated

more bluntly" (Clark 174–76). Peter Stallybrass writes of witchcraft's carnivalesque implications: "If kingship is legitimated by analogy to God's rule over the earth, and the father's rule over the family and the head's rule over the body, witchcraft establishes the opposite analogies, whereby the Devil attempts to rule over the earth, and the woman over the family, and the body over the head" (*"Macbeth* and Witchcraft" 192).

3. Although, as I mentioned in chapter 3, Shakespeare for some reason never mentions the autumn months by name, he alludes often to the fall festival when the dead walk, Halloween or All-hallowmas; in tune with widespread autumn rites propitiating spirits of the dead, he stresses battles occurring in autumn—Hotspur does battle on Holy-Rood Day, September 14; Henry V triumphs at Agincourt on St. Crispin's Day, October 25 (see *Wiv* I.i.188; *MM* II.i.125–27; *TGV* II.i.24–25; *R2* V.i.80; *1H4* I.ii.154, i.52).

4. St. Distaff's Day (the jocularly named day after Epiphany, when women resumed spinning and other housework after the Christmas season) was an occasion for sexual conflict: men burned women's flax, women doused men with water (Spicer 20). Two Eastertide sets of male/female holidays were rife with sexual conflict. Easter Monday was a male, Easter Tuesday a female holiday when members of the opposite sex were heaved into the air; on the Tuesday women sat drinking, and any invading male was pursued, heaved, and kissed (J. H. Bloom 118). A week later was another festive Monday/Tuesday: "Hock-day and Michaelmas divided the rural year into its winter and summer halves. Hock-day (the second Tuesday after Easter Sunday) was an important marker in the agrarian calendar, . . . celebrated by the carnivalesque seizing and binding of men by women (usually on Hock Monday) and of women by men (usually on the following Tuesday)" (Stallybrass, "'Wee Feaste'" 234); sexual conflict on this pivotal day suggests winter/summer combat in fertility rites. And in a May rite, a flitch of bacon went to a couple who had not, during the previous year, repented marrying. In its first three centuries, only three claimants succeeded; sexual conflict's permanence was thus wryly recognized.

5. On the misrule question, see also Sharp, Fletcher and Stevenson, and Macfarlane and Harris.

6. In our own day, literary criticism has its battle of ancients and moderns, "the treatment of previous criticism as a history of error which is always about to be set right in the present moment of critical breakthrough" (Mitchell 618). Some see the literary youth/age conflict as perennial in all periods since the Renaissance with its dawning of the "modern," individualized author: Harold Bloom's account of the strong male poet battling his poetic predecessor, a literary version of Freud's father/son battle, is another incarnation of the saturnalian struggle of youth against age.

7. The allegory possibly originates in simple confusion between Cronus and *chronus*, time. If so, the confusion set in as early as Plutarch and Cicero. Gods of time predated Cronus in other cultures: in the twelfth century B.C., "a god with a name that can be identified with the Persian word 'Zurvan,' i.e. 'Time,' was known" (Brandon 32–33); these may have contributed to the development of Cronus's allegorical *significatio*. See Macey, chaps. 1 and 2.

8. Laroque notes that "a document in the archives of Norwich Cathedral associates the 'Shrovetide festival' with a local 'bachery guild'" (59). Bernard Capp points out that the 1632 chapbook *The Pinder of Wakefield* concerns a youth group that enforces local laws, drinks together, plays football on Midsummer Day against youths from other towns, punishes jealous husbands, and subjects a scold and her husband to a skimmington ride. (Palmer reports a similar institution, "lewbelling" of adulterers by groups of young men in Warwickshire [96–97].) Elements of the Pinder of Wakefield story are present in the play *George à Green* but the youth group is much more prominent in the chapbook. *The Pinder* has other ritual motifs as well—a meeting with Robin Hood, riddling.

9. Noting however that this last passage refers to the reign of Henry VI, not memorable for wise counsel, Leggatt comments, "Shakespeare could be a little mischievous about the tendency to idealize" (51).

10. Jacobean city comedy, for example, is much more cynical: "Middleton's young men sound just like Plautus's wishing for the deaths of their elders. Fitsgrave asks the young gallants of *Your Five Gallants*, 'Are your fathers dead, gentlemen, you're so merry?' (IV.viii.288–89). Follywit explains filial coldness as a natural response to paternal closefistedness: 'they cannot abide to see us merry all the while they're above ground, and that makes so many laugh at their fathers' funerals' (I.i.45–47)" (Paster 156).

11. The temptation to desire his father's death, though, is structural: his "destiny is to replace his father as King Henry; his father's death is the legal condition for the creation of his own identity" (Montrose, "'The Place'" 37).

12. Freud's view in *Moses and Monotheism* of Christianity as a religion of the son, supplanting Judaism as a religion of the father, is saturnalian in its youth/age inversion: Time's saturnalia is at the heart of Freud's vision.

13. Laroque's theory that Caesar is literally trying to be crowned Lord of Misrule, as a first step toward becoming emperor, merits notice as perhaps this decade's most bizarre interpretation of Shakespeare: "Had the crowd elected him king-for-a-day, he could subsequently have tried unobtrusively to make permanent and to institutionalize what had been won 'in a moment of fun,' with the confusion and euphoria of the festival abet-

ting. If he had been elected king at the carnival, Caesar could have tried to prolong his reign beyond the period allotted for these seasonal rejoicings" (*Shakespeare's Festive World* 206).

14. I am indebted here to Troni Grande, who in her Ph.D. thesis "Marlowe and the Play of Dilation" makes a similar argument about Marlowe's tortured relationship to the literary authority of the Latin language and of Roman authors.

15. One Shakespearean exception is Tamora in *Titus Andronicus,* who orders her baby killed.

16. Links between evil-eye beliefs and breastfeeding/weaning have also been found in Lebanon, India, Greece, Romania, and many other cultures (see Harfouche; Dundes 270–71).

17. I am indebted for this insight to graduate student Simon Estok.

18. Jeanne Roberts develops a similar argument in *The Shakespearean Wild,* where she sees women, barbarians, and animals occupying a mental space she calls "the wild" in opposition to the civilized, human space associated with masculine values. What she calls the wild corresponds in some ways to what I would call the realm of misrule.

19. The excellent introductions to Babcock's *Reversible World* and Stallybrass and White's *Politics and Poetics of Transgression* provide background on this debate, which is at least as old as Marx's disagreement with Trotsky on the issue; see also Bristol 292; Hill 312; Le Roy Ladurie; Eagleton, *Walter Benjamin* 148; Stallybrass, "'Wee Feaste'" 234–37; Davis, "Reasons" 42, 54; Thomas, *Rule and Misrule* 42; Marcus, *Politics* 3–21; and Gluckman, "Rituals" 112–14. I also discuss the debate at some length in the introduction to Woodbridge and Berry's *True Rites and Maimed Rites.*

20. Similarly, in the realm of social saturnalia, history pressed into service that old ritual figure Robin Hood, symbol of rebellion and topsy-turviness, to ratify the Restoration. As Underdown recounts, "As part of the Coronation celebrations at Nottingham [where else?] in 1661 a short play was enacted, in which Robin's traditional loyalty to King Richard was carefully exaggerated to provide the basis for a commentary on the recent confusions. When the messenger arrives in Sherwood offering pardon to the outlaws if they will abandon their evil ways there are a few half-hearted protests. Little John utters some appeals to social levelling—'every brave soul is born a king'—and Robin wistfully recalls 'this gallant attempt we've boldly followed,' the Good Old Cause in other words. But like any repentant Roundhead he quickly gives up and leads his men in singing 'health unto our King'" (*Revel* 282–83).

Conclusion:
Owning Up to Magic

We shall not expect to understand other people's ideas of contagion, sacred or secular, until we have confronted our own.
—Mary Douglas

If there is one thing I hope I have demonstrated in this study it is the pervasiveness and longevity of magical thinking. Richard Kieckhefer shows that in the Middle Ages, magic belonged to everybody:

> Part of the inheritance passed down from classical antiquity to medieval and modern Western culture is the notion of magic as something performed by special individuals. . . . When we look at the people who were in fact using varieties of magic in medieval Europe, however, it becomes hard to sustain the stereotype. Instead of finding a single, readily identifiable class of magicians we find various types of people involved in diverse magical activities: monks, parish priests, physicians, surgeon-barbers, midwives, folk healers and diviners with no formal training, and even ordinary women and men who, without claiming special knowledge or competence, used whatever magic they happened to know. (56)

The situation had not changed very much by Shakespeare's day. The difficulty of eradicating the old mental structures appears, for example, in the fact that, as François Laroque shows, "despite the official abolition of the cult of saints, the old dating system was still used to refer to the events of secular life; the old calendar of feast days was still central to the life of the nation, being used more or less universally as a system for measuring time" (*Shakespeare's Festive World* 15); magical belief proved at least as difficult to root out as did the seasonal feasts, though Protestantism vigorously attacked both.

However strong was the pull upon Shakespeare of the new rationality and anti-ritualism of the Renaissance and Reformation, magical beliefs of his culture still washed daily against his mental shores. It is hard to swim in a sea of magical supposition without getting wet. The collision of the two—rationalism and magic—produced (as I have argued) an unconscious or semiconscious magical thinking that gave shape to many Shakespearean texts. Freud saw magical thinking as active in the unconscious world of everyone's dreams; I see it as subliminally active in that great dream work, Renaissance literature.

What the Thunder Said

Many other pieces of magical thinking, from large to small, remain to be explored in the works of Shakespeare and his contemporaries. For an example of an interesting small one, it would be good to know more about what lies encoded in the Elizabethan attitude toward thunder and lightning. Shakespeare does quite a lot with them: Cassius in *Julius Caesar* walks about in a thunderstorm with his breast bared, daring the lightning to strike him (I.ii.46–52), a suggestive analogue to his later offering his bare breast to Brutus to stab (IV.iii.100–101); Lear makes performative utterances, futilely commanding thunder to cease; Prospero's magic does command thunder and lightning. Thunder and lightning are important semiotic signs of evil and impending doom in plays by many writers, and often, as in *Dr. Faustus,* they are connected with magic and the demonic. Thoroughly conversant with classical thunder myth, with Jove as the thunderer, Shakespeare uses such beliefs to provide local color in plays set in classical antiquity—*Cymbeline,* for example, refers to "the thunder-master" and to "the thunderer, whose bolt . . . / Sky-planted batters all rebelling coasts" (V.iv.30, 95). He could also draw on contemporary magical belief: in his day witches were considered able to control weather, and medieval liturgical books had offered charms to drive away thunder (Thomas, *Religion* 32); "wax blessed on the feast of the Purification was thought effective against thunderbolts"; an Agnus Dei or sanctified wax lamb was a "protection against various evils, including death by lightning" (Kieckhefer 78).

Why did thunder and lightning prove so fascinating, and why were they so feared, if thunder is harmless and being struck by lightning statistically rare? I suspect it has to do with the fertility/sterility concept underlying the Renaissance notion of good and evil—thunder and lightning, as the voice of destructive storms, are threatening to crops. It is suggestive to find this antifertility force passing directly into the semiotics of moral evil in a case such as *Dr. Faustus*. The preoccupation with thunder and lightning also suggests that even as sin and grace were undergoing a process of interiorization during the Reformation and its successive waves of Puritan reform, the Protestant consciousness that considered God and the devil to be within the human heart was capable of subversion by the rising of a magic-minded unconscious that heard the voice of Judgment in the heavens, in thunder and lightning—a remnant of belief in the Sky God.

Magical Modernity

I have insisted that Shakespeare lived fairly early in the period that saw what Keith Thomas calls "the decline of magic"; but some believe that Thomas himself placed the decline of magic too early (see Fletcher and Stevenson 8), and there are many indications that magical thinking has not even now declined to the vanishing point. During the course of this study I have from time to time suggested modern equivalents to early modern magical thinking—in fear of the channel tunnel, in the sense that disease has been sent to us by a neighbor-enemy or is actually demonic, in the scapegoating of politicians or the resignation of cabinet ministers as a surrogate ruler killing, in the use of lawsuits to express the conviction that one has been harmed and an enemy must be blamed, in the sense that erotic desire is a kind of enchantment, in the tendency to blame society's troubles on women. In making such links between early modern magical thinking and our own, I hope I have suggested that to historicize Shakespeare's time with regard to magical thinking should not be to rusticate it, to exile it to a faraway land of historical irrelevance, to scapegoat it by projecting upon it the power hunger and superstition we ourselves wish to disown.

The body has not yet ceased to be an image of society: take for instance the contemporary United States, a society envisioning itself as beleaguered by enemies; when one enemy (the USSR) collapses, the United States immediately fixes upon others—Iraq, Japan. Its defense budget remains enormous. And as we might expect given Mary Douglas's model of besieged societies developing taboos to protect orifices, Americans are so obsessed with controlling diet that diet-related enterprises are one of its major industries. Is it accidental that the garrison-mentality isolationism that reared its head during the 1992 presidential election campaign is contemporary with a national cholesterol phobia that amounts to a food taboo? Much suggests that mirroring the national fear of external enemies is a residually magical fear of pollution to the body through vulnerable orifices.

The fortunes of the word *pollution* illustrate Gombrich's principle that the mind grasps the new by assimilating it to the familiar and also reminds us of the magical thinking underlying some of our scientific concepts. *Pollution* came into English in the late fourteenth century to render the magico-religious biblical notion of defilement, destruction of sacrality; in the midsixteenth century it was secularized and came to refer to any physical befoulment; in the midtwentieth century it acquired its scientific meaning, in reference to pollution of air and bodies of water.

In addition to food taboos, the modern mouth is guarded from pollution by a variety of purifying agents—toothpaste, floss, mouthwash, breath mints. Mary Douglas scoffs at the idea "that primitive ritual has nothing whatever in common with our ideas of cleanness, . . . [that] our washing, scrubbing, isolating and disinfecting has only a superficial resemblance with ritual purifications; our practices are solidly based on hygiene; theirs are symbolic: we kill germs, they ward off spirits." To the contrary, Douglas believes that "the resemblance between some of their symbolic rites and our hygiene is sometimes uncannily close" (*Purity* 32).

Sunglasses shield our eyes from penetrative rays; mirror sunglasses such as those worn by motorcycle police both hide the eye and mirror back the gaze of an onlooker—common features of evil-eye amulets. Moral guardians such as Jesse Helms seek to shield the national eyesight from the polluting filth of visual pornography. Washington wives rally to protect that old vulnerable orifice, the ear, from filthy rock lyrics, especially those that celebrate use of those body invaders, drugs. For protection of sexual orifices, the condom has become a kind of national amulet, replacing the eye magic of the national eagle.

I sometimes suspect that our planet is presided over by a cosmic joker who gives each culture the diseases most appropriate to it. The Middle Ages, obsessed with the transience of life, got that instantaneous killer without warning, bubonic plague. The Renaissance, delighting in the beauty of the human body and devoted to international trade, got that illness which trades back and forth between human bodies, syphilis. The Romantics got that pale, lingering, languishing malady consumption. The pattern holds when American culture, spending so much of the national budget on defense and so obsessed with defending bodily orifices, has been struck by AIDS, which enters through a bodily orifice and destroys the body's ability to defend itself. Be that as it may, the theory of scapegoating prompts us to look, in cases where a culture is fanatic about external enemies, for internal trouble, and with America's terrible divisions between rich and poor, between black and white, one does not have far to look. Magical thinking lies all around us—in ancient pollution beliefs, in self-protective strategies, in scapegoat thinking. And if magical thinking operates in our own time, we can hardly be surprised that it operated in Shakespeare's.

Another example—if printing came to seem demonic in its early days (see my essay "Patchwork"), if ancient magical belief provided schemata for understanding early modern technologies, similar magical thinking seems now to attend computing. The term *commands* suggests control of a genie by a magician. (Sometimes my Sanyo seems a spirit too delicate to act my earthy and abhorred commands.) When I hook my laptop to my PC to transfer files from one to the other, the word *master* comes up on the screen of one computer, the word *slave* on the other. Like a deferential waiter, a computer offers us menus. Much in computer language suggests that this magical electronic servant is an organic, sentient being: it has a memory, it reads files, it can be afflicted by bugs and viruses, it can "talk" to other computers. Like the Freudian psyche, it has "drives," and hidden codes lie under its text like the unconscious. The computer caters to our magical wish to be able to escape from any intolerable situation by providing a special key marked "Escape." Widespread folk beliefs in the doppelganger come to mind when one beholds the instantaneous replication of the text through a "copy" command. A command like "restore," bringing back lost text, bestows on the operator a godlike resurrective capacity. Underlying our attitude toward computers may be the memory of some magical tales, of the folk-tale group Max Lüthi has called "the living doll"—the story of a piece of human artifice that comes to life and becomes its creator's servant, companion, or nemesis—Pygmalion's statue, the broomstick of the sorcerer's apprentice, Pinocchio, Frankenstein. They are tales of culture's triumph over nature, but the magic by which they are mediated often exacts its revenge upon the presuming artificer—these tales have an aura of meddling with dark forces. One computer company named its magical servant Apple, recalling two mythic moments wherein widespread human evil was founded: the story of the Fall in Genesis and the story of the origins of the Trojan war in the Judgment of Paris. Both suggest a primitive evil attending this technology, just as the sixteenth century suspected that print was demonic.

People in the Middle Ages and Renaissance believed that a necromancer could "create the illusion of a boat or a horse which [would] take him wherever he wishe[d] to go. He [could] conjure forth an extravagant feast with banqueting and entertainment" (Kieckhefer 158); stage wizards in plays from *Dr. Faustus* to *The Tempest* bring to life this exciting belief. Nowadays computers are assisting in the creation of something similar—"virtual reality." Especially for consumers of computer technology or participants in virtual reality who have had nothing to do with their invention and manufacture, and know nothing of the material details of their hard wiring, such technologies will continue to have about them at least some aura of magic.

The first virtual reality, a universe in action but entirely artificial, was literature; or (more properly) folk tales in the oral tradition. There is something deeply magical in the whole experience of fiction: as Kirby Farrell says, "the unreal promises to free us from the prison of our limited mortal selves" (39), an experience resembling the *benandanti*'s capacity to walk forth out of the body by night. I suspect that all the narratology in the world will never pierce to the heart of the mystery involved in believing but not really believing in the doings of characters in a story, in worrying about what will happen to them, in caring about them intensely while knowing they do not exist. This is the mystery of tears for Hecuba that astounds so sophisticated a tale hearer as Hamlet. The double-mindedness of knowing Hecuba does not exist and weeping at her story anyway is not unlike the double-mindedness of knowing a computer is not a genie but feeling (as one issues it commands) half-consciously that it is; or the double-mindedness of knowing that making a scapegoat of a wicked king will not cure rivalries between thanes and uprisings among them, yet feeling somehow that the old magic of human sacrifice *will* purify, *will* cure everything. Because we still possess something of this under-mind that can think magically even while our conscious minds roll rationally on, we are in no immediate danger of losing our capacity to respond to the kind of tragedy that operates on scapegoating principles.

One of the most important (and sinister) kinds of magical thinking that is still with us is the scapegoat mentality behind witchcraft accusations. We still use the term *witch-hunt* for outbreaks of political hysteria, and it is apt and more than just a metaphor. Arthur Miller, in *The Crucible,* drew an implicit comparison between Salem witch trials and the McCarthy era purges; it is no accident that both are native to capitalist periods. Noting (as does Keith Thomas) that in the early modern period the reason for a witch's alleged anger was "almost always an unneighbourly action on the part of her future victim," Alan Macfarlane attributes the rise in witch persecution to the rise of an acquisitive, protocapitalist mentality, a shift away from traditional values of sharing, charity, and neighborliness:

> Witchcraft beliefs did not force people to examine their own conduct to see in what way they had deviated from traditional ideals of behaviour. If suffering had been accepted as the consequence of personal sin, then people would have had to admit that they had failed in charity, that the old woman was justified in laying a curse. The whole organic, distributive rather than acquisitive, communal rather than individual, "thou art thy brother's keeper," traditional Christian ethic would

have had to be adhered to. As it was, the enormity of the witch's reciprocal retaliation, and her association with foul behaviour and hidden power, so overshadowed the situation that the victim's original offence was forgotten. In a subtle way the whole traditional morality could be altered without appearing to change. ("Tudor Anthropologist" 147, 152)

This can easily be translated into modern North American terms, where the poor and especially the nonwhite classes are routinely scapegoated for national problems, from the national debt to our failure to compete with Japan. Because we have turned the poor away hungry, denied them social and economic justice, we think they want to harm us, and so, just as the early modern witch-hunter was obsessed with the danger from witches' supposed malice, we dwell on inner-city crime, call for law and order, a war on drugs, and so forth, the subtext of which is that decent, law-abiding citizens are in constant danger from criminal, riotous, drug-abusing riffraff—a clear case of projecting our own malice onto a scapegoated Other.

In the recent North American mania about illiteracy we can discern the familiar contours of scapegoat thinking. Examining the rhetoric about illiteracy in newspapers and magazines over the past four years in the United States, Donna LeCourt and Todd English show that nonliterates are portrayed as bestial and subhuman; literacy is equated with good family life by such organizations as the Barbara Bush Foundation for Family Literacy, and illiteracy is connected with drugs, welfare, and lawlessness. Like the clowns and servants in Renaissance drama who abuse language in malapropisms, modern nonliterates are clearly configured as language-abusing denizens of the land of misrule. Literacy is regarded as a panacea for social ills, illiteracy blamed for the sad state of the nation. Here we should invoke that crucial question, raised in my scapegoat chapter, about the relevance of the guilt: is the scapegoat's guilt directly responsible for the social evils that killing the scapegoat is supposed to cure? Even if nonliteracy is an evil (and it may not be), can it be held accountable for other social ills, for example unemployment? Many jobs have been lost because North American employers are hiring cheaper offshore workers, who are often illiterate. Or how about worker productivity? Shirley Brice Heath notes that companies sponsoring worker literacy programs often impatiently pull workers out of literacy classes when their productivity does not improve as a result—although reading skills are irrelevant to many assembly-line jobs, the scapegoat thinking that makes illiteracy responsible for all social ills leads employers to expect a simple relationship between mastery of the alphabet and more auto parts rolling off the assembly line.

There is much magical thinking in the periodic media crusades that briefly spotlight a small aspect of a large social problem. Two examples occurred recently in Canada. In the first, the media focused a blaze of publicity on a northern native community where five young people died at once from solvent sniffing and a number of other young attempted suicides reported that life was so dreadful in their community that they did not want to live. The media showed that the natives were living in this barren arctic spot against their will in the first place, that they had no running water or sewer system, and lived in appalling third-world conditions. After prolonged publicity, the federal government announced that it would move the entire community elsewhere and build a substance-abuse treatment center. The public was relieved and the media went away. In the second case, a group home for autistic adults in southern Alberta was the subject of a media exposé, with charges that living conditions were poor and residents sometimes abused. After intense media heat, the government closed down the group home and sent all the residents away (although no other facilities were available for many of them); the public was relieved and the media went away. Only small voices were raised against the magical thinking involved in these events: a solitary caller in a phone-in program noted that native people all over Canada live on reserves to which they were relegated against their will and that native people live in appalling third-world conditions not only in the distant high Arctic but within half an hour's drive of every Canadian city. A similar point could have been made about the group home: the mentally handicapped live in appalling nineteenth-century conditions all over Alberta. These periodic media forays into solitary islands of human misery represent classic scapegoat thinking: in a magical synecdoche, the part stands for the whole, and if conditions are ameliorated in one native community or "abuse" stamped out in one group home for the mentally handicapped, large social problems are solved for the whole country, just as Scotland is cured by the death of Macbeth. The mere training of the national gaze on one native community or one group home makes such problems seem to be rare and easily solvable. And eye magic as well as scapegoat magic operates in such cases: the electronic media control the public gaze in the same way the camera controls the film-viewer's gaze, as Laura Mulvey and other film theorists have shown; and when our gaze is directed toward something horrible, which is eradicated, and then directed away altogether from native communities and homes for the handicapped, we participate in the old magical thinking that what cannot be seen does not exist. We close our eyes to natives and the handicapped as Lucrece closes her eyes to Tarquin and Lady Macbeth to her murder weapon.

Alan Dundes argues that the modern practice of tipping waiters results from evil-eye beliefs—tipping averts the envy and possible evil eye of a waiter who is hungry while restaurant patrons eat, and extending the principle, Dundes suggests that "the collective guilt felt by citizens of the United States for their relatively high standard of living accounts for their attempts to 'tip' less fortunate countries by offering them substantial foreign aid" (295). Citing the fact that in evil-eye beliefs "a low profile is essential to avoid the envy of one's peers or the gods," Dundes again points to magical thinking that persists in modern life: "Certainly one element of the evil eye complex is the 'fear of success.' This is analogous to the underdog theme in American culture—politicians and athletic teams prefer to be the underdog because they ardently believe that front runners and the favored are likely to be overtaken and defeated" (296–97).

The early modern penchant for prognostication—visible in its almanacs, astrological forecasts, palmistry, physiognomy, witches' prophecies ("All hail Macbeth, that shall be king hereafter")—is a tendency that can hardly be said to have died out, as a glance at television weather forecasts or newspaper horoscopes reminds us. As Sydney Anglo says,

Astrology may be rejected as untenable, and numerology dismissed as an arcane absurdity. Yet modern states do not hesitate to implement the recommendations of statistical prognosticators, despite the existence of the very factors which undermined earlier divinatory superstitions: the fact that the figures are susceptible to as many conflicting interpretations as there are experts; and that the predictions are frequently wrong. If we remain abject before our own seers, it is not difficult to comprehend the force of [early modern magical] beliefs: . . . beliefs which fashioned a world where magic was not merely possible but normal; and where witchcraft was simply its most lurid manifestation. ("Evident Authority" 4)

I began this book by reminding readers that Shakespeare is old, that Shakespeare is *not* our contemporary. To the extent that he still shared a magical mind-set with his contemporaries, while we, in our modern rationality and scientific intelligence, have shaken off such magical thinking, it is true that Shakespeare cannot be our contemporary. But insofar as we can still discover traces of magical thinking in ourselves and our own modern culture—and I think that disconcertingly often, we can—perhaps Shakespeare is more our contemporary than one would have thought. It is not that he isn't so old after all; it is that we, after all, aren't so modern.

Works Consulted

A. *The Passionate Morris*. 1593. STC 1.

Abrahams, R. G. "The Literary Study of the Riddle." *Texas Studies in Literature and Language* 14 (1972): 177–97.

———. "Spirit, Twins, and Ashes in Labwor, Northern Uganda." *The Interpretation of Ritual*. Ed. Jean Sybil LaFontaine. London: Tavistock, 1972. 115–34.

Ackerknecht, Erwin W. *Medicine and Ethnology: Selected Essays*. Ed. H. H. Walser and H. M. Koelbing. Baltimore: Johns Hopkins University Press, 1971.

Adams, Hazard. *The Academic Tribes*. 2d ed. Urbana: University of Illinois Press, 1987.

Addis, William E., and Thomas Arnold. *A Catholic Dictionary*. London: Routledge and Kegan Paul, 1960.

Adelman, Janet. "'Anger's My Meat': Feeding, Dependency, and Aggression in *Coriolanus*." *Representing Shakespeare: New Psychoanalytic Essays*. Ed. Murray M. Schwartz and Coppélia Kahn. Baltimore: Johns Hopkins University Press, 1980. 129–49.

Aeneas Sylvius. *Opera*. Basel, 1571.

Alford, Violet. *Sword Dance and Drama*. London: Merlin, 1962.

———. *The Hobby Horse and Other Animal Masks*. London: Merlin, 1978.

Allen, Don Cameron. *Mysteriously Meant*. Baltimore: Johns Hopkins University Press, 1970.

Althusser, Louis. "Ideology and Ideological State Apparatuses (Notes towards an Investigation)." *Lenin and Philosophy and Other Essays*. Trans. Ben Brewster. London: New Left, 1971.

Anglo, Sydney. "Evident Authority and Authoritative Evidence: *The Malleus Maleficarum.*" *The Damned Art: Essays in the Literature of Witchcraft.* Ed. Sydney Anglo. London: Routledge and Kegan Paul, 1977. 1–31.

——. "Reginald Scot's *Discoverie of Witchcraft:* Skepticism and Sadduceeism." *The Damned Art: Essays in the Literature of Witchcraft.* Ed. Sydney Anglo. London: Routledge and Kegan Paul, 1977. 106–39.

Ardener, Edwin. "Belief and the Problem of Women." *The Interpretation of Ritual.* Ed. Jean Sybil LaFontaine. London: Tavistock, 1972. 135–58.

Argan, Giulio. "Ideology and Iconology." *Critical Inquiry* 2 (1975): 297–305.

Ariès, Philippe. *The Hour of Our Death.* 1977. Trans. Helen Weaver. New York: Knopf, 1981.

Aristophanes. *The Eleven Comedies.* New York: Liveright, 1943.

——. *The Frogs.* Trans. Benjamin Bickley Rogers. London: Bell, 1919.

Aubrey, John. *Remains of Gentilism and Judaism.* 1687. Ed. James Britten. London: Satchell, Peyton, 1881.

Austin, J. L. *How to Do Things with Words.* Cambridge, Mass.: Harvard University Press, 1962.

Babcock, Barbara A., ed. *The Reversible World: Symbolic Inversion in Art and Society.* Ithaca: Cornell University Press, 1978.

Bacon, Francis. *The Essayes or Counsels, Civill and Morall.* Ed. Michael Kiernan. Oxford: Clarendon, 1985.

Bakeless, John. *Christopher Marlowe: The Man in His Time.* 1937. New York: Washington Square, 1964.

Bakhtin, Mikhail. *Rabelais and His World.* Trans. Helene Iswolsky. Cambridge, Mass.: MIT Press, 1965.

Banerjee, Pompa. "Self, Other, and the Role of Demonic Parody in *Dr. Faustus.*" Paper delivered at the MLA conference, San Francisco, Dec. 1991.

Barasche, Moshe. *Light and Color in the Italian Renaissance Theory of Art.* New York: New York University Press, 1978.

Barber, C. L. "The Family in Shakespeare's Development: Tragedy and Sacredness." *Representing Shakespeare: New Psychoanalytic Essays.* Ed. Murray M. Schwartz and Coppélia Kahn. Baltimore: Johns Hopkins University Press, 1980. 188–202.

Barber, C. L. *Shakespeare's Festive Comedy: A Study of Dramatic Form and Its Relation to Social Custom.* Cleveland: World, 1959.

Barkan, Leonard. *Nature's Work of Art: The Human Body as Image of the World.* New Haven: Yale University Press, 1975.

Barker, Francis, and Peter Hulme. "'Nymphs and Reapers Heavily Van-ish': The Discursive Con-texts of *The Tempest.*" *Alternative Shake-speares.* Ed. John Drakakis. London: Methuen, 1985. 191–205.

Barnett, James Harwood. *The American Christmas.* New York: Macmillan, 1954.

Barroll, J. Leeds. "Shakespeare and Roman History." *Modern Language Review* 53 (1958): 327–43.

Basford, Kathleen. *The Green Man.* Ipswich: D. S. Brewer, 1978.

Baskervill, Charles Read. "Dramatic Aspects of Medieval Folk Festivals in England." *Studies in Philology* 17 (1920): 19–87.

———. *The Elizabethan Jig and Related Song Drama.* Chicago: University of Chicago Press, 1929.

———. "Mummers' Wooing Plays in England." *Modern Philology* 21 (1924): 225–72.

Beal, George. *Playing Cards and Their Story.* Newton Abbott and Vancouver: David and Charles, 1975.

Beaumont, Francis, and John Fletcher. *The Maid's Tragedy. The Dramatic Works in the Beaumont and Fletcher Canon.* Ed. Fredson Bowers. Vol. 2. Cambridge: Cambridge University Press, 1970. 28–124. 6 vols. 1966–85.

———. *Love's Cure; or, The Martial Maid. The Dramatic Works in the Beaumont and Fletcher Canon.* Ed. Fredson Bowers. Vol. 3. Cambridge: Cambridge University Press, 1976. 6 vols. 1966–85.

———. *The Woman-Hater.* 1607. STC 1692.

Belsey, Catherine. *The Subject of Tragedy: Identity and Difference in Renaissance Drama.* London: Methuen, 1985.

Benham, William Gurney. *Playing Cards.* London: Ward, Lock, 1931.

Bergeron, David M. "*Cymbeline:* Shakespeare's Last Roman Play." *Shakespeare Quarterly* 31 (1980): 31–41.

———. *English Civic Pageantry, 1558–1642.* Columbia: University of South Carolina Press, 1971.

Bergren, Ann L. T. "Language and the Female in Early Greek Thought." *Arethusa* 16 (1983): 69–95.

Berlin, Brent, and Paul Kay. *Basic Color Terms.* Berkeley: University of California Press, 1969.

Berry, Edward. *Shakespeare's Comic Rites.* Cambridge: Cambridge University Press, 1984.

Berry, W. Turner, and H. Edmund Poole. *Annals of Printing.* London: Blandford, 1966.

Billington, Sandra. *Mock Kings in Medieval Society and Renaissance Drama.* Oxford: Clarendon, 1991.

Birren, Faber. *History of Color in Painting.* New York: Reinhold, 1965.

Bloch, Marc. *The Royal Touch: Sacred Monarchy and Scrofula in England*

and France. 1961. Trans. J. E. Anderson. London: Routledge and Kegan Paul; Montreal: McGill-Queen's University Press, 1973.

Bloom, Harold. *The Anxiety of Influence: A Theory of Poetry.* New York: Oxford University Press, 1973.

Bloom, J. Harvey. *Folk Lore, Old Customs, and Superstitions in Shakespeare Land.* London: Mitchell Hughes and Clarke, 1929.

Boas, Franz. *The Central Eskimo.* Sixth Annual Report of the Bureau of Ethnology to the Secretary of the Smithsonian Institution, 1884–85. Washington, D.C.: GPO, 1888.

Bock, Philip K. *Shakespeare and Elizabethan Culture: An Anthropological View.* New York: Schocken, 1984.

Boose, Lynda E. "The Father and the Bride in Shakespeare." *PMLA* 97 (1982): 325–47.

———. "Othello's 'Chrysolite' and the Song of Songs Tradition." *Philological Quarterly* 60 (1981): 427–37.

Bord, Janet, and Colin Bord. *Earth Rites: Fertility Practices in Pre-industrial Britain.* London: Granada, 1982.

Boswell, John. *The Kindness of Strangers: The Abandonment of Children in Western Europe from Late Antiquity to the Renaissance.* New York: Pantheon, 1988.

Bourboule, Photeine. *Ancient Festivals of the "Saturnalia" Type.* Thessalonike, Greece: Hellenika, 1964.

Bourdieu, Pierre. "He Whose Word Is Law." *Liber* 1 (Oct. 1989): 12–13.

Brandon, S. G. F. *History, Time, and Deity: A Historical and Comparative Study of the Conception of Time in Religious Thought and Practice.* Manchester: Manchester University Press, 1965.

Brav, Aaron. "The Evil Eye among the Hebrews." 1908. *The Evil Eye: A Folklore Casebook.* Ed. Alan Dundes. New York: Garland, 1981. 44–54.

Brewer, Derek. *Symbolic Stories.* Woodbridge, Suffolk: D. S. Brewer; Lanham, Md.: Rowman and Littlefield, 1980.

Bristol, Michael D. *Carnival and Theater: Plebeian Culture and the Structure of Authority in Renaissance England.* New York: Methuen, 1985.

Brockbank, Philip. "Blood and Wine: Tragic Ritual from Aeschylus to Soyinka." *Shakespeare Survey* 36 (1983): 11–19.

Brody, Alan. *The English Mummers and Their Plays.* Philadelphia: University of Pennsylvania Press, 1969.

Bronowski, Jacob. "The Scapegoat King." *The Face of Violence.* Cleveland: World, 1967. 7–18.

Brown, Carleton, ed. *Religious Lyrics of the Fifteenth Century.* Oxford: Clarendon, 1939.

———. *Religious Lyrics of the Fourteenth Century.* Oxford: Clarendon, 1924.

————. *English Lyrics of the Thirteenth Century*. Oxford: Clarendon, 1932.

Brown, Paul. "'This Thing of Darkness I Acknowledge Mine': *The Tempest* and the Discourse of Colonialism." *Political Shakespeare: New Essays in Cultural Materialism*. Ed. Jonathan Dollimore and Alan Sinfield. Manchester: Manchester University Press, 1985. 48–71.

Browning, Robert. *The Complete Works of Robert Browning*. Ed. Roma A. King, Jr., Morse Peckham, Park Honan, Gordon Pitts, Jack W. Herring, Arthur N. Kincaid, and Allan C. Dooley. 8 vols. Athens: Ohio University Press, 1969–88.

Bryant, J. A., Jr. "Falstaff and the Renewal of Windsor." *PMLA* 89 (1974): 296–301.

Bryant, Mark. *Riddles Ancient and Modern*. London: Hutchison, 1983.

Bullinger, Heinrich. "Of the Sacraments of the Jews; of their sundry sorts of Sacrifices, and certain Other Things pertaining to their Ceremonial Law." *The Decades of Henry Bullinger*. Ed. Rev. Thomas Harding. Trans. H. I. Vol. 8. Cambridge: Cambridge University Press, 1850. 167–217. 8 vols. 1849–52.

Burke, Edmund. *The History of Archery*. London: Heinemann, 1958.

Burke, Peter. "Good Witches." *New York Review of Books*, 28 Feb. 1985, 32–34.

Burkert, Walter. "Greek Tragedy and Sacrificial Ritual." *Greek, Roman, and Byzantine Studies* 7 (1966): 87–121.

————. *Homo Necans: The Anthropology of Ancient Greek Sacrificial Ritual and Myth*. 1972. Trans. Peter Bing. Berkeley: University of California Press, 1983.

Burkert, Walter, René Girard, and Jonathan Z. Smith. *Violent Origins: Ritual Killing and Cultural Formation*. Ed. Robert G. Hamerton-Kelly. Stanford: Stanford University Press, 1987.

Burland, C. A. *Echoes of Magic: A Study of Seasonal Festivals through the Ages*. Totowa, N.J.: Rowman and Littlefield, 1972.

Buxton, John. *Elizabethan Taste*. London: Macmillan, 1963.

Bynum, Caroline Walker. *Holy Feast and Holy Fast: The Religious Significance of Food to Medieval Women*. Berkeley: University of California Press, 1987.

Caie, Graham D. "Christ as Warrior in Old English Poetry." *War and Peace in the Middle Ages*. Ed. Brian Patrick McGuire. Copenhagen: C. A. Reitzels Forlag, 1987.

Calderon, George. "Slavonic Elements in Greek Religion." *Classical Review* 27 (1913): 79–81.

Caldwell, Harry B. "Supplement: The Folk-Play and Related Forms (Selected Criticism)." *Twentieth-Century Criticism of English Masques,*

Pageants, and Entertainments: 1558–1642. Ed. David M. Bergeron. San Antonio, Texas: Trinity University Press, 1972. 43–49.

Campion, Thomas. *Campion's Works.* Ed. Percival Vivian. Oxford: Clarendon, 1909.

Capp, Bernard. "English Youth Groups and *The Pinder of Wakefield.*" *Past and Present* 76 (1977): 127–33.

Cary, Elizabeth. *Mariam, Fair Queen of Jewry.* c. 1613. Malone Society Reprint. Oxford: Oxford University Press, 1914.

Cassirer, Ernst. *Mythical Thought. Philosophy of Symbolic Forms.* Trans. Ralph Manheim. Vol. 2. New Haven: Yale University Press; London: Oxford University Press, 1955. 3 vols. 1923–57.

Cawte, E. C. *Ritual Animal Disguise: A Historical and Geographical Study of Animal Disguise in the British Isles.* Cambridge: Brewer; Rowman and Littlefield, 1978.

Cawte, E. C., Alex Helm, and N. Peacock. *English Ritual Drama.* London: Folklore Society, 1967.

Chambers, E. K. *The Elizabethan Stage.* Vol. 1. Oxford: Clarendon, 1923. 4 vols.

———. *The English Folk-Play.* Oxford: Clarendon, 1933.

———. *The Mediaeval Stage.* Oxford: Oxford University Press, 1903.

Chaucer, Geoffrey. *The Works of Geoffrey Chaucer.* Ed. F. N. Robinson. Boston: Houghton Mifflin, 1957.

Chrétien de Troyes. *Arthurian Romances.* Trans. W. W. Comfort. London: Dent, 1914.

Clark, Stuart. "King James's *Daemonologie:* Witchcraft and Kingship." *The Damned Art: Essays in the Literature of Witchcraft.* Ed. Sydney Anglo. London: Routledge and Kegan Paul, 1977. 156–81.

Clemen, Wolfgang. *English Tragedy before Shakespeare.* 1955. Trans. T. S. Dorsch. London: Methuen, 1961.

Clements, Forrest E. "Primitive Concepts of Disease." *University of California Publications in Archaeology and Ethnology* 32 (1932): 185–252.

Coleman, D. C. "Textile Growth." *Textile History and Economic History.* Ed. N. B. Harte and K. G. Ponting. Manchester: Manchester University Press, 1973. 1–21.

Copernicus, Nicolaus. *On the Revolutions of the Heavenly Spheres.* 1543. Trans. A. M. Duncan. New York: Barnes and Noble, 1976.

Cornford, Francis Macdonald. *The Origin of Attic Comedy.* Cambridge: Cambridge University Press, 1914.

Cornish, Vaughan. *Historic Thorn Trees in the British Isles.* London: Country Life, 1941.

Coursen, Herbert. *Christian Ritual and the World of Shakespeare's Trag-*

edies. Lewisburg: Bucknell University Press; London: Associated University Presses, 1976.

Cowie, L. W., and John Selwyn Gummer. *The Christian Calendar.* Springfield, Mass.: Merriam, 1974.

Crooke, W. *The Popular Religion and Folk-Lore of Northern India.* 2d ed. Vol. 1. Delhi: Munshiram Manoharlal, 1896. 2 vols.

Culler, Jonathan. *On Deconstruction: Theory and Criticism after Structuralism.* Ithaca: Cornell University Press, 1982.

Curtius, Ernst Robert. *European Literature and the Latin Middle Ages.* Trans. Willard R. Trask. New York: Pantheon, 1953.

Daniel, Samuel. *Sonnets to Delia. The Complete Works in Verse and Prose of Samuel Daniel.* 1885. Ed. Alexander B. Grosart. Vol. 1. New York: Russell and Russell, 1963. 19–77. 5 vols.

Davidson, Thomas. "Scoring Aboon the Breath: Defeating the Evil Eye." 1950. *The Evil Eye: A Folklore Casebook.* Ed. Alan Dundes. New York: Garland, 1981. 143–49.

Davis, Natalie Zemon. "The Reasons of Misrule: Youth Groups and Charivaris in Sixteenth-Century France." *Past and Present* 50 (1971): 41–75.

———. "Women on Top: Symbolic Sexual Inversion and Political Disorder in Early Modern Europe." *The Reversible World: Symbolic Inversion in Art and Society.* Ed. Barbara A. Babcock. Ithaca: Cornell University Press, 1978.

Davison, Francis. *A Poetical Rhapsody.* Ed. Hyder Edward Rollins. Cambridge, Mass.: Harvard University Press, 1931.

Deane, Tony, and Tony Shaw. *The Folklore of Cornwall.* London: Batsford, 1975.

Dean-Smith, Margaret. "The Life-Cycle or Folk Play." *Folklore* 69 (1958): 237–53.

De Gerenday, Lynn. "Play, Ritualization, and Ambivalence in *Julius Caesar.*" *Literature and Psychology* 24 (1974): 24–33.

de Heusch, Luc. *Sacrifice in Africa: A Structuralist Approach.* Trans. Linda O'Brien and Alice Morton. Manchester: Manchester University Press, 1985.

Dekker, Thomas, and Thomas Middleton. *The Honest Whore, Part 1. The Dramatic Works of Thomas Dekker.* Ed. Fredson Bowers. Vol. 2. Cambridge: Cambridge University Press, 1955. 1–130. 4 vols. 1953–61.

Delcourt, Marie. *Hermaphrodite: Myths and Rites of the Bisexual Figure in Classical Antiquity.* 1956. Trans. Jennnifer Nicholson. London: Studio Books, 1961.

Del Rio, Martinus Antonius. *Disquisitionum Magicarum.* Louvain, 1599.

De Mornay, Philippe du Plessis. *A Work Concerning the Trueness of the*

Christian Religion. Trans. Philip Sidney and Arthur Golding. 1587. STC 18149.

Dena, Dom Daniel Sour Dharim. *Annales de la propagation de la Foi* 60 (Lyons, 1888).

Derrida, Jacques. *Of Grammatology.* Trans. Gayatri Chakravorty Spivak. Baltimore: Johns Hopkins University Press, 1974.

———. "Plato's Pharmacy." *Dissemination.* Trans. Barbara Johnson. Chicago: University of Chicago Press, 1981. 61–171.

Detienne, Marcel. *Dionysus at Large.* 1986. Trans. Arthur Goldhammer. Cambridge, Mass.: Harvard University Press, 1989.

Dickenson, John. *Greene in Conceit: New Raised from His Grave to Write the Tragic History of Fair Valeria of London.* 1598. STC 6819.

Dieterich, Albrecht. *Mutter Erde: Ein Versuch über Volksreligion.* Leipzig: B. G. Teubner, 1905.

Dietrich, Julia C. "Folk Drama Scholarship: The State of the Art." *Research Opportunities in Renaissance Drama* 19 (1976): 15–32.

Dinnerstein, Dorothy. *The Mermaid and the Minotaur: Sexual Arrangements and Human Malaise.* New York: Harper, 1976.

Diodorus of Sicily. *Works.* Trans. Russell M. Greer. London: Heinemann, 1962.

Dollimore, Jonathan. *Radical Tragedy: Religion, Ideology, and Power in the Drama of Shakespeare and His Contemporaries.* Chicago: University of Chicago Press; Brighton: Harvester, 1984.

Dollimore, Jonathan, and Alan Sinfield, eds. *Political Shakespeare: New Essays in Cultural Materialism.* Manchester: Manchester University Press, 1985.

Donaldson, Ian. *The Rapes of Lucretia.* Oxford: Clarendon, 1982.

Donne, John. *The Poems of John Donne.* Ed. Herbert J. C. Grierson. Oxford: Oxford University Press, 1912.

Dorius, R. J. "A Little More Than a Little." *Shakespeare Quarterly* 11 (1960): 13–26.

Douglas, Mary. *Natural Symbols: Explorations in Cosmology.* New York: Pantheon, 1970.

———. *Purity and Danger: An Analysis of the Concepts of Pollution and Taboo.* London: Routledge and Kegan Paul, 1966.

Dover, K. J. "Greek Comedy." *Fifty Years (and Twelve) of Classical Scholarship.* Ed. Maurice Platnauer. New York: Barnes and Noble, 1968. 123–56.

Dubrow, Heather. *Captive Victors: Shakespeare's Narrative Poems and Sonnets.* Ithaca: Cornell University Press, 1987.

———. *A Happier Eden: The Politics of Marriage in the Stuart Epithalamium.* Ithaca: Cornell University Press, 1990.

Dundes, Alan. "Wet and Dry, the Evil Eye: An Essay in Indo-European and Semitic Worldview." *The Evil Eye: A Folklore Casebook.* Ed. Alan Dundes. New York: Garland, 1981. 257–312.

Dusinberre, Juliet. *Shakespeare and the Nature of Women.* London: Macmillan, 1975.

Eagleton, Terry. *The Ideology of the Aesthetic.* Oxford: Blackwell, 1990.

———. *Walter Benjamin: Towards a Revolutionary Criticism.* London: Verso, 1981.

Edwards, Viv, and Thomas J. Sienkewicz. *Oral Cultures Past and Present: Rappin' and Homer.* Oxford: Basil Blackwell, 1990.

Eisenstadt, S. I. *Generation to Generation: Age Groups and Social Structure.* Glencoe, Ill.: Free Press, 1956.

Eliade, Mircea. *Rites and Symbols of Initiation.* Trans. Willard R. Trask. Chicago: University of Chicago Press, 1956.

———. *Shamanism.* 1951. Trans. Willard Trask. New York: Pantheon, 1964.

Else, Gerald F. *The Origin and Early Form of Greek Tragedy.* Cambridge, Mass.: Harvard University Press, 1965.

Elton, G. R. "Scapegoats." *New York Review of Books,* Jan. 19, 1989, 48–50.

Elworthy, Frederick. *The Evil Eye: The Origins and Practices of Superstition.* 1895. New York: Collier, 1958.

Empson, William. *Some Versions of Pastoral.* London: Chatto and Windus, 1935.

Esler, Anthony. *The Aspiring Mind of the Elizabethan Younger Generation.* Durham: University of North Carolina Press, 1966.

Euripides. *The Bacchae.* Trans. Geoffrey S. Kirk. Englewood Cliffs, N.J.: Prentice-Hall, 1970.

Evans, Ifor M., and Heather Lawrence. *Christopher Saxton: Elizabethan Map-Maker.* London: Holland, 1979.

Fabri, Ralph. *Color: A Complete Guide for Artists.* New York: Watson-Guptill, 1967.

Falkener, Edward. *Games Ancient and Oriental.* 1892. New York: Dover, 1961.

Faludi, Susan. *Backlash: The Undeclared War against American Women.* New York: Crown, 1991.

Farley, Walter. *The Black Stallion.* New York: Random House, 1941.

Faron, Louis C. "Death and Fertility Rites of the Mapuche (Araucanian) Indians of Central Chile." *Gods and Rituals: Readings in Religious Beliefs and Practices.* New York: Natural History Press, 1967. 227–54.

Farrell, Kirby. *Shakespeare's Creation: The Language of Magic and Play.* Amherst: University of Massachusetts Press, 1975.

Felperin, Howard. *Shakespearean Representation: Mimesis and Modernity in Elizabethan Tragedy.* Princeton: Princeton University Press, 1977.

Fernández-Armesto, Felipe. *The Spanish Armada: The Experience of War in 1588.* Oxford: Oxford University Press, 1988.

Fiedler, Leslie. *The Stranger in Shakespeare.* New York: Stein and Day, 1972.

Fineman, Joel. "Shakespeare's *Will:* The Temporality of Rape." *Representations* 20 (1987): 25–76.

Fiorentino, Giovanni. *Il Pecorone.* 1558. Trans. W. C. Hazlitt. *Shakespeare's Library.* Vol. 1. London: Reeves and Turner, 1875. 319–53.

Fish, Lydia M. *The Folklore of the Coal Miners of the Northeast of England.* Norwood, Penn.: Norwood Editions, 1975.

Fitz, L. T. "Humanism Questioned: A Study of Four Renaissance Characters." *English Studies in Canada* 5 (1979): 388–405.

———. "Mental Torment and the Figurative Method of *The Tempest.*" *English Miscellany* 25 (1975–76): 135–62.

———. "The Vocabulary of the Environment in *The Tempest.*" *Shakespeare Quarterly* 26 (1975): 42–47.

Fletcher, Angus. *Allegory: The Theory of a Symbolic Mode.* Ithaca: Cornell University Press, 1964.

Fletcher, Anthony, and John Stevenson. Introduction. *Order and Disorder in Early Modern England.* Ed. Anthony Fletcher and John Stevenson. Cambridge: Cambridge University Press, 1985. 1–40.

Florio, John. Dedication to translation of *Essays* by Michel de Montaigne. London, 1603.

Fokkelman, J. P. "Genesis." *The Literary Guide to the Bible.* Ed. Robert Alter and Frank Kermode. Cambridge, Mass.: Harvard University Press, 1987. 36–55.

Foley, Daniel J. *The Christmas Tree.* Philadelphia: Chilton, 1960.

Foley, Helene. *Ritual Irony: Poetry and Sacrifice in Euripides.* Ithaca: Cornell University Press, 1985.

Fontenrose, Joseph. *The Ritual Theory of Myth.* Berkeley: University of California Press, 1971.

Forker, Charles R. "The Green Underworld of Early Shakespearean Tragedy." *Shakespeare Studies* 17 (1985): 25–47.

Foucault, Michel. *Discipline and Punish.* Trans. Alan Sheridan. New York: Pantheon, 1977.

———. *Power/Knowledge: Selected Interviews and Other Writings, 1972–77.* Ed. Colin Gordon. Trans. Colin Gordon, Leo Marshall, John Mepham, Kate Soper. New York: Pantheon, 1980.

Frankis, P. J. "The Testament of the Deer in Shakespeare." *Neuphilologische Mitteilungen* 59 (1958): 65–68.

Fraunce, Abraham. *The Third Part of the Countess of Pembroke's Ivy-church, Entitled Amintas Dale.* 1592. STC 11341.

Frazer, Sir James. *The Scapegoat.* 1890. Part 6 of *The Golden Bough.* 3d ed. London: Macmillan, 1913.

———. *The Dying God.* 1890. Part 3 of *The Golden Bough.* London: Macmillan, 1911.

Freedman, Barbara. *Staging the Gaze: Postmodernism, Psychoanalysis, and Shakespearean Comedy.* Ithaca: Cornell University Press, 1991.

Freud, Sigmund. *The Complete Psychological Works of Sigmund Freud.* Ed. and trans. James Strachey, Anna Freud, Alix Strachey, and Alan Tyson. 24 vols. London: Hogarth, 1953–74.

———. *Moses and Monotheism.* New York: Knopf, 1939.

Frost, William. "Shakespeare's Rituals and the Opening of *King Lear.*" *Hudson Review* 10 (1957–58): 577–85.

Frye, Northrop. *Anatomy of Criticism.* Princeton: Princeton University Press, 1957.

———. *The Great Code: The Bible and Literature.* Toronto: Academic Press, 1981.

———. "Myth, Fiction, and Displacement." *Fables of Identity: Studies in Poetic Mythology.* New York: Harcourt, 1963. 21–38.

———. *A Natural Perspective: The Development of Shakespearean Comedy and Romance.* New York: Columbia, 1965.

———. *The Secular Scripture: A Study of the Structure of Romance.* Cambridge, Mass.: Harvard University Press, 1976.

Frye, Susan. "The Myth of Elizabeth I at Tilbury." *Sixteenth-Century Journal.* Forthcoming.

Fuhrmann, Otto W. "The Invention of Printing." 1938. *Reader in the History of Books and Printing.* Ed. Paul A. Winckler. Englewood, Colo.: Information Handling Services, 1978. 237–83.

Geertz, Clifford. "Centers, Kings, and Charisma: Reflections on the Symbolics of Power." *Rites of Power: Symbolism, Ritual, and Politics since the Middle Ages.* Ed. Sean Wilentz. Philadelphia: University of Pennsylvania Press, 1985. 13–38.

———. *The Interpretation of Cultures.* New York: Basic Books, 1973.

Geertz, Hildred. "An Anthropology of Religion and Magic, 1." *Journal of Interdisciplinary History* 6 (1975): 7–89.

Giamatti, A. Bartlett. "Hippolytus among the Exiles." *Exile and Change in Renaissance Literature.* New Haven: Yale University Press, 1984. 12–32.

Gibson, George M. *The Story of the Christian Year.* New York: Abingdon Press, 1945.

Gill, Sam D. *Mother Earth.* Chicago: University of Chicago Press, 1987.

Ginzburg, Carlo. *The Night Battles: Witchcraft and Agrarian Cults in the Sixteenth and Seventeenth Centuries.* 1966. Trans. John Tedeschi and Anne Tedeschi. London: Routledge and Kegan Paul, 1983.

Girard, René. *Deceit, Desire, and the Novel: Self and Other in Literary Structure.* Trans. Yvonne Freccero. Baltimore: Johns Hopkins University Press, 1965.

———. "Lévi-Strauss, Frye, Derrida, and Shakespearean Criticism." *Diacritics* 3, no. 3 (1973): 34–38.

———. "Myth and Ritual in Shakespeare: *A Midsummer Night's Dream.*" *Textual Strategies: Perspectives in Post-structuralist Criticism.* Ed. Josué V. Harari. Ithaca: Cornell University Press, 1979. 189–212.

———. *The Scapegoat.* Trans. Yvonne Freccero. Baltimore: Johns Hopkins University Press, 1986.

———. *A Theatre of Envy: William Shakespeare.* New York: Oxford University Press, 1991.

———. "'To Entrap the Wisest': A Reading of *The Merchant of Venice.*" *Literature and Society.* Ed. Edward W. Said. Baltimore: Johns Hopkins University Press, 1980. 100–119.

———. *Violence and the Sacred.* Trans. Patrick Gregory. Baltimore: Johns Hopkins University Press, 1977.

Gluckman, Max. *"Les Rites de Passage." Essays on the Ritual of Social Relations.* Ed. Max Gluckman. Manchester: Manchester University Press, 1962. 1–52.

———. "Rituals of Rebellion in South-East Africa." *Order and Rebellion in Tribal Africa.* London: Cohen and West, 1963. 110–36.

Goldberg, Jonathan. *James I and the Politics of Literature: Jonson, Shakespeare, Donne, and Their Contemporaries.* Baltimore: Johns Hopkins University Press, 1983.

———. "The Politics of Renaissance Literature: A Review Essay." *English Literary History* 49 (1982): 514–42.

Golombek, Harry. *Chess: A History.* New York: Putnam, 1976.

Gombrich, E. H. *Art and Illusion: A Study in the Psychology of Pictorial Representation.* New York: Pantheon, 1960.

Goody, Jack. "Against 'Ritual': Loosely Structured Thoughts on a Loosely Defined Topic." *Secular Ritual.* Ed. Sally F. Moore and Barbara G. Myerhoff. Assen, the Netherlands: Van Gorcum, 1977.

Goody, Jack, and Ian Watt. "The Consequences of Literacy." *Literacy in Traditional Societies.* Ed. J. R. Goody. Cambridge: Cambridge University Press, 1968.

Gorfain, Phyllis. "Remarks toward a Folklorist Approach to Literature: Riddles in Shakespearean Drama." *Southern Folklore Quarterly* 41 (1977): 143–57.

———. "Riddles and Reconciliation: Formal Unity in *All's Well That Ends Well.*" *Journal of the Folklore Institute* 13 (1976): 263–81.

———. "Riddles and Tragic Structure in *Macbeth.*" *Mississippi Folklore Register* 10 (1976): 187–205.

Grande, Troni. "Marlowe and the Play of Dilation." Diss. University of Alberta, 1991.

Gray, John Henry. *China: A History of the Laws, Manners, and Customs of the People.* Ed. William Gow Gregor. Vol. 2. London: Macmillan, 1878. 2 vols.

Green, Marian. *A Harvest of Festivals.* London: Longman, 1980.

Green, Miranda. *A Corpus of Religious Material from the Civilian Areas of Roman Britain.* British Archaeological Reports 24. Oxford, 1976.

Greenblatt, Stephen. "The Eating of the Soul." Paper delivered at the meeting of the Shakespeare Association of America, Vancouver, B.C., Mar. 1991.

———. "Invisible Bullets: Renaissance Authority and Its Subversion, *Henry IV,* and *Henry V.*" *Political Shakespeare: New Essays in Cultural Materialism.* Ed. Jonathan Dollimore and Alan Sinfield. Manchester: Manchester University Press, 1985. 18–47.

———. *Renaissance Self-fashioning: From More to Shakespeare.* Chicago: University of Chicago Press, 1980.

———. "Shakespeare and the Exorcists." *Shakespeare and the Question of Theory.* Ed. Patricia Parker and Geoffrey Hartman. New York: Methuen, 1985. 163–87.

Greene, Gayle. "The Empire Strikes Back." *The Nation,* Feb. 10, 1992, 166–70.

Greene, Richard Leighton. *The Early English Carols.* Oxford: Clarendon, 1962.

Greene, Robert [?]. *George a Green, The Pinner of Wakefield.* 1590. STC 12212.

Guépin, Jean-Pierre. *The Tragic Paradox: Myth and Ritual in Greek Tragedy.* Amsterdam: Hakkert, 1968.

Gutierrez, Joannes Lazarus. *Opusculum de Fascino.* London: Philip Borde, 1653.

Hall, Joseph. *Virgidemiarum.* 1597. STC 12716. Book 1, Satire 7.

Hamilton, Edith. *Mythology.* Boston: Little, Brown, 1942.

Hand, Wayland. "The Evil Eye in Its Folk Medical Aspects: A Survey of North America." *The Evil Eye: A Folklore Casebook.* Ed. Alan Dundes. New York: Garland, 1981. 169–80.

Hansard, George Agar. *The Book of Archery.* London: Henry G. Bohn, 1841.

Hapgood, Robert. "Shakespeare and the Ritualists." *Shakespeare Survey* 15 (1962): 111–24.

Harbage, Alfred. "Shakespeare as Culture Hero." *Conceptions of Shakespeare*. Cambridge: Harvard University Press, 1966. 101–19.

Hardin, Richard F. "Chronicles and Mythmaking in Shakespeare's Joan of Arc." *Shakespeare Survey* 42 (1990): 25–35.

———. "'Ritual' in Recent Criticism: The Elusive Sense of Community." *PMLA* 98 (1983): 846–62.

Hardison, O. B. *Christian Rite and Christian Drama in the Middle Ages.* Baltimore: Johns Hopkins University Press, 1965.

Harfouche, Jamal Karam. "The Evil Eye and Infant Health in Lebanon." *Infant Health in Lebanon: Customs and Taboos.* Beirut: Khayats, 1965. 81–106.

Harley, J. B. "Meaning and Ambiguity in Tudor Cartography." *English Map-Making, 1400–1650.* Ed. Sarah Tyacke. London: British Library, 1983. 22–45.

Harrison, Jane. *Themis: A Study of the Social Origins of Greek Religion.* Cambridge: Cambridge University Press, 1912.

Hart-Davis, Duff. *Armada.* London: Bantam, 1988.

Hassel, R. Chris, Jr. *Renaissance Drama and the English Church Year.* Lincoln: University of Nebraska Press, 1979.

Hastrup, Kirsten. "The Semantics of Biology: Virginity." *Defining Females: The Nature of Women in Society.* Ed. Shirley Ardener. New York: John Wiley, 1978. 49–65.

Hawkins, Harriett. *The Devil's Party: Critical Counter-interpretations of Shakespearian Drama.* Oxford: Clarendon, 1985.

Hawkins, Sherman. "The Two Worlds of Shakespearean Comedy." *Shakespeare Studies* 3 (1967): 62–80.

Heath, Shirley Brice. "The Responsibilities for Literacy Conference: Significance, Accomplishments, Future Directions." Paper delivered at the MLA conference, San Francisco, Dec. 1992.

Heckscher, William S. "Shakespeare in His Relationship to the Visual Arts: A Study in Paradox." *Research Opportunities in Renaissance Drama* 13–14 (1970–71): 5–72.

Helm, Alex. *The English Mummers' Play.* Woodbridge, Suffolk: Brewer, 1981.

Henn, Thomas Rice. *The Harvest of Tragedy.* London: Methuen, 1956.

Herrick, Robert. *The Poetical Works of Robert Herrick.* Ed. L. C. Martin. Oxford: Clarendon, 1956.

Hewitt, Douglas. "'The Very Pompes of the Divell'—Popular and Folk Elements in Elizabethan and Jacobean Drama." *Review of English Studies* 25 (1949): 10–23.

Heywood, Thomas. *The Brazen Age. The Dramatic Works of Thomas Heywood.* Ed. R. H. Shepherd. Vol. 3. London: John Pearson, 1874. 165–256. 6 vols.

————. *The Iron Age, Part 2. The Dramatic Works of Thomas Heywood.* Ed. R. H. Shepherd. Vol. 3. London: John Pearson, 1874. 347–431. 6 vols.

————. *Troia Britanica; or, Great Britaines Troy.* 1609. Hildesheim, Germany: Georg Olms, 1972.

Hieatt, A. Kent. *Short Time's Endless Monument.* New York: Columbia University Press, 1960.

Hill, Christopher. *The World Turned Upside Down: Radical Ideas during the English Revolution.* London: Temple Smith, 1972.

Hoffman, Nancy Jo. *Spenser's Pastorals: "The Shepheardes Calender" and "Colin Clout."* Baltimore: Johns Hopkins University Press, 1977.

Holland, Norman. "Macbeth as Hibernal Giant." *Literature and Psychology* 10 (1960): 37–38.

————. *Psychoanalysis and Shakespeare.* New York: McGraw-Hill, 1964.

Holloway, John. *The Story of the Night.* London: Routledge and Kegan Paul, 1961.

Holmes, C. "Drainers and Fenmen: the Problem of Popular Political Consciousness in the Seventeenth Century." *Order and Disorder in Early Modern England.* Ed. Anthony Fletcher and John Stevenson. Cambridge: Cambridge University Press, 1985. 166–95.

Homans, George C. "Anxiety and Ritual: The Theories of Malinowski and Radcliffe-Brown." *American Anthropologist* 43 (1941): 164–72.

Hope, Robert Charles. *The Legendary Lore of the Holy Wells of England.* London: Elliot Stock, 1893.

Hubert, Henri, and Marcel Mauss. *Sacrifice: Its Nature and Function.* 1898. Trans. W. D. Halls. London: Cohen and West, 1964.

Hulse, S. Clark. "Shakespeare's Myth of Venus and Adonis." *PMLA* 93 (1978): 95–105.

Hunter, G. K. "Sources and Meanings in *Titus Andronicus.*" *Mirror up to Shakespeare: Essays in Honour of G. R. Hibbard.* Ed. J. C. Gray. Toronto: University of Toronto Press, 1984. 171–88.

Hunter, R. G. *Shakespeare and the Comedy of Forgiveness.* New York: Columbia University Press, 1965.

Ickis, Marguerite. *The Book of Festivals and Holidays the World Over.* New York: Dodd, Mead, 1970.

Indagine, Ihon. *Brief Introduction . . . unto the Art of Chiromancy, or Manual Divination, . . . and Physiognomy.* Trans. Fabian Withers. London: Johannis Day, 1558.

James I, King. *Daemonologie.* 1597. New York: Barnes and Noble, 1966.

————. *The Political Works of James I, Reprinted from the Edition of 1616.* Ed. Charles Howard McIlwain. Cambridge: Harvard University Press, 1918.

Johnson, Mark. *The Body in the Mind: The Bodily Basis of Meaning, Imagination, and Reason.* Chicago: University of Chicago Press, 1987.

Jones, Emrys. "Stuart *Cymbeline.*" *Essays in Criticism* 11 (1961): 84–99.

Jones, Francis. *The Holy Wells of Wales.* Cardiff: University of Wales Press, 1954.

Jones, Francis, and Regina Herzlinger. "Massport." Boston: Harvard Business School, 1979.

Jones, Louis C. "The Evil Eye among European-Americans." 1951. *The Evil Eye: A Folklore Casebook.* Ed. Alan Dundes. New York: Garland, 1981. 150–68.

Jonson, Ben. *Ben Jonson.* Ed. C. H. Herford and Percy Simpson. 11 vols. Oxford: Clarendon, 1925–52.

Jonson, Ben, George Chapman, and John Marston. *Eastward Ho.* Ed. C. G. Petter. London: E. Benn, 1973.

Jorgensen, Paul A. *William Shakespeare: The Tragedies.* Boston: Twayne, 1985.

Jung, C. G. *The Collected Works of C. G. Jung.* Trans. R. F. C. Hull. Ed. Herbert Read, Michael Fordham, and Gerhard Adler. Vol. 9, part 1. Princeton: Princeton University Press, 1959. 20 vols. 1957–59.

Kahn, Coppélia. *Man's Estate: Masculine Identity in Shakespeare.* Berkeley: University of California Press, 1981.

———. "The Rape in Shakespeare's *Lucrece.*" *Shakespeare Studies* 9 (1976): 45–72.

Keen, Sam. *Faces of the Enemy: Reflections of the Hostile Imagination.* San Francisco: Harper and Row, 1986.

Kerby, J. M. "Caxton to Computers." 1971. *Reader in the History of Books and Printing.* Ed. Paul A. Winckler. Englewood, Colo.: Information Handling Services, 1978.

Kermode, Frank. *The Sense of an Ending.* New York: Oxford University Press, 1967.

Kertzer, David I. *Ritual, Politics, and Power.* New Haven: Yale University Press, 1988.

Kieckhefer, Richard. *Magic in the Middle Ages.* Cambridge: Cambridge University Press, 1989.

Kilgour, Maggie. *From Communion to Cannibalism: An Anatomy of Metaphors of Incorporation.* Princeton: Princeton University Press, 1990.

Kirby, E. T. "Mummers' Plays and the Calendar." *Journal of American Folklore* 86 (1973): 282–85.

———. "Origin of the Mummers' Play." *Journal of American Folklore* 84 (1971): 275–88.

Kittredge, George Lyman. *Witchcraft in Old and New England.* Cambridge, Mass.: Harvard University Press, 1929.

Kluckhohn, Clyde. *Navaho Witchcraft.* Cambridge: Peabody Museum, 1944.

Kolodny, Annette. *The Lay of the Land.* Chapel Hill: University of North Carolina Press, 1984.

Kolve, V. A. *The Play Called Corpus Christi.* Stanford: Stanford University Press, 1966.

Kott, Jan. *The Bottom Translation: Marlowe and Shakespeare and the Carnival Tradition.* Trans. Daniela Miedzyrzecka and Lillian Vallee. Evanston, Ill.: Northwestern University Press, 1987.

———. *The Eating of the Gods: An Interpretation of Greek Tragedy.* Trans. Boleslaw Taborski and Edward J. Czerwinski. London: Methuen, 1974.

Krämer, Heinrich, and Jacob Sprenger. *The Malleus Maleficarum, 1486. Witchcraft in Europe, 1100–1700: A Documentary History.* Ed. Alan C. Kors and Edward Peters. Philadelphia: University of Pennsylvania Press, 1972. 113–89.

Kriedte, Peter, Hans Medick, and Jürgen Schlumbohm. 1977. *Industrialization before Industrialization.* Trans. Beate Schempp. Cambridge: Cambridge University Press, 1981.

Kuhn, Thomas S. *The Structure of Scientific Revolutions.* 2d ed. Chicago: University of Chicago Press, 1970.

Kunzle, David. "World Upside Down: The Iconography of a European Broadsheet Type." *The Reversible World: Symbolic Inversion in Art and Society.* Ed. Barbara A. Babcock. Ithaca: Cornell University Press, 1978. 39–94.

Lang, Andrew. *Magic and Religion.* London: Longmans, Green, 1901.

Langdon, Stephen. "An Incantation in the 'House of Light' against the Evil Eye." 1913. *The Evil Eye: A Folklore Casebook.* Ed. Alan Dundes. New York: Garland, 1981. 39–43.

Langman, F. H. "Comedy and Saturnalia: The Case of *TN.*" *Southern Review* (Australia) 7 (1974): 102–22.

Laroque, François. "Pagan Ritual, Christian Liturgy, and Folk Customs in *The Winter's Tale.*" *Cahiers Élisabéthains* 22 (1982): 25–33.

———. *Shakespeare's Festive World: Elizabethan Seasonal Entertainment and the Professional Stage.* 1988. Trans. Janet Lloyd. Cambridge: Cambridge University Press, 1991.

Latimer, Kathleen. "The Communal Action of *The Winter's Tale.*" *The Terrain of Comedy.* Ed. Louise Cowan. Dallas: Dallas Institute of Humanities and Culture, 1984. 125–42.

LeCourt, Donna, and Todd English. "'Who Do You Say That I Am?': 'Illiteracy' and the Popular Discourse of Power." Paper delivered at the MLA conference, San Francisco, Dec. 1992.

Leggatt, Alexander. *Shakespeare's Political Drama: The History Plays and the Roman Plays.* London: Routledge, 1988.

Le Goff, Jacques. *Medieval Civilization 400–1500.* Trans. Julia Barrow. London: Blackwell, 1989.

Le Roy Ladurie, Emmanuel. 1966. *The Peasants of Languedoc.* Trans. John Day. Urbana: University of Illinois Press, 1974.

Levin, Richard. *New Readings vs. Old Plays.* Chicago: University of Chicago Press, 1979.

Lévi-Strauss, Claude. *Structural Anthropology.* Trans. Claire Jacobson and Brooke Grundfest Schoepf. Vol. 1. New York: Basic Books, 1963. 2 vols.

———. *Totemism.* 1962. Trans. Rodney Needham. Boston: Beacon Press, 1963.

Liebler, Naomi Conn. "'Thou Bleeding Piece of Earth': The Ritual Ground of *Julius Caesar.*" *Shakespeare Studies* 14 (1981): 175–96.

Lindberg, David C. *Theories of Vision from Al-Kindi to Kepler.* Chicago: University of Chicago Press, 1976.

Livius, Titus. (Livy). *Livy.* Trans. B. O. Foster. Vol. 4. London: Heinemann; Cambridge, Mass.: Harvard University Press, 1948. 13 vols.

Lodge, Thomas. *Lodge's "Rosalynde" Being the Original of Shakespeare's "As You Like It."* Ed. W. W. Greg. London: Chatto and Windus, 1907.

Logan, Patrick. *The Holy Wells of Ireland.* Gerrards Cross, England: Smythe, 1980.

Long, George. *The Folklore Calendar.* London: Philip Allan, 1930.

Lowenstein, Joseph. "The Jonsonian Corpulence; or, The Poet as Mouthpiece." *English Literary History* 53 (1986): 491–518.

Lucian of Samosata. "Saturnalia." *The Works of Lucian of Samosata.* Trans. H. W. Fowler and F. G. Fowler. Vol. 4. Oxford: Clarendon, 1905. 108–12. 4 vols.

Lumiansky, R. M., and David Mills, eds. *The Chester Mystery Cycles.* London: Oxford University Press, 1974.

Lyall, Alfred C. *Asiatic Studies Religious and Social.* London: Murray, 1899.

McCartney, Eugene S. "Praise and Dispraise in Folklore." *Papers of the Michigan Academy of Science, Arts, and Letters* 28 (1942): 567–93.

Macey, Samuel L. *Patriarchs of Time: Dualism in Saturn-Cronus, Father Time, the Watchmaker God, and Father Christmas.* Athens: University of Georgia Press, 1987.

Macfarlane, Alan. "A Tudor Anthropologist: George Gifford's *Discourse* and *Dialogue.*" *The Damned Art: Essays in the Literature of Witchcraft.* Ed. Sydney Anglo. London: Routledge and Kegan Paul, 1977. 140–55.

———. *Witchcraft in Tudor and Stuart England: A Regional and Comparative Study.* London: Routledge and Kegan Paul, 1970.

Macfarlane, Alan, and Sarah Harris. *The Justice and the Mare's Ale: Law and Disorder in Seventeenth-Century England.* Oxford: Blackwell, 1981.

Mackenzie, Sir George. *Laws and Customs of Scotland.* Edinburgh: J. Glen, 1678.

Maclagan, R. C. *Evil Eye in the Western Highlands.* London: D. Nutt, 1902.

McLane, Paul E. *Spenser's "Shepheardes Calender": A Study in Elizabethan Allegory.* Notre Dame, Ind.: Notre Dame University Press, 1961.

McLuhan, Marshall. *The Gutenberg Galaxy: The Making of Typographic Man.* Toronto: University of Toronto Press, 1962.

Macrobius. *The Saturnalia.* Trans. Percival Vaughan Davies. New York: Columbia University Press, 1969.

Maddox, John Lee. *The Medicine Man: A Sociological Study of the Character and Evolution of Shamanism.* New York: Macmillan, 1923.

Magnus, Olaus. *Historia de Gentibus Septentrionalibus.* 1555. Ed. John Granlund. Copenhagen: Rosenkilde and Bagger, 1972.

Maloney, Clarence. Introduction. *The Evil Eye.* Ed. Clarence Maloney. New York: Columbia University Press, 1976. v–xvi.

Malory, Sir Thomas. *The Works of Sir Thomas Malory.* Ed. Eugene Vinaver. Oxford: Clarendon, 1967.

Maranda, Elli Köngäs. "The Logic of Riddles." *Structural Analysis of Oral Tradition.* Philadelphia: University of Pennsylvania Press, 1971. 189–232.

Marcus, Leah. *The Politics of Mirth: Jonson, Herrick, Milton, Marvell, and the Defense of Old Holiday Pastimes.* Chicago: University of Chicago Press, 1986.

———. *Puzzling Shakespeare: Local Reading and Its Discontents.* Berkeley: University of California Press, 1988.

Marett, R. R. *Sacraments of Simple Folk.* Oxford: Clarendon, 1933.

Marienstras, Richard. *New Perspectives on the Shakespearean World.* 1981. Trans. Janet Lloyd. Cambridge: Cambridge University Press, 1985.

Marlowe, Christopher. *Dr. Faustus.* Ed. John D. Jump. London: Methuen, 1962.

———. *Edward II.* Ed. H. B. Charlton and R. D. Waller. *The Works and Life of Christopher Marlowe.* Ed. R. H. Case. London: Methuen, 1933.

———. *Tamburlaine the Great, Part One.* Ed. Una M. Ellis-Fermor. *The Works and Life of Christopher Marlowe.* Ed. R. H. Case. London: Methuen, 1930.

Marx, Steven. *Youth against Age: Generational Strife in Renaissance Poetry, with Special Reference to Edmund Spenser's "The Shepheardes Calender."* New York: Peter Lang, 1985.

Mattingly, Garrett. *The Armada.* Cambridge: Riverside, 1959.

Maus, Katharine Eisaman. "Taking Tropes Seriously: Language and Violence in Shakespeare's *Rape of Lucrece.*" *Shakespeare Quarterly* 37 (1986): 66–82.

Mead, Margaret. *Male and Female.* New York: Morrow, 1949.

Menefee, Samuel Pyeatt. *Wives for Sale: An Ethnographic Study of British Popular Divorce.* Oxford: Basil Blackwell, 1981.

Merchant, Carolyn. *The Death of Nature: Women, Ecology, and the Scientific Revolution.* San Francisco: Harper and Row, 1980.

Merrifield, Ralph. *The Archeology of Ritual and Magic.* New York: New Amsterdam, 1987.

Miola, Robert S. *Shakespeare's Rome.* Cambridge: Cambridge University Press, 1983.

Mitchell, W. J. T. "*Critical Inquiry* and the Ideology of Pluralism." *Critical Inquiry* 8 (1982): 609–18.

Montrose, Louis Adrian. "'Eliza, Queene of Shepheardes,' and the Pastoral of Power." *English Literary Renaissance* 10 (1980): 153–82.

———. "The Elizabethan Subject and the Spenserian Text." *Literary Theory/Renaissance Texts.* Ed. Patricia Parker and David Quint. Baltimore: Johns Hopkins University Press, 1986. 303–40.

———. "*A Midsummer Night's Dream* and the Shaping Fantasies of Elizabethan Culture: Gender, Power, Form." *Rewriting the Renaissance: The Discourses of Sexual Difference in Early Modern Europe.* Ed. Margaret W. Ferguson, Maureen Quilligan, and Nancy J. Vickers. Chicago: University of Chicago Press, 1986. 65–87.

———. "'The Place of a Brother' in *AYL:* Social Process and Comic Form." *Shakespeare Quarterly* 32 (1981): 28–54.

———. "The Purpose of Playing: Reflections on a Shakespearean Anthropology." *Helios* 7 (1980): 51–74.

Moore, Clement Clarke. *A Visit from St. Nicholas.* 1823. New York: Onderdonk, 1848.

Morgan, Victor. "The Cartographic Image of 'The Country' in Early Modern England." *Transactions of the Royal Historical Society,* Fifth Series, 29. London: Royal Historical Society, 1979. 129–54.

Morrison, Toni. *Tar Baby.* New York: Knopf, 1981.

———. *The Bluest Eye.* New York: Holt, Rinehart, and Winston, 1970.

Moss, Leonard W., and Stephen C. Cappannari. "*Mal'occhio, Ayin ha ra, Oculus fascinus, Judenblick:* The Evil Eye Hovers Above." *The Evil Eye.* Ed. Clarence Maloney. New York: Columbia University Press, 1976. 1–15.

Mowat, Barbara. "Prospero, Agrippa, and Hocus Pocus." *English Literary Renaissance* 11 (1981): 281–303.

Mullaney, Steven. *The Place of the Stage: License, Play, and Power in Renaissance England.* Chicago: University of Chicago Press, 1988.

Munday, Anthony. *The Triumphs of Re-united Britania,* 1605. *Pageants and Entertainments of Anthony Munday.* Ed. David Bergeron. New York: Garland, 1985. 1–23.

Murray, Gilbert. "Hamlet and Orestes." 1914. *The Classical Tradition in Poetry.* London: Oxford University Press, 1927. 205–40.

Murray, Margaret Alice. *The Witch-Cult in Western Europe.* Oxford: Clarendon, 1921.

Myers, James P., Jr. *Elizabethan Ireland: A Selection of Writings of Elizabethan Writers on Ireland.* Hamden, Conn.: Archon, 1983.

Nast, Thomas. Christmas Illustrations. *Harper's Weekly,* Dec. 26, 1863, 824–26; Dec. 9, 1866, 824–25.

Nearing, Homer, Jr. "The Legend of Julius Caesar's British Conquest." *PMLA* 64 (1949): 889–929.

Neumann, Erich. *Depth Psychology and a New Ethic.* 1949. Trans. Eugene Rolfe. London: Hodder and Stoughton, 1969.

———. *The Great Mother: An Analysis of the Archetype.* Trans. Ralph Manheim. New York: Pantheon, 1955.

Newman, Arthur. *A Short Dialogue of a Woman's Properties, between an Old Man and a Young.* 1619. STC 18496.

Niles, John D. "The *Aecerbot* Ritual in Context." *Old English Literature in Context.* Ed. John D. Niles. Woodbridge, Suffolk: Boydell and Brewer; Totowa, N.J.: Rowman and Littlefield, 1980. 44–56.

Novy, Marianne. "Patriarchy, Mutuality, and Forgiveness in *King Lear.*" *Southern Humanities Review* 13 (1979): 281–92.

Oesterreich, Traugott K. *Possession and Exorcism among Primitive Races, in Antiquity, the Middle Ages, and Modern Times.* 1921. Trans. D. Ibberson. New York: Causeway, 1974.

O'Keeffe, Katherine O'Brien. *Visible Song: Transitional Literacy in Old English Verse.* Cambridge: Cambridge University Press, 1990.

Ong, Walter J. "Latin Language Study as a Renaissance Puberty Rite." *Studies in Philology* 56 (1959): 103–24.

———. *Orality and Literacy: The Technologizing of the Word.* London: Methuen, 1982.

Opland, Jeff. *Anglo-Saxon Oral Poetry: A Study of the Traditions.* New Haven: Yale University Press, 1980.

Ovid (P. Ovidius Naso). *Fasti.* Ed. and trans. Sir James Frazer. London: Heinemann; New York: Putnam, 1931.

Palmer, Geoffrey, and Noel Lloyd. *A Year of Festivals.* London: Warne, 1972.

Palmer, Roy. *The Folklore of Warwickshire.* London: Batsford, 1976.

Panofsky, Erwin. *Studies in Iconology.* New York: Harper and Row, 1939.

Parfitt, G. A. E. "Renaissance Wombs, Renaissance Tombs." *Renaissance and Modern Studies* 15 (1971): 23–33.

Parker, Patricia. *Literary Fat Ladies: Rhetoric, Gender, Property.* London: Methuen, 1987.

The Passionate Pilgrim. The Complete Works of Shakespeare. Ed. David Bevington. 3d ed. Glenview, Ill.: Scott, Foresman, 1980. 1567–72.

Paster, Gail Kern. *The Idea of the City in the Age of Shakespeare.* Athens: University of Georgia Press, 1985.

Patterson, Annabel. *Pastoral and Ideology: Virgil to Valéry.* Berkeley: University of California Press, 1987.

Pearce, T. M. "Beowulf and the Southern Sun (*Beowulf* ll. 603–6)." *American Notes and Queries* 4 (1966): 67–68.

Peele, George. *The Araygnement of Paris. The Life and Minor Works of George Peele.* Vol. 3. Ed. R. Mark Benbow. New Haven: Yale University Press, 1970. 61–114. 3 vols. Gen. ed. Charles T. Prouty. 1952–70.

Petrarca, Francesco. *Petrarch's Lyric Poems.* Trans. and ed. Robert M. Durling. Cambridge: Harvard University Press, 1976.

Pettitt, Thomas. "Early English Traditional Drama: Approaches and Perspectives." *Research Opportunities in Renaissance Drama* 25 (1982): 1–30.

Phillip, John. *Comedy of Patient and Meek Grissill.* 1565. Malone Society Reprint. London: Malone Society, 1909.

Pickard-Cambridge, A. W. *Dithyramb Tragedy and Comedy.* Oxford: Clarendon, 1927.

Pimlott, J. A. R. *The Englishman's Christmas: A Social History.* Hassocks, Sussex: Harvester, 1978.

The Pinder of Wakefield. 1632. STC 12213.

Pliny. *Natural History.* Trans. W. H. S. Jones. Vol. 8. Ed. T. E. Page, E. Capps, W. H. D. Rouse, L. A. Post, and E. H. Warmington. London: Heinemann; Cambridge: Harvard University Press, 1963. 10 vols.

Plutarch. *Moralia.* Vol. 8. Trans. Paul A. Clement and Herbert B. Hoffleit. Cambridge: Harvard University Press; London: Heinemann, 1969. 16 vols. 1927–69.

Pocock, D. F. Foreword. *A General Theory of Magic.* By Marcel Mauss. London: Routledge and Kegan Paul, 1972. 1–7.

Poole, Fitz John Porter. "Cannibals, Tricksters, and Witches: Anthropophagi Images among Bimin-Kuskusmin." *The Ethnography of Cannibalism.* Ed. Paula Brown and Donald Tuzin. Washington, D.C.: Society for Psychological Anthropology, 1983. 6–32.

Porter, Enid. *The Folklore of East Anglia.* London: Batsford, 1974.

Porter, Henry. *Henry Porter's "Two Angry Women of Abington": A Critical Edition.* Ed. Marianne Brish Evett. New York: Garland, 1980.

Preston, Thomas. *Cambyses. Elizabethan Plays.* Ed. Arthur N. Nethercot, Charles R. Baskervill, and Virgil B. Heltzel. Rev. ed. New York: Holt, Rinehart, and Winston, 1971. 83–108.

Propp, Vladimir. *Morphology of the Folktale.* Trans. Lawrence Scott. Ed. Svatana Pirkova-Jakobson. Bloomington: Indiana Research Center in Anthropology, Folklore, and Linguistics, 1958.

Rackin, Phyllis. "Anti-Historians: Women's Roles in Shakespeare's Histories." *Theatre Journal* 37 (1985): 329–44.

Ranald, Margaret Loftus. "The Degradation of Richard II: An Inquiry into the Ritual Backgrounds." *English Literary Renaissance* 7 (1977): 170–96.

Rhorer, Catherine Campbell. "Red and White in Ovid's *Metamorphoses:* The Mulberry Tree in the Tale of Pyramus and Thisbe." *Ramus* 9 (1980): 79–88.

Roberts, Jeanne Addison. "Falstaff in Windsor Forest: Villain or Victim?" *Shakespeare Quarterly* 26 (1975): 8–15.

———. "*The Merry Wives of Windsor* as a Hallowe'en Play." *Shakespeare Survey* 25 (1972): 107–12.

———. *The Shakespearean Wild: Geography, Genus, and Gender.* Lincoln: University of Nebraska Press, 1991.

———. *Shakespeare's English Comedy: "The Merry Wives of Windsor" in Context.* Lincoln: University of Nebraska Press, 1979.

Roberts, John M. "Belief in the Evil Eye in World Perspective." *The Evil Eye.* Ed. Clarence Maloney. New York: Columbia University Press, 1976. 223–78.

Robertson-Smith, William. *The Religion of the Semites.* Edinburgh: Black, 1889.

Robbins, Rossell Hope, ed. *Historical Poems of the Fourteenth and Fifteenth Centuries.* New York: Columbia University Press, 1959.

———. *Secular Lyrics of the Fourteenth and Fifteenth Centuries.* Oxford: Clarendon, 1952.

Roheim, Geza. "The Evil Eye." *American Imago* 9 (1952): 351–63.

Roscoe, John. *The Baganda: An Account of their Native Customs and Beliefs.* London: Macmillan, 1911.

Rossiter, A. P. *Angel with Horns.* Ed. Graham Storey. New York: Theatre Arts Books, 1961.

Rowe, Karen E. "To Spin a Yarn: The Female Voice in Folklore and Fairy Tale." *Fairy Tales and Society: Illusion, Allusion, and Paradigm.* Ed. Ruth B. Bottigheimer. Philadelphia: University of Pennsylvania Press, 1986. 53–74.

Rowlands, Samuel. *The Knave of Hearts. The Complete Works of Samuel Rowlands.* Vol. 2. London: Hunterian Club, 1880. 3 vols.

Runeberg, Arne. *Witches, Demons, and Fertility Magic.* Helsinki, Finland: Centraltryckeri Och Bokbinderi Ab, 1946.

Ryan, Alan. "The Nuclear Double Bind." *Times Literary Supplement,* Sept. 2–8, 1988, 971.

Sagan, Eli. *Cannibalism: Human Aggression and Cultural Form.* New York: Harper and Row, 1974.

Sahlins, Marshall. "Colors and Cultures." *Symbolic Anthropology.* Ed. Janet L. Dolgin, David S. Kemnitzer, and David M. Schneider. New York: Columbia University Press, 1977. 165–80.

Said, Edward. *Orientalism.* New York: Pantheon, 1978.

Sales, Roger. *English Literature in History, 1780–1830: Pastoral and Politics.* London: Hutchinson, 1983.

Schanzer, Ernest. "The Tragedy of Shakespeare's Brutus." *ELH* 22 (1955): 1–15.

Schoeck, Helmut. "The Evil Eye: Forms and Dynamics of a Universal Superstition." *The Evil Eye: A Folklore Casebook.* Ed. Alan Dundes. New York: Garland, 1981. 192–200.

Scot, Reginald. *The Discovery of Witchcraft.* 1584. Ed. Brinsley Nicholson. London: E. Stock, 1886.

Scott, Izora. *Controversies over the Imitation of Cicero.* New York: Teacher's College, Columbia University, 1910.

Seidel, H. "Krankheit, Tod, und Begräbnis bei den Togonegern." *Globus* 72 (1897): 21–25.

Selden, John. *Table-Talk.* London: Alex Murray, 1868.

Seligmann, Siegfried. *Der Böse Blick und Verwandtes.* Berlin: Bausdorf, 1910.

Shakespeare, William. *Complete Works.* Ed. David Bevington. 3d ed. Glenview, Ill.: Scott, Foresman, 1980.

Sharp, Buchanan. *In Contempt of All Authority: Rural Artisans and Riot in the West of England, 1586–1660.* Berkeley: University of California Press, 1980.

Sidney, Sir Philip. *The Countess of Pembroke's Arcadia* [*New Arcadia*]. *The Prose Works of Sir Philip Sidney.* Ed. Albert Feuillerat. Vol. 1. Cambridge: Cambridge University Press, 1962. 4 vols.

———. "The Defense of Poesy." *The Prose Works of Sir Philip Sidney.* 1912. Ed. Albert Feuillerat. Vol. 3. Cambridge: Cambridge University Press, 1962. 3–46. 4 vols.

———. *The Poems of Sir Philip Sidney.* Ed. William A. Ringler, Jr. Oxford: Clarendon, 1962.

Siebers, Tobin. *The Mask of Medusa.* Berkeley: University of California Press, 1983.

Simrock, M. Karl. *The Remarks of M. Karl Simrock on the Plots of Shake-*

speare's Plays. With Notes and Additions by J. O. Halliwell. London: Shakespeare Society, 1850.

Sir Gawain and the Green Knight. Trans. Marie Borroff. New York: Norton, 1967.

Skura, Meredith. "Discourse and the Individual: The Case of Colonialism in *The Tempest*." *Shakespeare Quarterly* 40 (1989): 42–69.

———. "Interpreting Posthumus' Dream from Above and Below: Families, Psychoanalysts, and Literary Critics." *Representing Shakespeare: New Psychoanalytic Essays*. Ed. Murray M. Schwartz and Coppélia Kahn. Baltimore: Johns Hopkins University Press, 1980. 203–16.

Smith, Hallett. *Elizabethan Poetry: A Study in Conventions, Meaning, and Expression*. Cambridge, Mass.: Harvard University Press, 1952.

Smith, Jonathan Z. "The Domestication of Sacrifice." In *Violent Origins: Ritual Killing and Cultural Formation*, by Walter Burkert, René Girard, and Jonathan Z. Smith. Ed. Robert G. Hamerton-Kelly. Stanford: Stanford University Press, 1987. 191–205.

Smith, Lacey Baldwin. "English Treason Trials and Confessions in the Sixteenth Century." *Journal of the History of Ideas* 15 (1954): 471–98.

Smith, Steven R. "The London Apprentices as Seventeenth-Century Adolescents." *Past and Present* 61 (1973): 149–61.

Smithsonian Institute. *Celebration: A World of Art and Ritual*. Washington, D.C.: Smithsonian Institute, 1982.

Smyth, Albert Henry. *Shakespeare's Pericles and Apollonius of Tyre: A Study in Comparative Literature*. 1898. New York: AMS Press, 1972.

Somerset Fry, Peter, and Fiona Somerset Fry. *A History of Ireland*. London: Routledge, 1988.

Sontag, Susan. "AIDS and Its Metaphors." *New York Review of Books*, Oct. 27, 1988, 89–99.

———. *Illness as Metaphor*. New York: Farrar, Straus, and Giroux, 1978.

Sophocles. *Dramas*. Trans. George Young. London: Dent, 1906.

Speed, John. *The Theatre of the Empire of Great Britaine*. Ed. John Arlott. 4 vols. London: Phoenix House, 1953–55.

Speirs, John. "Sir Gawain and the Green Knight." *Scrutiny* 16 (1949): 274–300.

Spencer, O. M. "Christmas throughout Christendom." *Harper's New Monthly Magazine*, Dec. 1872, 241–57.

Spencer, M. Lyle. *Corpus Christi Pageants in England*. New York: Baker and Taylor, 1911.

Spens, Janet. *An Essay on Shakespeare's Relation to Tradition*. Oxford: Blackwell, 1916.

Spenser, Edmund. *The Faerie Queene*. Ed. A. C. Hamilton. London: Longman, 1977.

————. *The Poetical Works of Edmund Spenser.* Ed. J. C. Smith and E. De Selincourt. London: Oxford University Press, 1912.

Spicer, Dorothy Gladys. *Yearbook of English Festivals.* New York: Wilson, 1954.

Stallybrass, Peter. "*Macbeth* and Witchcraft." *Focus on "Macbeth."* Ed. John Russell Brown. London: Routledge and Kegan Paul, 1982. 189–209.

————. "Patriarchal Territories: The Body Enclosed." *Rewriting the Renaissance: The Discourses of Sexual Difference in Early Modern Europe.* Ed. Margaret W. Ferguson, Maureen Quilligan, and Nancy J. Vickers. Chicago: University of Chicago Press, 1986. 123–42.

————. "'Wee Feaste in Our Defense': Patrician Carnival in Early Modern England and Robert Herrick's 'Hesperides.'" *English Literary Renaissance* 16 (1986): 234–52.

Stallybrass, Peter, and Allon White. *The Politics and Poetics of Transgression.* Ithaca: Cornell University Press, 1986.

Stein, Howard F. "Envy and the Evil Eye among Slovak-Americans: An Essay in the Psychological Ontogeny of Belief and Ritual." *Ethos* 2 (1974): 15–46.

Still, Colin. *The Timeless Theme.* 1936. Folcroft, Pa.: Folcroft Press, 1973.

Stirling, Brents. *Unity in Shakespearian Tragedy.* New York: Columbia University Press, 1956.

Strabo. *The Geography of Strabo.* Trans. H. C. Hamilton and W. Falconer. 3 vols. London: George Bell, 1903.

Strong, Roy C. *Portraits of Queen Elizabeth.* Oxford: Clarendon, 1963.

Strong, Roy, and Julia Trevelyan Oman. *Elizabeth R.* London: Secker and Warburg, 1971.

Stubbes, Phillip. *The Anatomy of Abuses.* 1583. New York: Garland, 1973.

Sundelson, David. "So Rare a Wonder'd Father: Prospero's *Tempest.*" *Representing Shakespeare: New Psychoanalytic Essays.* Ed. Murray M. Schwartz and Coppélia Kahn. Baltimore: Johns Hopkins University Press, 1980. 33–53.

Surrey, Henry Howard, Earl of. *The Poems of Henry Howard Earl of Surrey.* Ed. Frederick Morgan Padelford. Rev. ed. Seattle: University of Washington Press, 1928.

Sypher, Wylie. *The Ethic of Time: Structures of Experience in Shakespeare.* New York: Seabury, 1976.

The Tale of Gamelyn. Ed. Walter W. Skeat. Oxford: Clarendon, 1893.

Taylor, Archer. *English Riddles from Oral Tradition.* Berkeley: University of California Press, 1951.

Thistleton-Dyer, Rev. T. F. *Domestic Folk-Lore.* London: Cassell, Petter, Galpin, c. 1881.

Thomas, Keith. "Age and Authority in Early Modern England." *Proceedings of the British Academy* 62 (1976): 205–48.

———. "An Anthropology of Religion and Magic, II." *Journal of Interdisciplinary History* 6 (1975): 91–109.

———. "Fateful Exposures." *Times Literary Supplement,* Aug. 25–31, 1989, 913–14.

———. *Man and the Natural World: Changing Attitudes in England, 1500–1800.* London: Allen Lane, 1983.

———. "The Place of Laughter in Tudor and Stuart England." *Times Literary Supplement,* Jan. 1977, 77–81.

———. "The Relevance of Anthropology to the Study of English Witchcraft." *Witchcraft Confessions and Accusations.* Ed. Mary Douglas. London: Tavistock, 1970. 47–79.

———. *Religion and the Decline of Magic.* 1971. Harmondsworth, Eng.: Penguin, 1973.

———. *Rule and Misrule in the Schools of Early Modern England.* The Stenton Lecture, 1975. Reading: University of Reading Press, 1976.

Thorne, William B. "*Pericles* and the Incest-Fertility Opposition." *Shakespeare Quarterly* 22 (1971): 43–76.

Tiddy, R. J. E. *The Mummers' Play.* Oxford: Clarendon, 1923.

Tinkler, F. C. "*The Winter's Tale.*" *Scrutiny* 5 (1937): 343–64.

Tourney, Garfield, and Dean J. Plazak. "Evil Eye in Myth and Schizophrenia." *Psychiatric Quarterly* 28 (1953): 478–95.

Train, Joseph. *An Historical and Statistical Account of the Isle of Man.* Vol. 2. Isle of Man: Douglas; London: Simpkin/Marshall, 1845. 2 vols.

Turner, Victor. "Color Classification in Ndembu Ritual." *The Forest of Symbols.* Ithaca: Cornell University Press, 1967. 59–92.

———. *Dramas, Fields, and Metaphors: Symbolic Action in Human Society.* Ithaca: Cornell University Press, 1974.

———. *The Ritual Process: Structure and Anti-structure.* Chicago: Aldine, 1969.

Udall, Nicholas. *Respublica.* 1553. Ed. W. W. Greg. London: Oxford University Press for the Early English Text Society, 1952.

Underdown, David. *Revel, Riot, and Rebellion: Popular Politics and Culture in England, 1603–1660.* Oxford: Clarendon, 1985.

———. "The Taming of the Scold: the Enforcement of Patriarchal Authority in Early Modern England. *Order and Disorder in Early Modern England.* Ed. Anthony Fletcher and John Stevenson. Cambridge: Cambridge University Press, 1985. 116–36.

Usener, Hermann. *Kleine Schriften.* Osnabrück, Germany: Zeller, 1965.

Vairus, Leonardus. *De Fascino.* Venice: Apud Aldum, 1589.

Valenze, D. M. "Prophecy and Popular Literature in Eighteenth-Century England." *Journal of Ecclesiastical History* 29 (1978): 75–92.

Van Gennep, Arnold. *The Rites of Passage.* 1908. Trans. Monika B. Vizedom and Gabrielle L. Caffee. London: Routledge and Kegan Paul, 1960.

Velz, John W. "The Ancient World in Shakespeare: Authenticity or Anachronism?" *Shakespeare Survey* 31 (1978): 1–12.

Vernant, Jean-Pierre. "Ambiguity and Reversal: On the Enigmatic Structure of *Oedipus Rex.*" *Tragedy and Myth in Ancient Greece.* 1972. By Jean-Pierre Vernant and Pierre Vidal-Naquet. Trans. Janet Lloyd. Brighton: Harvester; Atlantic Heights, N.J.: Humanities Press, 1981.

Vickers, Brian, ed. *Occult and Scientific Mentalities in the Renaissance.* Cambridge: Cambridge University Press, 1984.

Vickers, Nancy. "'The Blazon of Sweet Beauty's Best': Shakespeare's *Lucrece.*" *Shakespeare and the Question of Theory.* Ed. Patricia Parker and Geoffrey Hartman. New York: Methuen, 1985. 95–115.

Vickery, John B., ed. *The Scapegoat: Ritual and Literature.* Boston: Houghton Mifflin, 1972.

Vigarello, Georges. *Concepts of Cleanliness: Changing Attitudes in France since the Middle Ages.* Cambridge: Cambridge University Press, 1989.

Villena, Enrique de Aragon. ca. 1422. *Tratado del Aojamiento.* Bari, Italy: Adriatica, 1978.

Vizedom, Monika. *Rites and Relationships: Rites of Passage and Contemporary Anthropology.* Beverly Hills: Sage, 1976.

Von Rosador, Kurt Tetzeli. "The Power of Magic: From *Endymion* to *The Tempest.*" *Shakespeare Survey* 43 (1991): 1–13.

Waddell, Laurence Austine. *The Buddhism of Tibet.* London: W. H. Allen, 1895.

Warner, Marina. *Alone of All Her Sex: The Myth and the Cult of the Virgin Mary.* London: Weidenfeld and Nicolson, 1976.

Watts, Harold. "Myth and Drama." *Cross Currents* 5 (1955): 154–70.

Webster, Graham. *The British Celts and Their Gods under Rome.* London: Batsford, 1986.

Webster, John. *The Duchess of Malfi.* Ed. John Russell Brown. London: Methuen, 1964.

———. *The White Devil.* Ed. Clive Hart. Edinburgh: Oliver and Boyd, 1970.

Weimann, Robert. *Shakespeare and the Popular Tradition in the Theatre.* 1967. Ed. Robert Schwartz. Baltimore: Johns Hopkins University Press, 1978.

Weiser, Francis X. *Handbook of Christian Feasts and Customs.* New York: Harcourt, Brace, and World, 1952.

Welsford, Enid. *The Court Masque: A Study in the Relationship between Poetry and the Revels.* Cambridge: Cambridge University Press, 1927.

———. *The Fool: His Social Literary History.* Gloucester, Mass.: Peter Smith, 1935.

Westermarck, Edward. *Ritual and Belief in Morocco.* 2 vols. London: Macmillan, 1926.

Weston, Jessie. *From Ritual to Romance.* Cambridge: Cambridge University Press, 1920.

Weyer, Johann. *De Praestigiis Daemonum. Witches, Devils, and Doctors: Johann Weyer: De Praestigiis Daemonum.* Ed. George Mora, Benjamin Kohl, Erik Midelfort, and Helen Bacon. Trans. John Shea. Binghampton, N.Y.: Medieval and Renaissance Texts and Studies, 1991. 1–584.

White, Harold Ogden. *Plagiarism and Imitation during the English Renaissance.* Cambridge, Mass.: Harvard University Press, 1935.

Wickham, Glynne. "From Tragedy to Tragi-comedy: *King Lear* as Prologue." *Shakespeare Survey* 26 (1973): 33–48.

Widdowson, J. D. A., and Herbert Halpert. "The Disguises of Newfoundland Mummers." *Christmas Mumming in Newfoundland.* Ed. Herbert Halpert and G. M. Story. Toronto: University of Toronto Press, 1969.

Williams, J. E. Caerwyn. "The Court Poet in Medieval Ireland." *Proceedings of the British Academy* 57 (1971): 85–135.

Williams, Raymond. *The Country and the City.* New York: Oxford University Press, 1973.

Willis, Deborah. "The Monarch and the Sacred: Shakespeare and the Ceremony for the Healing of the King's Evil." *True Rites and Maimed Rites: Ritual and Anti-Ritual in Shakespeare and His Age.* Ed. Linda Woodbridge and Edward Berry. Urbana: University of Illinois Press, 1992. 147–68.

———. "Shakespeare's *Tempest* and the Discourse of Colonialism." *Studies in English Literature, 1500–1900* 29 (1989): 277–89.

Wincor, Richard. "Shakespeare's Festival Plays." *Shakespeare Quarterly* 1 (1950): 219–42.

Witzschel, August. *Sagen, Sitten, und Gebräuche aus Thüringen.* Vienna: Braumüller, 1878.

Woodbridge, Linda. "Patchwork: Piecing the Early Modern Mind in the First Century of English Print Culture." *English Literary Renaissance* 23 (1993): 5–45.

———. "A Strange Eventful History: Notes on Feminism, Historicism, and Literary Study." *Exemplaria* 2 (1990): 692–96.

———. *Women and the English Renaissance: Literature and the Nature of Womankind, 1540–1620.* Urbana: University of Illinois Press; Brighton: Harvester, 1984.

Woodbridge, Linda, and Edward Berry, eds. *True Rites and Maimed Rites: Ritual and Anti-ritual in Shakespeare and His Age.* Urbana: University of Illinois Press, 1992.

Wood-Martin, W. G. *Traces of the Elder Faiths of Ireland.* Vol. 2. London: Longmans, Green, 1902. 2 vols.

Wright, A. R. *English Folklore.* London: Benn, 1928.

Wright, Thomas. *A History of Domestic Manners and Sentiments in England during the Middle Ages.* London: Chapman and Hall, 1862.

Wyatt, Sir Thomas. *Collected Poems of Sir Thomas Wyatt.* Ed. Kenneth Muir and Patricia Thomson. Liverpool: Liverpool University Press, 1969.

Yerkes, Royden Keith. *Sacrifice in Greek and Roman Religions and Early Judaism.* London: Black, 1953.

Index

LINDA WOODBRIDGE is past president of the Shakespeare Association of America, coeditor of *True Rites and Maimed Rites: Ritual and Anti-Ritual in Shakespeare and His Age,* and author of *Women and the English Renaissance: Literature and the Nature of Womankind, 1540 to 1620.* She is professor of English at the University of Alberta.